LUTHER'S WORKS

LUTHER'S WORKS

VOLUME 3

LECTURES ON GENESIS
Chapters 15—20

JAROSLAV PELIKAN

Editor

CONCORDIA PUBLISHING HOUSE · SAINT LOUIS

Copyright 1961 by
CONCORDIA PUBLISHING HOUSE
Saint Louis, Missouri

Library of Congress Catalog Card No. 55-9898

MANUFACTURED IN THE UNITED STATES OF AMERICA

Contents

General Introduction — vii
Introduction to Volume 3 — ix
CHAPTER FIFTEEN — 3
CHAPTER SIXTEEN — 42
CHAPTER SEVENTEEN — 75
CHAPTER EIGHTEEN — 176
CHAPTER NINETEEN — 239
CHAPTER TWENTY — 315
Index — 367

General Introduction

THE first editions of Luther's collected works appeared in the sixteenth century, and so did the first efforts to make him "speak English." In America serious attempts in these directions were made for the first time in the nineteenth century. The Saint Louis edition of Luther was the first endeavor on American soil to publish a collected edition of his works, and the Henkel Press in Newmarket, Virginia, was the first to publish some of Luther's writings in an English translation. During the first decade of the twentieth century, J. N. Lenker produced translations of Luther's sermons and commentaries in thirteen volumes. A few years later the first of the six volumes in the Philadelphia (or Holman) edition of the *Works of Martin Luther* appeared. Miscellaneous other works were published at one time or another. But a growing recognition of the need for more of Luther's works in English has resulted in this American edition of Luther's works.

The edition is intended primarily for the reader whose knowledge of late medieval Latin and sixteenth-century German is too small to permit him to work with Luther in the original languages. Those who can, will continue to read Luther in his original words as these have been assembled in the monumental Weimar edition (*D. Martin Luthers Werke.* Kritische Gesamtausgabe; Weimar, 1883 ff.). Its texts and helps have formed a basis for this edition, though in certain places we have felt constrained to depart from its readings and findings. We have tried throughout to translate Luther as he thought translating should be done. That is, we have striven for faithfulness on the basis of the best lexicographical materials available. But where literal accuracy and clarity have conflicted, it is clarity that we have preferred, so that sometimes paraphrase seemed more faithful than literal fidelity. We have proceeded in a similar way in the matter of Bible versions, translating Luther's translations. Where this could be done by the use of an existing English version — King James, Douay, or Revised Standard — we have done so. Where it could not, we have supplied our own. To indicate this in each specific instance would have been pedantic; to adopt a uniform procedure would have been artificial — especially in view of Luther's own inconsistency in this regard. In each volume the translator will be responsible primarily for matters of text and language, while the responsibility of the editor will extend principally to the historical and theological matters reflected in the introductions and notes.

Although the edition as planned will include fifty-five volumes, Luther's writings are not being translated in their entirety. Nor should they be. As he was the first to insist, much of what he wrote and said was not that important. Thus the edition is a selection of works that have proved their importance for the faith, life, and history of the Christian Church. The first thirty volumes contain Luther's expositions of various Biblical books, while the remaining volumes include what are usually called his "Reformation writings" and other occasional pieces. The final volume of the set will be an index volume; in addition to an index of quotations, proper names, and topics, and a list of corrections and changes, it will contain a glossary of many of the technical terms that recur in Luther's works and that cannot be defined each time they appear. Obviously Luther cannot be forced into any neat set of rubrics. He can provide his reader with bits of autobiography or with political observations as he expounds a psalm, and he can speak tenderly about the meaning of the faith in the midst of polemics against his opponents. It is the hope of publishers, editors, and translators that through this edition the message of Luther's faith will speak more clearly to the modern church.

J. P.
H. L.

Introduction to Volume 3

THIS volume continues our edition of Luther's *Lectures on Genesis* in English translation and contains his exposition of chapters 15 to 20 inclusive (Weimar, XLII, 550–XLIII, 137; St. Louis, I, 920–1369). Thus it is the next installment in his narrative of the story of Abraham, begun in Volume 2 of *Luther's Works* and scheduled for completion in Volume 4.

What we have said in our Introductions to Volumes 1 and 2 of *Luther's Works* applies to this portion of Luther's *Lectures on Genesis* as well, and very little needs to be added. The expository method at work in the first fourteen chapters continues to make itself evident here; so does the literary work of the compiler, Veit Dietrich, whose editorializing we have had occasion to observe in this volume as we did in its two predecessors. Luther's (or Dietrich's) continued use of Lyra's commentary has necessitated the identification of quotations from Lyra and borrowings from him. We have also tried to trace down hundreds of other quotations and references not properly identified — indeed, usually not identified at all — in any of the earlier editions of Luther's writings. In most cases our search has been successful in locating the specific reference to Scripture, the church fathers, the classics, or contemporary writers and events. In a few cases Luther's method of citation is so general as to preclude the identification of a single passage, and we have referred to the passage that seems to approximate the content of his citation. And in some cases neither our own memory nor the reference tools at our disposal were of any avail, and we have been obliged to admit that we do not know exactly where Luther got the idea or phrase he quotes. But even when our search has failed, we have contented ourselves with the knowledge that our edition of these *Lectures on Genesis* has managed to label many more references than any previous edition of Luther in any language.

With the determination of the chronology of these *Lectures on Genesis* we have been less successful. There are only three places in this volume where the transmitted text offers any hint at all about the time of the lectures. At the very beginning of the material translated here in Volume 3 (see p. 3) Luther complains of the many distractions that prevent him from giving adequate attention to his lectures. But this statement is of very little genuine help. Luther was subjected to continual pressure and harassment from friends and enemies, princes and publishers, students and clergy. Thus he could have said this at almost any time — and, in fact, did say something like this many times (see *Luther's Works,* 21, p. xx; 22, p. x; 23, p. xi). The other references to external events, however, are more helpful. Once he refers to earthquakes and floods "this year" in Naples and Puteoli (see p. 295, note 64); the year is probably 1538. A little later, discussing the feelings that must have gone through Abraham's mind as he contemplated the destruction of Sodom and Gomorrah, Luther refers to his own anxiety over Philip Melanchthon during the latter's stay in Frankfurt (see p. 303, note 75). From the correspondence of Luther and Melanchthon it is possible to determine the limits of the time span within which this comment must have been made. Melanchthon and Friedrich Myconius (1490—1546) left Wittenberg on January 31, 1539. They arrived at Weimar the next day. On February 5 Melanchthon left Weimar for Frankfurt, presumably accompanied by Myconius. On March 2, 1539, Luther wrote to Melanchthon that despite continuing ill health he was "beginning to take up Genesis again *[coepi hodie resumptum in Genesi]*." March 2 was a Sunday; on this ground Peter Meinhold suggests that Luther was referring to his preparations rather than to his lectures as such. Letters from Melanchthon under the dates of March 14, March 26, and April 22 indicate that he remained in Frankfurt throughout the rest of the winter and into the spring; but from the last of these letters we may gather that Melanchthon departed for Wittenberg well before the end of April and was probably back there about May 1. Thus it appears safe to conclude that Luther was lecturing on chapter 19 of Genesis about March or April 1539; for he would not have been anxious immediately after Melanchthon's departure. There seems to be no reliable way to figure backward or forward to the *terminus a quo* or the *terminus ad quem* of the other lectures in this volume.

J. P.

LECTURES ON GENESIS

Chapters 15—20

Translated by
GEORGE V. SCHICK

CHAPTER FIFTEEN

1. *After these things the word of the Lord came to Abram in a vision: Fear not, Abram, I am your Shield; your reward shall be very great.*

THIS is a chapter of the highest importance, and it should be read with much meditation. But I am so distracted by the affairs of the churches and of the court that I lack the leisure to devote myself more diligently to meditation.[1] Therefore we shall lecture on it at least so far as the language is concerned.

So far we have heard of Abraham's glorious victory and of the wonderful work through which God revealed Himself to that age in order thus to encourage all men to accept the God of Abraham, who alone is the Most High and All-powerful.

Now follow both trials and comforts, and Moses combines these in such a manner with the account of the victory that here as elsewhere he appears to have given little thought to a methodical arrangement of the historical account. Readers who are experienced in spiritual matters know that no pattern is more in accordance with the truth and more common than that new perils and new disturbances always follow comforting events. But he who is not fully experienced often thinks that the discourses and accounts of the prophets lack coherence.

Thus after this glorious victory of Abraham, by which his faith was undoubtedly strengthened greatly and his heart was buoyed up to an extraordinary degree — especially since Shem, the high priest, delivered such a serious discourse — there follows another trial, one that is new. Yet it is impossible to gather adequately from the account what kind of trial is was.

But this is sure and altogether reliable: that when God addresses Abraham in these words and commands him not to be afraid, these words are not without a reason. Elated and victorious a little while ago, Abraham was now surrounded by new dangers, cares, and terrors.

[1] On the significance of this comment for the determination of the chronology of these *Lectures on Genesis* see our Introduction, p. x.

If he was not at the point of despair over his defense or protection, or did not have doubts about his reward, what was the need of God's exhortation not to fear and of His promise of an abundant reward?

Here, therefore, we follow the general rule which Ps. 30:6-9 presents as the common example of all saints. "As for me," says David, "I said in my prosperity, 'I shall never be moved.' By Thy favor, O Lord, Thou hadst established me as a strong mountain; Thou didst hide Thy face, I was dismayed. To Thee, O Lord, I cried; and to the Lord I made supplication: 'What profit is there in my death, if I go down to the Pit? Will the dust praise Thee? Will it tell of Thy faithfulness?'"

This is the usual way of training saintly and godly men. For this reason Ps. 4:3 states that God rules His saints in a wonderful manner. Encouraged now by his miraculous victory, Abraham feels such joy of spirit and such a boundless sense of security with regard to God's goodness that he says in his heart: "I shall never be shaken." But immediately everything is reversed: "Thou didst hide Thy face, O Lord," says David, "and I was dismayed."

Why or how does God rule in this manner? Why does He not make this joy complete and lasting for His saints? I do not know, except for the fact that I observe this pattern and common example in all the saints, even in Christ Himself, their Head, who sometimes rejoices in spirit and joyfully gives thanks to God in the Holy Spirit. Afterwards He is again troubled in spirit, prays for protection, and laments that He has been forsaken in the hour of death, as one can see in Ps. 8:5 and in Ps. 22:1. Therefore one should learn this example and this pattern of the saints, yes, this method by which God governs His saints.

Abraham had rejoiced over such a notable victory. God had made his name renowned among all the neighboring nations. Therefore the danger of vainglory threatened him. There is nothing which this nature of ours is less able to bear than its own honors and God's favors. Consequently, God turns His face away for a little while and leaves man to himself. Then distress and hardship immediately arise.

Thus Paul says in 2 Cor. 1:9: "Why, we felt that we had received the sentence of death; but that was to make us rely not on ourselves but on God, who raises the dead."

God abhors the confidence which we have with regard to ourselves. But it is a natural shortcoming which troubles all the saints, especially the greatest. As a result, they sin against the First Table.

For lust has been sufficiently subdued in the saints so far as the Second Table is concerned. Theft, adultery, and murder do not harass them as they do young men whose flesh is still strong and sound. But other dangers, more serious and more troublesome, plague them, namely, those outstanding sins against the First Table: reliance on one's own strength, arrogance, and the presumption of righteousness and wisdom. Against these monsters the saints must constantly battle.

In this arena Abraham, Moses, Aaron, and David sweat to control and overcome presumption and pride.

Abraham appears to have been in a similar trial, as the words clearly bear out. Accordingly, when God sees that he is in danger of falling into presumption, He turns His face away and thus checks the temptation.

This is a shortcoming which we all have: when God bestows outstanding gifts, the old Adam exalts himself and becomes proud; for he sees that others do not have similar gifts. But to keep this sin from destroying the saints, God gives Paul an angel of Satan to harass him, lest he be elated because of his revelation (2 Cor. 12:7).

Therefore praise is properly given to what is related about a certain bishop who, when necessity forced him into the ministry of teaching, declined this office on bended knees or, if God insisted that he assume it, asked to be freed from ambition and the desire for vainglory.[2]

If Paul, the greatest apostle, is not free from this disease — indeed, if he cannot be delivered from this sickness except by being tormented and buffeted by Satan — why shall we not be afraid, we whose station is far below his?

By nature we cannot avoid being haughty because of the gifts of God, just as, conversely, we despair when His gifts are taken from us.

Nor is it necessary at this point to adduce historical accounts rather extensively. What else than this horrible presumption and ambition stirred up Münzer, the Anabaptists, the Sacramentarians, Zwingli, and Oecolampadius?[3] If someone is able to write four Greek words, to explain one psalm, he is puffed up by his knowledge as if by yeast.

[2] So prevalent did this idea become that the phrase *Nolo episcopari* was almost proverbial; many candidates for episcopal and papal office made a pretense of running away, but they were almost always caught in time.

[3] This reference to the pedantry of the autodidact seems to be directed especially at Zwingli; cf. *Luther the Expositor,* p. 125.

The result is that he thinks he is walking on the clouds, far above other human beings.

I learned to recognize this disease soon enough, since I was warned by so many accounts of the Holy Scriptures. At the beginning of the Reformation,[4] therefore, when God involved me in this faction (if I may call it that) against my will and by means of wonderful opportunities, I asked Him fervently to deliver me from this evil. He heard my prayer; for He kept me free from this temptation, although not so free that I did not feel it. He kept me occupied to such an extent with responsibilities, worries, perils, and hardships that all ambition was readily shut out of my mind.

Unless God delivers us in this manner, this untamed monster overpowers everyone. Youth feels its own evils; then manhood does. For the flesh is plagued by lust, the heart by greed, wrath, hatred, and similar emotions, which trouble the mind in various ways. But these conflicts involve the Second Table and gradually subside.

Therefore when the struggle seems to be over, this new and sharper battle involving the First Table confronts us, the fight against presumption, vainglory, and the confidence we have in ourselves because of our gifts.

To escape this pest, Paul feels the thorn of Satan in his flesh. "To keep me from being too elated by the abundance of the revelations," he says (2 Cor. 12:7), "a thorn was given me in the flesh, a messenger of Satan, to harass me."

Who would imagine when observing Paul that he was undergoing such a temptation? Who would not think that he himself had long since overcome it and laid it low?

Yet in Romans (7:23) he points out a greater danger, for he complains that he is being taken captive by sin or by "the law of sin."

When you observe these things in so great an apostle, you will not feel, will you, that you can be out of danger? Thus Abraham, too, was still in the flesh. Hence when he was distinguished by such an outstanding victory, is it surprising if he was elated in his heart and puffed up by his success? But to keep him from becoming presumptuous, the Lord sent upon him a great and severe trial to break his spirit and to humble him.

Even though we do not know what the nature of this trial was, we can nevertheless infer that he suffered what we have mentioned

---

[4] By the phrase *initium Evangelii* here Luther means the beginning of the Reformation.

above from the psalm.⁵ After winning his victory he sang a *Te Deum laudamus* with a joyful spirit and a loud voice. He said: "I shall never be shaken." But when the Lord turned His face away, there came a sadness which filled and troubled his heart so much that he completely forgot the glorious victory, and it seemed to him that he had been utterly forsaken and rejected by God.

Accounts of this kind should be carefully noted, in order that we may be able to comfort those who are in sorrow. For a trial is sent to keep us from exalting ourselves because of the gifts we have. But even though it is hard to suffer such distress of heart, we should nevertheless be buoyed up and, as it were, lighten those hurts, because we know that the forgiveness of sins is unimpaired and unchangeable. Let us keep this gift in mind and prefer it to others. Indeed, in comparison with this gift let us despise all the others, however great and glorious they may be. In this way our hearts will be eased a little.

God indeed gives great gifts to those who are His, just as here He gave Abraham a glorious victory. Nevertheless, He does not yet pour out all His gifts; nor does He give Himself completely. Although you may have greater gifts than either Abraham or Moses, still you do not yet have the Lord Himself. He withholds and, as it were, removes Himself from us, evidently in order that when we are not being tried and all is serene and quiet, we may still fear Him and not say, as the smug do: "I shall never be shaken." For if we sing this song, the words "Thou didst hide Thy face, I was dismayed" follow at once.

Therefore those who consider themselves invincible when they are not afflicted are struck with boundless fear when they are in the clutches of a trial.

But this is not because God may have changed His mind, as though He had withdrawn His grace and were refusing to grant forgiveness of sins. His will to save us through His Son, to whose kingdom He has called us, remains steadfast and unchangeable; but the awareness of this mercy is removed for a time.

Therefore those who experienced this trial in the monasteries have called it a spirit of blasphemy; but others have called it a suspension of grace, a milder and more suitable term.⁶ As a young man I indeed

⁵ See p. 4.

⁶ On the *suspensio gratiae* in medieval devotion see also *Luther's Works*, 2, p. 104, note 2.

read this in their discussions, but I did not understand it before I began to read Holy Scripture.

It is no small comfort, however, to know that grace has not been taken away but is truly immovable and unchangeable, although the awareness and experience of grace is taken away for a time, and dread and fear rush in, discouraging and troubling the spirit. Then man becomes impatient, concludes that he cannot bear the wrath of God, and simply makes a devil out of God.

Christ experienced this trial in the garden (Matt. 26:41), where nature was wrestling with the spirit, and the spirit indeed was willing, but the flesh was weak, terrified, fearful, and troubled. No one is truly sorrowful unless God forsakes him, just as, conversely, no one can be sorrowful when God is present. Therefore sorrow is an indication that God has departed from us and has forsaken us for a time, just as in the Song of Solomon (2:9) the bride complains that the bridegroom has concealed himself behind a wall and is looking through lattices. Then occurs what is written in Ps. 107:27: "They reeled and staggered like drunken men, and were at their wits' end."

When, on the other hand, as is written in the Book of Wisdom (3:7), God shines into our hearts with rays of mercy, then it is impossible for our hearts not to be glad, even though we, like Stephen, are being dragged to torture and death.

Therefore it is very profitable to consider these examples, namely, that the saints who are bold in the Holy Spirit are bolder than Satan himself. On the other hand, when they are in the clutches of a trial, they tremble so much that they are afraid even of a rustling leaf.[7] We are reminded of our weakness in order that no matter how great the gifts are that we possess, we may not exalt ourselves but may remain humble and fear God. From those who do not do this He turns His face away, and trouble and perplexity follow.

I want to preface these remarks to this chapter, in which we learn about what Ps. 4:3 says: "Know that God has dealt marvelously with the godly," that is, that He keeps those who are His occupied in various ways, lest they become heretics, be presumptuous with regard to their gifts, and be puffed up over against those who do not have these gifts. For those who do this are very close to destruction.

Therefore those who are chosen as teachers of the churches to rule

---

[7] For Luther's use of Lev. 26:36 in his description of the terrors of conscience see also *Luther's Works*, 1, pp. 170—174.

over others should offer special prayers that they be preserved from this affliction as from the greatest and most dangerous evil.

Other sins – such as wrathfulness, impatience, and drunkenness – naturally bring shame because of their foulness. Those who indulge in them know that they have sinned. Consequently, they blush. But vainglory and trust in one's own wisdom or righteousness is a sin of such a kind that it is not recognized as a sin. Instead, men thank God for it, as the Pharisee does in the Gospel (Luke 18:9-14); they rejoice in it as in an extraordinary gift of the Holy Spirit. Therefore it is an utterly incurable and devilish evil.

From this evil God preserves saintly Abraham by subjecting the glorious conqueror to such an affliction that it is necessary to comfort him with a divine word. Although, as I have said, the nature of the trial is not certain, yet the circumstances prove that it was so severe that Abraham was utterly disheartened.

Perhaps Abraham was troubled about his offspring, as his words indicate. God had promised him the land of Canaan and an eternal blessing; but since Sarah was barren, and the hope of children was almost entirely denied, he thought: "Why is it that God, who is so merciful toward you, does not give you a son? Perhaps you have offended Him, and He has changed His mind."

I dare not maintain that this was the affliction. Accordingly, I am going along with the general rule: that God makes His saints sad again after they have been gladdened, lest they become proud and smug; that after they have been made alive, He leads them down to hell, in order that He may lead them back from there. But if our surmise as to the specific and individual nature of the affliction now under consideration is not correct, we are not in error with regard to the general pattern.

The words "Fear not, Abram" are absolutely clear. They show that the saintly man did have great fear and the very affliction of mistrust. Otherwise why would God add: "I am your Shield; your reward shall be very great"? Therefore Abraham thought: "Perhaps God has chosen someone else, since He will fulfill this promise; and who knows whether this very victory is everything He has promised you?"

When God withdraws His hand, the flesh creates for itself an odd dialectic and rhetoric. Against these battering-rams, so to speak, with which Abraham's heart is pounded the Lord erects three grand bulwarks: "Fear not, Abraham; I am your Shield; your reward shall be very great." It is as though He were saying: "Whom will you fear if I protect you? What more will you demand for yourself if I am your Reward? Do you not have a greater prize than either the land of Canaan or the entire world would be?" This is a very extraordinary comfort, and it shows that the trial and fear which Abraham experienced were extraordinary too.

As to the statement of the text that the Lord spoke with Abraham "in a vision," we have not yet had this expression in Moses. In the twelfth chapter it is simply recorded that the Lord "said to Abram." Later on it is stated that the Lord "appeared to Abraham." In this passage, too, it is recorded that the Lord spoke with Abraham, but a new method is introduced, בַּמַּחֲזֶה.

This diversity of expressions sheds light on the three types of prophecy or the three classes of revelation that are clearly mentioned in Num. 12:6-8, where the Lord says: "If there is a prophet among you, I the Lord make Myself known to him in a vision, I speak with him in a dream. Not so with My servant Moses; he is entrusted with all My house. With him I speak mouth to mouth, clearly, and not in dark speech."

It is a vision or a form of apparition when God appears to people when they are awake, not as in dreams. Thus Abraham surely was not sleeping when the Lord spoke these words to him, for he went outside and was commanded to look at the heavens and count the stars. This appearance was not imaginary, for Abraham's eyes were open and awake.

But these visions are usually forms which require explanation, as, for example, Amos' vision of someone forming locusts when the crop is already growing into green blades (7:1). The locusts represent the king of Babylon, and the One forming the locusts is God, who inflicts this punishment upon His people. This Moses calls a semblance or an apparition.

Dreams are on a level below this. Scripture often mentions them. Even though a man is asleep and is not making use of his sense organs, some images present themselves to his mind while the body is sleeping and the sense organs are resting.

Thus Pharaoh and Nebuchadnezzar, while asleep, see images of future events.

There is extant a delightful account by Augustine concerning a certain physician who regarded the doctrine of the resurrection of the dead and the immortality of the soul as uncertain. While he is sleeping, a very handsome young man appears to him, addresses him familiarly and asks whether he knows him. When the sleeping physician says no and yet admits that he sees and hears him, the young man says: "How is it that you see me when your eyes are closed in sleep? How is it that you hear me when your ears are not open, but you are asleep?" [8]

Therefore learn and believe that there are other spiritual eyes with which those who believe in Christ see when the eyes of the body have been closed by death or have rather been entirely destroyed.

This image was received by the physician while he was asleep, and Scripture bears witness that God often revealed future events to the godly in this manner.

But at this point one asks what the criteria of true dreams are and, when visions occur, how one can know whether they are from God or from Satan. The heathen, too, saw that minds are deceived in various ways by phantoms in dreams. For this reason Cato warns against paying any attention to dreams,[9] and Sirach says (34:6-7): "Do not give your mind to them. For dreams have deceived many, and those who put their hope in them have failed."

But because superstition and curiosity plague the hearts of men in various ways, Satan also often mocks men on this account. Therefore it is not always easy to make a distinction.

Nevertheless, the historical accounts of Holy Scripture point out this principle:[10] through the dreams from God an impression of such a nature is made on the hearts that not only the intellect but also the will is troubled beyond normal. Nebuchadnezzar's dream had so disturbed his mind that he threatened the sorcerers with death if they did not tell the meaning of the dream he had seen, for his mind could not rest unless the dream and its interpretation were revealed anew.

But just as Satan causes both visions and dreams with which he deceives the unwary, so the third type of revelation is completely trustworthy, when God speaks to Moses face to face and adds His Holy Spirit to impress the word on the heart and to give encouragement.

When Abraham hears the promise concerning the Blessed Seed,

---

[8] Augustine tells this story in his letter of 415 to Evodius, *Epistola* CLIX, *Patrologia, Series Latina*, XXXIII, 699—700.

[9] *Catonis disticha*, II, 31.

[10] The Latin word used here for "principle" is *analogia*.

he receives the revelation of the Holy Spirit at the same time. Therefore his understanding of this revelation is different from that of the Jews. It is not concerned solely with the physical seed and the physical blessing, but there arises in his heart a new light with regard to the forgiveness of sins and reconciliation with God.

Accordingly, this kind of revelation — when God speaks face to face and enlightens hearts with the rays of His Spirit — is far more reliable than dreams and visions.

But when this passage states that the Lord spoke in a vision, we should take it to mean that Abraham heard the Lord speaking in the vision. That is, he not only heard the word; but the word was represented by a certain likeness of the Speaker, whatever its nature was. For Moses does not point this out.

2. *But Abram said: O Lord God, what wilt Thou give me; for I continue childless, and the heir of my house is Eliezer of Damascus?*

3. *And Abram said: Behold, Thou hast given me no offspring, and a slave born in my house will be my heir.*

These words reveal to some extent the nature of the trial with which Abram wrestled. Therefore it was necessary to comfort him with the divine words that the Lord would both defend and abundantly bless him.

It is not strange if Abraham in that very concern about descendants, gradually turned to the thought that God was angry with him. But, as I said previously, even though Moses does not state the nature of the trial, still when Holy Scripture relates the examples of the saints, it reveals clues, so to speak, on the basis of which it is possible to draw conclusions concerning trials. Accordingly, we have the general idea that Abraham began to have doubts as to the protection and the kindness of God; but there is no clear record of what occasioned these thoughts.

Nevertheless, Moses seems to imply that Eliezer, the manager of Abraham's house, became rather arrogant and confidently predicted that Abraham's entire blessing would fall to him, since Abraham's was a childless marriage.

In the first place, this is shown by the fact that Abraham laments his childlessness so sadly and not without sighing and sobbing. For these are not words of laughter or of joy; they are words of profound grief and sorrow: "I am without children; that man from Damascus will be my heir." What else did he have to look forward to at his age and with a barren wife? "Thou hast given me a glorious victory, and Thou hast blessed my house," he says, "but Thou art not giving me an heir, and my servant is now being encouraged to hope that all these things will fall to him after I am dead." His heart was deeply troubled by these thoughts.

Furthermore, the Lord's answer corroborates this interpretation when He says: "This man shall not be your heir; your own son shall be your heir."

Therefore Abraham's trial actually consisted in his fear that the promise would be diverted from his own offspring and seed to his servant.

This trial was no small thing, especially since the servant became insubordinate because of his hope. The flesh and the world have been corrupted to an extraordinary degree by ambition; they strive with great zeal after positions of authority. Thus because Cain despised his brother, he usurped both the secular authority and the priesthood. Ishmael and Esau did likewise. And when Sarah was indignant for a similar reason, she drove a mother and the son of that mother out of her house. Thus in all ages the ungodly have seized the name and title of the church and have adorned themselves with it.

Although there is nothing to which they are less entitled, the papists, the Anabaptists, the Sacramentarians, and the instigators of rebellion — Münzer and others — want to be the church and lay claim to this title even if it means bloodshed.

But the true saints, who are the true church, sigh and are saddened when they see how the ungodly so smugly appropriate to themselves the blessing and promises, just as we today are compelled to see and put up with the pretensions of the pope, who boasts that he is the head of the church, though it is certain that he has nothing else in mind than to fill the world with idolatry.

David, too, experienced this trial when he had been driven from his realm; he ordered Zadok to return to the city and to carry the Ark back with him (2 Sam. 15:25-26): "If I find favor in the eyes of the Lord, He will bring me back and let me see both it and His habitation; but if He says, 'I have no pleasure in you,' behold, here I am, let Him do to me what seems good to Him."

David had very clear and very sure promises about his everlasting kingdom. Yet so severe a trial befalls him that he has doubts about the outcome — whether he would be restored to the kingdom — and he commits the matter to God.

Just as the ungodly seize upon God's promises with inordinate smugness, so the saints, on the other hand, humble themselves under the mighty hand of God (1 Peter 5:6) and submit to God in fear and reverence.

Therefore even though Abraham had been assured by the Word of God about the future blessing, he nevertheless begins to have doubts when he considers both his own childless marriage and the hope and plans of his servant.

This, you see, is the way things go in the church and in the kingdoms of the world: they are at loggerheads with regard to the promises. The pope and his followers want to be the church of God; the Turk also wants to be the church of God. And yet neither of them is.

Thus the heretics, who are the originators of offenses and who subvert sound doctrine, "live as enemies of the cross of Christ," as Paul states with tears (Phil. 3:18-19), whose "god is the belly"; convinced that they are the church, they boast endlessly over against the true church.

Thus Abraham's trial seems to have been the arrogance and contempt of a domestic servant against his master.

Even though Abraham had a clear promise about his natural seed, as chapters twelve and thirteen prove, there were nevertheless those who scoffed at those promises, as heretics are in the habit of doing, and caused Abraham to waver.

This is what they said: that the promise was not to be understood to apply to his natural seed but to an adopted one belonging to the household; for Abraham was now an old man, Sarah was barren, and the Lord had given no word or any indication that Abraham should take another wife.

The promises, of course, were sure. But along came this demonic reasoning with its distinction between a natural and an adopted seed. This reasoning so disturbs and distresses the heart of the saintly patriarch that he humbles himself and submits to the will of God, but not without profound grief and sorrow; for he thinks that God is forsaking him and has changed His will.

Therefore the Lord comforts him and tells him not to fear. "I shall be your protection," He says, "I shall defend you from evils and shall overwhelm you with a blessing, and from your body there will come one who is to be your heir."

This analogy is in agreement with other examples in Scripture. Accordingly, even if we are wrong with regard to the specific nature of Abraham's trial, in general we are nevertheless following the analogy of Scripture.

Thus Abraham is very sad and finally concludes that God has forsaken him. Because great promises had been given to him, he was afraid that they might be transferred to his domestic servant, who perhaps had not only acted with great vigor in that contest but had many children besides.

This situation distresses the saintly man, and he thinks: "Why does God not give me children, when He gives my servant so many? Surely he will be my heir." Thus before God he pours out his complaint and the thoughts of a very troubled heart.

4. *And behold, the word of the Lord came to him: This man shall not be your heir; your own son shall be your heir.*

These words tend to reassure Abraham, in order that he may know the identity of the person to whom the blessing will come. "That heir," He says, "will come out of your own flesh and blood. Accordingly, you must not understand the blessing the way they explain it, for your seed will be a natural one. Therefore believe Me, not them."

This passage contains a hidden comfort and a profitable doctrine. The ungodly, as we have said, are obsessed with the ambition to apply and appropriate the promises to themselves. Therefore they oppress and harass the true church.

In these circumstances there is nothing else for us to do than to commend our cause to the Lord, as Moses did in that troublesome conflict with Korah, Dathan, and Abiram (Num. 16).

They were entirely incurable and so sure of their own cause that they were neither willing nor able to be instructed. Therefore Moses refers the matter to a divine judgment and prays the Lord not to regard their sacrifice. Thereupon the Lord pronounces judgment upon them and encourages the true church.

Münzer, the Anabaptists, and others similarly opposed us with great zeal, savagely defamed our character, and heaped every kind of abuse upon us.

Mindful of this rule, we remained steadfast in the Word and commended ourselves and our cause to God; but the glory and the triumphs we gladly left to our adversaries. For we knew that it was not necessary for us to fight about these. But we knew that the concern for the Word was entrusted to us by God, in order that we might keep it pure and unadulterated. As long as this is our task and endeavor, our opponents gradually fall one after another; but the truth stands unshaken.

Just as Abraham is strengthened by the divine Word, that he might be certain about the promise which his domestics were distorting, so it is God's regular custom to stand by and strengthen the church when it is in trouble.

At this point there is a philological dispute about the word מֶשֶׁק which I leave to the experts in this language.[11] Whether this Eliezer was the steward or the butler of Abraham does not matter; for us it is enough that this passage deals with the chief person in the household of Abraham, the person who arrogated the promises to himself because of his high rank and the number of his children.

Similarly, Cain, at the time of Adam — Esau, at the time of Isaac — Reuben, at the time of Jacob — and Judas, at the time of Christ and among the apostles — arrogated to themselves the first place and the possession of the promises.

Furthermore, the name Eliezer and Lazarus have the same meaning: "help of God." Perhaps this servant was also puffed up and thought that his name was in accord with the existing circumstances, since he had the highest rank in Abraham's household and was a native of a famous city of Syria.[12] Therefore he considered himself an infante of Spain above the rest and superior to Abraham himself, who did not have such a proud name, such a noble fatherland, or such an abundantly blessed marriage.

Whatever may be the facts about the word מֶשֶׁק, if we have not treated the linguistic question, we nevertheless have treated the theological aspects better than the rabbis.

Indeed, this is actually one of the colors used in Scripture when the saints are portrayed: they experience rebellions and factions even among their servants. They are living among ungodly people, who are by nature factious and exalt themselves. Accordingly, they harass the saints, who submit to God and commend their cause to Him.

[11] This information is taken from Lyra *ad* Gen. 15:4.

[12] The "famous city" is, of course, Damascus.

Eventually He comes and encourages the humble. But "He has scattered the proud in the imagination of their hearts" (Luke 1:51).

John states (1 John 2:19): "They went out from us, but they were not of us." For Satan leaves the saints and the church of God no peace; when one sect has been either overcome or humbled, another springs up, as Paul says in Acts 20:29-30: "I know that after my departure fierce wolves will come in among you, not sparing the flock; and from among your own selves will arise men speaking perverse things."

Adam, Abraham, Isaac, and Jacob endured the same thing. So did Christ Himself, who had His Judas, to whose place the pope, who troubles and harasses the church in various ways, has succeeded. Therefore let us commend our cause to God; and in due time these wolves will meet their just judge as did Korah, Dathan, and Abiram.

5. *And He brought him outside and said: Look toward heaven, and number the stars, if you are able to number them. Then He said to him: so shall your descendants be.*

Inasmuch as God's message to Abraham is so profuse and His encouragement so lavish, even adding signs, the trial which tormented the saintly man was not a light one. For God does not indulge in empty talk. It is our opinion that the promise so clearly set forth concerning the natural son who was to spring from Abraham's own body was sufficient. But a sign is added. Abraham is led out. He is told to look toward heaven and to count the stars. And innumerable descendants are promised him.

Therefore, as I have often said before,[13] these accounts are outstanding because the voice of God is heard in them. Thus this very passage, because of God's extensive conversation with Abraham, deserves to be regarded as highly important. For God speaks with Abraham in a manner that is no different from the way a friend speaks with a close acquaintance and another friend. It is God's practice to do so, and this is His nature. After He has properly afflicted His own, He shows Himself most benevolent and pours Himself out completely.

The fact that Abraham is commanded to look at the stars is proof that this vision occurred at night, at a time when Abraham was sighing and lamenting. It is characteristic of sublime trials to occupy hearts when they are alone. For this reason there is frequent mention

---

[13] See p. 3.

✓ in Holy Scripture of praying at night and in solitude. Affliction is the teacher of such praying.[14]

Thus because Abraham was occupied with these sad thoughts, he was unable to sleep. Therefore he got up and prayed; but while he is praying and feeling such great agitation within himself, God appears to him and converses with him in a friendly manner, so that Abraham, who is awake, is completely enraptured and carried away by the vision.

Thus when Peter was being delivered from prison by an angel (Acts 12:7 ff.), he did not realize at first that what was taking place was actually happening. He thought he was seeing a vision or was dreaming; but shortly after this, when he came to himself, so to speak, he saw that this was really happening.

In the same way this vision comes to Abraham. Yet he finally realizes that the event is actually taking place and that he is not being deluded by a dream. It is characteristic of such visions that they make people ecstatic, as Luke indicates when he says: γενόμενος ἐν ἑαυτῷ, "And Peter came to himself." Until then he had thought that he was seeing a vision in his sleep; he had not noticed that his deliverance from bonds and prison was really taking place.

This vision took place at night. Yet it was not a dream; it was an actual occurrence. Abraham heard the voice of the Lord, came out under the open sky from his chamber, looked at the heaven resplendent with stars, and finally heard the promise concerning his countless descendants.

Furthermore, I have stated before that there is a difference between this promise and the previous one in which he receives the promise of descendants like the sand of the sea.[15] Moses implies in a hidden fashion that this passage includes the promise about the spiritual and heavenly Seed, while previously he is speaking solely of physical descendants. Therefore in this instance he adds:

6. *And he believed the Lord; and He reckoned it to him as righteousness.*

No one has treated this passage better, more richly, more clearly, and more powerfully than St. Paul in the third to the twelfth chapters of Romans. Moreover, Paul treats it in such a way as to show that

---

[14] Luther seems to be thinking of Biblical passages like Ps. 42:8 and Matt. 6:6.

[15] See the discussion in *Luther's Works*, 2, pp. 253—257.

this promise concerning Abraham's descendants should not be interpreted to apply solely to the legitimate physical or temporal seed but to the spiritual and eternal heritage.

For Moses uses heavenly things to illustrate his point, not things that are earthly or temporal. Therefore the promise, too, is a heavenly one, not of children of the flesh but of the spirit, or, as Paul calls them, "children of the promise" (Rom. 9:8). This meaning is clear from what Paul says.

Moreover, when Moses adds that Abraham believed God, this is the first passage of Scripture which we have had until now about faith. For the others, which Moses mentioned previously — the passage about the Seed of the woman, for example, the command to build the ark, the threat of the Flood, and the command to Abraham to leave his country, etc. — merely demand faith; they do not praise or recommend it.

These promises as well as the threats are all words which require faith, but they do not commend faith as the passage before us does. Therefore this is one of the foremost passages of all Scripture.

And Paul has not only expounded this passage most carefully; he also takes great pains to commend it to the church when he adds this statement (Rom. 4:23): "But the words 'it was reckoned to him' were written not for his [Abraham's] sake alone" — who later on died — but (Rom. 15:4) "for our instruction, that . . . we might have hope."

This is truly an instance of treating the Scriptures in an apostolic manner and of establishing the universal statement which is so dreadful and detestable to the very gates of hell: that all who believe the Word of God are just.

Accordingly, lest my discussions obscure what the best interpreter says, I shall speak rather briefly here. Read Paul, and read him most attentively. Then you will see that from this passage he constructs the foremost article of our faith — the article that is intolerable to the world and to Satan — namely, that faith alone justifies, but that faith consists in giving assent to the promises of God and concluding that they are true.[16]

In conformity with this fundamental principle, the author of the Letter to the Hebrews learnedly includes the deeds of all the saints

---

[16] The terminology here is strongly reminiscent of Melanchthon's way of speaking about faith as assent; this passage may, therefore, show the touches of an editor's hand. Cf. the Introduction in *Luther's Works*, 1, pp. xi—xii.

in faith and maintains that everything was done by them out of faith. "For without faith it is impossible to please Him" (Heb. 11:6); and the very fact that God promises something demands that we believe it, that is, that we conclude by faith that it is true and have no doubt that the outcome will be in agreement with the promise.

Therefore if you should ask whether Abraham was righteous before this time, my answer is: He was righteous because he believed God. But here the Holy Spirit wanted to attest this expressly, since the promise deals with a spiritual Seed. He did so in order that you might conclude on the basis of a correct inference that those who accept this Seed, or those who believe in Christ, are righteous.

Abraham's faith was extraordinary, since he left his country when commanded to do so and became an exile; but we are not all commanded to do the same thing. Therefore in that connection Moses does not add: "Abraham believed God, and this was reckoned to him as righteousness." But in the passage before us he makes this addition when he is speaking about the heavenly Seed. He does so in order to comfort the church of all times. He is saying that those who, with Abraham, believe this promise are truly righteous.

Here, in the most appropriate place, the Holy Spirit wanted to set forth expressly and clearly the statement that righteousness is nothing else than believing God when He makes a promise.

At this point there arises an important debate concerning the Law and faith: whether the Law justifies, whether faith does away with the Law, etc.

In this connection Paul learnedly stresses the matter of time: that in this chapter Moses is speaking about righteousness and a righteous or justified Abraham prior to the Law, prior to the works of the Law, yes, prior to the people of the Law and before Moses, the lawgiver, was born. Accordingly, he says that righteousness is not only not from the Law but is prior to the Law, and that neither the Law nor the works of the Law contribute anything toward it.

Then what? Is the Law useless for righteousness? Yes, certainly. But does faith alone, without works, justify? Yes, certainly. Otherwise you must repudiate Moses, who declares that Abraham is righteous prior to the Law and prior to the works of the Law, not because he sacrificed his son, who had not yet been born, and not because he did this or that work, but because he believed God who gave a promise.

In this passage no mention is made of any preparation for grace, of any faith formed through works, or of any preceding disposition.[17] This, however, is mentioned: that at that time Abraham was in the midst of sins, doubts, and fears, and was exceedingly troubled in spirit.

How, then, did he obtain righteousness? In this way: God speaks, and Abraham believes what God is saying. Moreover, the Holy Spirit comes as a trustworthy witness and declares that this very believing or this very faith is righteousness or is imputed by God Himself as righteousness and is regarded by Him as such.

But because the words which the Lord is speaking relate especially to Christ, the spiritual Seed, Paul unfolds this mystery and declares clearly that righteousness comes through faith in Christ (Gal. 2:16). Let us, then, accept this statement and not allow ourselves to be dislodged from it by the ragings of Satan and the popes.

But how Satan hates this statement is proved not only by the fact that today he assails it in such a hostile manner and impudently blasphemes and condemns it; but here the rabbis of the Jews also reveal their folly and the wrath which they harbor against Christ.

They read this passage in the following manner: Abraham believed in God, and when he directed his thoughts to Him, he did so in righteousness. This means that Abraham believed the Lord and thought that God was just and would give him a seed because He was just, that is, because He would have regard for the merits and the saintliness of father Abraham.

Surely a thought worthy of the rabbis and enemies of Christ! For by it the entire sense is turned upside down, the promise and grace are excluded, and human righteousness is established — although Paul, on the basis of this very passage, most emphatically attacks this opinion as wrong and ungodly.

As for the verb חָשַׁב, I do not object very much whether you take it to mean either "to impute" or as "to think"; for the result remains the same. When the Divine Majesty thinks about me that I am righteous, that my sins have been forgiven, that I am free from eternal death, and when I gratefully grasp this thought of God about me in faith, then I am truly righteous, not through my works but through faith, with which I grasp the divine thought.

[17] Here Luther is contending against the scholastic definition of faith as *fides [charitate] formata*, "faith formed by love," and therefore not true faith until and unless love is present.

For God's thought is infallible truth. Therefore when I grasp it with a firm thought — not with an uncertain and wavering opinion — I am righteous.

For faith is the firm and sure thought or trust that through Christ God is propitious and that through Christ His thoughts concerning us are thoughts of peace, not of affliction or wrath.

God's thought or promise, and faith, by which I take hold of God's promise — these belong together.

Therefore Paul correctly translates the word חָשַׁב with λογίζεσθαι, which also refers to thinking, as does the word "to account"; for if you believe God when He gives a promise, God accounts you righteous.

It is not stated here that God wants to regard the Law, circumcision, or sacrifices as worthy of righteousness. Only His accounting, only that thought of grace concerning us, brings this about.

For righteousness is given to Abraham not because he performs works but because he believes. Nor is it given to faith as a work of ours; it is given because of God's thought, which faith lays hold of.

Therefore Paul is very adroit in putting such stress on the word "to account" or "to reckon as" (Rom. 4:4-5). "Now to one who works," he says, "his wages are not reckoned as a gift but as his due. And to one who does not work but trusts Him who justifies the ungodly his faith is reckoned as righteousness"; and a little earlier (Rom. 3:20): "For no human being will be justified in His sight by works of the Law."

But it is known what the works of the Law are. They are the highest and most beautiful virtues. Do these, then, contribute nothing toward righteousness?

"Nothing," says Paul; "all our virtues are rejected, and mercy alone avails."

Even though God demands our virtues and does not want us to be addicted to the lusts of the flesh but earnestly charges us not only to hold them in check but to slay them completely, yet our virtues cannot help us before God's judgment; for they are polluted and contaminated by lust. Therefore unless God averts His eyes from our sins, yes, even from our righteousness and virtues and reckons us as righteous because of faith, which lays hold of His Son, we are done for. Mercy alone, or the accounting alone, saves us.

Hence our doctrine that we are justified before God solely through His accounting mercy has its foundation in this passage.

This is the source from which Paul has drawn his discussions in Romans and Galatians, where he ascribes righteousness to faith, not to works or the Law. But look at the indifference, the sluggishness, yes, blindness of past times; even Lyra distorts this passage with his interpretation.[18]

Lyra declares that faith produced by love formally justifies the mind. Accordingly, he concludes that a faith which has not been formed by love is bare, and he rejects it. Is not this maintaining that God disregards faith and has regard for love and works?

But how does this agree with Moses and Paul? If faith is formed by love, then works are the main thing for which God has regard. But if it is works, then it is we ourselves. Therefore love or works are the living colors; but faith is a monogram, something crude and unattractive.

These insipid thoughts arise from a profound ignorance of sacred matters. As a result, the Law and the promise, faith and works, are jumbled, although a very great distinction should be made between them.

The chief and most important part of the doctrine is the promise; to it faith attaches itself, or, to speak more clearly, faith lays hold of it. Moreover, the confident laying hold of the promise is called faith; and it justifies, not as our own work but as the work of God. For the promise is a gift, a thought of God by which He offers us something. It is not some work of ours, when we do something for God or give Him something. No, we receive something from Him, and that solely through His mercy.

Therefore he who believes God when He promises, he who is convinced that God is truthful and will carry out whatever He has promised, is righteous or is reckoned as righteous.

After that there is also the Law; for God not only promises, but He also commands and enjoins. Moreover, it is the concern of the Law that you conform your will to it and obey God's commands.

Will you not say, however, it is extraordinary perverseness to conclude that the promise and the Law are the same thing? But if a difference has been established and faith alone lays hold of the promise but works serve the Law, what folly it is to invent an unformed faith [19]

[18] Lyra *ad* Gen. 15:6.
[19] See p. 21, note 17.

and to say that faith formed by love justifies! Why do they not leave each within its own fixed bounds?

Faith is assuredly nothing else — nor can it be anything else — than giving assent to a promise. But if this assent is reckoned as righteousness, why, you foolish sophist, do you make the same claim for love, hope, and other virtues?

I know that these are outstanding gifts of God and are required by Him, that they are called forth and sustained in our hearts by the Holy Spirit. I know that faith does not exist without these gifts; but the question now before us is: What is characteristic of each?

In your hand you are holding a variety of seeds; yet I do not ask which are related to which; I ask: What virtue is characteristic of each?

State clearly here what faith alone does, not with what virtues it is closely connected. Faith alone lays hold of the promise, believes God when He gives the promise, stretches out its hand when God offers something, and accepts what He offers. This is the characteristic function of faith alone. Love, hope, and patience are concerned with other matters; they have other bounds, and they stay within these bounds. For they do not lay hold of the promise; they carry out the commands. They hear God commanding and giving orders, but they do not hear God giving a promise; this is what faith does.

Here the testimony of Scripture is clear and beyond doubt. Righteousness is imputed to faith, that is, Abraham is reckoned as righteous by God because he believes God. Scripture makes no such statement about works.

These issues should have been decided on the basis of the sources, not on the basis of the foolish opinions of the sophists, who think as follows: "Behold, it is not enough that you believe; you must also do good works," as though we were concluding that God merely makes promises and does not also give the Law and impose definite duties!

When God makes a promise, there He Himself is dealing with us and is giving and offering us something. But when He gives a command through the Law, He is requiring something from us, and He wants us to do something.

Therefore this distinction must be retained: The only faith that justifies is the faith that deals with God in His promises and accepts them.

But it is love which deals with God when He gives commands; it carries out those commands and obeys God. Similarly, a distinction must be made between the promise and the Law, between faith and love, between the aim of faith and the aim of love; and that destructive gloss about a faith formed by love — the gloss which attributes everything to love and robs faith of everything — must be completely rejected.

Moreover, we must give heed to Holy Scripture, which proves abundantly that nobody can satisfy the Law. The Law demands that you love God with all your heart and your neighbor as yourself (Lev. 19:18). But who, I ask, is there who does this? Even the love of the saints is imperfect and is often troubled by fear, often by lack of trust, and often by impatience in misfortune. At such times what becomes of faith produced by love? If God will not consider you just unless you have loved Him with all your heart and have fulfilled the Law, you will never be justified.

Learn, therefore, not to attribute righteousness to your love or to your works and merits; for they are always unclean, imperfect, and polluted. Consequently, they call for a confession of our unworthiness and for humbling ourselves with a prayer for forgiveness. But attribute your righteousness to mercy alone, to the promise concerning Christ alone, the promise which faith accepts and by means of which it protects and defends itself against conscience when God sits in judgment.

This is the sound and true doctrine. On the other hand, the scholastic doctrine concerning an unformed and a formed faith is of the devil; it destroys the doctrine of faith and entangles us in Turkish and Jewish errors. Therefore let us reject it as a hellish pest.

We know indeed that faith is never alone but brings with it love and other manifold gifts. For he who believes in God and is sure that God is graciously inclined toward us, since He gave His Son and with His Son the hope of eternal life, how could he not love God with all his heart? How could he not revere Him? How could he not strive to display a grateful heart for such great blessings and to obey God while bearing hardships?

Thus faith brings with it a multitude of the most beautiful virtues and is never alone. But matters must not be confused on this account, and what is characteristic of faith alone should not be attributed to other virtues.

Faith is the mother, so to speak, from whom that crop of virtues springs. If faith is not there first, you would look in vain for those virtues. If faith has not embraced the promises concerning Christ, no love and no other virtues will be there, even if for a time hypocrites were to paint what seem to be likenesses of them.

Therefore the promise must be distinguished from the Law. The promise requires faith; the Law, works. The promise is certain and reliable, and is surely carried out, because God carries it out. But the Law is not carried out, because we, who try to fulfill it, are human beings, that is, weak sinners.

Accordingly, our righteousness does not depend on the Law and works, because we cannot perfectly fulfill the Law; it depends on the promise, which is sure and unalterable. Therefore this promise is surely carried out and fulfilled when faith takes hold of it; and it follows with infallible logic that faith alone justifies, inasmuch as faith alone accepts the promise.

The Law and works do not justify; yet Law and works must be taught and performed, in order that we may become aware of our wretched state and accept grace all the more eagerly.

This theology did not originate with us, as the blasphemous papists cry out; nor was it thought up or invented by us. St. Paul teaches it, and as a witness he quotes Moses, who says that Abraham believed God and that this was reckoned to him for righteousness, that is, that Abraham was reckoned as righteous when he believed the promise, since God had compassion on him.

Furthermore, every promise of God includes Christ; for if it is separated from this Mediator, God is not dealing with us at all.

Therefore the only difference between Abraham's faith and ours is this: Abraham believed in the Christ who was to be manifested, but we believe in the Christ who has already been manifested; and by that faith we are all saved.

7. *And He said to him: I am the Lord who brought you from Ur of the Chaldeans, to give you this land to possess.*

The Latin church has few commentators on Moses. The foremost is Lyra. His writings led to the emergence of other commentators: Hugo Carrensis, etc.[20] In connection with this passage Lyra draws attention to a fundamental principle that is most necessary for under-

---

[20] "Hugo Carrensis" was the Cardinal Hugo de Sancto Caro (*ca.* 1190 to 1263), whose *Postillae in vetus et novum testamentum* (Venice, 1487) were one of Luther's sources of knowledge about the exegetical tradition.

standing Scripture, namely, that many passages of Scripture have a twofold meaning: (1) a literal meaning pertaining to earthly things and (2) a meaning pertaining to spiritual and eternal gifts. Among these passages he includes the one before us.[21]

And in the schools of the theologians there is a widely known rule that Scripture must be understood in a fourfold manner:[22] (1) that the sense is historical or literal, (2) that it is tropological, (3) that it is anagogic, (4) that it is allegorical. I for my part am ready to concede that every one of these senses is richly represented; but if we want to treat Holy Scripture skillfully, our effort must be concentrated on arriving at one simple, pertinent, and sure literal sense.

For I consider it not only dangerous and unprofitable for teaching to assign a number of senses to a Scripture passage; this practice also makes light of the authority of Scripture, whose meaning should always be one and the same.

Therefore even though I do not oppose Lyra at this place, I nevertheless am unwilling to follow him. He explains that the less important promise deals with the possession of the land of Canaan, but that the important one deals with the spiritual promise and eternal life.

Thus it is Lyra's explanation that the statement of the psalm that "he will be my son, and I shall be his father" (cf. Ps. 89:26-27 and 2 Sam. 7:14) deals, in its less important meaning, with Solomon, the son of David; but he says that it must be understood as referring principally to Christ.

Lyra thinks that this fundamental principle helps students acquire the ability to extricate themselves from other obscure passages; but I am of the opposite opinion and maintain that to follow this fundamental principle in the church is neither safe nor profitable.

You must always strive to arrive at one sure and simple meaning of an account; and if you change it or depart from it, you should realize that you have departed from Scripture and, in addition, are following an uncertain and doubtful interpretation.

Accordingly so far as the passage before us is concerned, it is certain that Moses is speaking of both possessions, the spiritual as well as the earthly, but not, as Lyra supposes, with the same words. He

[21] Lyra *ad* Gen. 15:7.

[22] On the fourfold sense of Scripture see also *Luther's Works*, 1, p. 87, note 10.

uses words in such a manner that with some he points out the spiritual promise, with others the earthly one.

He does the same thing above, in the twelfth chapter.[23] There the Lord is talking about the possession of the land of Canaan. But finally He adds the brief statement (Gen. 12:3): "And in your seed all the families of the earth will be blessed." Thus He puts the spiritual promise concerning Christ in special words.

It is a serious mistake if Lyra, in keeping with his fundamental principle, tries to give the words a different meaning and to explain them as referring in a less important manner to the physical blessing of a physical Israel.

Thus this passage has the specific meaning — the one and only meaning — that the Lord is speaking about the physical promise of the land of Canaan. No twofold meaning of the account or literal sense must be allowed here.

If someone in search of an allegory should make hell, sin, and death out of Ur of the Chaldeans but eternal life out of the land of Canaan, no one will have any doubt that he is aiming at a foreign meaning and one that is alien to the words.

Even though the allegory is not inappropriate for teaching, its meaning is nevertheless weak and useless in a dispute. For who would prevent the devising of many such meanings, just as many shapes can be formed from a single piece of wax?

We, however, should be concerned about the sure and true meaning. This cannot be any other than that of the letter and the text, or of the historical account. Therefore just as Moses spoke shortly before of the spiritual promise and of true righteousness, so he is now speaking of the promise of the land of Canaan. No allegory is needed here to interpret Ur as sin and the Promised Land as immortality; for Moses has already stated that Abraham's faith in God was reckoned to him for righteousness, that is, that through faith his sins were forgiven and eternal life was granted to him.

That Abraham is the heir of righteousness and of eternal life through Christ — the literal sense itself reveals this if you treat it skillfully. Now because Abraham is not alone but has the promise of descendants, and his descendants are of the promise, that is, believe the promise, Paul transfers the promise from Abraham's physical seed to the believers among the Gentiles. Since the entire outcome depends

[23] Luther is referring to his earlier comments, *Luther's Works,* 2, pp. 253 ff.

on the fact that Abraham believed God and this was reckoned to him for righteousness, that is, that through believing he became righteous and an heir of the eternal kingdom, Paul constructs this universal proposition: that everyone who believes the promise as Abraham did is an heir of the eternal kingdom and righteous, whether he is a physical descendant of Abraham or not.

If Paul had not drawn this meaning from the literal and simple sense, he would never have seen it. "Those who are men of faith," he says in Galatians (3:9), "are blessed with Abraham, who had faith"; and likewise (Gal. 3:7): "It is men of faith who are the sons of Abraham." On the other hand (Gal. 3:10), "All who rely on works of the Law are under a curse."

What is the source of Paul's arguments? Where did he get them? Without a doubt from this passage; and if he had not undertaken its explanation in an apostolic spirit, we all would have passed it by as a useless and out-of-date statement.

Therefore we owe Paul special honor as the greatest teacher of Holy Scripture, and it is proper for us to follow him. In no circumstances shall we let lying sophists lead us away from his interpretation.

I have said this for the sake of those who are somewhat inexperienced. When they come across such passages in the writings of the doctors, they think they have found a jewel. Yet such passages are dangerous; they lead away from the true way, that is, from the literal and historical meaning, the only one that should be retained and stressed.

8. *But he said: O Lord God, how am I to know that I shall possess it?*

It is the custom of Holy Scripture to add signs to promises. Thus in Baptism and in the Lord's Supper there is not only the Word of promise but also a sign or work or ceremony. Therefore after Abraham has become more intimate with God and has been encouraged by Him, he has the courage to ask for a sign. At any other time this would be the sin of putting God to the test.

Putting God to the test is linked with doubting. Therefore the Virgin Mary seems to have acted more properly when she believed the promise without exacting a sign. Of his own accord the angel gives her the sign concerning Elizabeth (Luke 1:36).

But these matters must not be judged on the basis of reason; the person must be considered. Abraham is a believer and an heir of eternal righteousness, and so it pleases God to add to the promise the sign which he desires. But if he had been without faith, it would have been a sin to ask for a sign.

Thus Gideon and David ask for signs, and their plans are successful. The ungodly Ahaz does not ask for a sign, although he was commanded by the Lord to do so.[24] He persists in his habitual unbelief.

Thus one's judgment must be based either on the person or, to express myself more clearly, on the heart itself. "For whatever does not proceed from faith is sin" (Rom. 14:23). Conversely, whatever comes from faith pleases God.

David wages wars and is successful; another fights without success. For David remains in the faith and in his calling. By slaying his enemies he serves God. The calling, however, does not follow a set pattern. It takes place through signs, through the spoken Word, or even through an inner impulse of the spirit.

David and Samson kill lions without anyone's command; they are urged on by a divine impulse. He who does not have this impulse and attempts the same thing will most certainly become involved in danger.

Therefore just as these special works of a calling should not be adduced as a pattern, so Abraham's example should not be followed by everybody. You should not ask for a sign from God because Abraham asks for a sign. Abraham is described as righteous and full of the Holy Spirit through divine imputation. Therefore even when he asks for a sign without being commanded to do so, he does not sin but pleases God, who gladly listens to him. Unless you have the sunlight of the Holy Spirit guiding your way, you should never do this; but you must hold fast to the Word and command of God, which should be surer for you than any sign whatever.

I have often warned that much good sense is needed when passing judgment on the works of the saints. When the Spirit had come upon Saul, he cut oxen to pieces and threatened that the same thing would happen to the sheep of those who would not follow him and Samuel to war (1 Sam. 11). Success followed this impulse, which was both heroic and from the Holy Spirit.

After Münzer had aroused the peasants to take up arms, he was

---

[24] The reference to Gideon seems to be an allusion to Judges 6:17; the reference to David seems to be an allusion to Ps. 86:17; the reference to Ahaz seems to be an allusion to Is. 7:10-14.

also sure of victory in what seemed to him a just cause.[25] But he perished, and rightly so; for his actions came from his own spirit, not from the Spirit of God. Nor could he get any support from the examples of the Old Testament saints, the examples on which he was nevertheless relying.

For the most part, the examples of the saints are miracles. They should not be adduced as a pattern.

I have no command to walk with Peter on the sea; but I do have the command to love my neighbor, to be patient when under a cross, etc. When I do these things, I am not erring; and I am also out of danger.

In this passage Abraham is described as a friend of God (2 Chron. 20:7), who talks intimately with Him; and God, as his friend, is pleased with everything he does. When we are well-disposed toward someone, we endure and put up with everything and take offense at nothing, as Paul states (1 Cor. 13:7): "Love bears all things." But in an unfriendly and hostile person everything displeases, and we do not allow even the slightest fault to go unnoticed. The same thing happens here. Abraham comes forward with the utmost trust, through which he is righteous, and asks for a sign, not for his own sake — for he himself was not to possess the land — but for the sake of his descendants, lest their faith succumb during those terrible persecutions and obstacles which would confront them.

What trepidation there was when they were to be led out of Egypt, and how wretched they were while there! How often they grumbled in the wilderness itself because they were impatient! Why say more? Out of such a great multitude only two enter the land of Canaan. How could their faith have remained unshaken in so many dangers and difficulties had not this promise and similar ones given strength to their people? Hence this request for a sign was necessary and beneficial to the church.

9. *He said to him: Bring Me a heifer three years old, a she-goat three years old, a ram three years old, a turtledove, and a young pigeon.*

10. *And he brought Him all these, cut them in two, and laid each half over against the other; but he did not cut the birds in two.*

[25] In support of his militant action Münzer had cited the example of David and other saints in the theocracy of the Old Testament.

11. *And when birds of prey came down upon the carcasses, Abram drove them away.*

12. *As the sun was going down, a deep sleep fell on Abram; and lo, a dread and great darkness fell upon him.*

From this sign given by the Lord to Abraham his descendants were to learn that the promise concerning the land of Canaan is certain, no matter how long the Lord may delay it. Moses gives a well-detailed description of the sacrifice. Without a doubt this custom of sacrificing was handed down by Adam himself to his descendants; and gradually the heathen also adopted it, until it was reinstated by the Law.

Abraham seems to have been occupied throughout the day with the preparation of this sacrifice and with building the altars, until finally a deep sleep fell upon the tired man at nighttime. The text itself explains both what Moses mentions about the birds of heaven and what the entire sign means.

13. *Then the Lord said to Abram: Know of a surety that your descendants will be sojourners in a land that is not theirs, and they will be oppressed for four hundred years;*

14. *but I will bring judgment on the nation which they serve, and afterward they shall come out with great possessions.*

15. *As for yourself, you shall go to your fathers in peace; you shall be buried in a good old age.*

16. *And they shall come back here in the fourth generation; for the iniquity of the Amorites is not yet complete.*

This is the explanation of the sign. The slaughtered animals are the people of Israel, who were abused and afflicted in various ways in Egypt. The birds about to consume the pieces of flesh are Pharaoh and the Egyptians. Abraham, who is the father of this nation, drives the birds away; for the promise made to Abraham does not permit this nation to be completely crushed, even though it is severely oppressed.

Furthermore, the slaughtering of the four kinds of animals depicts the four-hundred-year affliction in Egypt of the descendants of Abraham. The birds denote the final period, during which Israel flew away from slavery to freedom and the Promised Land.

If you consider the time, it is hard to be oppressed by slavery that lasts so long. But the fact that there is the promise of sure deliverance in the end — this is comfort in greatest abundance.

Abraham no doubt impressed this sign on his descendants in sermon after sermon, urging them not to let themselves be overcome by their misfortunes and not to give up but to concentrate on the promise of the land of Canaan and on their deliverance in firm faith and unshaken hope. He also urged that just as he had driven off the birds to keep them from defiling the sacrifice, so his descendants, too, should thwart and overcome offenses until the Lord in His mercy would put an end to these evils and destroy the enemies of His people.

Thus Abraham not only had the promise of a temporal seed before this seed existed, but it had also been foretold to him that sufferings and hardships would precede the fulfillment of the promise.

Abraham was still alone. He was without an heir. But in the sight of God the nation had already been born at this time, yes, was being seized upon greedily by the birds, and the birds had been driven far away, even submerged in the sea, while the nation had been delivered and was safe. But Abraham sees these events only in the Word and in the promise, and he believes that they will surely happen in this manner.

This is the historical meaning of the passage before us. Through this sacrifice the Lord wanted to give Abraham a sign from which he might learn the events of the future. It is as though the Lord were saying: "In the world this nation will be for Me like the most acceptable sacrifice. Neither the birds of heaven nor the ungodly heathen will cease to assail it. But you will drive them away; that is, My promise, which I have made to you, will keep the nation safe. I Myself will judge the heathen and will lead out My people with great wealth." But this sign was necessary, not for the sake of Abraham, who believed God and was righteous, but for the sake of his descendants, who were to be afflicted among the heathen in various ways. It was necessary to keep them from despairing or being broken down in spirit.

Moreover, it is also the purpose of this passage to teach us what God's nature is. He is indeed the Deliverer and Liberator from death. But before He delivers, He destroys; before He makes alive, He plunges into death. For He is wont to act in this way "so that out of nothing He may make everything" (Heb. 11:3).

Thus when God wants to exalt this nation and to increase it beyond the number of the stars, He first permits birds to attack it and to trouble, oppress, and harass it in various ways.

This was the reason for the tyrannical imposition and exacting of work and for the boundless cruelty practiced at the command of the Egyptian tyrant on the children when they were born (Ex. 1:8 ff.).

It was likewise Satan's intention to devour Moses when he was exposed on the water (Ex. 2:3). Therefore this nation is rightly compared to a sacrifice, because it was frequently slain in the flesh.

This is also the reason for the fright by which Abraham is seized in the night. For the flesh cannot refrain from grieving and sobbing when it feels the cross.

At this point there arises a question about the number of years, namely, where one should start counting. The end of the exile is definitely the departure from Egypt, but as to its beginning there are various opinions.

Lyra proves clearly enough from the account in Ex. 6:16 ff. that the Jews were not in Egypt for 400 years.[26] For Levi had three sons before he went down to Egypt. Kohath was born in Canaan and lived 133 years, but he died in Egypt. His son Amram lived for 137 years and was born and died in Egypt. The son of Amram is Moses, and in his eightieth year the people departed from Egypt.

Therefore this computation must not begin from the entrance into Egypt; for if you add up the years of the lives of these patriarchs, they amount to only 286.

Accordingly the Jews begin their computation from the birth of Isaac; but here, too, many years are unaccounted for.

Therefore one must begin computing from the year in which Abraham was called out of Ur of the Chaldeans, for from that time until the descent into Egypt there are exactly 215 years. But the stay in Egypt also amounts to 215 years. Together these now make 430 years, just as they are reckoned in Ex. 12:40 and in Gal. 3:17.

Abraham was 75 years old when he left Ur. From that year it is 25 years until his hundredth year, during which Isaac was born to him. But from the birth of Isaac to the descent into Egypt there are 190 years. Together these amount to 215 years. If you add the 215 of the stay in Egypt, they total 430 years.

[26] Lyra *ad* Gen. 15:13. On Luther's own chronological works cf. *Luther's Works*, 1, p. 334, note 1.

I consider this calculation correct, for Moses in Exodus and Paul in Galatians count 430 years.

When in this passage Scripture mentions only 400 years, it does not reckon the time accurately; it indicates that the people will be in exile approximately 400 years. We are in the habit of doing the same thing. At times we count something accurately; at times our count is inaccurate.

But why, you will ask, do you begin the computation with the departure of Abraham from Ur, although the text clearly states that the seed of Abraham will be in exile for so many years?

My answer is: "When Abraham was called out of Ur, he was at that time already being declared the father of this people; and so far as the promise was concerned, he already was a father, even though he was still childless."

The Epistle to the Hebrews (7:9-10) states: "By Melchizedek a tithe was exacted from Levi when he was still in the loins of Abraham"; for when a tithe was exacted from Abraham alone, who through the promise was the father of this nation, a tithe was exacted from his entire posterity, which was still hidden in his loins. When Abraham is an exile, his descendants are exiles; when the desendants of Abraham are afflicted, Abraham himself is afflicted. Nevertheless, toward the end, when deliverance was nearest, everything was in a most disturbed and wretched state.

Similarly today, now that the Day of the Lord and the deliverance of the true church is near, the outburst of violence is most powerful and bitter; for more blood is being shed by the Turk and the pope than was shed during any previous period.

Here, too, we are reminded of the excellence of the sacred accounts. For in all the books of the heathen what do you find to compare with them? Here the events of 400 years are predicted. Accordingly, Abraham sees the history of his descendants predicted for a long time to come, their afflictions in Egypt and finally their glorious liberation.

Thus it is evident that God "calls into existence the things that do not exist" (Rom. 4:17). For with God there is no past or future; with Him everything that for us is far in the future exists at the present time.

Therefore this chapter is one of the foremost in the entire Holy Scripture; through the Holy Spirit the prophets have drawn much from it. From this source the psalm (100:3) declares: "Know that the Lord is God! It is He that made us." And Ps. 139:1 — "O Lord, Thou hast searched me" — is also based on it. From this source stem all the prophecies concerning the tribulations of the righteous.

This is a marvelously powerful text if the Holy Spirit comes and explains it to us. "In Thy book," says David (Ps. 139:16), "were written, every one of them, the days that were formed for me, when as yet there was none of them." Have you not in this passage (Gen. 15:13-16) a clear example of David's statement? The years are numbered, and a manifold affliction is predicted; but so far no one of those who will be living during these years exists, for the people of whom the Lord is speaking here have not yet been born. In this manner the holy prophets, enlightened by the Holy Spirit, drew their sermons from Moses.

But it is a very great comfort to know that the divine truth deceives neither with regard to the past nor with regard to the future. Therefore through this promise Abraham, even though he is still without an heir, nevertheless is sure about the possession of the land of Canaan and about his whole posterity; so far as his faith is concerned, he is already in possession of the land.

Moreover, the passage before us is also useful for strengthening our faith in opposition to the Jews. If God so loved the seed of Abraham that He fixed a definite time when they were to be set free, how will the Jews of our time defend themselves, now that they have been wandering and roaming for more than fifteen hundred years without any prophecy, in a hard exile without any end in sight, without a form of worship, and without a government, especially since there are very important prophecies in Jeremiah and elsewhere, such as "David shall never lack a man to sit on the throne of the house of Israel" (Jer. 33:17), etc.?

During the Babylonian captivity, when it seemed that the people had been completely cast aside, the godly were nevertheless clinging to the prophecy of Jeremiah, who, through the Holy Spirit, had set a limit to the time of the captivity, namely, that they would return to Canaan after seventy years.

Are not our Jews forced to admit that ever since the time of Christ's crucifixion no man has sat on the throne of David before the face of God?

What now? God is not lying, is He? No, but the Jews themselves are lying when they deny that Christ has come and are now waiting in vain these many years for the Messiah.

But if their hope were reliable, and the Messiah were near, you do not suppose, do you, that they would be without prophets to remind them of the time of His arrival? But because they have been deprived of the ministry of prophets for so long a time and have no knowledge of a definite or indefinite time when their captivity is to end, it is certain that their expectation is vain and their faith of no avail, but that the Word of God is sure and reliable; for it promises that until the coming of the Messiah a descendant of David will never fail to sit on the throne of David.

It also follows that the Jews are no longer the people of God but have been cast aside by Him because of their unbelief in not accepting the promised and manifested Messiah.

Therefore keep this reasoning in mind; it cannot be evaded in any way. God keeps His promise and keeps it to such an extent that He is concerned even about those who have not yet been born, as we see in this passage. How, then, could He disregard those who have already been born and let them wander about for so long a time without prophets if they were the people or the seed of Abraham? Accordingly, their lot proves conclusively that they are not the people of God but have been rejected by God.

Even though the church of the Gentiles has been oppressed in various ways during these last times, it nevertheless has evidences of God's concern for it.

The Turkish religion and the papacy are most powerful monsters. In recent times the church has been severely afflicted by them; yet amid the ragings of the dragon and the lion Baptism remains, the Eucharist remains, the power of the Keys remains, and the text of the Bible, or Holy Scripture, remains. Certainly this is not through human power; otherwise the Turk and the pope would have long since done away with these. But through His power God preserves these, so that when the Word and the sacraments remain, faith and the church remain in spite of the pope and the Turk.

Therefore inasmuch as God is still speaking with us, He has not forsaken His church, even though He allows it to be afflicted.

The Jews are unable to adduce anything like this; for because they themselves also have Sacred Scripture, there has been added the punishment that their table becomes a snare for them (Ps. 69:22).

Isaiah (29:11-12) compares them to someone who is holding a book but does not know the letters and for this reason is unable to read.

He also calls Scripture a closed and sealed book which they cannot open. Hence the Jews are certainly in error.

For through prophets God always reveals to His people a definite time both of affliction and of deliverance. Therefore it is characteristic neither of God nor of His people that for about fifteen hundred years now they are exiled and without prophets.

We Christians, on the other hand, are as certain as anyone can be that nothing remains to be fulfilled except the Last Day and our redemption. Meanwhile God speaks with us, encourages and instructs us, in order that we may be ready every day and hour. This is positive proof that we are the people of God and the true church, which God does not forsake to such an extent that He does not carefully forewarn the descendants of Abraham, who as yet have not even been born, about the length of their exile.

For with God both the future and the past are the present. For God the descendants of Abraham were living at that time; therefore He is speaking to them and giving them instruction.

Thus even the dead exist and are alive in the sight of God; for just as I was alive for God before I came into existence and before I was born, so I shall also be alive and exist for God even when I am dead.

The text before us asserts powerfully that God is the God of the living and that those who are not yet in existence or through death have ceased to be among the living are just as alive for God as those who are in existence. The holy prophets have based many of their sermons on this passage.

What follows in the text — "As for yourself, you shall go to your fathers in peace" — is a most beautiful comfort. For our thoughts are as follows: Abraham dies as an exile, and not until long after his death do his descendants obtain the promise of the land of Canaan. What, then, becomes of what God said above: "Fear not, Abram, I am your Shield; your reward shall be very great"? What good is this to one who is dead? This is indeed something great, and I pray that what God promises concerning a pleasant old age and a peaceful death may happen to me. But what is this in comparison with such a magnificent promise?

Since Abraham had been enlightened by the Holy Spirit, he realized that these words referred to the resurrection of the dead and to the life of the future world, and as a sign or an evidence of this he pointed to the physical promise concerning the land of Canaan. Therefore he concludes that God will be his rich reward when he is already dead and resting in the dust of the earth.

And above all one should note the very pleasing description of death this passage contains. God does not use the term "death." No, He tones down this name, so to speak, with pleasing words. "You will be gathered to your fathers," He says, "and will sleep with Noah and other heroes." Likewise: "You will be buried, that is, you will not be snatched away, as Enoch was, but will be buried in the earth; and you will be reduced to dust at a peaceful old age, when the measure of your days is full and you have become weary, as it were, of this life."

Accordingly, God declares that Abraham will die; yet He promises that He will be Abraham's reward. How are we going to harmonize these statements unless we conclude that after this life there remains another life, one that is better and eternal, to which we shall be awakened out of the very dust of death by the Son of God? [27]

The saintly fathers had such tokens of a life to come. With them they sustained themselves in this troubled and wretched life. But those previous statements about imputed righteousness, that is, about the free forgiveness of sins and deliverance from eternal death, serve this same purpose.

"But these words — were written not for Abraham's sake alone," says Paul (Rom. 4:23-24), "but for ours also," in order that we, too, may believe that there has been laid up a reward for us when we shall lie buried in the earth, and indeed such a reward that we may live with God as long as He Himself will live, that is, forever. With this hope Abraham is satisfied. Even though he does not obtain the promise of the land of Canaan, yet he is cheerful. He disregards and despises death, for he knows that he will live with God in all eternity.

Therefore you must take careful note of this passage. It is like an ocean and a great sea in which the prophets have found many brilliant sermons on justification, on redemption from sin, on the resurrection of the dead and eternal life.

These things, as we have said, were not written for Abraham's benefit. They are of service to us, in order that when we, with Abraham, believe in the woman's Seed, we may through this hope over-

[27] On this principle for interpreting the Old Testament see also *Luther's Works*, 13, pp. 126 ff.

come death and no longer have a horror of departing from this life. Our bodies will indeed be buried in the earth; yes, they will decay in the earth and will be reduced to dust. But in due time the earth will return this deposit to Him who has promised that He will be our reward. This hope is sure and firm.

It is the purpose of the last statement — the one about the fact that the iniquities of the Amorites are not yet complete — to point out the patience of God. For just as there has been assigned to the godly their portion in the land of the living, so the ungodly have their portion assigned in hell. Therefore let us too endure their iniquities for a time; for they will not go unpunished forever.

Thus the iniquities of the pope and of the Turk are not yet complete. God, who is long-suffering and patient, does not punish evildoers immediately. But this does not mean they escape entirely, for the time has been appointed when they will be brought to trial and will pay the penalties their crimes deserve.

Thus Peter says (2 Peter 3:7) that the ungodly are being reserved for the Day of Judgment in order to be punished, and Paul declares (Rom. 2:4) that the punishments are delayed with the intention that God may grant time for repentance. But the imprudent and complacent flesh misuses the long-suffering of God as a license to sin and, because the punishment is not inflicted immediately, dreams of perpetual security.

This is what the Lord promises in this passage concerning the Canaanites: "I shall still spare them and grant time for repentance; meanwhile, My dear Abraham, have patience, you and yours; perhaps some of them will be converted and will repent."

17. *When the sun had gone down and it was dark, behold, a smoking fire pot and a flaming torch passed between these pieces.*

18. *On that day the Lord made a covenant with Abram, saying: To your descendants I give this land, from the river of Egypt to the great river, the river Euphrates,*

19. *the land of the Kenites, the Kenizzites, the Kadmonites,*

20. *the Hittites, the Perizzites, the Rephaim,*

21. *the Amorites, the Canaanites, the Girgashites, and the Jebusites.*

The rite of sacrificing did not begin here but was passed on by Adam and the rest of the holy fathers down to Abraham. The writings of the heathen also contain evidences that sacrifices were used in making covenants, and Jeremiah's account of the servants who were to be restored to liberty is also familiar.[28] After the sacrificial animal had been slain and cut up, those who were making the covenant would pass between the pieces. Then they would burn one part and keep another part for a feast.

This custom was also observed in our own lifetime. When Maximilian, King Louis of France, and Pope Julius were making the covenant which has been called the most holy covenant, they divided a eucharistic host into three parts and partook of it together. But this sacred covenant lasted barely six months![29]

It appears, therefore, that this way of making covenants is ancient. Because God is making a covenant with Abraham which specifies that the land of Canaan will surely be handed over to Abraham's descendants, He Himself observes this practice and passes between the pieces of the sacrificial animals like a flame; and He sets fire to them for a sign that this sacrifice is pleasing to Him.

In this manner Abraham has been encouraged in this chapter and has been appointed the heir to eternal and temporal life. I confess that this matter is worthy to the highest degree of a longer and more careful discussion; but I am too busy for more elaborate reflections, and the seeds of the very great things which Moses wanted to stand out in this chapter have been pointed out as well as it has been possible for me.

[28] Apparently a reference to Jer. 34:8 ff.

[29] The Weimar editors suggest that Luther is thinking of the holy alliance entered into by Pope Julius II, Spain, and Venice against King Louis XII of France. They add that in the League of Cambrai in 1508 Julius II and Louis XII (as well as Maximilian I) were allied against Venice.

CHAPTER SIXTEEN

1. *Now Sarai, Abram's wife, bore him no children. She had an Egyptian maid whose name was Hagar;*

2. *and Sarai said to Abram: Behold now, the Lord has prevented me from bearing children; go in to my maid; it may be that I shall obtain children by her.*

ABRAM had been delivered from his anxiety about an heir, which had made him afraid that his Damascene servant would come into the possession of the promise as his legal and not his natural heir since he himself had no heir. For this reason the Lord expressly promises Abram that he will have a natural heir, one from his own body.

Now follows another trial, which distresses his wife Sarah. Thus the life of this godly couple was full of trials and incessant troubles. People who are coarse and lack experience in spiritual matters see only the fact that she brings her maid to her husband. Because they themselves burn with lust, they do not consider the promise which gave occasion for this action; they consider only those filthy deeds of the flesh. The Jews do the same thing.

Thus I have heard all too often in school — not only from jurists but also from theologians — that the writings of Moses contain nothing but the lustful deeds of the Jews, since he devotes a great deal of attention to the recording of genealogies and marriages.[1]

Such opinions give proof of foul minds, which pass rash judgments on the deeds of the saints on the basis of their own character. The godly husband and wife do not resort to these plans because they have been spurred on by lust; they succumb to temptation, both because they are concerned about offspring on account of the promise and because they are eagerly waiting for the Seed promised to Adam in Paradise. Therefore Sarah, who knows that she is both exhausted and barren, shares her plan with Abram and has her maid Hagar lie

---

[1] See a reference to the same accusation, *Luther's Works*, 1, p. 240.

with him, in order that she may be built from her. Even though she is not in doubt concerning the promise, yet she does have doubts about the persons whom God wants to choose for this work.

This passage praises the fruit of matrimony, namely, the propagation of the human race. The writings of the heathen also give lavish praise to this fruit. Even though the world is unable to understand these thoughts which trouble Abraham, it nevertheless both approves of marriage and condemns promiscuous lusts.

It has always been the wish of respectable parents that their children be joined in respectable marriage rather than associate with rakes and prostitutes.

In the first place, reason is aware of the respectability which will exist in this lawful union of a man and woman; in the second place, it considers the enormous advantages; for it sees that from this source flow states and households, which would necessarily collapse and perish if there were no lawful and secure marriages.

But Abraham bears in mind not only the opportunity of increasing his offspring but also the redemption of the entire world, which he knows will come to the world through the promised Seed. This he longs to have accomplished in any manner whatever.

In his seventy-fifth year Abraham left Ur of the Chaldeans; but this is already the tenth year of his exile, and so far there appears to be no hope of a child. To be sure, he has the promise; but it is being delayed, and in his own opinion it is being delayed too long.

If we consider what he did — so much wandering and so many journeys, then the battle with the four kings — this decade was very short; but if you think of the delayed promise, it was long indeed. Month after month and year after year passed by. Yet Sarah remained childless.

Here there were no lustful thoughts, but the anxious expectation of the seed racks his mind. Moreover, what conversations, sighings, tears, and mutual comfortings there must have been between the saintly spouses during these years as a result of this trial! For the longer the promise was delayed, the more heavily the cross lay on them and the more unbearable the trial became.

Hence in this chapter Moses wanted to portray the extraordinary trial of Sarah. Abraham's doubt about an heir had been removed through the promise, for he knew that an heir had to be born from him. Assured that a descendant would come from his own body, he now has doubts about the mother — and not without good reason, for Sarah was barren by nature and also too old to have a child.

As an example to all women Sarah is described as having been a very wise woman and most faithful to her husband. She had followed him into exile after giving up all her friends and relatives. While in exile she steadfastly bore all the inconveniences and hardships. She humbly obeyed her husband in all things. Now, after all circumstances have taken away every hope of a child, she nevertheless does not abandon her faith; nor does she doubt the promise.

Even though Sarah sees that the fulfillment of the promise is being delayed and even though she despairs — both because of her barrenness and because of her age — of being a mother, she nevertheless relinquishes the glory of motherhood in the utmost humility and is content if her maid Hagar becomes pregnant by Abraham.

Therefore she holds fast to her faith and hope in the mercy of God. In the utmost humility she bears the disgrace of barrenness and willingly concedes this honor to her maid.

The wives of Job, Tobias, and David would not have acted this way.[2] They would have cast doubt on the promises of God and would have said indignantly that they had been deluded by Satan. They would have quarreled with Abraham for having left his native country because he had been deceived by Satan's tricks. But if they had resorted to none of these tactics, they would in any event have had doubt about God's good will toward them and would have considered barrenness a sign of God's wrath.

But Sarah distinguishes most beautifully among the gifts of God. Even though she is barren, she believes that He loves her. For this reason she willingly concedes the glory of fertility to her maid. Thus the virtue of this woman is extraordinary in every respect.

Therefore Sarah is deservedly held up by Peter (1 Peter 3:6) as a pattern for the entire female sex. But under the papacy accounts of this kind were held in contempt because they conflict with celibacy, even though you see that this wife had far more virtues than anyone of all the celibates. For who will ever be able properly to explain and praise the fact that she relinquishes the glory of maternity of her own accord and is willing to be considered rejected, as it were, in this respect, provided that she remains in the grace and compassion of God and the promise is fulfilled through another woman?

[2] The passages Luther seems to have in mind are Job 2:9; Tobit 5:17; and perhaps 2 Sam. 6:16.

Abraham's virtuousness is also outstanding. Although he had the right to take another woman, as was customary — for at that time polygamy was in vogue — yet he does this only at the urging of his wife. This was a rare example on the part of both. Abraham could have taken another woman than that Egyptian servant, one who was more distinguished, more refined, and in better circumstances; but he yields to his wife, who has her maid lie with him. Sarah herself intends to remain the mother and the mistress in the household; she herself intends to have the promised Seed — if not the natural one, still the legal one.

Take note of Sarah's temperate language: "The Lord," she says, "has prevented me from bearing." She does not indignantly blame Satan, as we are in the habit of doing; she acknowledges the act of God with humility and says: "So far it has not been the Lord's will that I should bear children."

Accordingly, Sarah acknowledges that matrimony is a way of life established by the Lord and under God's control; she voluntarily endures her barrenness with equanimity. She would have thanked God most sincerely if He had blessed her womb.

Because of its modesty the Hebrew manner of speech is very pleasant. "Go in to Hagar," says Sarah. In like manner Scripture says of David (Ps. 51): "He went in to Bathsheba."

Furthermore, the verb "to build" connotes the blessing of offspring; for when offspring are given, the house is built and a household is properly established, because the parents know for whom they are working and whom they will have as heirs of their possessions.

Here, too, the faith of this most saintly woman is shown. Sarah has her maid lie with Abraham in order that she, Sarah, may lay claim to the offspring as her own. She intends to be a mother legally, even though she cannot be a mother naturally.

And this reason induced Abram to obey his wife when she urged and entreated him. Because the promise was there and yet it was by nature impossible for Sarah to give birth, they conclude that offspring must be sought from another mother, lest the promise be obstructed.

But this case should not be set up as a pattern, as though we were allowed to do the same things; for it is necessary to consider the circumstances. The promise of the Seed has not been made to us, as it was to Abraham; and no matter if your marriage is completely barren, there is no danger whatever from this source, even if your entire lineage should die out if God so wills.

Abraham, however, not only had the promise of the Seed, but it was also an assured fact that Sarah was barren.

These circumstances do not exist in your case. Therefore this unusual action of these spouses should in no wise be adduced as a pattern, especially not in the New Testament.

For the Old Testament permitted polygamy also for the sake of children, and in Moses there is a law which states that if anyone has ravished a maid, he must keep her as his wife (Deut. 22:29). But regulations concerning ceremonial or legal matters have come to an end, and Abraham's case is far different from the one which appears in Moses.

And Abram hearkened to the voice of Sarai.

3. *So, after Abram had dwelt ten years in the land of Canaan, Sarai, Abram's wife, took Hagar the Egyptian, her maid, and gave her to Abram her husband as a wife.*

Moses states clearly that Abraham obeyed Sarah; he does not say that he was glad to do so. I for my part am completely convinced that he obeyed Sarah unwillingly; for he loved her very much, as the account shows. Yet he yielded to her reasons when she mentioned her barrenness and her old age. Therefore he does this in compliance with his wife's wish, not as the polygamists of the Old Testament were in the habit of doing.

And Moses has reason to continue to call Sarah Abram's wife, and Abram her husband. He does so in order to show that Abram did not become an adulterer and that the earlier marriage of Sarah and Abram had not been dissolved by this new arrangement. Abram remains the chaste husband of his very chaste wife. He lies with Hagar only to prevent the promise of God from being obstructed.

4. *And he went in to Hagar, and she conceived; and when she saw that she had conceived, she looked with contempt on her mistress.*

Here a new trial begins. The fact that Moses mentions the ten years — this the Jews bring into conformity with the rule and law that a husband should live with his wife for ten years, but that in case she remains childless for a decade, then it is right for the husband to take another wife, in order that he may not die without an heir.³ I do not know whether this law was observed or not.

Nevertheless, I do not approve of their taking this historical account as a pattern; for, as I stated previously, it has its own particular circumstances.

And why should the Jews use Abraham's example to justify polygamy when this practice was commanded in the Law (Deut. 25:5)? For the widow of a brother who died without children had to become the wife of her deceased husband's brother, in order that the latter might bring forth offspring for him who had died.

When we reflect on this command, we commonly assent to the opinion that much license was given to sexual lust among the Jews, since polygamy was not only permitted but even commanded.

But my opinion is different, for we see the ways of nature. As soon as the law orders us to do something, we do it unwillingly and incline toward what is forbidden.⁴ Nor did polygamy lack disadvantages. We see the boundless weakness of women. They indulge their moods and are controlled by them. One is irritable and quarrelsome; another is proud. This one is unsuited to manage a household; that one is negligent in bringing up children, etc. Therefore it was a serious matter to marry the wife of a deceased brother, for the Law could not be evaded under any pretext. Hence this Law did not give license for lust; but it did increase trouble, toil, and worries.

And through Adam's disobedience nature has become so stubborn and rebellious that it cannot bear any law. Thus since marriage has been enjoined so that every man may have his own wife in order to avoid fornication (1 Cor. 7:2), we find that celibacy is extolled by some with immoderate praise and that young people are more inclined toward promiscuity.

In the comedy the old man says: All who have amours are reluctant to marry.⁵ And before our eyes there are countless instances to show that spouses who love each other most fervently come to hate each other for the most insignificant reasons, forsake each other, and associate with others.

³ Cf. Lyra *ad* Gen. 16:4.

⁴ Ovid, *Ars amandi*, III, 4, 17. The same passage is quoted earlier in the *Lectures on Genesis, Luther's Works*, 2, p. 329.

⁵ Terence, *Andria*, I, 2, 20.

So savage and corrupt is human nature. Marriage is necessary as a remedy for lust, and through marriage God permits sexual intercourse. Not only does He cover the sin from which we are unable to abstain, but He also blesses the union of the male and the female. And yet the whole world shuns this legitimate, divinely instituted union and prefers to indulge in promiscuous relations, which are harmful in more than one way. Property is squandered, bodies are damaged by serious diseases, God is provoked to inflict horrible punishments, and, worst of all, states and households are destroyed.

Why do we not avoid these great evils? Why do we not prefer to seek the blessing of God through a legitimate union? Obviously because our nature is corrupted by sin, rebellious, and intolerant of laws, and does not want to be tamed or restrained.

So indescribable and pernicious a malady is our inborn disobedience. From it stem those sayings of the Greeks and the Latins which condemn marriage and advise against it because of the annoyances of the flesh it brings with it.[6] And yet those who were more prudent esteemed respectability more highly and declared that marriage was the inseparable union of a male and a female.[7]

This union must be brought about with the consent and will of each spouse. After they have been thus united, they plan and work together, provide food for themselves and their children, bring up their children in the fear of God, and rule the household.

It is when domestic discipline is maintained in this way that ministers are provided for the churches; capable rulers are supplied for the community; and the church, which alone has the true knowledge of God, is extended.

This is profitable instruction, and young people must often be reminded of it in order that early in their lives they may receive and learn true and honorable ideas.

And this is the point of the text before us. For what the Jews dream up concerning the ten years when they adduce these words about Abraham as a pattern is nonsense.

To teach hearts what true piety is it is useful for us to observe how the godly spouses take counsel together when they are tried;

---

[6] Luther may be thinking of classical passages such as these: *Greek Anthology*, X, 116; Juvenal, *Satires*, VI, 28.

[7] Luther is citing the legal definition of marriage: *coniugium esse individuam coniunctionem maris et foeminae.*

how Abraham, the husband, gives assent to the honorable and godly plans of Sarah; and how both hold fast to the hope they have in the mercy of God.

For Abraham, who loved his wife so tenderly and had lived with her for so many years, it was a difficult thing to lie with her maid, and an Egyptian at that; and yet he overcomes this antipathy and obeys Sarah when she implores him. This was a great humiliation for the saintly patriarch. But what was the outcome?

Sarah, a very saintly woman, does not begrudge the maid her husband and voluntarily grants her the honor of motherhood; but when the maid becomes a mother, she begins to despise her mistress Sarah in comparison with herself. Such are the ways of human beings. Kindness is an indispensable and praiseworthy virtue; but not to be offended by ingratitude, or to put up with ungrateful persons — this is a far greater virtue and one that is even more indispensable and deserving of greater praise than kindness. Here there is no middle ground. The kingdom is either God's or the devil's. It is characteristic of the kingdom of God to show kindness, give counsel, do good, yes, even to be subject and to serve. But to repay kindness and all favors with ingratitude is characteristic of the kingdom of the devil.

Therefore if you want to be godly and to hope for the life to come, it is necessary to observe this universal rule: Do good to all men, have pity on all who are in distress, expend your very property and life, and yet expect no gratitude for all this; but steel your heart in the certain knowledge that evil deeds instead of good deeds will be your reward.

But he who does not want to do this, let him look for another world, a world in which there are only grateful human beings; and let him deliberate more wisely about bestowing kindnesses than saintly Sarah and humble Abraham did.

But we know from experience that very few steel their hearts in the way I have mentioned. We all expect thanks for our kind deeds; but when we do not get the thanks we desire, then complaints, reproaches, blows, and irreconcilable indignation result, as can be seen from the examples of the poets, particularly the tragic poets.[8]

When I was a student at Erfurt, the burgomaster was hanged on

---

[8] Luther is thinking of passages like Aeschylus, *Prometheus Bound*, ll. 221 ff.

the gallows by a man whom he himself had saved from the gallows.[9] And Christ's complaint in the psalm (41:9) is well known: "Even My bosom friend in whom I trusted, who ate of My bread, has lifted his heel against Me."

Therefore not only in the church but also in the state and in the household one should follow the rule of showing kindness to ungrateful people. For such are the ways of human beings, and that word of Christ (John 13:18) is properly employed as a proverb: "He who eats My bread — that is, to whom I am giving food and clothing, whom I am cherishing as My dearest son, and whom I am supporting on My bosom — has lifted his heel against Me."

You must arrange your life in such a manner that in the first place you are a servant of God, that is, that you trust in God not only so far as this temporal life is concerned but also because He is forever our God, whom we shall have and keep forever, even if everything else should fail and cease to be.

In the second place, you should show kindness not only to friends but also to enemies. If they have thanked you, it is well, and your favor has been conferred so much more auspiciously; but if they trample you underfoot and substitute hatred for thanks, your kindness has nevertheless not been wasted, and you have followed the example of your Father in heaven, who lets His sun rise over the good and the evil (Matt. 5:45).

Such are the ways of human beings. One must not maintain that these are chance occurrences. No, they are inevitable and cannot be otherwise, to use a statement by Aristotle.[10]

There is no greater and more glorious work than a correct and genuine training. If, then, you are a teacher or the director of a school, what should you do? You must educate, teach, correct, and admonish the young people who have been entrusted to your faithful care. You must do so in the expectation that some will do their duty, others not. For whoever wants to do a kindness is bound to waste it, because there are always more who spurn sound advice than there are who follow it. The fact that our kindness has not been completely wasted should be sufficient for us; and if among ten lepers one returns and acknowledges the kindness, this is enough (Luke 17:18).

---

[9] Luther had studied at the University of Erfurt from 1501 to 1505.

[10] A reference to Aristotle, *Metaphysics*, Book V, ch. 5, 1015 a.

If among ten pupils there is one who submits to improvement and studies diligently, this is enough. For then the kindness has not been completely wasted. God's example directs us to show kindness to the grateful and the ungrateful.

The world is ignorant of this or at least refuses to do it. It expects gratitude and holds that favors are bought by favors. When this expectation fails, it becomes indignant and follows the example of the misanthrope Timon, who hates everybody alike and shows kindness to no one.[11]

You must shun this inhuman conduct and show kindness to others in such a way that you do not hope for a reward in this life, just as your Father in heaven is kind to the ungrateful world.

Let us follow His example and not that of the world, for that familiar saying is true: "He who ate of My bread has lifted his heel against Me" (Ps. 41:9). And many examples prove that the expectations of men are deceptive.

A man looking around for a wife carefully selects for himself one of whom he hopes that she will reflect his own ways in the most pleasing manner. But the hidden recesses of the heart are inscrutable. Gradually pride, jealousy, and irascibility come to the fore. Learn, therefore, that such is the character of the world; for just as God is God, that is, just as He is kind and good, so the world is the world; it is ungrateful and evil. Therefore let those who want to live under God be ready to serve everybody, and let them accustom themselves to putting up with ingratitude.

The monks, who had no knowledge of God or of people, withdrew into the deserts and there lived for themselves. But this is by no means Christian. You should remain in the world and among people; and you should endure the annoyances of the world and of Satan, and not be overcome by the flesh. For to overcome the malice of human beings is the mark not only of a man but of a Christian.

The legends or accounts of the saints which we had under the papacy were not written according to the pattern of Holy Scripture. For to wear a cowl, to fast, and to undertake similar seemingly difficult tasks is nothing in comparison with those inconveniences which domestic life brings with it and which the saints bore and overcame with patience. Sarah had a right to feel painfully wronged

---

[11] Timon of Athens was legendary for his misanthropy; cf. also *Luther's Works*, 24, p. 267, note 39.

by the fact that a purchased slave is puffed up and treats her mistress with disdain. Hagar had nothing in this world except food and clothing; she was elevated to this honor of bearing the offspring of such a great patriarch, not because of any merits, standing, or worth of her own but solely because of the kindness and the love of her mistress.

But the Holy Spirit does not disdain to describe such domestic troubles; He describes them for our comfort, in order that we may see what training the saints have had in this life. The fact that the four kings pillaged the whole land of Canaan was an evil that affected the state. The kings had led Lot away captive with his whole household and all his possessions.[12] This evil — that Sarah is scorned in such a manner by her maid — concerns the household.

But even though it seems to be a small and inconsequential matter, still the Holy Spirit considered this account worthy of being described at great length as a comfort to all believers and to give them an example and instruction, in order that they, too, might expect similar things, bear them in patience, and hope for eventual deliverance.

This is the purpose of the account about Hagar, the wretched and poor maidservant. Although she owes her very life, so to speak, and what she has to her mistress, she nevertheless exalts herself and acts haughtily toward her mistress.

Learn, therefore, to do good to others. Yet be prepared to put up with ingratitude. The things that we wish for do not happen, and the hopes we entertain about others are disappointed. For nature is corrupt and depraved, and the fickleness of hearts is astounding.

When fortune smiles, no one is so spiritless that he does not behave insolently toward those whom he is in a position to treat in this manner. As the German proverb points out, no living being is prouder than a louse on a scabby head.[13] The filthy little vermin places its nest on the head and there is king and rules. Ungrateful Hagar behaves in this insolent manner toward her mistress. But what does Sarah do?

---

[12] To clarify the meaning of this sentence we have followed the example of earlier editors and have omitted one *captivum*.

[13] In his *Sermons on Genesis*, delivered in 1523—24 (Weimar, XIV, 358) Luther cites this proverb as "When a louse gets into the scabs, it becomes haughty."

5. *And Sarai said to Abram: May the wrong done to me be on you! I gave my maid to your embrace, and when she saw that she had conceived, she looked on me with contempt. May the Lord judge between you and me!*

This is a domestic discussion and a just remonstrance with her husband, for Sarah has good reason to be angry. She had lived for so many years with her husband and yet had remained childless. Now she is despised by her maid, who had become a mother thanks to what she, Sarah herself, had counseled. This means that the louse is finding a nest and is now lording it high on the crown of Hagar's head.

Abraham gave the occasion for this unfortunate situation. Now that he was sure of an heir, he treated the pregnant maid more generously and gave her a place at his table. Consequently, she was no longer Sarah's maidservant; she was her companion.

Now Abraham did this in accordance with natural and divine right; but, as happens, Hagar's servile nature abused the goodness of the patriarch. She thinks that because she is being treated more generously, she no longer has to acknowledge her mistress as a mistress but may despise, and be indifferent to, her in comparison with herself.

Therefore, as is customary among women, Hagar no doubt occasionally burst into these words: "I am Abraham's real wife. You are not, for you are barren. God has cast you aside and has been unwilling to bless your marriage; but He has chosen me, who became pregnant at once. For who would deny that this is a most certain sign of divine favor?"

These statements were unbearable to Sarah. Accordingly, she accuses her husband and says: "My wrong is upon you. You are causing this unfortunate situation by not treating the maid like a servant."

Why does the Holy Spirit mention these quarrels? Was there nothing more important or more profitable to record?

But surely no insignificant matter is being dealt with here. In this historical account the Holy Spirit depicts the source of all the dangers that arise not only in the household but also in the state and in the church. In the state you will find it to be true that for the most part those least capable of conducting the affairs of state administer them. Likewise those who are not the church arrogate to themselves the government of the church. We also heard above about Abraham's servant Eliezer that he dreamed he would inherit Abraham's blessing.[14] Similarly, here Hagar wants to be the mistress.

These accounts pertain to our consolation, lest we be offended when something similar to Sarah's desire to hold down Hagar and Abraham's desire to hold down Eliezer happens to us; for by His marvelous counsel the Lord defers His help, and those who trust in His goodness triumph in the end (Is. 28:29).

Moreover, you should note that Sarah not only remonstrates with her husband Abraham but also appeals to God as Judge against him. Hence there must have been considerable disagreement between the spouses. But such is the life of married people. It is impossible to avoid all occasions for offense, just as this is also impossible in the state and in the church, although here they are sharper and more dangerous.

Therefore this example serves to instruct us about life among men. The language, of course, is harsh: "May the Lord judge between you and me." But the extraordinary wrongs, which, as Sarah knew, were a great sin, wrung these words from her.

The pregnant Hagar wanted to be the mistress of the household. She wanted to be the heiress of everything Abraham had, and Sarah was unable to restrain her in any way. Hagar's haughtiness was assuming such proportions because of the gift of an offspring. But consider what the great patriarch Abraham does and answers in this situation:

6. *But Abram said to Sarai: Behold, your maid is in your power; do to her as you please.*

This husband must be carefully considered. He deserves commendation and praise. He could have said: "Dear Sarah, why are you so disturbed? These difficulties should have been overcome by patience, and no such great quarrels should have been stirred up. You see that by a gift of God she is pregnant and that from me she has the offspring destined to have the promises made to me. Therefore bear with the pregnant mother, and protect her until she has given birth. Then we shall deliberate further."

This way of thinking would have been honorable and completely fair. In a similar situation I would have concurred in it. "My dear lady," I would have said, "you are barren. God has deprived you

---

[14] See pp. 12 ff. on Eliezer.

of the fruit of the womb and has given it to this woman. Therefore show some forbearance."

But Abraham does not do this. He prefers his barren and aged lady to the pregnant mother. Without giving any consideration to his progeny, he lets his wife decide how she will want to deal with the maid. He would rather cast aside the mother together with her offspring than make his godly wife sad.

This little section is intended to describe not only the perils of marriage and of the household but also the trials.

Abraham went through a trial concerning his servant Eliezer, and no one was able to relieve him of that trial except God through His Word. Here Sarah goes through a trial, and the Lord comforts her through her husband. Therefore the Lord is at hand to oversee and direct marriages and households. He shows that He takes delight in that game, so to speak, of human relations.

In the household, quarrels and disputes arise between husband and wife. In the state the peace is disturbed in various ways. In the church sects are established. The result is that he who observes these things rather carefully almost begins to despair of a happy outcome.

But these accounts teach and admonish us to be prepared to bear troubles and to overcome them with patience, and not to be among those who want to be husbands or rulers of the state without having any trials; for these are futile thoughts of people who know nothing about this life.

If you are a husband, it is impossible for you not to have either a Hagar or a troublesome Eliezer in your home.

A similar situation obtains in church government, where disturbances are caused by sects and other offenses. Therefore let us remember this example, and let us, too, together with faithful Abraham, trust in God and, as much as is possible, preserve harmony. Since we must live among ungrateful and wicked people, no place will fail to present occasions for discord and trouble. This is the moral import of the passage before us; it is exceedingly useful for the conduct of life.

But this passage also contains a theological meaning, with which the allegory Paul employs in Gal. 4:29-30 is almost in agreement. For just as Hagar, whose status was that of a purchased maid or a slave, was puffed up by the gift of God and wanted to lord it over Sarah and to make Sarah subject to Hagar, so the false church condemns, despises, and afflicts the true church and arrogates to itself alone the title "the people of God."

This dispute continually troubles the household of the church. Those who are not the church want to be the church. On the other hand, those who are the true church are harassed and suppressed by the false church.

Cain, Ham, Ishmael, and Esau — these men all boasted of the title "church" and sought to grab the promises for themselves, as though they themselves were the heirs.

And that well-known dispute among the apostles of Christ — what else was it than a trial concerning rank and prestige (Matt. 20:20-28)? From this source heresies and sects spring up in the church later on.

But just as Hagar acts haughtily toward her mistress and thinks she has a right to conduct herself in this way, so the false church — because it has more resources, prestige, and power — persecutes and condemns the true church, which does not have this protection and is afflicted.

Moses points this out in an excellent manner by saying that Hagar "saw." When Hagar "saw that she had conceived, she looked with contempt on her mistress." The verb "to see" connotes that Hagar's awareness of the gift was combined with haughtiness and high spirits.

To recognize that one is learned, wise, and rich is not evil; for it would be ingratitude to despise these gifts. But to be haughty because of these gifts is devilish and a vice stemming from original sin.

Thus after Adam and Eve had sinned, their eyes were open, and they knew good and evil (Gen. 3:7). But as for those whom the Holy Spirit rules, the more they excel in gifts, the more they become aware that they must work harder and be more zealous in serving others, who do not have such gifts. But most of us are like Hagar; because of our gift and blessing we act haughtily toward those who are inferior to us.

If Hagar had said: "Thanks to the kindness of God I am pregnant, but this does not mean that I cease being a maid. Therefore I shall obey my mistress just as I did in the past, and I shall do so all the more zealously now because I have become a mother at her wish and request. She did not begrudge me her husband. Therefore I, in turn, shall please her in whatever way I can." If Hagar had done this, she would have done what was right; but she follows the custom of our corrupt nature and, because of her gifts, acts haughtily toward her mistress; for she is sure that she will be the mother of the promised Seed through whom the blessing is to come to all nations.

Sarah is aware of this wrong, but she does not disregard it. Even though one must show patience and wait for help, yet one must by all means guard against justifying the sins of others.

Thus I am bearing the excommunication of the pope and the hatred of the entire world, but I do not for this reason approve or praise the pope as though he were doing what is right when he opposes the true doctrine and condemns and murders the members of Christ solely for the purpose of maintaining his rule.

Christ endured all wrongs, but He did not disregard them. He boldly rebuked the servant of the high priest and said (John 18:23): "Why do you strike Me?" Patience and confession must go together; for if there is no confession, the cause which must be defended against Satan and the world is betrayed.

But here it is evident how great the weakness of human beings is. Sarah rightfully complains about the wrong done to her, yet she lets some human frailty creep in when she deals so harshly with her innocent husband and invokes the judgment of God against him.

For Abraham's intention was not what she imagined. To be sure, he was glad that because of the Lord's blessing he would finally have an heir, and he treated the mother in a kindly manner even though she was a servant; but this did not cause him to cast his Sarah aside.

Hence this is a family quarrel like those that often take place between husband and wife when one of the two yields too much to moods and suspicions;[15] for if Abraham had been the kind of man Sarah accuses him of being, he would undoubtedly have defended Hagar and would have told Sarah: "What business is it of yours if I want her to be the mistress? You are not giving up anything. Remain in your position, as before; but let me honor her who, as I see, has been honored by the Lord with a blessing that makes her happy."

But you hear nothing like this; Abraham simply turns over his authority to Sarah and puts the haughty maid under her control. Sarah may deal with Hagar as she pleases.

This action clears the very virtuous patriarch of all suspicion of lust and proves that whatever he did was done at the urging of

---

[15] Instead of the *superstitionibus* in the text we have followed earlier editors and translated *suspicionibus*.

his wife, lest the promise be obstructed. Nevertheless, he loves his aged Sarah so much that he would rather abandon even his hope of offspring than be at odds with her. Where would anyone find a husband who loves his wife so much and is so eager to preserve harmony in the household?

This is indeed an instance of ruling a wife with love and discernment, as Peter says (1 Peter 3:7). For if Abraham had wanted to return like with like and to reply too harshly to his aroused wife, and if he had been unwilling to yield any part of his right, the bond of marriage, namely, love,[16] would have been broken.

But Abraham, who was full of the Holy Spirit, thought: "Behold, I am a man; but Sarah is a woman, a weak vessel (1 Peter 3:7). Therefore I shall preserve peace by being patient."

It is an outstanding virtue for a man so great to yield with such love to his wife, lest the demon of the household called Asmodeus [17] gain control. Men without experience, who regard it as praiseworthy if they are rather harsh toward their wives and their households, give vent to anger when such a trial presents itself. They give excellent support to the efforts of Satan.

Therefore it is profitable for the head of a household always to keep carefully in mind the example of this householder. For a household cannot be ruled without disturbances of this kind. Neither can the church or the state. But we must cling to the comfort that we shall be defended and preserved by the angel of the Lord.

Then Sarai dealt harshly with her, and she fled from her.

The verb עָנָה means "to humble," "to vex," "to afflict." Thus Christ is called עָנִי by Zechariah (9:9), poor and afflicted; and the same thing is said about Moses in Num. 12:3.

Therefore the meaning in this passage is this: Hagar had become haughty and wanted to occupy the place of her mistress Sarah and to have possession of everything. But Sarah, unwilling to put up with the affront, humbled her and ordered her to carry out her servile duties. Perhaps she punished her in accordance with that people's custom, of which I have no knowledge. Moreover, it is

---

[16] The text reads *vinculum matrimonii amoris;* we have accepted the emendation of earlier editors, *vinculum matrimonii, amor scilicet.*

[17] An allusion to Asmodeus in Tobit 3:8, which had become the *Hausteufel* of medieval legend.

a very bitter experience to be hurled down from the pinnacle of glory and prestige and to be degraded.

This humiliation hurt Hagar more than any blows. Yet she remained incorrigible. Her body had been humbled, but her heart not only persisted in its haughtiness but even added hate and anger to the haughtiness.

Haughty Hagar, like a person gone mad, plans revenge and wants to deprive the mistress not only of her maid's body but also of the offspring. For she thinks that she has with her an excellent guarantee that will compel Abraham to look for her of his own accord and to restore her with honor to the house from which, as it seemed to her, she had been cast out with dishonor.

Such indeed is the righteousness of the Law; for when only the Law is present, it puffs men up and provokes them to anger. Hearts are stirred up against God when He does not permit the realization of the things we desire and puts us under a cross. It is for this reason that Paul says (Rom. 4:15): "The Law brings wrath." Moreover, civil punishments and the sword belong to the Law; for by these the wicked are compelled to do their duty against their will, just as Scripture also states that fools must be corrected by stripes (Prov. 10:13). But just as children cannot bear blows without tears, so it is impossible for adults to endure punishments without grumbling and hatred.

Today the Turks are masters of almost the entire world. They keep their people in subjection by means of strict discipline. Their prisoners are given black bread and water, and not enough at that. But a fixed amount of labor is prescribed; and if the prisoners loaf on the job or are somewhat careless, they are urged on with clubs.[18]

And, to be sure, sluggish natures cannot be treated otherwise; nor should they be. Nevertheless, it is true that they are not improved by this method. Hagar, who formerly had been a good woman, becomes haughty after she has been honored with the kindnesses of her mistress. She becomes a very bad woman. When Sarah plans to remedy this evil, Hagar just runs away.

Accordingly, here you also have the state of the world depicted as in a painting. We see that it is futile to warn and correct people with words. Even blows are futile, as Isaiah (49:4) complains about his Jews. To be sure, we are in the habit of wailing and complaining

---

[18] In 1529 Luther had concerned himself at some length with the problem of Christians captured by the Turks (W, XXX-2, 160—197).

when we feel the blows; but we should have wailed in the first place because of the sins that provoked God's wrath.

When the nation was compelled to spend the entire seventy years of exile in Babylon among the heathen, there was no lack of complaints, tears, sighs, and prayers. But what do the prophets say, yes, even God through the prophets? "I," He says (Jer. 7:25; 35:15), "sent prophets, cried aloud, and wept to call you back on the way; but you killed them. Therefore I shall let you, too, weep in vain."

Thus today Germany has so far not cried, not wept, and not grieved over the awful sins we are committing. But now that punishments are coming, we are beginning to moan and wail, although this should have been done long ago.

For when the punishments are being inflicted, we cry out and wail in vain. But those who wail before punishment comes — by their sighs the Lord is moved, and He mitigates the punishments, as is promised in Ezek. 9:4-6, where God, who is about to inflict punishments on the priests and the people, commands that those who are sobbing because of idolatry be picked out and saved, lest they perish together with the ungodly.

Thus Hagar is an example of the carnal human being who cannot be improved either by chastisement or by kindnesses. She is puffed up by the kind acts of her mistress; and when she is punished, she promptly runs off. Yet here, too, an example of mercy is set forth.

7. *The angel of the Lord found her by a spring of water in the wilderness, the spring on the way to Shur.*

8. *And he said: Hagar, maid of Sarai, where have you come from and where are you going? She said: I am fleeing from my mistress Sarai.*

9. *The angel of the Lord said to her: Return to your mistress, and submit to her.*

This is a very fine example to show that God loves domestic establishments and protects them through the ministry of His angels. It had been the work of Satan that the excited Hagar had fled into the wilderness and had left her mistress; but the angels, who were assigned to the head of this household as guardians, bring Hagar back, in order that the promise in which God had given the assurance that He would be the God of Abraham and of his seed may be kept.

Moreover, Abraham as well as Sarah undoubtedly prayed for Hagar after she had fallen into such a serious sin. For she had not only removed her body from her mistress, but she had also become guilty of kidnaping by carrying off Abraham's son.

The wilderness of Shur is located between Judea and Egypt. Therefore Hagar intended to return to Egypt and her native country, and this wicked plan did not fail to cause great uneasiness for the godly spouses. Sarah repented of the rather severe way she had treated her pregnant maidservant, and Abram reproached himself for having been too complaisant toward his wife.

This is a singular change. Those who were saintly and without guilt bear the consciousness of sin. Hagar, who alone was the cause of all the sins, was untroubled, as though she had committed no sin at all.

This evil is also to be found in the household, in the state, and in the church. Those who have sinned excuse themselves and do not acknowledge their sin.

Moses does not identify the angel who spoke with Hagar. Hilary thinks that it was God Himself and in general connects such appearances of the angels with the mystery of the Trinity.[19]

Even though human beings are also called angels, I nevertheless think that this angel had assumed the appearance of a human being; for when angels appear before people, they assume the form of the body in which they appear.

Thus the angel who was assigned to Paradise as a guard could be seen with the eyes; likewise those two who led Lot out of Sodom, who sat by the Lord's tomb, and who gave instruction to the disciples about the return of Christ from the clouds.[20]

It is a regular practice of the angels to appear in human form, either of a young or of an old person. Just as we do not always wear the same garment but, though we now put on one and now another, lose or change nothing of our body, so the angels remain the same spirits even if they do not always show themselves to people in the same form but change it like a garment.

But Hagar immediately recognized the angel who calls her by name. Because she has lived in the home of the holy patriarch for

[19] Hilary, *De Trinitate,* Book IV, ch. 23, *Patrologia, Series Latina,* X, 113 to 114.

[20] The passages Luther has in mind are Gen. 3:24; Gen. 19:1 ff.; Mark 16:5; Acts 1:10.

a long time, she has often heard from him that human affairs are directed through the ministry of the angels. Therefore she now drops the conceit she had displayed in Abraham's home against her mistress, and when asked by the angel, she answered that she was fleeing from her mistress Sarah.

Thus she accuses herself of disobedience and rapine, inasmuch as she admits her flight and acknowledges Sarah as her mistress.

The angel, too, judges her from her own words. "If," says he, "Sarah is your mistress, return to her and submit to her; for this is the duty of a maid."

This, therefore, is a preaching of the Law; and the Law has the power to produce terror. For the frightened Hagar tells the truth, which she never would have done had she not been frightened.

When Sarah was speaking with her maid Hagar, the face of Moses was still covered; but here, when the angel is speaking, horns come forth from the face of Moses, or unbearable rays of light, at which the wretched woman is terrified.[21] She would surely have died from anguish if the angel had not again cheered and comforted her.

This is the way the Law works. When it strikes hearts with its rays, it simply drives to despair, as we see in the cases of Judas and Saul. Therefore it is proof of God's inexpressible goodness that He not only terrifies through the preaching of the Law but also gives encouragement and comfort through His promise.

Moreover, this passage serves to confirm that domestic life is pleasing to God and the object of His care. He does not want people to change or abandon their vocations, as under the papacy it was considered piety to have given up one's customary way of life and to have withdrawn into a monastery.

Thus Hagar could have remained in the desert, but the Lord wants her to serve in her vocation and obey her mistress.

Therefore no one should change his position in life because of his own judgment or desire. God will change it either through death or because of the desire and judgment of those who are your superiors. If this does not happen, those who give up their vocations commit a sin.[22]

Thus contrite Hagar asks with Paul: "Lord, what wilt Thou have

[21] Cf. also *Luther's Works*, 13, p. 299.

[22] By *vocatio* here Luther seems to mean "social station" rather than "calling" in the sense of occupation.

me do?" (Cf. Acts 9:6.) It is the radiant face of Moses, not his divine face, that causes her to do so. Before this contrition she haughtily made light of her mistress Sarah.

Now there follow most glorious words of comfort — words owed to Abraham, whose offspring was Ishmael, because of the promise, not to Hagar because of piety.

10. *The angel of the Lord also said to her: I will so greatly multiply your descendants that they cannot be numbered for multitude.*

This is an extraordinary promise. By it the terrified Hagar is again encouraged. For these are the divine successions: Comfort follows affliction, hope follows despair, and life follows death.

Satan has the habit of doing the opposite. First he makes glad, then he disturbs, and eventually despair follows complacency in sins.

Therefore let no one be disturbed in his heart when he experiences terrors and dangers, but let him take courage to hope that the Lord will again give comfort and encouragement. Because the godly have this sure hope, they pray so diligently and fervently for deliverance.

But even though this promise is not on a par with the one made to Isaac, it is nevertheless highly praised by the descendants of Hagar, who call themselves Saracens, and is preferred to that of Isaac. In their reliance on it they exalt themselves above all the people of the earth, and in their Koran they invent the colossal lie that Abraham spared Isaac and wanted to sacrifice Ishmael in his place.[23]

This they invent solely for the purpose of transferring to themselves the promises that were made to Abraham and of showing that they are the legitimate sons of Abraham.

Thus the popes, too, prattle and boast that all the promises of Christ have lost their effect in all the apostles and have remained firmly attached to Peter alone.

So great is the vanity of hearts. From it, as from a fountain, there have arisen these boastful statements of the Saracens and of the popes.

Furthermore, the power of the Saracens was great when the name of the Turks was still unknown to the world. The Saracens plagued Greece, Italy, and Africa severely until they themselves were reduced to slavery by the Turks and finally became one nation with the Turks.

Thus here, too, we see that when the pride of the flesh is able

[23] Cf. the Koran, XXXVII, 100.

to defend itself with the Word of God, it shamefully abuses the Word of God and becomes worse.

Accordingly, God is provoked to abase again those who have been exalted and to humble the descendants of Hagar, who put themselves on a higher plane than the true descendants of Abraham because Ishmael was his first-born.

But Paul argues learnedly (Gal. 4:23) that those born according to the promise are the sons of Abraham, not those born of Abraham's flesh. This the ungodly heathen did not see. They boasted of the prestige of primogeniture. To this they attached the promises, and they were sure that for this reason they would never be overcome.

But the physical promise was fulfilled long ago; for twelve kings were descendants of Ishmael, and their power lasted for a long time. They gained possession of the East but seriously harassed the West, until finally Gog and Magog, that is, the Turks, humbled them.

11. *And the angel of the Lord said to her: Behold, you are with child and shall bear a son; you shall call his name Ishmael, because the Lord has given heed to your affliction.*

On the basis of this passage the Jews have invented strange and ridiculous nonsense; for they say that Hagar, tired out by the journey and surrounded by cares and troubles, gave premature birth in the wilderness, but that then she conceived the fetus again and gave birth in due time. Furthermore, they say that the angel announces this miracle here in order to comfort the unfortunate woman.[24]

To this they refer the angel's words "The Lord has given heed to your affliction," that is, the death of the fetus in the womb. But this prattle is not worth repeating.

The angel undoubtedly calls that an affliction which Hagar felt to be an affliction, namely, the fact that she was a slave and had been disciplined by Sarah. It is as if he were saying: "Do not resent being a maidservant. God loves maidservants and free women alike. He is no respecter of persons (Rom. 2:11; Eph. 6:9; Col. 3:25). Therefore bear this; be subject to your mistress even though you are pregnant. God loves Sarah; He also loves you, and this position in life does not harm you before God. He compensates for this disadvantage with a blessing that brings much joy. Sustain yourself with this."

---

[24] This comes from Lyra *ad* Gen. 16:11.

This is my own understanding of the passage before us. Those who want to understand it as referring to the discomfort of contrition resulting from the Law, may do so for all I care. But this is simpler: "God hears that you resent being a maidservant and a slave, and that you have nothing of your own. But He has regarded your unhappy state and wants to bless you. Therefore be of good cheer, and do not despair."

In this manner we, too, should comfort one another. The circumstances of this life differ greatly. Poor Lazarus is hungry and is tortured by disease, while the rich man lives sumptuously and is happy (Luke 16:19-21). The situation of a king seems more pleasant than that of a private person. This inequality is often disturbing, and it often agitates hearts so much that people change their situation by sinning.

But one should hold fast to the comfort given here and think: "Behold, I am a manservant, a maidservant, one who is stricken with poverty and overburdened with work, etc. So be it! But let this be my comfort, that my God regards all alike — kings and servants, rich and poor, sinners and those who are righteous."

He is the God of all, and He wants us all to rely on His mercy and favor. The difference there is among people in this life does not make different persons before God. God hears all alike — you in your menial state and another in his free state.

This comfort is necessary and must often be impressed upon men, for it makes hearts confident and prevents the dangerous abandoning of a calling, the abandoning that is never attempted without sin. For by nature hearts shun the cross and strive with blind ambition for what is high.

The name יִשְׁמָעֵאל means "God hears" or "God, hear"; for we regard verbs in the past tense as dealing with the present. It is a very beautiful name and was undoubtedly also a cause of the haughtiness of the Saracens; for the names Abraham, Isaac, and Jacob are not so glorious.

We also learn from this passage that God dispenses His best gifts even to the ungodly. God is so solicitous for the distressed Hagar that because of her He seems to have forgotten Abraham and Sarah. Indeed, He is not only solicitous for Ishmael, who was not yet born, but He even honors him with a very rich blessing.

Yet a limitation is added, lest this be put on a par with the promise to Abraham and his true seed. It is not enough to have said: "I will so greatly multiply your descendants." No, a description of Ishmael and the nation to be born of him is added. This limitation must be considered with special application.

12. *He shall be a wild man, his hand against every man and every man's hand against him; and he shall dwell over against all his kinsmen.*

Strictly speaking, this description applies to the Arabs, who do not stay in a definite place but carry all their possessions with them in carts and live mostly on plunder.

The word פֶּרֶא is almost the same as our "wild," for those accustomed to wildernesses and forests are wild. The Jews say it means "wild ass"; but what sort of animal that is I do not know, for I have never seen one. We, however, in our own German translation of the Bible, have used the general word "wild."

In the first place, therefore, you see that Ishmael does not have possession of a definite and permanent part of the world, as does Abraham, to whose descendants the land of Canaan is expressly promised.

Thus Ishmael's manners and disposition are really at variance with everybody else's; for other people remain in definite cities or districts, but Ishmael is fond of wildernesses and is wild and roaming: Today he lives with his family under one tree, tomorrow under another, just as the Arabs and the cave dwellers do today, who, as Breitenbach [25] reports, consider it their rightful privilege to live by plundering and robbery.

This the angel indicates when he calls him פֶּרֶא, a wild man, who will not be bothered with cities, laws, and ordinances necessary for preserving human society.

And yet, when the Gospel began to be spread abroad in the world, it also reached these parts, and the Lord had a large church there. Hermits commonly withdrew into these wildernesses, and Jerome has written much about them.[26] In this way a people that was born for war and was wild eventually also became a partaker

---

[25] Georg Breitenbach was professor of law at Leipzig and rendered service as counsel to the Duke of Saxony, later to the Duke of Brandenburg as well.

[26] Much of Jerome's material on the hermit fathers in the desert had been taken over and reworked in the devotional and hagiographic works with which Luther was familiar from his own days as a monk.

of the spiritual promise. They often harassed the Romans and Persians with their marauding.

The prattle of the Jews of which I spoke above proves that they know nothing about sacred matters. Yet they win over to their view great men, such as Lyra, and, in our own time, men who are very well versed in their language and frequently admire such prattle.

But this happens to the Jews because they have lost the knowledge of the subject matter. For knowledge is of two kinds: (1) what the words means, (2) what the subject matter is. To him who has no knowledge of the subject matter the knowledge of the meaning of the word will be of no help.[27]

There is an old saying: Do not talk about anything you do not know well. Our age has produced very many examples; for many very learned and eloquent men are inordinately awkward and silly because they speak about things they do not understand.

Every time Erasmus, a marvelously learned and eloquent man, begins to speak about justification and matters of faith, he stammers most wretchedly and talks like a fool. When he discusses other matters, he reveals a very high degree of ability.[28]

You can see the same thing in the case of Sadoletus.[29] On the other hand, he who knows the subject matter — even if he lacks eloquence and halts in his speech — teaches correctly, makes an impression, and is convincing.

Thus Cato won out over Cicero in the senate, even though he made nothing but paradoxical statements and presented them in an unpolished manner and without any oratorical display.

The same thing is happening to the Jews, for they know only the meaning of the word; they have lost the subject matter completely.

When a philologian unfamiliar with the subject matter hears the proverb "There is a wolf in the story,"[30] he thinks that the story is being discussed. But if there is a wolf in the story, it follows that the wolf is being discussed. Who would not laugh at such a scholar? Yet great men permit the same thing in the most serious discussions.

---

[27] See also *Luther's Works*, 1, pp. 21—22.

[28] A reference to Luther's conflict with Erasmus in 1524—25 over the freedom of the will.

[29] Cardinal Jacob Sadoleto (1477—1547), widely criticized even within Roman Catholicism for his Semi-Pelagianism.

[30] The saying was *Lupus est in fabula*.

Because the Jew has no knowledge of the universal statement of Holy Scripture that God wants all people of lower rank to be subject to their superiors, he prattles most disgracefully about affliction and invents a new and unusual miracle where there is absolutely no need for a miracle.

How much more proper and profitable it would be for directing one's life to teach that God loves, and does a kindness to, those who know that He is chastising them!

Hagar is being punished by her mistress Sarah, and Hagar does not bear this punishment calmly but tries to help herself through flight. Even though she sins by doing this, God nevertheless has regard for her affliction and comforts her. What could be called more benevolent? [31]

Therefore let us accustom ourselves to patience and calmly bear even lashes and blows — children from their parents, subjects from the magistrate, and pupils from the teacher. For if we allow ourselves to be disciplined, obedience is pleasing to God.

But when nature feels the blows, it not only grumbles; it also despairs of the grace and mercy of God. These evils arise from ignorance of sacred matters.

Those who know that they are being cared for by God when they are disciplined and afflicted either by their parents, by the head of the family, or by a magistrate will lighten their grief and sorrow with that hope and will wait for the Lord's blessing, which, as they see, came to Hagar even when she was wrongfully running away.

Thus if you have a firm grasp of the subject matter, the language is easy, as Horace also points out. Words, he says, are not reluctant to follow where the subject matter has been discerned well beforehand, understood, and considered.[32] But where there is no knowledge of the subject matter, there a knowledge of the words is worthless.

I am pointing this out to you in a rather wordy manner in order that when you read the rabbis at some time or other, you may know what kind of teachers you have before you. They know what the words mean; they do not know what the subject matter is. Therefore they are unable to teach anything that is sound.

[31] The text has the Greek word φιλάνθρωπον.
[32] Horace, *Ars poetica*, 311.

By the grace of God we have this knowledge of the subject matter; they are blinded. Therefore even though they know the language, they do not know the true meaning of Scripture. To them, as Isaiah says (29:12), Scripture is a book they cannot read. Who, then, will set them up as a pattern?

But you must not understand this to mean that I am condemning the study of language, which is altogether necessary. Unless, however, you learn the subject matter together with the language, you will never become a good teacher. For speech, as Horace maintained, must originate in the heart, not in the mouth.

Accordingly, you know who Ishmael is and what sort of people he begets, namely, a people without laws and accustomed to wildernesses, hunting, plundering, marauding, etc.

For Isaiah thus explains the word פֶּרֶא when he calls the people mangled and patched, ravaging and ravaged.[33] It ravaged all the neighboring nations and eventually was also ravaged by the Turk, who himself is also an Ishmaelite; for his hand is against everybody, etc.

13. *So she called the name of the Lord who spoke to her: Thou art a God of seeing; for she said: Have I really seen God and remained alive after seeing Him?*

14. *Therefore the well was called Beerlahairoi; it lies between Kadesh and Bered.*

The Word of God is never without fruit. Therefore the rebellious, proud, and disobedient Hagar is changed when the angel speaks; she returns to her mistress and patiently submits to her authority. And not only this; she acknowledges God's mercy, praises God, and calls upon Him by a new name, in order to proclaim abroad the kindness through which He had manifested Himself to her.

Thus in the New Testament we call Christ the Redeemer because of the work through which He has manifested Himself to us. We call the Holy Spirit the Paraclete. Thus Hagar calls God the Seeing One because He had regard for her lowliness or affliction.

This example is also profitable for giving us instruction, in order that everyone may come to know the kindnesses of God in his calling, may be thankful for them and proclaim them. Likewise, that we

---

[33] The Weimar edition has a marginal reference to Is. 18:2.

may bear with patience the chastisements inflicted by our superiors, because God takes pleasure in such patience and sends help.

Thus Scripture, as Paul says (2 Tim. 3:16), is profitable for instruction and is not a useless grammar, in which we dispute about letters, points, and words. For by Hagar's example we are also taught to give praise to God, who has comforted us, and to say: "Lord, Thou hast delivered me from sickness, Thou hast enriched me, Thou hast given me a good wife," etc.

It is a sacrifice of thanksgiving and a service most pleasing to God if you acknowledge and proclaim His acts of kindness and call Him רֳאִי, He who sees me, as if you were saying: "I thought I had been completely forsaken by God. But now I see that He had regard for me and did not cast me aside when I was in trouble."

This is a most beautiful name for God. Would that we all could bestow it on Him, that is, conclude with certainty that He has regard for us and cares for us, especially when He seems to have forgotten us, when we think we have been forsaken by Him. For he who can say in affliction: "God sees me" has true faith and can do and bear everything, yes, he overcomes all things and is triumphant.

Therefore I certainly conclude that Hagar should be counted among the saintly women; for the fact that Paul (Gal. 4:30) compares her to Sarah and calls her a maid who has no place in the home is in no wise a hindrance.

For in Scripture even the saints frequently symbolize the ungodly. Thus Isaiah, Jeremiah, and Hosea symbolize the ungodly synagog, although they themselves are saintly and pious. I believe that Ishmael, too, was saved together with many of his descendants; nor does it do him any harm that his mother symbolizes the synagog.

For the entire church symbolizes eternal damnation, since it is cruelly afflicted and slain by its enemies. Yet it is not abandoned.

Thus Simeon calls Christ a sign (Luke 2:34) on the basis of Is. 8:14, which calls Him "a stone of offense." Thus Hagar, justified and sanctified by the Word of God, symbolizes the ungodly without detriment to herself.

The words "Have I really seen God and remained alive after seeing Him?" cause the philologists a great deal of trouble. But before referring to what others consider to be the meaning of these words I warn you not to give any credence at all to the rabbis when you read their explanations. To be sure, grammar is necessary. What it says is true. But grammar should not rule the subject matter;

it should serve it. The blinded Jews, however, have lost all knowledge of the subject matter and confine themselves to grammatical discussions of the words.

Rabbi Solomon thinks that Hagar's words show amazement at seeing the angel in the wilderness, since she has been accustomed to see angels in Abraham's home.[34]

Lyra follows the lead of Rabbi Kimalthi and translates thus: "I saw after my seeing," that is, "At first I did not recognize the angel; but when he suddenly disappeared before my eyes, then I realized for the first time that it was an angel."

Thus because they have no knowledge of the subject matter, they confine themselves to the explanation of the words; but they never arrive at the true meaning. They do not realize that Hagar, who was troubled in various ways before, has now been comforted by the angel, is giving thanks to God, and is in a cheerful mood.

Therefore the subject matter must be considered first. "Thou, O God," says Hagar, "seest me. Thou dost not forsake me when I am afflicted, but Thou dost visit and comfort me. Therefore whenever I think of this well or come to it, I shall proclaim this great favor that here I saw Him who saw me."

Hence these are words of one who is glad and filled with wonder. "Ah," says Hagar, "how incredulous I have been! I did not think that God was concerned about me, and I assumed that I was seeing God from behind, not His face; that is, I assumed that God had turned away from me. But now I realize that the back which He showed me is His face.[35] He indeed saw me before; but I, preoccupied as I was with my afflictions, was not able to look closely. Now, however, I know that He loves me and that He cares for me."

These words are, therefore, like a universal hymn of all the godly. When there is affliction, we see God from behind; that is, we conclude that God has turned away from us, as He says in Isaiah (54:8): "For a moment I hid My face from you, but with everlasting love I will have compassion on you"; that is, "At first I acted as though I did not know you, as though I had abandoned you." This is the view from behind, when we feel nothing but affliction and doubts; but later, when the trial has passed, it becomes clear that by the very

---

[34] This is taken from Lyra *ad* Gen. 16:12.

[35] See also *Luther's Works* 22, p. 157, note 25, on this way of speaking about divine revelation.

fact that God has showed Himself to us from behind He has showed us His face, that He did not forsake us but turned away His eyes just a little.

1 Peter 1:11 says that the prophets predicted "the sufferings of Christ and the subsequent glory."

This, therefore, is the hymn of the whole church. With Hagar it sings: "Here I have seen Him who sees me. I have seen Him from behind"; that is, God first turned His back to me, for during trials we come to the conclusion that we are being neglected by God. Eventually, however, we realize that what we saw from behind was the true face of God and that the Lord not only saw us, but that we also saw Him.

He who does not learn this when he is troubled despairs. Hence the well-known words (Ps. 31:22): "I am driven far from Thy sight"; that is, God does not see me and does not concern Himself about me. Likewise (Ps. 31:16): "Let Thy face shine on Thy servant."

When the heart has this awareness of the wrath of God, it should rouse itself through faith and not allow itself to be crushed. It should hope that the time will come when it will sing with Hagar: "I have seen Him who sees me. I have seen Him from behind." For these are the words of a rejoicing and triumphant heart which now leaps for joy, even though previously it had almost lost courage because it was weighed down with despair.

If anyone cares to look for allegories, let him do so. I am satisfied with this literal meaning which the historical account itself presents.

Lyra calls the back the imperfect knowledge of God, but the face he calls the perfect knowledge.[36] It is simpler, however, to understand the back as a sign of wrath, when God turns away from us and considers us unworthy of being looked at, that is, when our hearts conclude that God has become angry. But when His face is turned toward us, this is a sign of favor. Therefore Hagar is saying: "I did not realize that my bondage and submission were pleasing to God, but now I see that the back which He showed me was His real face and that I am the object of His care."

It is not grammar — the only thing the rabbis have — that gives us this meaning; it is the knowledge of sacred matters. Since the rabbis lack this knowledge, they should be completely disregarded.

As for yourselves, see to it first that you are thoroughly familiar

---

[36] Lyra *ad* Gen. 16:16.

with the subject matter; after that it will be easy to learn the grammar. He who sins in the matter of grammar commits a venial sin, but to sin in the subject matter is a mortal sin.

Furthermore, I consider knowledge of the subject matter nothing else than a knowledge of the New Testament; for when this is understood well, the entire Scripture of the Old Testament is clear. But because the rabbis are not only unacquainted with Christ but utterly reject Him, what can we learn from them? Nevertheless, today many outstanding and learned men consider it great wisdom to be familiar with all the prating of the rabbis.

Him who not only has an extensive vocabulary but also knows his subject matter the rhetoricians call an orator. And there is a well-known saying that the heart makes eloquent.[37] Those whose words originate in their mouths are talkative but not eloquent. All the rabbis without exception are like that, for they have nothing but deceptive husks of words and empty bubbles.

Therefore let us retain the meaning of this passage — the meaning conveyed, not by their grammar but by a knowledge of the subject matter. It is evident that this is a hymn for the instruction of every one of us. While we are feeling affliction, we conclude that we have been cast aside by God and receive no consideration, that God does not have us in His care. Eventually, however, we sing: "I have seen Him who sees me. I have seen Him from behind." God has not cast me aside; He has not neglected me, as I suspected. No, He has had regard for me. This I have seen after seeing Him from behind, that is, after the affliction has been removed.

Furthermore, as a sign of gratitude — because she wants to confess God and to accord Him fitting veneration for the kindness He has bestowed on her — Hagar gives a name at the same time both to God and to the place, and she calls the place a well of the living God who sees.

Each of the two names is full of comfort; for if God is the living God, then we who are His people shall also live His life, that is, an everlasting life.

Since this is a great blessing, it is proper to compare the one fact with the other, because the living God is the seeing God, who does not forsake the afflicted but has regard for them and helps them.

---

[37] Quintilian, *Institutio oratoria*, Book X, ch. 7, 15, has almost these exact words: *Pectus est, quod disertos facit.*

With this statement saintly Hagar honors God and makes this well famous. And this is the true worship we must accord a God so kind.

Kadesh, in relation to the Holy Land, is located toward the south, in that area which later fell to the tribe of Judah; and the road from the Holy Land to Egypt runs through it. But by mentioning the place in the wilderness where the well was located Moses wanted to draw his people's attention to such an outstanding blessing.

15. *And Hagar bore Abram a son; and Abram called the name of his son, whom Hagar bore, Ishmael.*

16. *Abram was eighty-six years old when Hagar bore Ishmael to Abram.*

You see that after this revelation Hagar, who had been rebellious and impatient of her yoke, has become an entirely different person. Accordingly, she returns home and obeys Sarah. She tells Abram himself the words spoken by the angel who gave a name to the son who had not yet been born. And Abram is pleased with what has happened. Therefore he does not change the name.

Moses adds the remark about Abraham's age to inform us that Abraham would still have to wait thirteen years before Sarah herself would give birth for him to Isaac, the son of the promise.

CHAPTER SEVENTEEN

1. *When Abram was ninety-nine years old, the Lord appeared to Abram and said to him: I am God Almighty; walk before Me, and be blameless.*

Thus far Moses has told the story of Abraham up to the birth of Ishmael, concerning whom a sufficiently clear promise had been made through the angel of the Lord. The angel not only persuaded Ishmael's mother, who was impatient of the yoke of her mistress and was a fugitive, to return and submit to her; but, when she was frightened by the Law and acknowledged her sins, he also buoyed her up with the promise and brought her to the true knowledge of God. As a result, she believed that God had her in His care and had regard for her. Through this faith she was sanctified and absolved of her sins.

When Hagar returns to Abraham's house, she bears a son and gives him the very charming name Ishmael. In this way she also gives evidence of her faith that God listens to the sighs and the prayers of the afflicted.

Now Moses proceeds with his account and passes over a period of thirteen whole years without recording a word about what Abraham did or experienced during that entire time.

But it seems that after Ishmael's birth Abraham was content and, because of the promise given by the angel, was under the impression that Ishmael was the heir of the promise which the Lord had given above in chapter twelve.

Therefore Sarah, too, showed the utmost affection toward this son of her servant and cherished him with the greatest care. But since both Abraham and Sarah are now untroubled, and all danger seems to have been removed by the birth of Ishmael, Moses covers with eternal silence everything that happened from that time until Abraham became ninety-nine years old. Nevertheless, it is probable that so great a man had much important business to attend to after such a glorious victory, and this among heathen, who were strangers to his religion.

But when quiet reigns and there is freedom from danger, God comes and explains the earlier promises concerning Abraham's descendants in a new sermon and completely excludes Ishmael from the promised inheritance. Thus the promises are gradually unfolded and become clearer.

When Abraham heard the promise given in chapter twelve, he believed that he would become a father through Sarah; but since, as time went on, there were many evidences that Sarah was barren, Hagar is brought to him in order that he may become a father at least through the maid.

For although here Abraham is confronted by a great trial because Hagar flees secretly before giving birth, still she bears Ishmael after she has returned home. Now Abraham concludes that the promise has been fulfilled. For at times God lets the greatest saints simply believe, even if they do not understand everything.

Therefore at this point Moses begins a new account and, after passing over everything that happened during the thirteen intervening years, he first tells about the new covenant of circumcision that has been established among the people. In the second place, he tells about the further unfolding of the promise that the Lord will give Abraham an heir from the barren and sterile Sarah herself.

This chapter, therefore, is outstanding because of the institution of circumcision, which the Jews single out for unrestrained praise and are proud of beyond measure. Indeed, because of the very fact that they are known to be circumcised the Saracens, too, conclude that they are the heirs of the promise.

Therefore Paul attacks the Jews so vigorously in order to free them from this carnal presumption. Indeed, while circumcision itself and the Law were in force, the prophets and Moses himself (Deut. 10:16) had to contend unremittingly against circumcision by calling the people uncircumcised in heart and lips and exhort them to be circumcised in their hearts (Jer. 9:26).

For this reason I have often marveled that after Satan at this time has incited sects of every kind to hate the Gospel, so far there have been none who urged circumcision and maintained that it is necessary for salvation.

If someone should diligently stress this chapter, he will find countless supporters and pupils, for in it Moses assembles such powerful arguments in favor of circumcision that St. Paul had to resist with all his might.

But if Jerusalem had not fallen and been totally laid waste, and if both the Mosaic priesthood and the Mosaic rule were still flourishing to some extent as at the time of the apostles, surely a great amount of exertion would hardly make it possible to restrain our people from being circumcised and becoming Jews.

How much trouble this one article caused the apostles in the beginning, since even the godly and those who believed the promises concerning Christ considered circumcision necessary!

And Paul's well-known thundering — "If you receive circumcision, Christ will be of no advantage to you. I testify again to every man who receives circumcision that he is bound to keep the whole Law. You are severed from Christ, you who would be justified by the Law; you have fallen away from grace" (Gal. 5:2-4) — does it not prove that his opponents fought for circumcision with much vigor?

Thus this plague agitated the church violently at the very beginning of Christ's kingdom because ignorant men began to confuse Gospel and Law. In like manner, the Mohammedan monstrosity, the Koran, where it is best, is nothing but a hodgepodge of statements of the Law and of the Gospel; for from both fanatical men have culled what serves their purpose and the flesh.

I hear that in Austria and Moravia some Judaizers are today advocating both the Sabbath and circumcision.[1] If they were to move against those who are not fortified beforehand by the Word of God, they would surely cause much harm.

Therefore this discussion concerning circumcision should not be slighted but should be carried on most diligently, not so much to confute the Jews as to strengthen and fortify our own people.

St. Paul presents chiefly two arguments against circumcision. The first is that Christ is the end of the Law; for if the Law looks to Christ and the Jews are commanded by Moses himself in Deut. 18:15 to hear Christ, it follows that the Law must keep silence when Christ preaches and that they who previously heard the Law as a doctrine inadequate for salvation should now hear Christ, whose Word is the Word of life.

The second argument is that Abraham was righteous before his

[1] On these "Judaizers" see the comments in *Luther's Works*, 2, pp. 361—362.

circumcision and because of faith, without circumcision. Hence circumcision is of no avail for righteousness.

These two arguments no one will ever be able to invalidate or refute. Therefore there is no danger among strong Christians and those fortified by the Word if some fanatic should insist on circumcision.

But among the weak there is great danger; and this is the fault of the papists, who persecute and banish godly and learned preachers and let wretched human beings who have been exposed to the devil and all the sects be without the Word and go astray.

Accordingly, they have the experience a foolish shepherd had.[2] When he had killed his dogs, he could not keep the wolf away from his sheep. Now that the guardians had been removed, the wolf went about at will. If you have not received clear instruction from the Word of God, how are you going to show that circumcision is not an eternal law which all who want to be the people of God are compelled to observe?

In the first place, therefore, you must not think that Moses makes clear mention of Abraham's age without a purpose when he says that circumcision was commanded thirteen years after the birth of Ishmael and fifteen years after Abraham was justified by faith and sanctified.

In the second place, you must devote careful attention to what the Lord says before He gives the command concerning circumcision.

The Jews simply pass over these words. But who would suppose that such a lofty statement was made without a definite reason? "I am God Almighty; walk before Me and be blameless." What else did God want than that Abraham should continue in the righteousness and faith because of which he had been declared righteous and that he should be uncorrupted, blameless, and perfect?

But if blamelessness is required of Abraham before the law of circumcision is given, who does not see or understand that this covenant of circumcision does not bring about blamelessness but that blamelessness by faith is required of man before the establishment of this covenant? The only requirement is that man remain in this blamelessness.

We have stated several times what walking before God means,

[2] An allusion to a story that has assumed various forms in the history of folklore.

and the explanation given by the author of the Epistle to the Hebrews (11:5-6) is well known. He says: "By faith Enoch was taken up so that he should not see death; and he was not found, because God had taken him. Now before he was taken he was attested as having pleased God. And without faith it is impossible to please Him. For whoever would draw near to God must believe that He exists and that He rewards those who seek Him."

Accordingly, the righteousness of faith is inculcated on Abraham before God commands him to be circumcised. Since he is commanded to remain righteous and blameless, as he had begun to be, he was righteous at that time.

That the noun תָּמִים in this passage is plural — be a man of perfections or of integrities — one can appropriately relate to the fact that there is a twofold righteousness: (1) the perfect righteousness, through which we are righteous before God through faith; (2) the imperfect righteousness, through which we are righteous before God and men so far as our conduct and reputation is concerned.

The blind Jews pass over this important preface as though it had been put there for no purpose and did not pertain to them. Furthermore, the only thing they stress is circumcision, as if righteousness and salvation resulted from it alone. They do so in spite of the fact that their own father Abraham was righteous for such a long time before circumcision, when he still had his foreskin, and that here the only instruction given to him is that he persevere in this righteousness of faith and this pure life.

But does not he who is righteous before God already have more than circumcision is able to give? But it is futile to say this to the deaf and blind Jews.

For us, however, this is the strongest proof that circumcision does not bring about righteousness. Thus on the basis of this very chapter, which the Jews imagine to be the foundation of their faith, circumcision is made ineffective; for Moses declares that Abraham was righteous before this, and here the only instruction the Lord gives is that Abraham persevere in the righteousness which had its beginning long ago. Accordingly, circumcision finds Abraham already righteous, holy, and blameless before God.

But just as David was not pronounced righteous when the kingdom was promised to him by the prophet, so Abraham is not pronounced righteous by the fact that circumcision is enjoined upon him.

Accordingly, the statement that circumcision does not produce a people of God is true and beyond doubt, and from it there follows the true and sound conclusion that it is not necessary for all nations to be circumcised.

"What, then, is circumcision?" you will ask. Nothing but a work of obedience and an exercise of faith, such as the sacrifice of Isaac and other similar works which God assigned to some men.

For this reason Paul does not call circumcision righteousness; he calls it a sign of righteousness. For to be justified through works and to do works after being justified are not the same.

First the person is righteous. Then he is commanded to be circumcised, not to become righteous through circumcision. When these facts have been carefully considered, they will disclose the error and the godless arrogance of the Jews.

But what purpose does the new name of God serve — the name which Moses uses for the first time in this passage? Up to now he has called God אֱלֹהִים; here he calls him שַׁדַּי, undoubtedly to indicate some mystery. Even though there can be various ideas with regard to the matter, depending on each person's opinion, I think that the main thing this name signifies is that this command concerning circumcision does not apply to all creation but indicates that by means of circumcision this people was to be separated from the other peoples of the earth.

The word אֵל means "strong"; but it is sometimes used substantively, as in Deut. 28:31: "Your ass shall be violently taken away before your face, and shall not be restored to you; your sheep shall be given to your enemies, and there shall be no אֵל to help you"; and in Prov. 3:27: "When it is in your power to do it," that is, when you have the ability to do it.

Likewise in the First Commandment (Ex. 20:5): "I the Lord your God am God, a zealous, mighty one." It is from this noun that the names of the angels Raphael, Uriel, Michael, and Gabriel are derived; also the name Ishmael, of which we have just spoken.

In short, this name indicates the might and power of God. It means that He alone is powerful, is all-sufficient of Himself, has power over everything, needs no one's help, and is able to give all things to all.

The other designation, שַׁדַּי, is commonly translated "almighty"; and I am wasting no time at this point on the quarrels of the linguists about its origin. I am indeed not against their compounding it of a pronoun and a noun, so that its meaning is "having sufficiently from himself," even though I do not believe what they say. It has nothing whatever in common with the noun שֵׁד, a designation for the demons to whom the Jews sacrificed, or with שָׁדַד, which means "to lay waste."

But no matter what its origin, it seems to me that Moses did not want to use אֱלֹהִים, the general term employed by the whole human race, but made use of this unique and new designation to indicate a mystery, namely, that he does not want the whole world to be bound by this covenant of circumcision which he commands here but wants circumcision to pertain specifically to the descendants of Abraham.

Therefore Moses wanted to anticipate the rabid pride of the Jews, who maintain on the basis of this text that the entire world must be circumcised; but it does not follow as a sound conclusion that because circumcision is enjoined upon the Jews, all who want to be the people of God must be circumcised.

There are very clear examples to disprove this claim. When Jonah had been sent to the Ninevites, he converted them; but he did not circumcise them, for they believed God and improved their life. Thus they became people of God without circumcision, which would certainly not have happened had circumcision been commanded with the idea that it was necessary for all nations.

After Joseph had been sold into Egypt and had been miraculously appointed to the highest position of authority, he no doubt planted the true knowledge of God in Egypt; but he did not circumcise the Egyptians.

The patriarchs understood well that the command concerning circumcision extended no further than to the descendants of Abraham and that the descendants of Abraham did not have to observe it forever but only up to the time of Christ, the true Seed of Abraham.

In all ages, therefore, even uncircumcised persons — for example, Job, Cyrus the Persian, the widow of Zarephath, and Naaman the Syrian [3] — became members of the church. And at the time of Christ many — for example, the eunuch, Cornelius, and others — worshiped in the temple even though they were not circumcised.

Accordingly, Paul is right in contending that circumcision must

---

[3] On the Gentile saints cf. Augustine, *The City of God,* Book XVIII, ch. 47.

not be extended to the heathen but must be restricted to אֶל and שַׁדַּי, that is, to the people which was still under Moses before the coming of the true Seed of Abraham.

For this law concerning circumcision was imposed on the Jews, not in order that they might be justified by it — for then Christ would have been promised in vain — but in order that they might be a people separated from all other peoples, in order that it might be known from what people, from what part of the world, the Savior was to be born.

Therefore Moses, who so carefully describes the beginnings of circumcision, greatly irritates the Jews when he commands them (Deut. 10:16) to circumcise the foreskins of their hearts. The prophets Isaiah and Jeremiah (9:26) do the same thing. "All these nations," they say, "are uncircumcised, and all the house of Israel is uncircumcised in heart."

Is this not a terrible statement to make against the glory of the circumcised nation? Yet necessity compels the prophets to make it and to take away a most pestilential trust in righteousness from their people, who affirmed so stubbornly that circumcision of the flesh produces a people of God and makes righteous.

Therefore let us adhere firmly to the conviction that circumcision does not concern other nations but pertains only to this one nation to which the promise concerning Christ was made. But it concerns this nation in such a way that after the promised Christ has come into the flesh and has been revealed to the world, circumcision should then cease entirely.

For because, in accordance with the command of the eternal Father (Matt. 17:5), He alone is to be heard who does not teach circumcision but teaches Baptism, henceforth all who want to be the true people of God must be baptized, not circumcised.

For circumcision serves the promise, and the promise is included in circumcision. Therefore when the promise has been fulfilled, what further need is there of circumcision?

Thus if the promise were not included in Baptism, we would be baptized in vain. But when this promise of Baptism is fulfilled in the life to come, then Baptism will no longer be required either

It is absurd, yes, even an act of godlessness, for some Jews to say that שַׁדַּי is derived from שָׁדַד, "to destroy," because God alone destroys heavenly and earthly things. This name with such a meaning fits the demons more truthfully than it fits the God of life and light; for God is a God of kindness, not a God of destruction.

It is more correct to derive it from the stem שַׁד, which denotes a breast. Similarly, the Greeks called a goddess πολύμαστον, or "having many breasts," and attributed to her the blessing of sustenance; and we call God the Sustainer, who sustains the entire human race and not only has power from Himself but gives all others enough to sustain them.[4]

This meaning pertains properly to the Jews, to whom alone the promise concerning the land of Canaan had been given. For them, therefore, He was אֵל; for He had sufficient power to defend His people against the heathen.

He was also שַׁדַּי, as though you meant to say "breasts to support and sustain them." Even though He defended and sustained the heathen too, He was nevertheless compelled to sustain the Jews because of His promise.

This seems to me to be the true reason for this name. Even though I do not set myself up as a judge of these quarrels among the philologians, the fact that God cherished this people, defended it, and, as Paul states in 1 Tim. 6:17, bestowed everything in abundance, is in accord with my opinion.

Therefore just as this is a new covenant with a new people, a people that is to come into existence, so God takes on new names, like a new garment and a new character, to show that He is making this covenant, not with all peoples but with this one single one which was to originate from Abraham.

I gladly impress this on you, for the question concerning circumcision is very difficult and complicated; and if St. Paul had not stepped in and dealt with it so profusely and seriously, we would hardly have avoided errors.

For we read in Acts 15 that after Christ's resurrection the Jews who had been converted to the faith continued to stress the Law and to compel those who had been baptized to observe not only circumcision but also the entire Law; for they maintained (Acts 15:5): "It is necessary to circumcise them, and to charge them to keep the Law of Moses."

[4] The source of this information is Jerome's preface to his *Commentariorum in Epistolam ad Ephesios libri tres, Patrologia, Series Latina,* XXVI, 470, where he refers to Acts 19:34. The Greek word πολύμαστος does not appear to be of classical origin.

Accordingly, this was a serious question — a question which, as is apparent in the early church, caused trouble for the apostles themselves and compelled Paul to go to Jerusalem and to confer with the apostles about it.

Furthermore, this question in Acts is not a single question. It has two parts: (1) whether man is justified on the basis of works; (2) whether circumcision is necessary.

For circumcision was enjoined upon the descendants of Abraham long before the Law was given to them. And the Law binds not only the Jews but also the heathen, for it is the eternal and immutable decree of God concerning the worship of God and the love of one's neighbor. Moreover, God's decree has been written in the hearts of all men from the beginning of the world. Therefore it will be worthwhile to see how Paul carries on this discussion.

So far as circumcision is concerned, this presentation is faultless, and the conclusion is unquestionable and well known from Holy Scripture itself that Abraham was righteous before circumcision and without it. Therefore it follows that circumcision must not be imposed for the sake of righteousness.

Thus with regard to the second question there is the indisputable presentation which the same Paul employs. He stresses it skillfully in Romans and Galatians, where he says that Abraham was accounted righteous, not because of some work, but simply because he believed God.

But to be righteous because of divine imputation is something different from being righteous because of one's own works and merits.

Hence these conclusions are in agreement and are proved not only by argumentation and dialectics but also demonstratively. If Abraham is not righteous as the result of circumcision, he is righteous much less because of any Law of Moses, a Law which was not yet written when Abraham was pronounced righteous.

Indeed, Moses himself and those who were under him were not justified on the basis of the Law. For righteousness is not fulfillment of the Law; it consists in believing God when He makes a promise.

Thus Paul stresses this one little word in a truly learned and sagacious manner. And if either the papists or the Jews cry out against this conclusion, this is due to their own fault and sin, not to any fault or sin of ours.

For these facts are clear and sure: Abraham was righteous before circumcision; and because he is accounted righteous through faith, righteousness comes about, not because of the Law or works, but simply from faith, or trust in the promise.

The written Law was given to the Jews alone, but the heathen have the Law written in their hearts, that is, born with them; and we today, after the Gospel has been revealed, are compelled to teach the Law diligently and to impress it on the people. But even under the guidance of nature and from the very light of reason we are able to conclude that the Law does not make righteous.

Aristotle argues that a work is not good unless it results from proper reasoning and a good will.[5] Therefore since the will is evil and reason errs, as experience proves, it surely follows that this imperfection of the will and of reason is not remedied by works, no matter how good they appear to be.

Hence the philosophers, too, conclude that before doing any good work the person must be good; that is, the will must be good and reason must be right before anything is properly done. It is impossible to refute this conclusion.

But the Jews, on the contrary, insist that this passage deals with an everlasting covenant and, in addition, that he who is not circumcised shall be completely removed from this people. Thus the debate consists in the denial of the contrary.[6] But the conclusion that this is why circumcision makes righteous must be rejected.

Why, then, they say, was it given? Paul answers (Rom. 4:11) that it might be a seal of righteousness; that is, this work had to be there in order to place the seal upon righteousness. Circumcision had to be a document, as it were, for the purpose of acknowledging that the promise is true.

In short, circumcision was a sacrament by which they were to be reminded that they were the people of God. But they did not become the people of God through circumcision.

In reply the Jews stress the circumstance that circumcision was commanded, not as a work that concerns Abraham alone, but that at the same time it is imposed upon his entire posterity and that the promise includes his entire posterity, not only the person of Abraham; for the text contains the words "to be God to you and to your descendants after you."

[5] Apparently a reference to Aristotle, *Nicomachean Ethics*, Book III, ch. 5.
[6] Luther appears to mean that the logic of the case refutes the Jewish position.

Hence if those who have not been circumcised are compelled to be without this promise and are not the people of God, it follows conversely that through circumcision the descendants of Abraham become the people of God.

This argument is no longer philosophical, like the previous one, that a right reason and good will are required for a good work, and precede it. No, it is a theological argument against which Paul, who understood it best, particularly contends.

Nor must one be misled by the idea that the promise pertains solely to this physical life. For God is not speaking with stones, pieces of wood, oxen, or asses; He is speaking with human beings and the descendants of Abraham, and He promises him that if they keep this covenant of circumcision, He will be their God not only in this life but also in the future and eternal life.

For here the word "God" indicates a relationship; it refers to Him whom the descendants of Abraham believe to be God and who, in turn, reveals Himself to the descendants of Abraham as God and as the eternal Benefactor.

Nor is there any room here for the scoffing that water, sun, and moon also understand God; for they, too, do God's will. Here we are speaking of the true Promiser and of the Word of the promise. Surely no sun, no pieces of wood, no ox, and no ass understand that Word.

Therefore it follows (so the Jews argue) that circumcision makes righteous. For it includes the promise, yes, it validates the promise that God would be God for the descendants of Abraham. For unless they were circumcised, there would be no occasion for the promise, since the uncircumcised are to be removed completely; that is, they do not have God.

What are we going to say in this connection? Although it has been stated that Abraham was righteous before circumcision, here the opposite is established: that circumcision has the effect that God is God for us.

My answer is: Circumcision was given to Abraham in order that through him this sign of the covenant might be transmitted to his entire posterity. Therefore there was one reason for circumcision in the case of Abraham and another reason in the case of Abraham's descendants. God was the God of Abraham before this time, as Moses clearly testifies. Accordingly, it was not through circumcision that Abraham began to be a son of God. Nevertheless, because God commanded that he be circumcised, he was in duty bound not to offer any resistance whatever to the will of God.

But for the descendants of Abraham circumcision was a symbol that they were the heirs of the promise which had been given to Abraham before he was circumcised.

Thus it is necessary for us to make a distinction between act and act. When Christ was baptized and when we are baptized, there is, so far as the act itself is concerned, no difference at all between the Baptism of Christ and that of other believers. Both are washed with water in the Jordan; both receive the comfort that God wants to forgive sins. But there is a very great difference in the persons.

Christ is baptized, not in order to be made righteous — for He is the Son of God and endowed with eternal righteousness so that we may be made righteous through Him — but as an example, so to speak, for us, in order that He may precede us and we may follow His example and also be baptized.

In almost the same way circumcision is a sacrament for the descendants of Abraham because, since they have the promise, they are made righteous by believing this promise and making use of the sacrament in faith. But those who do not believe are not made righteous. Yet they are circumcised. But this was not the purpose of Abraham's circumcision; for, on the one hand, he had the promise before he had this sign, and, on the other hand, through faith in this promise he was made righteous before he was circumcised.

Many similar examples can be cited. A teacher instructs his pupils in grammar, not to learn it himself, for to him it is already familiar and fixed by use, but to have the pupils learn it. We ourselves, too, read the Holy Scriptures in public, not for our own sakes but for the sake of the hearers; for we can study them in private. Indeed, we have already studied them.

Thus circumcision was enjoined upon Abraham in order that for his descendants it might be a sacrament through which they would be made righteous if they believed the promise which the Lord had attached to it. In the case of Abraham, who had already been made righteous, there was a different reason for this work, although for him also it was a seal of righteousness.

This is the kind of answer one can give. But the Jew is not yet satisfied; for he insists that if the descendants of Abraham were made righteous because of circumcision, it follows that all who want to be made righteous must be sons of Abraham. Because it is by nature impossible, however, for all to be born from the flesh and blood of Abraham, it remains that they be circumcised and freed from the foreskin, in order that in accordance with this work, which has this promise, they may become like Abraham, as the proselytes among the people were, Herod and others.

The belief that Christ has come has refuted this insistent claim. You will hardly satisfy a contentious person by citing from the Old Testament, but those who believe that Christ came in the flesh know that righteousness should not be sought on the basis of circumcision; they know that one must seek it solely from Christ, in whom all the promises are yea and amen (2 Cor. 1:20).

Although Christ Himself was circumcised, He does not command circumcision; but He does command that we be baptized in His name. For a godly person this reason takes the place of a proof. But to the Jews, who do not believe in Christ, it is presented in vain. Therefore it is necessary to confront them in another way.

Whatever may be the state of affairs regarding the descendants of Abraham and the command of circumcision, it is certainly impossible for the Jews to prove that the heathen must be circumcised in order to attain righteousness. From this text they will be able to prove only that circumcision was enjoined upon the descendants of Abraham and that those who are descendants of Abraham cannot be the people of God unless they are circumcised. They will by no means be able to prove that none but Jews are made righteous and are the people of God.

For, in the first place, Moses himself states that Abram is to be made the father of many nations. If he is to be the father of nations, and not of the Jews, and God is the God of the descendants of Abraham, then the nations, too, will be the descendants of Abraham, and God will be the God of the uncircumcised as well. Thus the Jews are under compulsion; they cannot say anything else than that circumcision is necessary for the physical descendants of Abraham.

Then, however, there is another proof *a posteriori,* or from the effect. For our conclusion is correct when we say that when Joseph instructed Egypt, Pharaoh acknowledged God and through that knowledge became righteous, even though he had not been circumcised. The text states clearly that because of circumcision it is an abomination for the Egyptians to eat with the Jews. Therefore even the uncircumcised are made righteous.

Thus King Nebuchadnezzar, like Darius and Cyrus, has the extraordinary testimony that he acknowledged God. Yet he was not circumcised.

Job, the widow of Zarephath, and Naaman the Syrian were righteous. The Jews are so overwhelmed by these examples that they cannot deny that uncircumcised Gentiles are also the people of God and please God, and that the command of circumcision does not apply to the Gentiles.

Therefore as long as the Jews do not believe in Christ, they are under the Law and bound to circumcision; but they cannot prove that the heathen should be circumcised.

Christ had this in mind when He said in Matt. 23:15: "Woe to you, scribes and Pharisees, hypocrites! For you traverse sea and land to make a single proselyte, and when he becomes a proselyte, you make of him twice as much a child of hell as yourselves."

Jonah did nothing of this sort when he instructed the Ninevites; nor did Elisha when he cleansed Naaman. Indeed, Elisha let Naaman continue in his way of life and permitted him to enter the temple of the idol in the company of his king, provided that he worshiped the God of Israel in his own heart. And the earth which had been brought to the heathen from the temple in Jerusalem bore witness to his faith. Thus it follows clearly *a posteriori* that God is the God not only of the Jews but also of the heathen.

But it is a remarkable state of affairs that Ishmael's descendants are excluded from circumcision and yet are included in the promise that God will be their God. What blindness or stubbornness, then, it is on the part of the Jews to boast that because of circumcision they alone are the people of God!

Do not these examples, which have been cited in opposition, show clearly that before the birth of Christ circumcision was necessary for the Jews and not for the heathen, but that for the Gentiles faith in the promise, or trust in the promised Seed, was necessary for salvation, just as Abraham was accounted righteous, not because of circumcision but through his faith in the promise before he was circumcised?

You say: "Why, then, was he circumcised?" I want you to give the answer by telling me why Christ was baptized. We are made just through Baptism when we believe the promise. Yet Christ, even though He was baptized, was not made righteous through Baptism; for He was baptized, not for His own sake, but for the sake of the succeeding generations of believers.

Nor was Abraham circumcised for his own sake. I am using this comparison to clarify the matter, even though I realize that it contains many dissimilarities. This is not the place to discuss them; they are clear in themselves to one who is moderately learned.

It is true that we cannot take circumcision away from the Jews as a people. They do not believe in Christ, and as long as they cling to their erroneous conviction that Christ has not been revealed, they are compelled to bear the burden of circumcision. Nevertheless, it is certain that circumcision does not apply to the Gentiles. Therefore he who imposes it on the Gentiles as necessary for salvation commits a sin, as did those of the converted Pharisees about whom we read in Acts.

But because even in Moses, who says (Deut. 18:15): "The Lord your God will raise up for you a Prophet like me from among you, from your brethren — Him you shall heed" — those who know Christ have the express command to listen to Christ, they know that Christ is the end of the Law; they know that not only circumcision but the Law of Moses itself must come to an end in Christ.

For Christ is the Do-all:[7] "In Him the whole fullness of deity dwells bodily" (Col. 2:9); and "From His fullness have we all received, grace upon grace" (John 1:16). Therefore we can tell the Jews that the promise given to Abraham has been fulfilled, that now the prophecies and visions have been fulfilled, as is written in Daniel (9:24), and that for this reason not Abraham, not circumcision, but the Lord of both rules.

And here belongs Paul's simple statement (Rom. 2:25) that circumcision is nothing; for it was given to Abraham as a sign of righteousness not bestowed on Abraham through circumcision but to be transmitted to his descendants until Christ, the promised Seed, should come.

Moreover, if the Jews were not so blind, they should be especially impressed by the expression which the Lord adds here time and time again. "I will establish My covenant between Me and you and your descendants after you throughout their generations" (Gen.

---

[7] The original is *Christus enim est fac totum.*

17:7). "You shall keep My covenant, you and your descendants after you throughout their generations" (Gen. 17:9). Likewise: "And I will give to you, and to your descendants after you, the land of your sojournings" (Gen. 17:8).

This expression, "throughout their generations," should be carefully noted. He could simply have said: "My covenant shall be everlasting between you and your descendants after you"; but because He adds "throughout their generations," He indicates its continuance for a fixed time. Therefore the meaning is: This covenant, or circumcision itself, will continue as long as your generation continues.

It is also certain that Abraham's descendants no longer continue to exist, for after the capture of Jerusalem no kingdom, no people, no family, and no sacrifice remained. But if his descendants were still in existence, surely a home or some form of his kingdom would still be in existence; for what did God promise Abraham if He did not promise this?

But now, what is most important, even Moses remains silent about this throughout his writings. How, then, will it be possible to insist on circumcision if there are none to be circumcised; that is, if there are no longer any who have a definite generation, a definite place, in which they are found? Therefore after Christ had come, circumcision had to give way as a shadow gives way when the sun comes.

For what benefit, then, was circumcision given? To make known that the Savior was to be born from this circumcised nation and not from the Gentiles. He who was desired by all the nations did not become incarnate among all the nations; He became incarnate among this one people which had been commanded by God to be circumcised.

And the special rite was instituted that it might be an outstanding reminder for the entire world that Christ would come from the Jews; for He had been promised to the Jews alone, even though the Jews would not be the only people to derive benefit from Him.

I have spoken at sufficient length about circumcision. But if the Jews believe that Christ has come, they will readily concede that it is not necessary for the whole Law, together with circumcision and all the other ceremonies, to endure longer than up to the time of Christ. For Moses commands them to hear Christ (Deut. 18:15). Christ, therefore, is to bring a new doctrine and new ceremonies, which Moses commands His people to accept after discarding those of the Law, just as Christ's command is definite (Matt. 28:19):

"Go therefore and make disciples of all nations, baptizing them in My name."

But as for the Jews, who stubbornly cling to their error and are waiting for the Messiah, we shall not only be unable to release them from circumcision; but, because they acknowledge that they are the descendants of Abraham, they are under obligation to the entire Law.

Whether the Jews believe, however, or do not believe, whether they cling to circumcision or not, for us this statement remains certain: that we Gentiles are free from the Law and from circumcision, just as before the Law and in the Law many of the Gentiles were converted to God and yet remained free from the Law and from circumcision.

But we Christians are free from the Law and from circumcision to a far greater degree. We know that according to the Father's command it is the Son of God who must be heard, not Moses. Even though He was circumcised, He did not command us to be circumcised; He commanded us to be baptized. This statement is true and unchangeable.

But just as we no longer have any need of the Sacrament of Baptism when the promise of the New Testament is fulfilled in eternal life, so circumcision is no longer necessary, since the promise given to Abraham has been fulfilled through Christ.

Therefore let the Jews be either converted or condemned under the Law, which it is impossible for them to keep even according to the letter.

But it is also necessary to consider the purpose of this chapter. The increase of the descendants of Abraham, to whom the promise is given here that he will be the father of many nations, is drawing near. But because it did not suit God to make a new covenant with each generation and to confirm new promises — as He did to Abraham, Isaac, and Jacob — He gives all the descendants of Isaac a common revelation or seal by which they are not only to be distinguished from the rest of the nations but are also to be reminded as by a sacrament that they are the people of God and that God, in turn, will be a God to them, that is, will do good to them in this life and in the eternal life, and will do all this because of Christ, the promised Seed of the Woman.

In the first place, therefore, the Jews are a people set apart from all the nations in order that their own generation may not be confused with other nations and the promise concerning Christ may be sure to those on whom it is to be conferred. In the second place, circumcision is for them a sign of righteousness; for by this very deed that is done to them — if I may express myself in this way — they are reminded that they are the people of God and that God has them in His care.

Observe, I beg you, what a remarkable conclusion Paul draws from this. For from this very separation of the descendants of Abraham from all the nations he concludes on the authority of Moses that the Gentiles are most closely connected with the Jews and the true descendants of Abraham. For this is what the text says: "I have made you the father of a multitude of nations." What else is this but that the Gentiles, as sons and heirs of Abraham, will come into possession of the promise made to Abraham? Otherwise how can Abraham be the father of many nations? Nevertheless, you see that the Gentiles are set apart from the Jews. For the descendants of Abraham are commanded to be circumcised; the Gentiles are not commanded to be circumcised.

These most excellent consequences result from Moses himself. To share in the promise, the Gentiles must be united with the Jews, who are set apart from all the Gentiles by means of circumcision. Yet the Gentiles are not obliged to be circumcised.

In this manner Ishmael is set apart from the descendants of Abraham and is not set apart as the rest of the Gentiles are.

So far as outward relationship and physical association are concerned, Ishmael and the Gentiles are set apart from the Jews; for the Jews alone have that seal of righteousness, but the Gentiles are not set apart from the promised Seed.

This is the source of the distinction which Paul, a learned man, makes between the children of Abraham who are children according to the flesh and those who are children according to the promise. John, too, refers to this distinction when he applies the term "children of God" to those "who were born, not of blood nor of the will of the flesh nor of the will of man, but of God" (John 1:13).

This also serves to point out the mystery of circumcision. Because it has been imposed by God until the coming of Christ, the Jews bear it as long as Christ has not yet been revealed. They do so in order that it may be a reminder to the other nations and may give them the opportunity to believe the same God — the God who had promised Abraham the Blessed Seed — and to hope for Christ.

Accordingly, there is a twofold result. The Jews are set apart from and united with the Gentiles. This gives rise to that excellent statement which Paul is at pains to stress in Romans:[8] that it is not enough to be children of Abraham according to the flesh, but that the Jews themselves, who are the physical descendants, are required to become children of the promise, as the text says: "Through Isaac shall your descendants be named" (Gen. 21:12).

This is the origin of the chief doctrine of theology: that God is the God of the Jews and of the Gentiles, rich toward all, even at that very time when the Law and circumcision flourished.

For other nations heard Abraham, heard the prophets, saw the worship at Jerusalem, and believed that the God of the Jews was the only true God.

Meanwhile the Jews alone had this seal of righteousness because of which they were conspicuous among all the nations. And even though the Gentiles were not circumcised, they nevertheless called upon and worshiped the same God who revealed Himself to the Jewish people through circumcision.

Therefore we do not slight St. Paul, the best and most learned interpreter of Moses. For concerning this chapter he teaches us that so far Moses has written about the birth of the son Ishmael and a descendant of Abraham according to the flesh but has said that this descendant was born without the promise. For God did not speak to Abraham about the son who would be born of the maid; it was Sarah's plan that Abraham should consort with the maid. It was not a command of God. Far less was it a command with a promise.

Thus a human plan or, to express it somewhat more reverently, love prevailed in that instance and not faith; for there was no promise concerning Ishmael, who was born of the servant.

But with regard to Isaac the matter is different. He is born as the result of the promise, and the promise is attached to him. When this difference is recognized, it will shed a bright light on this discussion about circumcision.

But the Jews, immersed in thoughts about the Law, pay no attention to the promise and make no distinction between Law and

---

[8] Although the original has "Rom. 11," the reference is actually to Rom. 9:6-8.

Gospel. Indeed, they have absolutely no knowledge of the Gospel; they persecute and loathe it.

Nevertheless, they cannot deny that even though Ishmael was a true son of Abraham according to the flesh and was also circumcised in accordance with God's command, he is not counted among the seed of Abraham. Only Isaac, who was born according to the promise, has this distinction.

But one must not take this to mean that we condemn Ishmael on this account. I am of the opinion that he clung to the knowledge of the true God and was saved. It is the purpose of this discussion to teach the Jews, an ungodly and haughty people, that physical birth, of which they themselves boast so much, is of no avail.

It is as Christ says (John 3:6): "That which is born of the flesh is flesh." Likewise (John 3:3): "Unless one is born anew, he cannot see the kingdom of God."

This is a necessary doctrine, and it alone squelches the stiffnecked Jews; for they cannot deny that Ishmael was cast off from the possession of this promise. Yet he was a true descendant of Abraham, that is, a descendant according to the flesh. But this was not enough, for it was necessary for him to become a believing son of believing Abraham if he wanted to be saved.

Thus it is clearly seen that birth according to the flesh carries with it no prerogative, not even in the case of Isaac; for everything depends on the promise. But the promise can be accepted solely by faith. So far as birth according to the flesh is concerned, we are all born in sin. Hence those who are to be saved must be born again through water, that is, through Baptism, not through circumcision, and through the Spirit, who kindles faith in the promise and thus frees and saves from sin.

But, as I have already stated repeatedly, this people is circumcised for the purpose of designating it with a distinctive mark, in order that the Gentiles, prompted by admiration, may learn to acknowledge the God of the Jews until Christ should come and provide a new mark — a mark by which both the Jews and the Gentiles would be certified as sharers in the eternal grace which, through the Son of God, falls to the lot, not of those who are favored because of the prerogative of birth according to the flesh but of those who believe, or have been born again through water and the Spirit.

Thus Paul has looked carefully at Moses' text, which states that the Jews were set apart from the Gentiles by means of circumcision and that in spite of this the Gentiles were associated with the true children of Abraham through faith — as a sure proof by which it should become known to the whole world that before God birth according to the flesh is of no avail and that the way to grace is open even to the Gentiles.

A similar statement was made above about the descendants of Cain. Although through sin he lost the promise which was transferred to godly Seth, it is nevertheless likely that many of his descendants were saved after they had united with Seth. But these were not saved by a definite promise; they were saved by a promise that was indefinite, if I may say so, just as Pharaoh in Egypt certainly did not have a definite promise, as did Isaac concerning his salvation, and yet, because he hears Joseph and worships and calls upon Joseph's God, he himself is also saved.

Thus he who does not have the promise obtains the promise; but, as Paul says, the Jews, who had the promise, did not attain the righteousness of the Law by following the Law.

Therefore let no one glory in his birth according to the flesh, in his ancestors, in his wisdom, riches, and power; but let him glory "in this, that he understands and knows Me, that I am the Lord" (Jer. 9:24). For God is the God of the Jews and of the Gentiles; and although there is a difference in this respect, that the Jews have the promise and their own distinctive marks by which they are known to be the people of God, God nevertheless does not exclude the Gentiles from the promise, provided that they embrace it in faith.

Thus the descendants of Esau, who are the wise men in Teman, had many outstanding saints, although they were not circumcised and did not know the Law of Moses. They were satisfied with the indefinite promise [9] and thanked God for it.

Thus from the beginning to the end many of the Gentiles were saved, even though the promise had not been given to them; and, what is more remarkable, because of their pride the Jews lost the promise which was theirs and was due them. But the heathen, to whom it was not due, appropriated it and took the place of the Jews, in accordance with John's statement in Matt. 3:7, 9: "You brood

---

[9] See the similar term used above, *Luther's Works*, 2, p. 177, note 64.

of vipers! . . . I tell you, God is able from these stones to raise up children to Abraham."

This pride and obstinacy ruined the Jews. They kept contending that they were the people of God. If you asked why, they would reply: "We are the descendants of Abraham, and we are circumcised."

If this reason is valid, what else follows than that all other nations are condemned? For they are not the descendants of Abraham, nor are they circumcised.

Therefore Paul emphatically refutes this idea. He states indeed that the promise was given to Abraham and that through circumcision Abraham's descendants were set apart from all the Gentiles; but because he sees that Moses calls Abraham a father of many nations, he draws the correct conclusion that the Gentiles are also the people of God if they embrace the promise together with believing Abraham.

The Gentiles are not circumcised, and they do not have the promise of the future Christ. This promise was denied Japheth and Ham and was given to Shem alone; and yet Japheth dwells in his tents, and many Hamites were also saved. For the Gospel must be spread abroad among all nations.

Hence both statements are true. Salvation is from the Jews (John 4:22), but the Jews are not the only ones who are saved; the Gentiles, too, attain to the promise of salvation.

In this manner the Holy Spirit wanted to forestall the error of the Jews, but in their blindness they do not notice it. They note only this one thing, that circumcision is commanded with the promise that they will be the people of God; but that Abraham is told that he will be the father of many nations — this they do not see.

Therefore this horrible downfall must not be attributed to the Holy Spirit, who took pains to prevent this error; it must be attributed to the blindness of the Jews themselves.

Similarly, the Holy Spirit forestalls the heresy of the papists concerning celibacy, inasmuch as He points out that Adam was joined in marriage with Eve by God's ordinance.

Thus the Jews are warned in this passage not to boast of their birth according to the flesh; for the children of God are born not of the flesh but of the grace and mercy of God.

For just as God gave to those not yet born the sign and the promise out of His mercy and not because of their merits, so the promise and salvation are bestowed on the Gentiles also out of mercy.

But we discuss these matters with the Jews in vain. Because

they do not accept Christ, the veil remains before the eyes of Moses — the veil which is not lifted unless one believes in Christ. Therefore the Jews must be left to their own evil genius, just as the Turks and the papists, who either do not understand the clearest testimony of Scripture or jeer at it, because they are crazed by their own opinions. Let this be enough concerning the essential points of this chapter. Now we shall explain the text.

Abraham's ninety-ninth year is very remarkable, for everything that Moses includes in the next four chapters took place in that year: circumcision was instituted, through it Abraham's descendants were set apart from all the Gentiles, Ishmael was sent away with his mother, and the proud and ungodly Sodomites were punished, etc. These are magnificent accounts, as will become clear later on. Therefore one must take careful note of this chapter. About the names אֵל and שַׁדַּי we have spoken above.[10]

It has also been noted above that Abraham is commanded to walk before God and to be blameless. This includes both Tables: the First, that he should believe in God, call upon Him, preach the Word, and practice godliness. God includes all this when He commands Abraham to walk before Him.

Even though He includes what pertains to the worship of God when He adds that Abraham should be blameless, He is giving primary consideration to the Second Table.

The meaning of תָּם is "perfect and blameless," that which is completely perfect, unspoiled, without defects, and uncorrupted.

But here this word appears in the plural. "Be you perfect ones"; that is, let your life be blameless and uncorrupted, and walk before men without offense. The use of the plural is not without purpose; for the head of a family and everyone who holds some administrative position owes it not only to himself to commit no offense but also to those who are in his charge.

Thus Paul (1 Tim. 3:2) wants a bishop to be תָּמִים. Not only should his own life be blameless, but by strict discipline he should restrain his people from becoming guilty of anything unworthy of them. But those who do not want to be corrected should be expelled either from the home or from the church rather than be an offense to others. In this manner every ruler should be תָּמִים, not תָּם, not only in one commandment; he should be תָּמִים in all the commandments. So much for the exhortation to lead a blameless life.

---

[10] Cf. pp. 80 ff.

2. *And I will make My covenant between Me and you, and will multiply you exceedingly.*

Here, as on several previous occasions, an increase is promised, and, as a confirmation of the promise, there is added a covenant or compact, the purpose of which we have stated at sufficient length. Undoubtedly, however, Abraham had the hope that Ishmael would be the heir of this promise.

Although the promise which the angel gave to Hagar herself concerning Ishmael clearly indicated that Abraham would have another child, Abraham, absorbed in his own ideas, was satisfied with Ishmael. For what hope could he entertain about Sarah, who was already ninety years old and by nature barren?

Accordingly, both parents guided their son with careful instruction and bestowed all their love on him as the stock from which such an abundant progeny would result. But suddenly the Lord intervened and gave Abraham complete information about the heir of the promise, namely, that a son would be born to him from Sarah.

3. *Then Abram fell on his face; and God said to him:*

4. *Behold, My covenant is with you, and you shall be the father of a multitude of nations.*

5. *No longer shall your name be Abram, but your name shall be Abraham; for I have made you the father of a multitude of nations.*

6. *I will make you exceedingly fruitful; and I will make nations of you, and kings shall come forth from you.*

The fact that Abraham falls prostrate to the ground is a sign not only of reverence but also of joy and thanksgiving. The saintly patriarch realizes how great a kindness it is that God will fill his temporal life with manifold gifts and, after removing the curse under which all the nations were because of sin, will restore the blessing and eternal life.

And this is the text about which I stated above that Paul discusses it learnedly. Just as the people of the Jews is set apart from all the Gentiles by circumcision, so the Gentiles are again united and joined with the Jews through the promise. Consequently, they are one and the same people in the same grace and under the same God.

The fact that God changes Abraham's name is not devoid of

a mystery. Abraham's former name is אַבְרָם, which means "lofty father." His later name, אַבְרָהָם, is longer by one letter for a ה is inserted between ר and ם in the Hebrew. The text itself points out the etymology. It states that this name comes from הָמוֹן, which means "a multitude." Hence it is made up of the three words אָב, "father," רָם "lofty," and הָמוֹן, "multitude," from which comes the word "mammon," which denotes an abundance or multitude of riches. The name should be pronounced אָב רָם הָמוֹן; but since the syllable ־ָם repeated twice produces an unpleasant sound, it is used only once. These matters, however, are not without their mystery, as we shall perhaps discuss more extensively later on.[11]

The passage concerning circumcision is of primary importance. Therefore we must strive to explain it first. Whether the Jews keep circumcision or give it up is of no concern to us. In the first place, it is sufficient for us to state in opposition to them that circumcision does not pertain to the heathen; for it is enjoined upon the seed of Abraham.

In the second place, they cannot deny that circumcision did not make Abraham righteous; for he was justified before he was circumcised, as Moses points out above in the fifteenth chapter. But if Abraham was not justified through circumcision, how dare his descendants assert that they are justified by it?

In the third place, even if the Jews were justified through circumcision most of all — which, of course, is not true — still it is certain that circumcision was not instituted as something permanent; it was to continue only until the coming of Christ, that is, as long as the generation of Abraham should last and should have possession of the land of Canaan and be a people or a kingdom. For this is the meaning of the text, and Moses bears witness that when Christ comes, He will establish a new seal. For this reason Moses admonishes the Jews to obey Christ and to listen to Him. These three points are certain and should be carefully noted.

"What, then, is circumcision?" the Jew will ask. In the first place, it cannot be stated according to natural reason and in philosophical parlance that circumcision is a work like the works enjoined by the ceremonial law and the moral law. For moral works, as they call them — such as the obedience of children to their superiors, in conformity with the Second Table, and invoking God and the giving

[11] See p. 113.

of thanks, in conformity with the First Table — these have been enjoined in such a way that they must always be performed every day, yes, every hour.

Circumcision, however, took place only once during an entire lifetime; nor could it be repeated, just as in the New Testament it is sufficient to be baptized in the name of Jesus only once, and it is sinful to repeat Baptism.[12]

In this respect circumcision differs from moral works. Ceremonies, too, are repeated. It was not enough to have sacrificed only once, to have worshiped in the temple only once, to have been reconciled with the church only once, etc.

In the second place, circumcision is an affliction and a cross rather than a work. For he who is circumcised does not perform it; he suffers it from others and indeed with pain. Therefore if it is not a moral or a ceremonial work, then, what is it?

Paul is an excellent definer and an expert dialectician; for he defines circumcision as a sign or seal of the righteousness which Abraham had before he was circumcised, in fact as a sign imprinted on the very flesh of Abraham and of all males who descended from him (Rom. 4:11).

But if someone calls circumcision a ceremony, he will concede in spite of this that it differs from the rest of the ceremonies in that it, like Baptism, is a passive ceremony.

Furthermore, when it has been established that circumcision is a sign which does not make Abraham righteous but indicates the righteousness which Abraham already has, the question arises whether this seal was an empty sign or something that was implemented together with the seal.

My answer to this question is that in Abraham's case circumcision is a mere sign without implementing anything; that is, it is a sign in such a way that it does not implement what it signifies but merely signifies. For the argument with which Paul proves that Abraham was righteous before he was circumcised is irrefutable. Hence circumcision is a sign that merely signifies righteousness but does not confer it, for it finds Abraham already righteous. It does not make him righteous.

But the situation of Abraham's descendants was different. Circumcision does not find them righteous like Abraham. Therefore it

---

[12] A reference to passages like the following: Acts 2:38; Acts 8:16; Acts 10:48; Rom. 6:3; Gal. 3:27.

was a seal of righteousness in such a way that righteousness was implemented by it. For thus it is written below (v. 14): "Any uncircumcised male who is not circumcised in the flesh of his foreskin shall be cut off from his people; he has broken My covenant." Here spiritual and eternal destruction is meant.

This negative statement implies the positive one that a male who has been circumcised on the eighth day will be saved and will be counted among the people of God. Therefore circumcision was efficacious among the descendants of Abraham; that is, it brought righteousness, not because of the work alone, which was merely passive, but because of God's promise, which was joined to this passive work.

But if circumcision was efficacious by reason of the promise, and the promise can be accepted only through faith, it follows not only that the little boys who were circumcised were received into the people of God and justified, but also that, because of the co-operation of the Holy Spirit, the little boys have faith.

This is a weighty passage, as people say. Therefore we must note it well, for it is clear evidence that God received the children of the Jews into the fellowship of the people of God and of eternal grace. The Jews are ignorant of this glory of circumcision; they merely boast of the suffering, and to this they attribute righteousness as something that is merited. But they give no thought to the promise, to the work of the Holy Spirit, or to faith.

This is great blindness; for circumcision as circumcision achieves nothing. Faith in the Word must be added to it. When this is present, then indeed circumcision is a seal of righteousness and implements righteousness.

The Jews give a very foolish reason for circumcision. They maintain that the foreskin is removed because no other part of the whole human body is so useless and superfluous, as though there actually were no other parts that could be regarded as more superfluous, such as the hairs and nails which we cut because we consider them superfluous, or as though God were the kind of master builder who creates superfluous things.

These are arguments of a mind that is blind and without a scintilla of sound understanding. Therefore let us follow Paul (Rom. 4:11), who calls circumcision a seal of righteousness and relates it to faith in this manner because it has the promise attached to it; for when circumcision is separated from faith, it is truly dead and amounts to nothing. It is of such a circumcision in the carnal sense that the Jews boast.

But here another question arises. If the uncircumcised males of the Jews are lost, what is one to conclude about infants who died before the eighth day? What about the other sex, the girls? Likewise, what about our own infants, either those who are stillborn or those who die shortly after birth, before they are baptized?

Concerning infants who died before the eighth day the answer is easy, just as it is easy to give an answer about our own infants who die before Baptism. For they do not sin against the covenant of circumcision or of Baptism. Since the Law commands them to be circumcised on the eighth day, could God condemn those who die before the eighth day?

Accordingly, the souls of those infants must be left to the will of the Heavenly Father, whom we know to be merciful. Furthermore, what Paul says in a gentle manner about "those whose sins were not like the transgression of Adam" (Rom. 5:14) and about Jacob and Esau — "though they were not yet born and had done nothing either good or bad" (Rom. 9:11) — holds true in their case too.

Even though infants bring with them inborn sin, which we call original sin, it is nevertheless important that they have committed no sin against the Law. Since God is by nature merciful, He will not let their condition be worse because they were unable to obtain circumcision in the Old Testament or Baptism in the New Testament.

With regard to the girls among the Jews the answer is easy. For because this sign was prescribed only for the male sex, it does not pertain to the girls. Nevertheless, since the girls are Abraham's descendants, they are not excluded from Abraham's righteousness; they attain it through faith. But those adults who despised circumcision or who despise Baptism are surely damned.

But it is necessary to take note of the command concerning circumcision when opposing the ravings of the Anabaptists.[13] They hold that Baptism must be repeated and that only adults should be baptized, because, as they maintain, infants have no understanding. Where there is no understanding, they say, there is no faith either.

But tell me! Circumcision, as we have said, profits only by reason of faith. Yet God gave the command that infants should be circum-

---

[13] The parallel between circumcision and Baptism seems to go back to Col. 2:11-12, but this argumentation occurs more often in Melanchthon's writings against the Anabaptists than in Luther's.

cised on the eighth day, and the promise that He will take care of them and save them is very strong. Hence the command to circumcise either served no purpose or infants, who are without any understanding, also believed and through circumcision obtained by faith the righteousness which Abraham obtained while he was still uncircumcised.

Those who are circumcised are given the promise that they are the people of God and that God wants to be their God. This means that they are in the fellowship of the kingdom of God, since they have been justified by the justifying faith which the Lord grants them through His Spirit.

If this was brought about with the Jews in the Old Testament through the medium of circumcision, why would God not do the same thing with the Gentiles through the medium of the new covenant of Baptism?

The command (Matt. 28:19) pertains to all: "Go therefore and make disciples of all nations, baptizing them. . . ." Hence whereas circumcision was commanded only to the descendants of Abraham, Baptism is commanded to all the nations, with the promise of salvation if they believe.

But if, by virtue of the promise, Abraham's descendants had the blessing that those circumcised on the eighth day would receive the gift of faith and become the people of God, why would this be denied the nations now united with God through the covenant of Baptism?

For the situation of Baptism will not be worse than that of circumcision, especially since circumcision pertained only to the males, while Baptism includes the other sex.

But just as a Jew who fell away from this covenant of God through sin did not have to be circumcised again but was received into grace if he returned to this covenant and took courage from this promise, so those who fall away from grace do not have to be rebaptized. They should rely with firm faith on the promise once given and hope for pardon through Christ.

This is a powerful argument against those who say that because little children have no understanding and do not believe, they should not be baptized. For here the command is given that little children are to be circumcised on the eighth day, and the promise is added: "I will be their God."

Hence both the command and the promise bear witness that righteousness was imputed to infants through the medium of circumcision, just as it was imputed to Abraham through faith before circumcision; for it is impossible to please God without faith (Heb. 11:6).

But the covenant of circumcision was to last only till the coming of Christ. Because He intended to include the Gentiles in the kingdom of God, He wanted to introduce a new sign after the old sign or covenant had been done away with, just as He says (John 3:5): "Unless one is born of water and the Spirit, he cannot enter the kingdom of God."

Something like this — though the similarity is by no means perfect — can be found in affairs of state. A person has exerted himself strenuously in defending his native land against the enemy and in saving it. Because of his valor the emperor presents him with special decorations, with towns, districts, and castles. All his descendants enjoy these gifts and are incited to emulate their ancestors in valor.

But if the descendants of this man should degenerate — the emperor gave gifts to their ancestors and can take them away from descendants who have degenerated.

Thus to Abraham, the most illustrious victor who not only conquered his enemies but also overcame sin and death, God gives circumcision as a decoration for valor — a decoration which Abraham is to wear on his flesh. But God does not give it as an empty sign. No, Abraham's descendants, too, are to rejoice in it and to have the benefit of it, provided that they follow in the footsteps of their valorous father.

Therefore even though only the family of Abraham was under obligation to bear this sign or distinctive mark before the whole world, yet through it the Gentiles, too, were urged to learn to know Abraham's God and to serve Him.

For this reason Paul states in Rom. 4:11 that circumcision was given to Abraham as a sign, that it might be a seal of the righteousness of faith which he had before he was circumcised; and Paul immediately adds that "the purpose was to make him the father of all who believe without being circumcised and likewise the father of the circumcised who are not merely circumcised but also follow the example of the faith which our father Abraham had before he was circumcised" (Rom. 4:11-12).

The correct definition of circumcision is this: It is a public mark by which all, whether circumcised or uncircumcised, are urged to follow in the footsteps of Abraham or to emulate the faith of Abraham.

For Abraham is the common father of the Gentiles and the Jews. He has been distinguished with a new sign in order that the Gentiles might hasten to him as to a standard-bearer and might acknowledge, confess, and worship the same God. The Gentiles are also invited to the same righteousness of faith, in order that Abraham, in accordance with the promise, may become the father of many nations.

Thus Job, Pharaoh, and countless others were saved throughout the entire period of the Law and before, though they were not descendants of Abraham; for Abraham had to be the father not only of the Jews but also of the Gentiles who believe.

Even though foreigners are not forced to be circumcised, yet they are received into the fellowship of righteousness. Meanwhile, however, circumcision is also efficacious to the end that a definite kind of people may remain until the coming of Him to whom all things are referred, who is to set up a new banner or sign, not among one particular people but throughout the whole world.

The church is no longer to be confined to one particular nook, the way the Roman pontiff does not recognize the churches that do not recognize him. For the banner which Christ has raised when He said (Mark 16:15): "Go into all the world" is not in one specific nook or in one particular family. For this reason it is called the catholic church. Yet this church consists only of those who are baptized. For apart from Baptism there is no salvation, just as at that time salvation resulted from circumcision, not because of circumcision alone but because of faith in the promise which was attached to circumcision and, as it were, embodied in it.

From the beginning of the world divine wisdom has so ordained and arranged things that there was always some public sign toward which all peoples might look, in order that the Gentiles, too, might find, worship, and pray to the true God, although not all who had that sign believed and had use of it for righteousness.

Thus prior to circumcision the sacrifices were signs. The brothers Abel and Cain bring sacrifices. For Abel the sacrifice is a seal of righteousness, because he believes. For Cain, however, it is not a seal of righteousness, because he does not believe but retains the bare work without faith.[14]

Thus circumcision is raised up as a sign or a banner to be looked

---

[14] Cf. *Luther's Works*, 1, pp. 257 ff.

at by those who are to be saved. For because through the divine blessing Abraham was to be multiplied into peoples and kingdoms, the church is embodied, so to speak, in his flesh for a time, and a universal sign is given — a sign which pertained to the church in such a way that even if those who believed did not have it, they were not excluded from the church.

Augustine defines a sacrament as a visible form of invisible grace.[15] His definition is correct. At the same time he points out why the sacraments are commonly despised by those who have them as their own, as Isaiah states (65:1-2): "I was ready to be found by those who did not seek Me. . . . I spread out My hands all the day to a rebellious people, who walk in a way that is not good, following their own devices."

This is a judgment of God that must be borne. God establishes a sign of grace, in order that it may be recognized by sinners and sinners may be saved; but it commonly happens that those for whom the sign is set up despise it.

Thus Baptism has been established as a sign of righteousness for all who believe in Christ. The papists also boast of Baptism; but they do so in vain, because they do not believe. They condemn and persecute the doctrine of justification. Thus the voice of John, which cried out in the wilderness, and Baptism had been established as a banner; but the Pharisees paid no attention. Similarly, Isaiah says (11:10) that a root is to be set up as a sign; but the Jews reject this sign. The Gentiles, however, put their hope in it.

We say the same thing about circumcision, with which the Gentiles are not burdened but are nevertheless invited to the same faith, in order that Abraham may be the father of the circumcised as well as of the uncircumcised.

Therefore many of the Gentiles believed, but the Jews kept their hearts uncircumcised. Thus circumcision was an opportunity for salvation even for the Gentiles and was profitable for them. For we have need of marks and signs of this kind, in order that they may lead us to the knowledge of God, since human reason is unable to find God unless such signs instituted by God lead us by the hand, so to speak. And nothing is more dangerous than if one devises his own way to God and relies on his own speculations.

We were in the habit of doing this sort of thing under the papacy.

---

[15] Augustine, *De catechizandis rudibus*, ch. 26, *Patrologia, Series Latina*, XL, 344, is one form of this familiar definition of a sacrament.

For one dreamed that he would find God in Rome; another, in Spain; and still another, in a different part of the world. When each attempted this for himself, the outcome was that we all went astray and accomplished nothing, as Ps. 14:3 states.

Why did we not follow the signs which the Lord Himself had established for the purpose of gathering us into the unity of faith, that is, the Word of God, Baptism, and the Lord's Supper?

Thus when the Jews had the temple, circumcision, and a definite form of worship, for which they, as people who acknowledged one God as their Leader, were to assemble as under a military standard, they disregarded all this and turned to their own endeavors. Everyone devised his own way of worshiping God and followed it to his own certain destruction.

When God reveals Himself in some sign, no matter what its nature, one must take hold of Him in it. But Satan continually strives to remove the true signs from our sight and to set up false signs, just as he displays lights to those who get lost in the night and, when heedlessly following these lights, fall either into abysses or into water.[16]

Therefore in Matt. 24:23 Christ earnestly exhorts us to avoid such snares when He says: "If anyone says to you: 'Lo, here is the Christ!' or 'There He is!' do not believe it."

Christ must be sought where He has manifested Himself and wants to be known, as in the Word, in Baptism, and in the Supper; there He is certainly found, for the Word cannot deceive us. But it generally happens that reason disregards those signs and turns aside to the harlot sitting at the gate (Prov. 7:10 ff.).

Therefore let everyone remember to walk on the way God Himself has prescribed, not on the one we ourselves have chosen; for our own choice is sinful and delusive.

Thus the prophet says (Is. 66:3): "These have chosen their own ways"; and Paul (Col. 2:18, 23) condemns self-elected religions. For it is certain that a human being cannot find God through his own wisdom; and for this reason, too, there is great danger that Satan transforms himself into an angel of light (2 Cor. 11:14) and surrounds himself with divine majesty while producing signs and wonders to confirm his errors.

We shall be safe from these dangers if we follow that visible

---

[16] On this phenomenon cf. *Luther's Works*, 2, p. 147, note 27.

form or those signs which God Himself has set before us. In the New Testament we have as a visible form the Son of God on the lap of His mother Mary. He suffered and died for us, as the Creed teaches. Besides, we have other visible forms: Baptism, the Eucharist, and the spoken Word itself. Therefore we cannot complain of having been forsaken.

In the first place, however, Satan, and, in the second place, his servants, the pope with his entire church, strive to divert us from these divinely appointed visible forms to their own forms: the canonization of the saints, the invocation and worship of the departed saints, and the statues set up in special places for the sake of gain, etc.

Therefore we must be fortified against these plots in order that we may say: "Just as I have no knowledge of any church before Christ's coming except the one which was in the home of Abraham and was marked by circumcision, so after Christ's coming I know nothing except Christ and Him crucified, who reveals Himself to us in visible forms: in the use of the Keys and in the Eucharist. I know that I find God there and that I receive forgiveness of sins there and nowhere else."

"No," say the papists, "God has given a variety of gifts to His saints. How many miracles adorn the sanctuary of St. James at Compostela! How many miracles grace Rome! Hence God wants to be sought and found there too. Thus Francis certainly left behind a rule suitable for saints. How could those who follow it fail to please God? And these gifts, too — in accordance with the custom of the fathers, who approved them — serve a purpose."

Thus Satan strives hard to lead us away from the forms prescribed by God. But you must adhere to and follow this sure and infallible rule: God in His divine wisdom arranges to manifest Himself to human beings by some definite and visible form which can be seen with the eyes and touched with the hands, in short, is within the scope of the five senses. So near to us does the Divine Majesty place Itself.

It is the height of wisdom to hold fast to these visible forms. But the examples of all the patriarchs, prophets, and godly men teach that Satan strives continually to find ways to obscure those forms and to set others before us.

Thus circumcision, too, was a visible form which was not instituted by human beings but was instituted by God Himself, in order that He might be known through it and that not only the Jews but also the heathen might believe in that God who had revealed Himself to the Jews in such a manner.

Therefore I am convinced that all the circumcised infants of the Jews who died at an early age were saved. For they were found in Abraham's bosom, that is, in the promise that God wants to be their God.

I hold the same opinion about our baptized infants. But adults who let sin deprive them of faith are not saved; for even though they have been baptized, they do not believe. Nothing like this happens to infants. Therefore they remain in the deliverance they have received, and they are saved.

This doctrine is necessary, and it bestows high praise on the sacraments, which fanatical men shamefully underestimate because they pay no attention to the Word. For the frequent repetition of what is said here about circumcision — "I shall be their God and the God of your descendants after you" — is no game or jest. Circumcision was the outward and visible sign by which the Jews were to be recognized among the Gentiles and were to recognize one another.

But circumcision not only brought this people together politically and served as a password among them; but it was also a sacrament, that is, a sign of the divine will and therefore a sign of eternal salvation for those who believed. For it showed that God was the God of this circumcised people. "He is not God of the dead, but of the living" (Matt. 22:32). Therefore through circumcision, to which faith is added, they are not only citizens in that state which was established apart from other nations; they are also heirs of eternal life. For God is immortal and eternal. Therefore He bestows immortality on those who are His.

Let us by all means take the same stand with regard to Baptism in the New Testament and with regard to the Eucharist, lest we, like the fanatics, think that these are external signs instituted merely for the purpose of distinguishing Christians from the heathen.[17] They do make a distinction, it is true; but they do more than this, for those who believe the promise and make use of these signs become the people of God and are saved.

But it is necessary to note what I stated above: that circumcision

---

[17] This phrase, which is almost a direct quotation from the Augsburg Confession, is developed in Luther's *This Is My Body: These Words Still Stand* (W, XXIII, 269).

was enjoined only upon the descendants of Abraham and only upon the male sex. Yet neither the females of the Jews nor the Gentiles were excluded from the grace which circumcision confirmed.

For circumcision as a work had no validity per se, but faith in the promise that was added to circumcision did have validity.

Before circumcision the sacrifices and the ministry of the Word were the visible signs of the invisible grace; but circumcision, which was instituted under Abraham, had validity up to the coming of the Blessed Seed.

Since the coming of Christ we have holy Baptism, the Eucharist, and the Keys; by these signs God reveals Himself and saves those who make use of them in faith. When the descendants of Cain who were instructed by the Word of God had this faith, they were saved; for Cain was not cast aside to such an extent that God denied salvation to his descendants.

The reason for Cain's sentence was a different one, namely, that the church might be more definitely marked and recognized, and that it might not seem that there was a twofold church; for throughout all ages there had to be one definite family from which alone it would be believed that Christ was to be born.

With this intention Ishmael, too, is cast out. Yet he is admitted into the fellowship of the promise; for Abraham prays for him and has the promise that he will also be the father of many nations. Therefore Ishmael was not cut off from salvation and eternal life; he was cut off from the glory of being the father of Christ. Yet Christ would be among his people.

In this way the pride in his physical birth was to be held in check, in order that he might not boast of being Abraham's son but might embrace Abraham's faith. And I believe that he really did embrace the faith of Abraham.

But let us return to the exposition of the text. Abraham hears that both covenants are being confirmed: the material one involving the land of Canaan and the spiritual one involving the eternal blessing. Therefore when he learns of the favor God confers on him by choosing to establish in his family the church in which He may surely be found by all the nations that call upon Him, He falls prostrate on the ground and gives thanks.

For it is a most glorious and truly magnificent promise when God confirms with a covenant that from the descendants of Abraham there will arise the church which is to have its home in the land of

Canaan until Christ is born, in order that both the Gentiles and the Jews who will believe what Abraham had believed may be saved.

The seal of circumcision is given to him to the end that all may be saved through the righteousness of faith which is in Abraham and that the church may be transferred from the sacrifices of the early fathers to this one circumcised church.

"Lo, I." These are wonderfully glowing words, as though God wanted to say: "You are now not hearing a God who is different from the God you heard before, when I called you out of Ur of the Chaldeans; but I am promising you that your family will be the church for the entire world. It is to be like a lap and bosom of grace in which all nations, not only your descendants, are to find salvation, provided that they persevere in your faith."

For in Christ, who is promised to Abraham, all peoples are gathered, whether they are little children, who are not deceived by the sin that lives in the flesh, or adults, who are easily deceived and yield to the flesh, and for whom, on this account, as Peter says (2 Peter 2:21), it would be better if they had never known grace than if through sin they fall again from the grace they have known.

But note here also a strong passage against the empty boasts of the Jews concerning circumcision. Abram's name is changed, and he is called Abraham, that is, father of many nations, before circumcision is enjoined upon him.

Hence God wants the faith of Abraham to be spread abroad, not only among the descendants of Ishmael, Isaac, and the other sons, who were born from Keturah but also among the nations who were not born from the flesh of Abraham.

For the Jews must not be allowed to prate that in any nation only those are saved who have been circumcised and that all nations must observe the Law, but especially circumcision. This is nonsense that befits blinded minds.

God wanted Abraham to bear this sign for the benefit of his descendants, yet in such a manner that through it the Gentiles would also be invited to faith. For the Gentiles could become the people of God through faith in the Blessed Seed, not through circumcision.

Thus the Queen of Sheba and Hiram acknowledged the God of circumcised Solomon, even though Hiram remained uncircumcised. This, then, is the bosom of Abraham into which the Gentiles, too, are gathered, namely, the faith of Abraham, by which they themselves also obtain the promise, even though they do not obtain the visible sign that is added to the promise. For this sign was required of the descendants of Abraham, not of the Gentiles.

We have spoken above about the change of Abraham's name.[18] But be that as it may, a mystery is connected with the insertion of the letter ה in the middle of the word. This letter represents a weak *h* sound and a soft hissing, as it were. Perhaps the Lord wanted to signify that the Holy Spirit would come with a very gentle hissing and would call the heathen to the fellowship of faith and of the promise.

It is also stated that the letter ה includes the two words הֲמוֹן גּוֹיִם "multitude of nations," so that Abraham has the name together with the fact and is appointed father of the church or high priest, not because of circumcision, which was merely the seal of righteousness and not righteousness itself, but because of faith in the promise concerning the blessed Seed. And all those who have this faith, whether they live in Egypt or in the land of Canaan, are the sons of Abraham; they and Abraham himself, the father of nations, have been breathed on by the same Spirit of God, in order that in this manner the unity and the certainty of the church may remain and there may be only one way, not many ways that are really uncertain and deceptive.

The addition of the words "I will make you exceedingly fruitful; and I will make nations of you" also contradicts the dreams of the Jews; for the statement is explicit that the descendants of Abraham are to be increased, not to become one nation but to become many — to such an extent that many kings will come from him.

But "nation" is the term applied to one definite people which has its own government, head, and laws. A mob of brigands who live without law — likewise hermits; likewise the Jews, who are scattered today — cannot be called a nation; for the Jews have been without a head or a kingdom for more than 1,500 years. They are like an army in the field without a banner and without a leader.

Therefore the Jews have lost this promise, no matter how much they boast of their father Abraham. And not only does circumcision serve no purpose, but whatever they do in conformity with the Law is done in vain. They are no longer the people of God.

But it is necessary to note that this text sanctions civil government. Peoples and kings cannot exist without laws. They must wage wars, defend their subjects, and punish criminals. All these activities are

[18] See p. 100.

approved of in this passage as just and lawful. For this reason Scripture calls them judgments of the Lord, wars of the Lord, etc.

In like manner, we have administrative agencies in the church — agencies that are approved of on the authority of Christ and of the apostles. But not only the officials who are in the church and profess the faith together with us but also the governments of the heathen have this approval. Similarly, this passage sanctions not only the rule of the descendants of Abraham but also that of Ishmael's descendants and of the neighboring nations that sprang from him.

7. *And I will establish My covenant between Me and you and your descendants after you throughout their generations for an everlasting covenant, to be God to you and to your descendants after you.*

I have repeatedly stated that the accounts of the patriarchs are superior because God is speaking with them, and the account of Abraham is preferred to all the rest because God is not found speaking so often with any other patriarch.

Therefore because Abraham is a father of faith and God's special friend, it is right to call him a patriarch. God speaks with him in such a friendly manner when He so frequently promises him the increase of his descendants and not only the possession of Canaan and a physical kingdom but also a church. This church is to have its home solely among the descendants of Abraham, and as a distinguishing mark God instituted circumcision, which was to be a definite sign and a visible form in the world. In circumcision God would reveal Himself or appear not only for the benefit of the family of Abraham but also for the benefit of all nations. They would see this sign or banner for their salvation, and it would give them the opportunity to come to the knowledge of God. Accordingly, circumcision led to the salvation of many of the Gentiles.

Concerning the letters of princes it is stated in a proverb that they should be read three times; but surely the letters of God — for this is what Gregory calls Scripture — should be read seven times three, yes, seventy times seven or, to say even more, countless times.[19] For they are divine wisdom, which cannot be grasped immediately at the first glance. If someone reads them superficially like familiar and easy material, he deceives himself.

[19] Luther frequently quoted this proverb about the letters of princes; cf. W, *Tischreden*, 1, 155; 3, 383. See also p. 126, note 32.

It is certainly evident that the prophets meditated day and night on the writings of Moses and especially on these accounts of the patriarchs, and that they drew wonderful conclusions from them. For the Holy Spirit comes to the aid of their diligence. Therefore because it does not displease God to converse with Abraham at such great length, we shall consider everything somewhat more carefully.

As I have often stated, what God repeats about establishing and confirming the covenant is to be understood not only of Abraham's physical descendants but also of the Gentiles who will believe in the God of Abraham, as King Pharaoh did at the time of Joseph and Abraham did at the time of Abimelech, and just as from among the Gentiles there were many who acknowledged the true God and were saved.

Therefore the words "I will establish or set up My covenant" must be understood in a very broad sense. But when God adds that the covenant will be everlasting — this the Jews distort to mean that even the Gentiles must be circumcised if they want to become the people of God. But they make this mistake on purpose; for why do they not consider the words that are added: "between Me and you and your descendants after you throughout their generations"?

Accordingly, the text states that this covenant will be in force among the descendants of Abraham and is never to be changed while the generations of Abraham continue to exist.

This limit was added, and the time was precisely defined, as it were. As long as the generations of the descendants of Abraham continue to exist, that is, as long as a state, a kingdom, a priesthood, and some definite form of a people remain, this covenant must remain unchangeable.

Accordingly, the generation of Abraham comes to an end in Christ, who is the Head and Founder of a new generation. But just as the previous generation had circumcision added as a distinguishing sign, so the new generation of Christ has other distinguishing signs.

The generation of Abraham lasts up to a definite time, as Mary beautifully states in her hymn (Luke 1:50): "His mercy is on those who fear Him from generation to generation." She points out that God will preserve this people if it fears Him; but since the ungodly synagog ceased to fear God when it killed the Son of God and persecuted His Word with inhuman hatred, circumcision did not have such value that on its account such great sins went unpunished.

At that time, therefore, the physical generation of Abraham came to an end and was succeeded by the new generation of the Son of God — the generation concerning which the prophet says (Is. 53:8): "Who shall declare His generation?"

Accordingly, circumcision and this covenant of Abraham had their duration. Nevertheless, they were subject to change and limited as to time, and no human being was permitted to change them while the generations of Abraham still remained.

But Christ, the Founder of the new generation, did not change the covenant; He changed the sign of the covenant. Therefore the Jews boast in vain that circumcision is perpetual, that is, unrestricted as to the extent and the time of its practice, and that for this reason it must be imposed on the Gentiles too.

There was a definite time for circumcision to remain in force, and during this time it was to be retained in the house of Abraham. But after the spiritual descendants promised to Abraham had come, the physical generation ceased and along with it the sign of the physical generation — the sign appointed not only for the sake of Abraham's descendants but also for the sake of the Gentiles, as we said above. This sign was everlasting and unchangeable so far as men were concerned, but God finally changed it.

The words "to be God to you" have been mentioned above at various times.[20] They embrace not only the material promise concerning handing over the land of Canaan but also the spiritual one of which Scripture said (Gen. 15:1): "I am your shield; your reward shall be very great."

By means of a plain covenant and in very clear words God points out that the church must be in the house of Abraham and that the house of Abraham will be in the land of Canaan. Here, however, Abraham himself was a sojourner. For "to be God" not only means to be the creator of something but includes the worship of God.

God is also the God of the heathen, for He created them; but He is neither acknowledged nor worshiped by the heathen.

When God says: "I shall be your God," He points out that Abraham will always have the Word of God in his family and house, in order that his descendants may learn from it to know God and to worship Him aright.

Thus the First Commandment says: "I am the Lord your God"

---

[20] Cf. *Luther's Works*, 2, pp. 253 ff., on the meaning of this phrase.

(Ex. 20:2), that is, "I reveal Myself through the Word, and you shall worship Me and acknowledge Me."

The name God must be understood in a relative sense, to mean the God who is worshiped and adored, not in an absolute sense, to mean God according to His essence and majesty.[21] "I shall be your God," that is, "In your house I shall set up My worship, and among you and your people I shall be the God who is worshiped, and among your descendants I shall manifest Myself by means of signs and visible marks, by means of miracles and wonders, in order that they may know Me beyond all doubt and may adore and worship Me." For the true worship of God is accomplished in this twofold manner.

To adore God is to go to Him for help when you turn your face toward Him and call upon Him in trouble, when you give thanks for deliverance, when you recall and proclaim His acts of kindness by declaring that He is the Creator, the Benefactor, the Promiser, and the Savior.

Because of a natural instinct the heathen also have this understanding; they know that there is a supreme deity, that he must be worshiped, called upon, and praised, and that one should take refuge with him in all dangers. Paul says that they have a natural knowledge of God (Rom. 1:21).

For God has implanted this knowledge in the hearts of all human beings. They call God a helper, kind, and forgiving, even though afterwards they are in error as to who that God is and how He wants to be worshiped.

But when it is recognized that God is gracious, placable, and kind, then I go out and turn my face from God to human beings, that is, I tend to my calling. If I am a king, I govern the state. If I am the head of a household, I direct the domestics; if I am a schoolmaster, I teach pupils, mold their habits and views toward godliness.

These works are rightly called a worship of God. For in all of them we serve God, who wanted us to do such things and, so to speak, stationed us here.

This doctrine concerning the worship of God is very necessary.

---

[21] Luther is operating here with the distinction he develops in his exposition of Ps. 51: "David is not speaking this way with the absolute God." For, Luther says a little earlier, "he is speaking with God as He is dressed and clothed in His Word and promises." *Luther's Works,* 12, p. 312.

For the entire world knows of the monstrous fictions invented by the papists, who finally went so far as to maintain that it is worship to be buried in a monks' cowl.[22] But the real chief points of godliness and of true religion are these: faith toward God, through which we receive remission of sins; invocation; thanksgiving; and confession; next, the works of our calling with reference to our neighbor, that you rule, prescribe, teach, comfort, exhort, make a living by working, etc.

In the schools the sophists have debated whether God was in some category.[23] But hallucinations of this kind reveal that the sophists have absolutely no understanding of sacred matters. For he who wants to ask what God is should consider the worship of God, which consists in its entirety of adoration and service (Matt. 4:10).

In the second place, it is not enough to teach about God in this manner, namely, that He is the God who is worshiped and who reveals Himself through His Word. It is necessary to add that this God, who tells us how to worship Him, is the Giver of eternal life, as Christ argues against the Sadducees (Matt. 22:32). For the God who is worshiped and adored — I am expressing myself thus for the sake of teaching — is the one necessary part that belongs to this life.

But this worship or adoration must not be Saducean or Epicurean. For the Sadducees and the Epicureans maintain that God is the God of the dead. Christ, on the other hand, teaches (Matt. 22:32) that God is the God of the living. Therefore He is the God of the godly, the God of Abraham, for example, of Isaac, and of Jacob; these are living and are not dead, even though they are dead so far as we are concerned.

Therefore with these words, with which He promises to be the God of Abraham, the Lord calls not only Abraham but also all his descendants, yes, even all the Gentiles who believe as faithful Abraham did, to the hope of eternal life. He promises that they will live as long as God Himself lives, that is, forever.

As authority for this conviction we have the Son of God Himself, who says: "God is the God of the living." Hence though Abraham, Isaac, and Jacob are already dead, they are nevertheless living, and indeed eternally.

---

[22] Cf. *Luther's Works*, 24, p. 327.

[23] Luther is alluding here to the discussions of the medieval logicians about whether God could be classified; the discussions ended with the conclusion that God is *sui generis*.

8. *And I will give to you, and to your descendants after you, the land of your sojournings, all the land of Canaan, for an everlasting possession; and I will be their God.*

These statements seem to contradict each other. Abraham is promised the everlasting possession of the land of Canaan, and yet he is said to be a sojourner. This is really what the ancient dialecticians used to call a contradiction in terms.[24] But the contradictions are duly brought into agreement by this mediating fact, that the God of Abraham is the God of the living. And so Abraham, who worshiped and served God in this life, was a sojourner; yet, in view of the promise, he at the same time had possession of the land of Canaan. Though he died, he is not actually dead; he lives and has possession of the promised land through his descendants.

Stephen says (Acts 7:5): "He gave him no inheritance in it, not even a foot's length." Therefore both statements — that Abraham has possession of the land after his death and is a sojourner in the land while he is living — are true. Thus even though he died, he is not dead; he lives, according to the promise: "I shall be your God."

From these facts it is easy for us to conclude what Abraham's feelings were and what kind of thoughts he had. He saw the promise, and he felt that it was true beyond all doubt. He also saw that he had nothing of his own but was a sojourner in the land.

But because the promise could not fail and he himself, while he was living here, did not gain possession of the land of Canaan, he concluded with certainty that though he would die, he would not be totally blotted out but would rise again and be brought to life in his own person.

For what else could he think or feel? He is a sojourner in this life, and yet he is promised the possession of the land of Canaan. Therefore this is sure proof that he will not die. For the pronoun points expressly to his person — "To you I shall give" — lest we say that although Abraham died in his person, he lives and possesses the land in his descendants. This is a sophistic explanation; for God says privately and personally to Abraham: "To you and your descendants," not to your descendants alone. No, the possession of the land of Canaan was also to come to Abraham himself. Yet it did not come to him while he was alive. Therefore to be the heir of the land of Canaan, he had to be alive after he had died.

[24] The technical phrase is *oppositum in adiecto*.

Therefore Abraham has the promise that after his own death the God whom he worshiped and adored in this life will remain in his house and among his descendants. But Abraham's house will remain in the land of Canaan. After his death, however, he himself will live as the true possessor of this land.

The Word of God is such a great treasure and brings such marvelous revelations concerning invisible and impossible things that Abraham concludes with certainty that he will live after he has died and that after his death he will possess the land which he was not to possess in this life. Thus he will live with God eternally.

Therefore why would he not be glad, and why would he not give thanks to God after he is certain that the church and the faith which has been sealed by circumcision will remain in his house and among his descendants in spite of Satan and the world, and that he himself will also remain in eternal life with God?

Accordingly, he waited joyfully for the hour of his departure. And what else could he do throughout his life but give thanks to God and proclaim the mercy of Him who speaks with him in such a friendly way and so amicably comforts him?

If I could have such thoughts and could conclude with certainty (yet I pray God every day that I may be able to do so, and I know that He will hear me) that when I die I shall not die but shall live and declare the works of the Lord (Ps. 118:17);[25] likewise, that the Word of God and the true worship of God will remain among those students whom I leave behind when I die; and that my students will be the cause of salvation for the whole world — in what frame of mind do you suppose I shall meet death? You do not suppose, do you, that I shall be afraid and not prefer to say with Simeon: "Lord, now lettest Thou Thy servant depart in peace" (Luke 2:29)?

Accordingly, Abraham is a truly remarkable man in his faith. Nor is it surprising if he was calm in dangers and bore misfortunes with the greatest patience. For he knew that the church would remain in a definite place, among definite persons, and up to a definite time, namely, up to the time of Christ, who was not of the generations of this world. Moreover, he knew that after his death he would live eternally. Nevertheless, he did not yet have the son in whom that blessing was to have its beginning — the blessing which embraced

---

[25] On Luther's affection for Ps. 118 cf. his remarks in *Luther's Works*, 14, p. 46.

not only the Jews but also all the Gentiles who were willing to adore the God of Abraham and to believe in Him.

I have said this to give you an understanding of what it means to be God; and my view agrees with what Daniel says about Antiochus but Paul (2 Thess. 2:4) says about the Antichrist, namely, that he will exalt himself above all that is God and above all worship. The Antichrist, that is, the pope and Turk,[26] do not elevate themselves above God in His essence, who is the unknown and "hidden God," as Isaiah (45:15) calls Him, but above God in the category of relation, who is the God proclaimed by the Word and manifested by the worship.[27]

Both not only disregard but even loathe and persecute the Word of God and worship. Thus the pope has exalted himself above God and has set himself up in God's place in such a way that he, instead of God, is worshiped and served after the Word and the worship of God have been suppressed.

Examine the canons, and you will see that transgressions of the traditions of the pope are punished with far greater severity than transgressions of the Law of God. Indeed, Christ, who alone should be adored and worshiped — Him the pope treads underfoot and blasphemes; he wants people to cherish his own dogmas, to fear him, and to place confidence in what he himself teaches. This is truly setting himself above the proclaimed and worshiped God. Therefore it is proper to call him the Antichrist.

Before the light of the Gospel came, how many do you suppose there were even among the teachers who could recite the Commandments of the Decalog or the petitions of the Lord's Prayer? The necks of all were burdened with human traditions; and when we had met the demands of these, we thought that our worship was perfect.

This was truly being exalted above God and sitting in the temple of God, not in the heaven of the essential God, where the unrevealed and hidden God dwells, but in the place of the God who has been proclaimed and is taught in the Word and the God who is worshiped and served.

The pope not only did away with divinely instituted matrimony, but he sullied it outright, as though it were an unholy kind of life and were displeasing to God.

[26] See pp. 122 f. for a fuller exposition of this identification.
[27] See the passage cited in note 21, p. 117.

From the Sacrament of the Eucharist the pope has not only removed the cup and — contrary to what is right — taken it away from the church; but he has changed Christ's testament into a sacrifice and a work that is done for profit. In short, he has buried Christ completely and has attributed righteousness to his own traditions and to forms of worship that have been established beyond and contrary to the Word. This is truly exalting oneself above everything that is called God.

But I understand God in a relative sense as the adored God to whom we turn our faces, to whom we give thanks, upon whom we call as the author of all good things, material and spiritual. Him we then serve in love and in discharging our obligations toward our neighbor when we obey the government and our parents and when we serve our children by providing for their sustenance and instructing them faithfully. For all these things must be done for the sake of God, who has revealed Himself in His Word.

This the pope, the Turk, and the Jews do not do; but they exalt themselves above God by despising His commands, and when they think they are most saintly, they take for granted that they are worshiping and understanding God in His essence. From such a God, however, no life is to be hoped for, because such a God does not speak with us. But the God who has revealed Himself by visible marks, who has given the Word of promise and has instituted the sacraments, is the true God and Savior whom we are able to take hold of and to understand.

Yet you must guard against either adding to or subtracting from the things by which God has manifested Himself. But if you depart from this God whom we are placing in the category of relation and investigate Him in the category of substance or quantity, you will be overwhelmed by His majesty. If you search Him in the category of quality, you will be consumed; for God is "a consuming fire" (Heb. 12:29) and "dwells in unapproachable light" (1 Tim. 6:16).[28]

Therefore stay with God in the category of relation. Above Him the Antichrist, that is the Roman pope and also the Turk, exalts himself. Yet it is more in accordance with the truth to say that the Turk is the beast, because he is outside the church and openly persecutes Christ.

The Antichrist, however, sits in the temple of God. Therefore,

---

[28] Luther is referring to some of the terms defined and discussed by Aristotle in Book V of the *Metaphysics*.

strictly speaking and by logical definition, he who sits in the church is the Antichrist. Here appear the visible forms of God which he himself treads underfoot. He invents new forms, etc.

Thus we see the character and the greatness of Abraham, who was endowed with such great promises that on the basis of them he concludes with certainty that he will live eternally. When the Lord says: "I shall be your God and the God of your seed after you," He thereby not only assigns to the church a definite place in the family of Abraham but at the same time promises immortality and adds a sign on Abraham's body, namely, circumcision.

If these things were promised by some prince of the world — namely, that he wanted to be our most gracious emperor or king — and a letter of attestation were added to the promise, they would bulk large. Yet it could happen that a human being might change his mind, just as the German proverb compares the favor of princes to April weather, which is not clear and is most changeable.[29] And memorable to all succeeding generations are the examples of many whom kings and princes ultimately brought to the gallows or subjected to other punishments after they had been held singularly dear. Thus among deceitful and fickle human beings even insincere and deceitful favor is welcome.

But Abraham had God as the Promiser, and he knew that God could not change or deceive. God promises: "My dear Abraham, just keep My covenant, walk before Me blameless and perfect, and know for sure that I want to be your God and the God of your descendants after you, yes, because of you, also of all the heathen who will believe in Me according to your example."

These are manifestly words which concern not only this life but also everlasting life. And we think that if God said the same things to us, we would easily overcome by hope whatever evils can befall in this life. Yet we have this promise far more abundantly than Abraham himself had it.

Abraham and his people occupied only a small nook in which the voice of God might be heard and the visible signs of God might be seen. Today the entire world is filled with these signs of God, just as the seraphim in Isaiah (6:3) sing: "The whole earth is full of His glory."

Abraham had circumcision as the sign of this promise. We have

---

[29] On this proverb see also *Luther's Works*, 13, p. 180, note 46; and *Luther's Works*, 14, p. 232, note 11.

Baptism, which was instituted with a far more magnificent form; for we are baptized in the name of the Father, of the Son, and of the Holy Spirit.

Not satisfied with this sign of grace, the Son of God left the church His body and His blood as a testament. He wanted us to eat His body and to drink His blood in this life unto eternal life, in order that there might remain no doubt that the salvation accomplished by the suffering and death of the Son of God belongs to us and not only — as we used to think under the papacy when we were corrupted by the doctrine of the pope — to Peter, Paul, Mark, and other servants of God who were distinguished by outstanding qualities.

The pope's doctrine left us uncertain about salvation. Indeed, it was an act of piety to doubt whether you were in grace or not. This doubt Christ wanted to remove from us not only by His Word but also by these visible signs of His grace. Therefore He added such clear promises to these signs — promises that are applied to the individuals when they make use of these signs.

Accordingly, just as Abraham had circumcision and the glorious words "I shall be God to you and your descendants after you" added to circumcision, so we have several visible signs. In the first place, we have Baptism itself, which is adorned with the most important and pleasing promise that we shall be saved if we believe. But because in this weakness of ours it is very easy for us to fall, there have been added to Baptism the Keys or the ministry of the Word — for these must not be separated — which in itself is also a visible sign of grace bound to the Word of the Gospel in accordance with Christ's institution (Matt. 18:18): "Whatever you loose on earth shall be loosed in heaven." When you take hold of this Word in faith, you will be restored to grace, and the life which was lost through sin is given back.

The same thing takes place in the use of the Holy Eucharist, for the words (Matt. 26:26-27) "My body given for you, My blood shed for the remission of your sins" are certainly not without meaning; they admirably strengthen the hope of the remission of sins.

Thus you see that we have the promise of eternal grace far more richly than Abraham himself had it. Therefore we should also take pride in this gift over against Satan and the world, and we should buoy ourselves up with this comfort in all misfortunes, just as the saintly patriarch did.

But we are hampered by our wretched and sinful flesh, and we are living in the last times, which have been corrupted by evils of every kind. Therefore we neither see nor marvel at these eternal riches.

In this one way St. Stephen, St. Lawrence, Sebastian, Fabian, and men like them overcame death and all tortures.[30] Because they kept the faith of Abraham and comforted themselves with these visible signs of grace, all tortures — as an often repeated statement of Vincent [31] puts it — were amusement, pastime, and, so to speak, child's play for them.

So great a thing is faith when God reveals Himself through a promise and hearts embrace this promise seriously. This very promise, "I shall be your God," sounds forth continually in the church. Therefore the prophets and apostles diligently meditated on it and splendidly elucidated it in their sermons. They taught that this life should be devoted to the service of one's neighbor, in order that as many as possible may be brought to the knowledge of God. And if some hardship is encountered, the hope of deliverance should be retained, and the name of the Lord be called upon. For inasmuch as He has promised to be the God of those who believe in Him, eternal joy and life will follow the miseries of this earthly life.

9. *And God said to Abraham: As for you, you shall keep My covenant, you and your descendants after you throughout their generations.*

We are devoting many words to the discussion of this passage. But it is highly necessary to do so, not only because of the Jews, whom we can readily esteem lightly, but also because of consciences. It is for this reason that Paul, too, discusses circumcision itself so carefully and then the entire Law.

And it is truly wisdom above all wisdom to be able to distinguish properly between Law and Gospel and to be a good dialectician in this matter. By their very nature these are indeed two distinct things; but when there is a conflict in the conscience, it is not so easy to see to what extent the Law binds and to what extent it does not bind.

The Jew maintains that circumcision was divinely commanded,

---

[30] Of these saints only Stephen is Biblical. Lawrence died as a martyr under Valerian, Sebastian under Diocletian, and Fabian under Decius.

[31] Vincent of Lerins, *Commonitorium*, V, *Patrologia, Series Latina*, L, 643 to 645, is a discussion of martyrs and may be what Luther has in mind here; see the similar story about SS. Agatha and Agnes, *Luther's Works*, 24, p. 118.

and we acknowledge that this sign or covenant was entrusted to Abraham as to a standard-bearer, in order that through circumcision all nations might have a definite place and a definite person in whom God would appear visibly and in association with whom they would find the true God, who was to be found nowhere else in the entire world.

This was a great kindness of God. But other matters remain to be considered; for you observe that persons are specifically referred to: "You shall keep My covenant, you and your descendants after you" and also "throughout their generations." These words, which are impressed and reiterated so often, show that circumcision is limited and confined, as it were, within definite bounds and does not concern the nations of which it is certain that they are not the descendants of Abraham.

Likewise, the statement concerning the descendants of Abraham that this covenant is to be kept throughout their generations proves conclusively that this burden is not being imposed as one that is everlasting. We have the evidence before our eyes that the generations have now ceased to exist for more than 1,500 years; for they are without a temple, without a priesthood, and without a kingdom. This surely means that the generations are at an end. What folly it is, therefore, still to insist on circumcision!

Thus circumcision was commanded in such a way that it should have its fixed time during which it had to continue in existence. It should not be insisted on as an unchangeable and eternal law.

Time brings repeal with it; for inasmuch as the generations have ceased, circumcision ceases to be necessary. In fact, when the law itself was given, a relaxation of the law was necessary; for although the command states that males are to be circumcised on the eighth day, Ishmael is circumcised in his fifteenth year; but Abraham is circumcised in his ninety-ninth year.

In the matter of laws it is great wisdom to see where they must be strictly kept and where a dispensation must be granted. Therefore it is correct to say that the letters of princes should be read three times and that the letters of God should be read far more frequently.[32] There is a difference between the thoughts and opinions of princes and those of private individuals. All the concerns of princes are grand, but those of private persons are small and insig-

---

[32] See p. 114, note 19.

nificant. Therefore if princes either write or say something, it must be carefully pondered. But with how much greater propriety we do this in those matters which divine wisdom prescribes and commands!

Thus here God's own words refute the argument of the Jews, who maintain that circumcision is to continue forever and want it imposed upon the Gentiles too; for He expressly says: "You and your descendants shall keep your covenant." Hence this covenant does not concern the Gentiles. In addition, He says: "Throughout their generations," that is, as long as the kingdom and the priesthood continue to exist.

If this were either a general or an eternal command, these restrictions would certainly not be attached, nor would the Lord give such an express command concerning the purchased slaves in the house of Abraham; He would include in general all the males and slaves of the Gentiles.

Therefore it is certain that the Gentiles who are not a part of the house of Abraham do not have to be circumcised. For circumcision is prescribed specifically for the house of Abraham and is temporary; it is to remain in effect during the fixed and definite time the generations of Abraham continue to exist. This a sensible Jew — provided that there is one who is sensible — will never deny.

And this very fact that circumcision was restricted in such a way undoubtedly disturbed and troubled Abraham greatly. His own house is chosen as the church into which God moves, as it were, through the visible form of circumcision in order to dwell in it. But as a result of this arrangement of God, Abraham undoubtedly felt tempted to be concerned about the rest of the nations, those that were not a part of his house.

For Abraham thought as follows: "If my house alone will be the church in which God will dwell, all the rest of the nations will not be condemned on this account, will they? God will not abandon them, will He?" For it is our nature not to be able to be unconcerned about others.

Thus when Peter had heard what the Lord said about him (John 21:18), he immediately asked what would happen to John. And this is a weighty question: whether only those who have circumcision and the Law are saved or others, who do not have the Law, are also saved.

But this precise designation of the person — "you and your descendants" — seems to exclude outright all the Gentiles from divine mercy and salvation, and to confine mercy and salvation to the house of Abraham alone. This debate or trial of Abraham is indicated here in a few words, just as it is later, when he says (Gen. 20:11): "There is no fear of God at all in this place."

For because God says: "As for you, you shall keep My covenant, you and your descendants after you," Abraham thought: "What, then, will happen to the rest of the nations?" Nor was this a light trial — to be intent on his own calling and not to be curious about other people.

The pope and his followers succumbed to this trial. He had the way of salvation set before him: faith in Christ. But he abandoned it and chose for himself other ways — the sacrifice of the Mass, vows, and the like.

Thus every person surely has a calling. While attending to it he serves God. A king serves God when he is at pains to look after and govern his people. So do the mother of a household when she tends her baby, the father of a household when he gains a livelihood by working, and a pupil when he applies himself diligently to his studies.

This sure life of godliness the monks and nuns have abandoned, for they considered these works to be too insignificant and looked for others seemingly more burdensome. At the same time they departed from the faith and became disobedient to God.

Therefore it is great wisdom when a human being does what God commands and earnestly devotes himself to his vocation without taking into consideration what others are doing. But surely there are few who do this. The majority do what the poet censures: "A lazy ox wants a saddle, a lazy nag wants to plow." [33]

There are very few who live satisfied with their lot. The layman longs for the life of a cleric, the pupil wishes to be a teacher, the citizen wants to be a councilor, and each one of us loathes his own calling, although there is no other way of serving God than to walk in simple faith and then to stick diligently to one's calling and to keep a good conscience.

Thus Abraham sees himself and his descendants burdened with the law of circumcision, but he accepts it with humility and with thanksgiving. But the concern about the salvation of the heathen he leaves to God and asks no prying questions about them.

Abraham could likewise have been under trial with regard to the

[33] Horace, *Epistles*, I, 14, 43.

other sex. What about the females? Will God not mark them too by some sign, just as He marked our males? But he dismisses this concern, too, and is intent on doing what he knows has been commanded him. Meanwhile he fosters and keeps in his heart this hope, that, as Peter says (Acts 10:34), "God shows no partiality, but in every nation anyone who fears Him and does what is right is acceptable to Him." In this manner the saintly man overcomes the trial.

But the men who labor in the vineyard and see that the same reward is distributed among those who labor for only one hour are unable to overcome this trial. Therefore they incur the displeasure of the householder, for since they have devoted a fixed amount of time to their work, they want to be given preference over the others (Matt. 20:12).

Accordingly — just as the godly are exposed to trials of various kinds — Abraham could have thought: "Behold, I and my people are chosen to be circumcised, and God promises that He will be God to me. What, then, will become of the Gentiles? God will not condemn them and cast them aside, will He?" In like manner, the Jews say in the Gospel: "We have borne the heat of the sun and the labors of the day; therefore we alone are holy." But the Spirit of God guides him — lest he sin in this trial — and gives him other thoughts. Consequently, he reflects: "What concern is it of mine what God intends to do with the Gentiles? If He denies them circumcision, He does not for this reason deny them salvation. He has imposed upon me what pleases Him. Therefore I shall bear and do it, and I shall not be inquisitive about others."

Peter is clearly in such a trial when he asks concerning John (John 21:21-22): "But what about this man?" But the Lord gives him the answer: "If it is My will that he remain until I come, what is that to you?"

Thus the Lord wanted me to be a preacher, that is, He wanted me to bear the envy and the hatred of the world for the sake of the Word. To others He assigns manual labor. When I look at them, they seem to me to be happy; for labor gives them pleasure, they live without worry and without any rather burdensome annoyance, and they would dislike a life of inactivity. Moreover, by labor bodies are made strong and health is preserved. While another person, like a boy seven years old, does his work as though he were at play, I am severely plagued by perils and trials. Yet that workman is saved just as I am.

What now? Shall I become impatient or refuse to follow my calling? No. I shall rather reflect that God has manifold graces or forms of activity and allots them in accordance with His will. But it is our duty to obey God when He calls (Rom. 12:6; 1 Peter 4:10).

Because the hands are compelled to work, they appear to be in a more troublesome situation than the eyes. But the feet support and carry the entire body, and if you consider the burden they bear, they are the most unfortunate members of the entire body. Better is the situation of the tongue, which tastes what is agreeable to it and is sumptuously fed. The gifts are of various kinds, but the burdens must be borne the way they have been laid upon each person. God gives the ability to bear them, and one must keep in mind Paul's well-known statement (2 Cor. 12:9): "My grace is sufficient for you." Although the feet alone support the bulk of the body, they nevertheless derive their power and healthy state from the body and enjoy all the benefits of the body. The eyes, precious members though they are, cannot assume this seemingly small and easy function; for they were created to be different and to serve a different purpose.

Therefore it is necessary to observe the rule that everyone should remain in his calling and live content with his gifts but should not be inquisitive about other people.

The monks foolishly fit on all feet a shoe made over one last and govern everybody in accordance with one rule. Thus when I entered the monastery, they used to say to me: "As was done to me, so let it be done to you too." But how much more correct Augustine's statement is! "Not alike for all," he says, "because you are not all constituted alike." [34]

It is arithmetic proportion for the eyes and the feet, inasmuch as they are members of one body, to bear the same and equal burdens. But this brings about anarchy and destroys order. Hence geometric proportion must be applied in these affairs of government and of the household.[35]

Arithmetic proportion, however, has its place in the kingdom of God. There it is proper for all things to be equally distributed among unequals, because, as we quoted above from Acts, God is not προσωπολήπτης (Acts 10:34). God finds that all of us are sinners,

[34] This is a verbatim quotation from Augustine's monastic rule, *Regula ad servos Dei*, I, *Patrologia, Series Latina*, XXXII, 1378; it will be remembered that Luther was an Augustinian monk.

[35] On a similar distinction cf. *Luther's Works*, 13, p. 120, note 68.

even though some are more cautious, more reasonable, and — if I may say so — more restrained than others.

Because reason rates these gifts highly, it considers God unfair when He distributes His grace equally. Therefore the men in the Gospel who labor more boast of the burden and the heat of the day and are displeased when the same reward is distributed among those who have labored for only one hour (Matt. 20:12).

But the godly patriarch does not behave in such a manner. He is entirely without arrogance and pride, and he regards God's counsel with wonder and praises it. He does not say: "Why does God impose circumcision on me and not on the Gentiles?" He does not even say: "Why is it not imposed on my brother's son Lot, who lives close by, and on his family?" He is glad that they are his fellow believers, and he bears with the utmost willingness the burden laid particularly on him as a special sign of God's good will; and even though the Gentiles do not have this sign, he knows that they are in grace if they believe.

This will become clear below. The people of Gomorrah and of Sodom did not have circumcision. Yet Abraham hopes that there are fifty righteous men among them. But if circumcision, when it was practiced very extensively, was not imposed through the patriarch Abraham on the Gentiles and on his kinsman Lot — indeed, if Abraham himself was accounted righteous before he was circumcised — why do the wretched Jews dispute about burdening the Gentiles with it?

Therefore the conclusion is this, that everyone should look at his own calling and follow it. It may be that Antony [36] and other hermits were saintly men; but you are committing a grave sin if you abandon your calling and follow their example by secluding yourself in a hiding place; for what the Lord has commanded you to do is something else, namely, to obey your parents, the government, and your teachers.

Thus before the birth of Christ it was the calling of the Jews to be circumcised. It was their duty to practice circumcision, not to impose it on others.

Now there is the universal calling not to be circumcised but to believe in Christ and to be baptized in His name. Let the person who is baptized and believes — whether mother, father, or prince — then do what is required. In this way that person will be saved. Now the law itself — the law of circumcision — follows:

[36] See p. 217, note 46.

10. *This is My covenant, which you shall keep, between Me and you and your descendants after you: Every male among you shall be circumcised.*

11. *You shall be circumcised in the flesh of your foreskins, and it shall be a sign of the covenant between Me and you.*

This entire passage has five parts. In the first place, God commands the males to be circumcised. Hence the females are excluded from this law. The Gentiles, who are not descendants of Abraham or in the house of Abraham, are also excluded.

The verb מוּל is ambiguous. In Ps. 118:10-12 it denotes "to cut down with the sword," the way trees are usually cut down. Therefore in order to make the matter clear, the Lord adds that the flesh of the foreskin is to be cut off in such a manner that the rest of the members of the entire body remain unharmed. The second part of this passage states that God chooses only this part of the body.

In the third place, after the women, the Gentiles, and all the other parts of the body have been excluded, the eighth day after birth is appointed for circumcision.

In the fourth place, the purchased slaves and those born in Abraham's house are added to the descendants of Abraham. God commands that these too be circumcised.

In the fifth place, a promise and a threat are added to the law. The promise is: "I shall be your God." The threat is: "The soul of him who has a foreskin shall be utterly destroyed." Promise and threat are correlative in civil matters and in theology. Christ says (Matt. 19:17): "If you would enter life, keep the Commandments." Here is included the threat that he who does not keep the Commandments will enter hell. In the state it is said: "If you want to have peace, respect the sword." This promise includes the threat that those who show no respect for the sword will perish by the sword.

Hence ancient teachers said that there are four things a preacher should keep in mind in all his sermons; he should give consideration to vices and virtues, to punishments and rewards.[37] And they did well to give this advice, provided that they retained Christ. For the Law concerns itself with these four things: vices contrary to the Law, virtues in accordance with the Law, punishments in accordance with the Law, and rewards in accordance with the Law. But this doctrine does not produce Christians. It is the doctrine of the Law, which does

---

[37] This motto goes back at least to Vegetius in the fourth century A. D.

not bring about perfection. The Gospel of grace must be joined to this doctrine of the Law! Then at last the Christian is made complete.

The Jews adduce a reason for the fact that the Law requires only the males to be circumcised. No other part of the human body, they say, is superfluous; the body can do without this part. But I have said that this statement is a proof of the extreme blindness among the Jews.

The historical and true reason, however, is this, that God wanted to condemn the male, not the female, manifestly because it was the male who sinned. For if Eve had been alone and Adam had not agreed, or had rebuked his wife, he would have escaped the punishment. But because he gives his consent to his wife's sin, he is the cause of evil and is properly brought to punishment through circumcision, while the woman is let go, although she herself also bears her share of the punishments.

Thus through circumcision, which has been imposed on the males, God shows that original sin has spread from our first parent to the entire human race, as Paul also states in Rom. 5:12 ff. Everywhere he calls Adam the author of sin; about Eve he is silent.

With regard to the question concerning the women, who are the other part of the human race, likewise concerning the infants who died before the eighth day, I made a statement above. The Master of the Sentences also deals with the question how the women were saved without circumcision.[38]

The answer is simple. The Law itself excludes the women and prescribes circumcision only for the males. Hence when the women are not circumcised, they do not sin against this Law; neither do the small children who do not get to be eight days old. For the Law compels only those who have become eight days old to be circumcised.

Thus both the women and the infants who die before the eighth day are really excluded from circumcision, but they are not excluded from the salvation and faith of Abraham. Therefore the uncircumcised women live with their circumcised husbands, and both are saved by faith. Thus Ruth, who followed her mother-in-law Naomi, says (Ruth 1:16): "Your people shall be my people, and your God my God." Although she did not belong to the holy people — for she was a Moabitess — she was nevertheless saved because she clung in faith to the God of Israel.

[38] Peter Lombard, *Sententiae*, Book IV, Dist. 1, *Patrologia, Series Latina*, CXCII, 840—841.

The women have their own circumcision, which is burdensome and painful enough. Concerning it Moses says: "In pain you will give birth to your children." It is then that they are circumcised unto death. There is wrath in the word "pain," but there is mercy in the statement "You will give birth."

Although the female sex, too, is condemned because of original sin, it is nevertheless not done away with for this reason; nor does it perish utterly. This burden was not imposed on Eve alone; it was imposed on all who give birth. Therefore believing matrons comforted themselves in their pains with the thought that even though these pains are a definite evidence of sin and of the wrath of God, it is nevertheless a sure sign of divine blessing that through birth the human race and the very church of God are being rebuilt.

If God had merely wanted to be angry and to punish and not also to forgive and have compassion, He would have said: "You shall remain barren" or: "I shall create a new Eve, who is not a sinner but a saint." But the merciful God does not do this. No, He speaks these words of mercy: "You will bear children." Yet in order that sin may not go unpunished, He adds: "You will give birth in pain and distress."

Comforted by these words, Eve gained the sure hope of salvation, inasmuch as both a holy Seed had been promised and the blessing of giving birth and of multiplying had remained, which God did not take away, even though He altered it somewhat when He added the pains which would not have resulted when nature was perfect.

Consequently, saintly women have always regarded childbirth as a great sign of grace. Rachel is rude and exceedingly irksome to her husband when she says (Gen. 30:1): "Give me children, or I shall die!" She makes it clear that she will die of grief because she sees that barrenness is a sign of wrath.

And in Ps. 127:3 [39] there is a glorious eulogy of offspring: "Lo, sons are a heritage from the Lord, the fruit of the womb a reward [that is, a gift of God]." Surely it is a magnificent name that children are the gift of God!

Therefore Hannah laments so pitiably (1 Sam. 1:10), and John's aged mother Elizabeth leaps for joy and exults (Luke 1:25): "The Lord has taken away my reproach."

Thus when the world was still in a better state, barrenness was considered a sign of wrath; but childbirth was considered a sign of grace.

[39] The original has "Ps. 137."

Because of the abuses of lust, however, this remnant of the divine blessing gradually began to be obscured even among the Jews, just as today you could find many greedy men who regard numerous offspring as a punishment.

Saintly mothers, however, have always regarded this gift — when they were prolific — as a great honor, just as, conversely, they have regarded barrenness as a sign of wrath and as a reproach.

Therefore when poor Sarah sees that she is barren, she is almost undone by this trial. No doubt godly Abraham often had to cheer her up with his comforting words. Thus her sex was condemned to be punished with pain, but the blessing was not completely taken away on this account.

The woman's members were condemned to punishment, but they were not condemned to sterility. The same thing happened when the males were circumcised. The males are required to be circumcised, and through circumcision of the foreskin it is shown that their birth is cursed and full of sins. Yet there the comfort is added: "I am the Lord your God."

Thus God burdens and slays the church according to the flesh. Yet through faith He justifies it and revives it according to the spirit. Thus a promise has been added to the punishment, and to the terrors there has been added a comfort by means of which the godly should encourage themselves in perils and misfortunes.

The heathen forgot both the punishment and the blessing and gave themselves up to monstrous lusts. But the saintly fathers saw the disasters that were inundating the human race because of sin. Therefore they humbled themselves and checked the desires of the flesh. Then they comforted themselves with the restraint God had shown by leaving behind a blessing. So much about the fact that circumcision was imposed only on the males.

But God's command that the flesh of the foreskin be circumcised and the fact that He applies the law of circumcision to this so-called lewd member, which has to do with the procreation of the entire human race, and does not apply it to a part of the ear or of the lip, to the hair, or to the beard, which are respectable members and do not shun being seen by people — about this the Master of the Sentences argues that God wanted to point out that this member is misused more than the rest and that its disobedience is greater.[40] Let others judge how much validity this statement has.

[40] See the passage referred to on p. 133, note 38.

The source of all evil is the fact that hearts are full of ungodliness and unbelief. Consequently, both this member of the body and all the other members are misused. And if someone should make a careful comparison, does the tongue not sin more gravely, and do the eyes and the ears not arouse carnal desires?

Therefore the following reason states the case more truthfully: this member is the member for the propagation of all flesh and was created solely for the purpose of procreation. God selects this member because he wants to point to original sin, not to actual sin — to our innate sin, which grows while we grow.

This is the reason why the male is condemned in that member because of which he is called a male. Yet this is not actually a condemnation; it is rather a threat and a display of wrath. For although God seems to condemn the entire member, yet He preserves its use.

This is the historical reason, and it is in harmony with other works of God. For just as He condemns childbirth and preserves it, just as He kills and makes alive, and just as He threatens and promises, so He condemns and preserves the male organ at the same time through circumcision; for He is wonderful in His counsels and deeds.

Moreover, here the mystery of the incarnation of the Son of God is pointed out; for because of the Virgin Mary alone, from whom Christ was to be born, God spares the entire female sex, and only the males are required to be circumcised. There was to be a woman who would give birth without a man. Because of her God spares the entire sex, and with this seemingly foolish law He burdens only the males.

Therefore circumcision was a sign in which God foreshadowed the sum total of theology, that is, sin and grace in both sexes; for circumcision performed on so shameful a member not only reminds us of sin — namely, that by nature we are children of wrath (Eph. 2:3) and have sin born with us — but it is also a sign of grace because not the entire member but a small part of it is cut off, and procreation, which is necessary for the church and for the state, is preserved.

In the other sex, on which circumcision is not imposed, there is a sign of grace. For it is pointed out that He who is to do away with circumcision and to deliver from sin and death will be born of a woman. These mysteries the Jews do not understand; they must be diligently sought out and noted by us.

Concerning the third part there is the question why God wanted the males circumcised on the eighth day, and the Master of the Sentences and the scholastic teachers have treated this matter with what seems to them to be great zeal.[41]

I myself, however, think that this question should be dealt with briefly; for what concern is it of mine why God wanted it so, when the fact that He did want it so is sufficient? One should not inquire into the reason for God's will, just as one should not inquire into the reason for His wisdom, His omnipotence, and His goodness. For these things are inscrutable, and the condition we are in demands, not that we ask why but that we obey Him who commands.

This is the simple and true explanation we may use against seditious spirits and those who flaunt their own wisdom. Nevertheless, without danger to our faith we may imagine and search for a similar situation and for a reason that is useful either for teaching or for consoling.

Above all, however, maintain with certainty that the males who died before the eighth day were not condemned by reason of this law; for they in no wise sinned against this law. Neither did the women, who although they were not circumcised, nevertheless were part of the people of God.

The Master of the Sentences and other teachers argue that such infants perish; but we have here a clear text on which we can safely rely, a text which states that God condemns neither the uncircumcised infants nor those who have been circumcised after the eighth day. But if you were to debate about the original sin of infants, that is a different question. Here we are asking about circumcision, concerning which the Lord makes the statement that the soul of the infant the flesh of whose foreskin is not circumcised on the eighth day must be rooted out of the people of God.

This threat must not be extended or given a wider scope than God gave to it. But from this law, which deals with infants who were uncircumcised after the eighth day, it follows with sound logic that those who do not get to be eight days old will not be condemned.

A well-known rule states that kindnesses must be increased but that stern measures must be restricted. Here we are doing this to the glory of God. For it is His nature to forgive and to have com-

---

[41] Peter Lombard, *Sententiae*, Book IV, Dist. 1, *Patrologia, Series Latina*, CXCII, 841.

passion. Therefore we do not maintain that He is too severe toward the infants of His own people whom death has prevented from being able to obtain this covenant; for He "desires all men to be saved" (1 Tim. 2:4).

This statement must be adduced against those teachers, and the promises must be given the widest scope. Wrath and harshness, however, must be curtailed. With much greater justification this maxim, which is drawn from the experience of ordinary life, will have validity here! Christ says (Matt. 7:11; Luke 11:13): "For if you who are evil can give good gifts to your children, how much more will your heavenly Father give the Holy Spirit to them that ask Him?"

Therefore let us not debate about the little children who were uncircumcised before the eighth day; let us leave them to the goodness of God. But let us debate about things that are not uncertain and unknown, about things that have been enjoined upon us by the divine Word. Let us not be concerned about what God does with others. As for ourselves, let us listen to Christ, as the Father's voice from heaven commands. But the secrets of the Divine Majesty which God has not revealed to us in His Word — let us pass them by and leave them untouched. Then we shall not be cast down headlong.

Accordingly, Sirach is right when he warns (Ecclus. 3:22): "Seek not the things that are too high for you," for the exploration of the Divine Majesty has not been committed to us. Nor is it expedient for us. For he who searches out majesty is overwhelmed by it (cf. Prov. 25:27).

As I have often said, God in His essence is incomprehensible and dwells in a light which we cannot approach even with our thoughts (cf. 1 Tim. 6:16), and to want to inquire into His judgments is truly to strive for things that are impossible.

Therefore we must stay with the Word; there we must hear what He promises us and what He threatens. This is done with profit, as the first and the 119th psalm teach. The other things, which have not been revealed in the Word, must simply be dismissed; for one cannot meddle with them without danger.

I stress these facts gladly and often; for it is a doctrine that is very necessary because of original sin, Satan, and the fanatical spirits. If Adam had followed this rule, he would not have fallen into sin. But because he turns from the command which the Lord had given him and heeds Satan, who discusses the reasons why God has forbidden him to touch this tree, he is hurled headlong into sin and death. He should not have inquired into the reasons for the divine command; for this is to judge the will of God and to search out His ways, which are unsearchable, and to try to comprehend His judgments, which are incomprehensible.

I have no doubt that the sin of Lucifer was something like this, that he wanted to find out and know more about the unknown God than became his station, that is, about the God who has not been revealed and disclosed through the Word. What He is, what He does, and what His will is does not concern me. But this does concern me, that I know what He has commanded, what He has promised, and what He has threatened. When you reflect on these things carefully, you find God, yes, He Himself takes you on His lap. If you fall out of it, that is, if you presume to know anything beyond what has been revealed in the Word, you plunge into the depths of hell.

Therefore the well-known hermit was right when he gave the advice: If you see a young monk ascending to heaven and so to speak, putting one foot in heaven, pull him back at once; for if he puts both feet there, he will see that he is not in heaven but in hell.[42]

This saying gives no other advice than that we should restrain our curiosity and remain within the definite bounds that are placed before us by God. He wanted us to walk on the earth, not on the clouds. He wanted us to learn the revealed Word painstakingly, not to give thought to those things that are too high for us. He wanted us to follow His Word and command, not to inquire with inordinate diligence into the reasons for His commands. When Adam and Eve do this, they perish; for they put themselves in the place of God the Creator and forget that they are creatures.

It is just as Satan says: "Then you will be like gods." You will no longer be creatures who will be concerned about carrying out the commands of God; you yourselves will be gods, you will judge God, and you will do other things — things that are proper for God alone.

Oh, the wretched divinity with which Satan surrounded us through sin when he had this one design, that we should disregard the commands and promises of God. Therefore it is original sin to become a god. Against this disease we must fight throughout our entire life, and we must say with Paul (1 Cor. 2:2): "I know nothing except Jesus Christ and Him crucified."

Perhaps some of you will read those discussions of Peter Lom-

---

[42] On the source of the story mentioned in this paragraph see p. 275, note 49.

bard and his followers. Therefore learn not to yield to them. Abide with your churches by the promises and commands of God, lest, in accordance with the poisonous promise of Satan, you turn out to be similar to gods. Let God recognize good and evil; but as for you, remain His humble creatures.

As to the question which has been raised about infants who died before the eighth day I know this: that they are not condemned by this law concerning circumcision. But my answer to the question what God does with them is that I know that I do not know. If they became eight days old and were not circumcised, they would not belong to the people of God. But when they die before the eighth day, this is a matter of God's judgment, of which I have no knowledge; it is beyond me, except that I know that God is merciful. This good thing God wanted me to know, for He informs me to this effect in His Word. But He did not want me to know the other things.

In this way we stay on the road which God Himself has pointed out to us through His command and promises. On it one cannot go astray. On the other hand, those who disregard this road as they bend their course toward God are hurled down and overwhelmed; for, as Sirach says, it is not good to eat much honey (cf. Prov. 25:27).

Therefore let the first answer to this question why God wanted the infants to be circumcised on the eighth day be: Because God wanted it this way. In the second place, one can give reasons that are probable and are not fraught with danger, namely, that God had consideration for the weakness of the infant, lest it die, since it was already weakened by the hardships of birth.

Thereby praise is given to the benevolence and great mercy of God, which is so concerned about the little infants that it does not burden them with circumcision before they have recovered to some extent and are able to endure it.

Thus you learn here, too, what the psalm (30:5) says: "In His favor is life." Likewise (Ezek. 18:23): "Have I any pleasure in the death of the wicked?"

Even though this is the historical reason, it nevertheless serves to extol the mercy of God and to nourish and increase faith in the godly, just as, conversely, the fact that in the Flood and in the destruction of the Sodomites infants also perished serves to frighten the ungodly and the obdurate.

The mystic reason which the Master of the Sentences and other teachers adduce is passable. They maintain that circumcision was deferred to the eighth day because in the resurrection, which is signified by the eighth day, we shall be perfectly circumcised, in order that we may be free from every sin of the world.

We not only do not reject this thought, but we confirm it as godly and learned. In an allegorical sense the eighth day signifies the future life; for Christ rested in the sepulcher on the Sabbath, that is, during the entire seventh day, but rose again on the day which follows the Sabbath, which is the eighth day and the beginning of a new week, and after it no other day is counted. For through His death Christ brought to a close the weeks of time and on the eighth day entered into a different kind of life, in which days are no longer counted but there is one eternal day without the alternations of night.

This has been thought out wisely, learnedly, and piously, namely, that the eighth day is the eternal day. For the rising Christ is no longer subject to days, months, weeks, or any number of days; He is in a new and eternal life. The beginning of this life is perceived and reckoned, but there is no end. In that life the true circumcision will be carried out. At that time not only the foreskin of the heart will be circumcised — which happens in this life through faith — but the entire flesh and all its essence will be cleansed of all depravity, ignorance, lust, sin, and filth. Consequently, the flesh is then immortal.

This allegory is a prophecy that when Christ rises again there will be a spiritual, true, and perfect circumcision outside time in eternal life. In Holy Scripture the number seven denotes a cycle [43] of time; for when the seventh day is reached, the series is again repeated.

For this reason chroniclers have generally divided the world into seven ages or seven days, during which the week of this finite life is brought to a close.[44] The first is reckoned from Adam to Noah; the second, from Noah to Abraham; the third, from Abraham to Moses; the fourth, from Moses to David; the fifth, from David to Christ; and the sixth, from Christ to the end of the world. But the

---

[43] The original has *revelationem*. Because it makes much more sense in this context, we have conjectured the reading *revolutionem* and have translated accordingly.

[44] It was customary for medieval chroniclers to work with four monarchies and seven ages of the earth; these latter were an allegory on the seven days of creation.

seventh they called the age of the sleeping, after the example of Christ, I suppose, who rested in the tomb during the Sabbath.

These divisions are arbitrary. Therefore they should not be accepted as articles of faith. The eighth age comprises the resurrection into eternal life.

12. *He that is eight days old among you shall be circumcised; every male throughout your generations, whether born in your house, or bought with your money from any foreigner who is not of your offspring,*

13. *both he that is born in your house and he that is bought with your money, shall be circumcised. So shall My covenant be in your flesh an everlasting covenant.*

Generally speaking, these words belong to the fourth part of the command concerning circumcision; for we have divided this entire section into five parts. Here God specifies those who are to be circumcised and distinguishes three separate kinds of males:

The male from the stock, that is, born from the flesh of Abraham with the very stock of Abraham; the male born in the house from his own servants; and the male who was not born in the house but was brought into the house by purchase.

This clear designation of the persons is proof that circumcision does not pertain to all males. Accordingly what folly it is for the Jews to maintain that the Gentiles, too, must be circumcised!

In the second place, this passage shows that there are various ranks in this life. If you should consider their lot, the position of the head of the household is better than that of a slave, and that of an emancipated slave or one who has been granted freedom is better than that of one who is still in the position of a slave. But because God commands that all be circumcised without distinction and affirms through circumcision that He will be their God, do not those who are unlike in the world because of their positions share in the same glory and grace before God?

Therefore let us not exalt ourselves above others because we are above them by reason of our position; but let us acknowledge that although in this life grace has many forms and there are various kinds of vocations, the same God is the God of all, whether they are slaves or free, whether they are rich or poor, provided that they hold fast to the Word and persevere in the faith.

This is a profitable doctrine. It confirms the fact that there are various stations in life, and it proclaims the mercy of God, who takes pity on all in the same manner. If a person believes according to the example of faithful Abraham, it makes no difference whether he is descended from Abraham or from a slave of Abraham.

14. *Any uncircumcised male who is not circumcised in the flesh of his foreskin shall be cut off from his people; he has broken My covenant.*

This threat is added in order that this sign of grace, which seemingly is not only trivial and paltry but even foolish, may not be held in contempt. For no matter how worthless the rite seemed to be, it was nevertheless established for the salvation of many, not only of those who were circumcised but also of those of the Gentiles who believed.

Furthermore, here it is customary to ask whether this passage is to be understood concerning civil or spiritual death. Some declare [45] that Moses is speaking of a civil cutting-off, namely, that the little boy who was not circumcised had to be excluded from the state, that he had to be kept away from the altars and the sacrifices and was not to have the benefit of ordinary laws and privileges of this people. But this interpretation is wrong; it proves that such teachers do not understand what God intended to accomplish through circumcision.

Therefore the words must be understood of a cutting-off from the church. This, however, does not pertain to the Gentiles at all — something we have now stated rather frequently — for even though the Gentiles are excluded from circumcision, they are nevertheless not excluded from the blessing if they believe with faithful Abraham.

But for the Jews bodily circumcision was also necessary over and above faith; for if they slighted circumcision, they ceased to be the people of God and were not only excluded from the government of this people but from the blessing which the Seed that was promised those who were circumcised would bring. Heaven was closed to them, their sins were retained to them, and their reward was hell and its fire. This is truly being excluded from the people of God.

This statement, as we have also pointed out above, does not involve infants who died before the eighth day. Even though they

---

[45] Although the original has *indicant* here, the reading *iudicant* seems very plausible.

have original sin, a merciful God will nevertheless find a way to deliver them, just as He does with other sinners. But so far as this threat is concerned, they are delivered from it, because they have committed no sin against the law of circumcision. There remains in them the guilt of birth or of original sin and no guilt so far as circumcision is concerned.

One must have the same opinion about the little boys who were not circumcised either because of the carelessness or the wickedness of their parents, just as today there are some who are not baptized, as, for instance, Pope Clement VII, about whom there was a persistent rumor that he had not been baptized.[46] Such little children should be committed to the dispensation of the goodness of God. For what guilt against this law have the little children who either die or are neglected by ungodly parents? Therefore they should be left to the goodness of God and should not be condemned as the scholastics have condemned them. Let this be enough concerning the fifth part of this passage. Now let us see what is added about Sarah.

15. *And God said to Abraham: As for Sarai your wife, you shall not call her name Sarai, but Sarah shall be her name.*

16. *I will bless her, and moreover I will give you a son by her; I will bless her, and she shall be a mother of nations; kings of peoples shall come from her.*

We have finished with the command concerning circumcision, which God so surrounded with His own bounds that He excluded not only the Gentiles but also the entire female sex and likewise the males who died before the eighth day. Hence the Jews, who want circumcision to be universal, clamor in vain. The part of the body which is to be circumcised was also designated. Hence the priests of Baal cut and slashed their bodies in vain (1 Kings 18:28).

When Christ came, this law was abolished; for circumcision was not given as an everlasting law but for the preservation of the seed of Abraham until Christ should be born from it. At His birth not only circumcision but the entire law, with its ceremonies and forms of worship, came to an end.

What now follows unfolds the promise concerning Christ, for it gradually began to become clearer and more distinct. First Abraham

---

[46] Luther recites this story and other gossip about Pope Clement VII (1478—1534) in his *Table Talk*, W, *Tischreden*, III, No. 3577B.

had doubts concerning an heir, and he came to suspect that if he should die without an heir, his Damascene servant would get possession of the blessing. But later on he is assured by a word of God that an heir shall be born to him from his own body. When he has this explanation and assurance about the promise, there follows another uncertainty — about Sarah, who was advancing in years and was barren. Therefore he acquiesces in her plan and lies with the maid Hagar. From her he begets Ishmael, whom he fully expects to become the heir of the blessing. But now at last the saintly couple is delivered even from this error, for Abraham is promised an offspring from the aged and barren Sarah herself.

In the course of time the promise is transmitted to Jacob, not to Esau; and when Jacob had twelve heirs, the promise falls to Judah alone. Eventually David is designated as the heir of the promise. From his house came the Blessed Virgin Mary, the mother of Christ, who was the end of the Law and of circumcision.

Therefore the Jews achieve nothing when they contend both for the eternal duration of circumcision, as though it had to continue in existence forever, and for its unlimited practice, if I may say so, as though it had to be extended to all nations.

There was need of circumcision for a fixed time as a visible sign to which the children of God might look and to which they might come when they were about to hear and worship God, just as there had previously been the sacrifices of the fathers instead of a sign at which the Gentiles might gather.

These marks, by which God has manifested Himself to the world, must be regarded more highly than any miracles. For there even the Gentiles heard God speaking through His instruments, and they were saved if they believed the Word. Therefore it is great praise of God's mercy that He did not let the human race walk and go astray in its own thoughts but set up for those who feared Him public signs at which they might gather.

Abraham and all his descendants were circumcised in order that the heathen might be attracted and also obtain salvation themselves. Therefore we justly give thanks to so merciful a God, who manifested Himself in this way at all times and gathered a church for Himself.

But these facts also have validity against the awful darkness of human traditions. For reason seeks God and roams through countless errors of its own endeavors in an effort to find Him. This led to the origin of so many orders of monks, each of which maintained that it was nearest to God. This led to many kinds of worship and works. But all these are undertaken in vain, for God does not want us to go astray in our thoughts; He shows Himself not only in the invisible thought of the heart but also in signs that are visible and tangible.

Thus in the New Testament there are Baptism, the Keys, and the Eucharist. He who makes use of these in faith does not believe in vain and does not stray from God but surely hears and finds God.

Therefore these signs must be learned, followed, and held fast with the utmost zeal. "In every place I cause My name to be remembered I will come to you," says the Lord (Ex. 20:24). Therefore other places, other forms of worship, new things, and other endeavors are sought in vain. God is not found there; but where He causes His name to be remembered, that is, where the Word of God resounds, there He comes, not with curses but with blessings.

This must be diligently impressed over against the awful raging of Satan, who, arrayed in divine and angelic splendor, does not cease to lead the world astray in order to obscure or entirely to remove from the eyes those most pleasing signs of grace through which God has manifested Himself to the human race.

Therefore we should give hearty thanks to God for our ability to hear His Word, to see His signs, and also to make use of them. But alas, they are becoming cheap because of their constant presence, and they are being loathed like daily food. A black or white hood and similar articles devised by men without the Word are prized more highly than these infallible signs of eternal grace. Therefore the world deserves to be continually immersed in errors and perils because of this extreme ingratitude. But let us concern ourselves with Sarah.

Just as the Lord changes Abraham's name because of the promise concerning the blessing, so He also changes Sarah's name. It is derived from the verb שָׂרָה, which means "to rule," "to wrestle," "to overcome," "to triumph." From it comes the name Israel, because Jacob wrestled with God (Gen. 31). And Sarah denotes a female wrestler, a pugilist, a mistress, a princess. The vowel "i" added at the end is a possessive pronoun. Thus Sarai in Latin is *domina mea*, and the Italians say *madonna, misersi*, "my lady." Thus the root of this word means "to contend"; and by metonymy it is used for "to rule," "to overcome," "to govern." Hence Sarah, like the word *Frau* among the Germans, is a noun which denotes not only a sex but also the mistress of a household.

But just as the Lord calls Abraham by the new name of father, in order that he alone may possess the name "father" because of the blessing, so Sarah is called the mistress and manager of the home, in order that she alone may be the mother of countless families in the church.

This appellation serves to praise the unity of the church, for God does not want a large number of churches. It is for this reason that He unites all nations in such a manner that one is their father, namely, Abraham, and one is their mother, namely, Sarah, and that thus their descendants, even though they are spread over a very wide area, become indivisible and remain in perfect unity, with the result that just as there is one God, so one church is to be gathered from many kings and peoples, whose father is Abraham and whose mother is Sarah.

Thus at that time there was no church outside the house of Abraham. Yet in the house of Abraham there was not only Isaac but also Ishmael; yes, there were even slaves purchased from the Gentiles, and also girls, virgins, and wives. They all belonged to that church and were the people of the same God.

Christ says in the New Testament (Matt. 23:8): "You are not to be called rabbi, for One is your Master in heaven." And James states (3:1): "Let not many of you become teachers." God does not want many to be teachers; He does not want the church to be in many houses or families. Not that the persons cannot be numerous; for Christ had twelve apostles, and there was a large number of prophets among the holy people. But God does not want everyone to take it upon himself to form a church. Hence these statements were made against heretics, as though Christ intended to say: "Do not tear My church apart and form sects," as Paul states (1 Cor. 1:10). "It is My desire that just as there is one God, one Christ, and one Baptism, so there should also be only one father Abraham and one mother Sarah."

Furthermore, the promise made to Sarah here is altogether inestimable. To us indeed who read these accounts of the Old Testament with indifference it does not appear at first glance what is most excellent. But St. Paul examined them carefully. He therefore enlarges on this passage in a rhetorical manner (Rom. 4:19 ff.).

"Abraham did not become weak in faith, and he considered neither his own body, which was already dead, since he was almost a hundred years old, nor Sarah's dead womb; but he was mindful of God's promise and did not doubt because of unbelief but was strengthened in faith. He gave glory to God and was certain that He who made the promise is able also to fulfill it. Therefore this was accounted to him for righteousness. But the statements that this was accounted to him were written, not only for his own sake but also for our sakes. For us, too, it will be accounted if we believe in Him who raised our Lord Jesus Christ from the dead."

Paul considers the fact that so far the promise consists of words only but that the reality is not yet at hand. Therefore the godly couple was not lightly disturbed, for what could be expected from a dead womb and one that also because of age was useless for birth? Sarah was like a corpse from which no fruit can be expected.

Accordingly, what this story sets forth is analogous to the resurrection of the dead, inasmuch as from a dead womb there is born not only an offspring but a male who is appointed to be the father of many nations and of many kings and peoples.

Therefore it is a most extraordinary account. In it we must direct our attention chiefly to the Word of God. Here God speaks with Abraham at such length and so intimately that the reader is compelled to forget the Divine Majesty and to think of a guest or an intimate friend.

Moreover, it must be noted especially that these promises include Christ Himself, yes, eternal life, even though they appear to be speaking, not of Christ but of Isaac. For this reason Paul adds (Rom. 4:23-24) that this was written, not for Abraham's sake but for the sake of us, who would believe after the example of Abraham; for the promise is temporal, like a nut which covers the kernel, namely, Christ and eternal life. When Christ comes, the shell or hull in which the kernel is enclosed is broken; that is, the temporal blessing comes to an end, and the spiritual blessing takes its place.

Abraham did not see these promises fulfilled. He saw his son Isaac and his little grandsons Esau and Jacob, the sons of Isaac. But Sarah was called out of this life before these men were born. You will say: "What is this in comparison with such grand promises? They did not benefit Abraham and Sarah; they benefited the descendants of Abraham and Sarah."

Such is commonly our thought, and this is an offense especially to the Jews, who see only the shell but do not see the kernel — Christ and eternal life — which is enclosed in this shell or hull, as it were, of the material blessing concerning the land of Canaan and the descendants of Abraham.

But Sacred Scripture points out very clearly that eternal and spiritual blessings are included in the material blessings. For we were not created like oxen and asses; we were created for eternity. Therefore when God speaks with us to give a promise, He is not speaking with us for the sake of temporal things only; nor does He concern Himself with the belly only. No, He wants to preserve our soul from destruction and to grant us eternal life.

Thus the external promises are like a shell; but the essential part of the nut and its real nature is Christ and eternal life, because when God gives a promise, He is not speaking with asses and oxen — as Paul says (1 Cor. 9:9): "Is it for oxen that God is concerned?" — but with an intelligent creature created in the image of God that it may live with God in eternal life.

Moreover, the material promises are like nuts and apples with which we attract children to ourselves. Thus we are led and attracted to the love of eternal things, and the hope of immortality is nourished, so to speak, by the material promises.

Thus God gives me bread and water, not in order that I may eat and drink like a horse or a mule, which have no understanding (Ps. 32:9), but that from this physical gift I may gain a knowledge of the goodness of God and may encourage and comfort myself with it in other needs too. If He gave you only straw, He still wants you to know that He is the eternal God and that His goodness is boundless. If you believe this, you have eternal life.

Even though Abraham did not see those promises during his lifetime, he nevertheless believed God. Therefore he had eternal life and could not die but still lives. For he believed God when He promised kings, peoples, and a son as the heir of the blessing. Therefore he closed his eyes and withdrew into the darkness of faith. There he found eternal light.

The promises must be amplified in such a way that even though they speak only of physical things, we nevertheless — because of the Person who is speaking — apply them to eternal life. For He is eternal, and even by means of physical things He spurs us on to believe Him. Moreover, he who believes God has eternal life; for he is not an ox or a mule. He understands and sees that God is good, and this knowledge is eternal life.

But at this point, too, we shall argue with the Jews for a while. They cannot [47] deny that this temporal blessing is now at an end. For the shell has been opened and broken, and the chaff or hull has been removed from the kernels and the grain, just as John the Baptist prophesies in his sermon that it would happen (Matt. 3:12). The nut had to be broken when the kernel was revealed, and 1,500 years have now elapsed. Meanwhile they have had no king and no definite place. Moreover, with the destruction of the temple their worship ceased completely.

Therefore I ask what vestiges or what signs they retain of the promise made to Sarah and Abraham. The fact that the Jewish nation was completely destroyed and was scattered throughout the entire earth — this does nothing for them, for Abraham is promised a kingdom.

But we do not understand kingdom in a material sense; we understand it in a formal sense, namely, a state established by laws in a definite place, together with everything that pertains to a people or to the government and administration of the people. A band of brigands certainly cannot be called a kingdom, even though they choose a head for themselves and occupy a definite place. In a kingdom, as in the human body, there are various functions and various duties. Nevertheless, all these functions and duties have been provided to the end that the body may remain healthy and have its proper strength. But a body that is torn in pieces — where no hands, no eyes, and no feet perform their duty — is more properly called a cadaver than a body. Thus the descendants of the Jews are like a cadaver and not like a kingdom, as even they themselves bear witness. For what similarity is there to that people which was in existence before and after the captivity up to the coming of Christ?

What, then, shall we say? God does not lie. His promises are true and firm. They do not promise that some dregs of a people will come from Abraham; they promise kings and peoples. Where, then, has the kingdom remained during these 1,500 years? Where have their laws remained, the institutions of the fathers, and their worship? What else are the Jews today than a body miserably torn to pieces and scattered throughout the entire world? They have no definite place and no offices that are necessary for the establishment of a state; they are servants, and they seek their livelihood solely

---

[47] Although the text of the original has *possum* here, we have followed the reading *possunt*, which is recommended also by the Weimar editors.

through sins. Hence God is either lying in His promise, or the Jews are no longer the people of God but have been rejected by God and put out of the church.

Therefore this promise helps to strengthen our faith. Consequently we are sure that since the Jews are without a kingdom and the hull of the nut has been broken, Christ must necessarily have been revealed and that the multitude of the Gentiles has taken the place of the Jews.

For the promise made to Sarah cannot lie. "Kings and nations shall come from you," it states. But mention to me one king or prince the Jews have now had during 1,500 years.

History itself will indeed compel one to admit that the restoration of the people and of the kingdom was repeatedly attempted, but most unsuccessfully. Moreover, they were especially to keep possession of the land of Canaan. But because they were deprived of it and have been scattered throughout the entire world in most wretched bondage, history declares that they are no longer the people of God or the seed of Abraham to which God promised and also gave kingdoms up to the time of Christ.

It is altogether absurd for the Jews to continue to hope so tenaciously for a kingdom and for a restoration of the land of Canaan, nor is there anything to encourage them. In the first place, they have no promise. Therefore they hope in vain. In the second place, how is it possible for them to hope for a return to the land of Canaan from which they have now been exiles for a longer time than they dwelt in it? Moreover, what kind of promise is this which is unfulfilled for a longer time than it is fulfilled?

But their retention of circumcision and their use of the Law even though they are outside the land of Canaan — it is not right for them to do this. For it is only in the land of Canaan that they are obliged to use the Law. Circumcision, like the whole Law, must continue as long as the people continues, as long as their descendants continue, as long as the possession of the land of Canaan continues.

Hence this promise itself serves to strengthen our own faith and to weaken the obstinacy of the Jews. For we maintain that long ago, while their state was still in existence, the promise both of the shell and of the kernel was fulfilled, that is, the physical promise. The spiritual promise, which, as we have said, is included in the physical promise, was also fulfilled.

From the womb of Sarah there came not only kings — David, Solomon, etc. — but also peoples, the Edomites and others, who are reckoned among the descendants of Esau. This is the physical promise. When Christ was born of the Virgin Mary, the spiritual promise was also fulfilled.

That was the real time of blessing. Then there were valiant kings: the apostles and their successors. Next came Gentiles who, because of faith in the Blessed Seed, are also descendants of Abraham, not according to the flesh or by nature but "engrafted," as Paul calls them in Rom. 11:17.

Of course, the promise concerns the spiritual seed, that is, the believers, more than it does the physical descendants. And although Isaac himself was born from the flesh of Abraham, he was nevertheless a son of the promise; for he was not born according to the flesh, inasmuch as the bodies of Sarah and Abraham were dead, as it were, so far as procreation was concerned.

Just as we correctly call Isaac a son of faith and not of the flesh — for if you consider the flesh, Abraham and Sarah are like two corpses which procreate in spite of this, not by virtue of the corpse but by virtue of faith — so all who believe according to the example of Abraham are descendants of Abraham and partakers of the blessing, whether they are Gentiles or Jews, whether they are circumcised or uncircumcised. This is the apostolic argument, which abounded in ill will and hatred when the Jewish nation was still in existence; for it put the Gentiles on the same level with the Jews. Paul calls them fellow citizens of the prophets and the apostles (cf. Eph. 2:19-20).

But today, after the Jews have ceased to be a people and are miserably scattered throughout the world, this discussion does not seem to be of such great importance. Therefore we know that the promise has been fulfilled. For wherever Christ, the Blessed Seed, rules, there the church is, and there are kings and peoples born of the faith of corpselike Abraham who have the promise and believe. But because the physical descendants of Abraham refused to accept the promised Christ, they were rejected according to the prophecies of Moses and other prophets, like Hos. 2:23: "I will say to Not My People, 'You are My people,'" Moses (cf. Deut. 32:21): "I shall vex you among a foreign nation," and Christ (Matt. 21:43): "The kingdom will be taken from you and given to a nation producing the fruits of it."

The same thing happened to the papists in our time. They rejected knowledge, they did not want to teach, and they did not want to be bishops; but they did want to rule and be princes of the world. Therefore when they had been rejected, God raised us from the dung and the dirt and set us with the princes of His people, in order that through our ministry Germany might be linked to the kingdom of God and come to the true knowledge of God. For God does not care for the pomp and show of the world. If those who are anointed and called are unwilling to teach, let those teach who are not anointed. Let them keep the name, but let us keep the matter. Naturally they bear this with indignation and cry out that the harmony which should be in the church is being disturbed.

The Jews did the same thing; but when they had been scattered, the church of the Gentiles continued to exist. Thus when the pope, the cardinals, the bishops, the abbots, the monks, and the doctors have been rejected, the church remains among the poor, despised, and wretched little group of the believers, in accordance with the statement of the prophet (Hos. 4:6): "You have rejected knowledge; I will reject you too." For the Lord is not complaining about wealth and prestige; He is complaining about knowledge, as is stated in another passage (Hos. 6:6): "I desire the knowledge of God rather than burnt offerings." He wants the people to be taught, in order that they may learn to know God and so come to eternal life. Hence if we, too, were to keep silence to please the pope and his followers, God would stir up pieces of wood and stones rather than that there should be no true knowledge of God and, as a result, no church in the world.

17. *Then Abraham fell on his face and laughed, and said to himself: Shall a child be born to a man who is a hundred years old? Shall Sarah, who is ninety years old, bear a child?*

This passage is full of emotion and is an outstanding example of faith. For this reason I shall be unable to treat it as it deserves. To me indeed it seems that Christ had this very passage in mind when He said (John 8:56): "Abraham saw My day and was glad."

Even though Abraham had no doubts about the promise, yet so far he was mistaken with respect to the person. For he thought that Sarah would not bear a child and that the promise would be diverted to Ishmael. But here a perfect circle is closed, so to speak, and Abraham sees that a true heir will be born to him from Sarah.

Consequently, he is full of joy. Exulting and triumphing in the most beautiful and perfect faith, he falls to the ground and laughs. Full of wonderment, he says: "Shall a son be born to me, a man one hundred years old, and from Sarah at that?"

These are words of one who in no wise doubts but is astonished and transported with joy, just as the laughter is also evidence of a heart overflowing with joy. Accordingly, these matters transcend all eloquence and have to do with experiences that are spiritual. Just as no one can put the sorrow of afflicted hearts in words, so this exultation and joy of the spirit is altogether inexpressible.

Now Abraham puts Ishmael out of sight and out of his mind. Up to this time he had loved him most tenderly as the hope of the blessing. Now he forgets about his own dead body, even about corpselike Sarah, and sees with certainty that an heir is to be born to him from Sarah. Therefore he laughs and rejoices, and later on, as a result of this very laughter and this spiritual and inexpressible joy, a name is given to the son, and he is called Isaac for an everlasting remembrance and an eternal monument of a faith so glorious, steadfast, and sure that when these words had hardly been uttered by the Lord, the saintly man is filled with such great joy.

Abraham falls to the ground and laughs. This, as Christ explains in John 8, is the gesture of a heart that exults and overflows with joy; for now at last he is sure that he will be the father and Sarah will be the mother of Jesus Christ, the Son of God, through whom salvation and blessing will come to the entire world.

Accordingly, Abraham did not fall down from fright, nor did he laugh because he had doubts about the promise; he laughed because he was filled with great gladness and joy.

Below (Gen. 45:27), when it is announced to Jacob that Joseph is alive in Egypt, the text states that Jacob was like one who had been roused out of a deep sleep and that he still did not believe it. Therefore he gave no signs of joy. But after he had seen the wagons and the gifts which Joseph had sent, then at last his spirit revived. Unusual and sudden emotions, whether of joy or of sorrow, cause people to become thunderstruck and devoid of sensation, and there are accounts of some who died from sudden joy. Thus Abraham, too, full of joy, falls to the ground and laughs as he gives thanks to God for His so unexpected kindness. For what else could he do than marvel at this and rejoice over it?

Furthermore, when we read such accounts, we should justly be ashamed that a like fervor of the spirit is not felt in our hearts, although, as I have also stated above, we are either on a par with Abraham or even above him so far as the gifts of God are concerned; for we, too, have God speaking to us in the Word, in Baptism, and in Communion.

But what is it that He says to us? Is He frightening us? Is He threatening us? Is He accusing us? By no means. Indeed, the church constantly hears those familiar words: "Take heart, My son; your sins are forgiven (Matt. 9:2). I am gracious toward you through My Son; you will be an heir of eternal life," etc.

Although we have the Word of God in such richness, our hearts are nevertheless harder than an anvil and, like rocky soil, keep the root of the Word without sap and fruit, while the saintly patriarchs marveled at this inexpressible benevolence of God to the point of being overcome.

I myself feel in me this hardness of heart, and I hate it and also offer prayers against it every day. Just as the prophet Isaiah says (6:10): "It is a people with a heavy heart and with sleeping eyes," so we, who have the Word in such great richness, feel that our ears and hearts are slow and our eyes heavy with sleep.

This, however, is not the fault of God, who speaks with us in a friendly manner and, as Paul says in Titus 3:4, converses with us in the most kindly fashion when He gives us the ministry of the Word, His sacraments, and His pledges of eternal grace. But we have soundly sleeping eyes and dull ears, and we despise these gifts as something ordinary and paltry. Moreover, what is far more outrageous and disgraceful, we apply ourselves meanwhile to the study of decretals and human traditions.

Therefore we should ask God to give us a joyful heart for such joyful promises, in order that we, too, may exult and be glad with saintly Abraham because we are the people of God. But oh, the wretched and corrupt flesh which restrains the spirit and does not permit us to laugh! If the flesh did not hamper us and we were true Christians, we could sing nothing throughout our entire life but the *Magnificat,* the *Confitemini,* the *Gloria in Excelsis,* the *Sanctus,* etc.

I for my part believe that the saintly patriarch was dazed at first and in a state of ecstasy, so to speak, for great joy, that he also trembled, but that he then wept for joy, until he finally regained his composure, as it were, and laughed when at last he felt this joy with a calm heart, a feeling which is a part of eternal life.

When, as we read in Isaiah,[48] Hezekiah hears from the prophet that he can expect to live and that his sickness is to be cured, he debates with himself (2 Kings 20:8): "Of what nature is this sign? Shall I again go up into the house of the Lord?" For his recovery was not expected. In like manner, Abraham says to himself: "What? Shall a son be born to me from Sarah?" No one can experience this joy of the spirit without faith.

But I have also pointed out above that one must give careful consideration to the circumstance that so far not one of these promises has been fulfilled. Abraham and Sarah have the Word. This they hear. They do not yet have the fulfillment. Still they believe. Indeed, Sarah saw none of her descendants except Isaac. Abraham saw his two grandsons. This physical promise itself, therefore, points to the spiritual promise of eternal life. For no promise is given to dead people, since they do not believe. Indeed, they do not exist. But the Promiser is eternal, and he who believes the eternal Promiser will himself also live eternally through his faith.

Thus even the physical promises, when they do not demand our works or do not have a legal stipulation, include the promise of eternal life. But the promises that are not given gratis but involve merit, that is, have a stipulation of the Law attached to them — like those given to the people concerning the land of Canaan if they keep the Law of Moses — are purely temporal; for they include our own works, and we need God's patience in order to obtain them. Such is not the nature of the promises that are given gratis and depend solely on God's mercy, where God alone wants to be the Doer and Worker and demands nothing from us except faith. Even though these promises are physical, they nevertheless include the eternal salvation which God wants to give us, not in consideration of our merits but out of His grace, which regards and accepts faith alone. "But the righteous shall live by his faith," says the prophet (Hab. 2:4).

Paul makes this distinction between the promises in Rom. 4:5, where he states that faith is reckoned as righteousness, not to him who works but to him who believes. To Abraham three promises

---

[48] Despite the reference to Isaiah the passage Luther has in mind seems to be 2 Kings 20:8.

concerning physical things were given gratis. But he regarded not only the physical things; for he died without having attained these promises, but after he had greeted them from afar, as it were, as the Letter to the Hebrews (11:10) declares: "For he looked forward to a city which has foundations, whose Builder is God."

18. *And Abraham said to God: O that Ishmael might live in Thy sight!*

God promised Abraham a son from the aged Sarah, and He added the promise that Sarah was to be blessed in such a manner that kings and peoples would spring from her. When Abraham hears this and receives far greater things than he would ever have had the courage to ask for, he says: "O that Ishmael might live in Thy sight!" As though he were saying: "O Lord, why dost Thou promise me such great things — things that I accept with the utmost gratitude and joy? I would have been satisfied and would have thought that I would have enough mercy and blessing if Ishmael had lived in Thy sight. Therefore since Thou art about to give me a son, the true heir, from Sarah, give some consideration also to Ishmael, the other son, and do not reject him." Thus it appears here that Abraham was very fond of Ishmael, since he is so concerned about him and is at such pains to intercede for him.

19. *God said: No, but Sarah your wife shall bear you a son, and you shall call his name Isaac. I will establish My covenant with him as an everlasting covenant for his descendants after him.*

20. *As for Ishmael, I have heard you; behold, I will bless him and make him fruitful and multiply him exceedingly; he shall be the father of twelve princes, and I will make him a great nation.*

21. *But I will establish My covenant with Isaac, whom Sarah shall bear to you at this season next year.*

22. *When He had finished talking with him, God went up from Abraham.*

I am pointing out repeatedly that these accounts should be valued because of the conversation God carries on with the saintly patriarch at such great length, not so much because of the subject matter itself. Moreover, one may observe here that God always grants more than we are able to ask for or to understand.

Accordingly, one should learn that those who want to pray properly should accustom themselves to pray with confidence and not to be deterred either by the greatness of the things to be granted or by the unworthiness of their praying.

Paul's statement in Eph. 3:20 is well known. "To Him" he says, "who is able to do far more than we ask or think." Therefore God's title and true name is this, that He is a Hearer of prayers. But we, the petitioners, are called those who do not know how to pray or what to pray for. Our hearts are too feeble for us to be able to grasp the importance of the matter; we trouble ourselves with questions about when, where, and by what means God is willing to hear us. These matters we picture to ourselves beforehand within such narrow bounds that we wrestle constantly with unbelief.

Therefore we must combine these two incomparables, as they are called: the finite and the infinite.[49] Our narrowly defined petitions and our desires and vows are something finite and are exceedingly petty in comparison with that boundless and immeasurable return which God constantly wants to put into practice toward us.

Abraham, not to mention ourselves, never understood. Still less did he have the courage to ask for or to have in mind a promise so great and so rich. To be sure, he longs for a son and is content with the fact that Ishmael is born to him by the maid. This he considers a suitable means — and the only means — of obtaining the blessing for his descendants. God, however, makes use of a different way, one that is more acceptable, even though it is unexpected, and gives him a son, not only from his own flesh but also from the aged, barren, and dead Sarah, for whom it was impossible to conceive when she was still younger and because of her age was in a better condition to give birth. Nor is this enough. To this promise there is attached the promise of the forgiveness of sins and of eternal life. How could Abraham have thought of these things, or how could he have had the courage to ask for them?

Thus we are weak, and our heart does not understand the boundless mercy of God. Consequently, we groan so much when we feel that we are being hard pressed by the Turk, when we are aware of the hatred of the pope and of his insatiable thirst for our blood, and when we reflect on the fury and malice of Satan, whose aim it is to destroy the churches utterly and to reduce us to nothing. We are frightened from both sides, by the immensity of the evils that

---

[49] The terms are *proportio infiniti* and *proportio finiti*.

confront us and by the magnitude of the future favor which we must seek to obtain.

Therefore we think: "What shall we wretched people do, we who have been living in all the sins against the First and the Second Table? Shall we short-lived sinners (Ps. 103:15) really approach the infinite and eternal God and ask Him to alleviate these evils?"

Such are truly the sentiments of all human beings. Yet we must learn that we should pray even in the most desperate evils and hope for the unexpected and the impossible. And it is for this reason that these examples of the holy patriarchs are set before us. They show that the patriarchs, too, were afflicted by sundry cares and trials and yet received more good than they either understood or had been bold enough to ask for.

For we have a God who is able to give more than we understand or ask for. Even though we do not know what we should ask for and how, nevertheless the Spirit of God, who dwells in the hearts of the godly, sighs and groans for us within us with inexpressible groanings and also procures inexpressible and incomprehensible things.

It is profitable to teach these things, because even though we begin to believe and to pray, our hearts are nevertheless deterred by the magnitude of the things for which we are asking and then also by the Person of the Listener. Therefore these accounts incite our hearts to open our mouths toward God and to pray with confidence, without being deterred by the fact that we who are nothing are approaching Him who is everything.

James and John prayed that one should sit at the left of Christ and the other at His right, but He told them (Matt. 20:22): "You do not know what you are asking." Yet He heard their ever so foolish request, but He did so in a manner that was far different from what they themselves had thought. For they are not at the left or at the right of some worldly king; they are princes and judges of the entire world on the Last Day.

Therefore if we want to describe our prayers, they are really nothing else than the stammering of children who ask for bread or a morsel before meals. For we do not know what we should ask for. The things we ask for are beyond our comprehension, and He who bestows them is greater; and the things are also too great for our narrow hearts to be able to understand.

Thus there is the very beautiful example of Monica, the mother of Augustine, who prayed for her son and asked for nothing else than that he be delivered from the foolish ideas of the Manichaeans and be baptized. Like an anxious mother, she also considered betrothing a girl to him if in this way he might be converted. But the more she prayed, the more unyielding and stubborn her son became. Apparently, her praying came to be a sin. But when the time had come for the anxious prayer to be heard (for God is wont to delay His help), Augustine is not only converted and baptized; he devotes himself completely to the study of theology and becomes a teacher who shines in the church up to this day and teaches and instructs it.[50]

Monica had never asked for this. She would have been satisfied to have her son delivered from his error and become a Christian. But God wants to give greater things than we are able to ask for, provided that we do not tire of praying.

For praying is no small task, as those who have no experience think. Those who do have experience in spiritual matters have said that no task can be compared to the task of praying. For praying does not mean to recite a number of psalms or to bellow in the churches, as the monks are accustomed to do; it is a serious meditation, in which the heart makes a comparison between the person praying and the Person hearing, and reaches the firm conviction that even though we are wretched sinners, God will nevertheless be gracious, will alleviate our punishments, and will hear our prayers.

But even though our hearts, strengthened by the Spirit and the Word of God, believe this, it is nevertheless certainly true that no one has so bold a heart that he dares ask for what God has determined to give. Thus we are hampered on both sides; the grandeur of Him who bestows and the unworthiness of him who prays hamper our prayer, so that we actually do not understand what we are praying for.

The petition for daily bread is of little consequence among the rest of the petitions. Yet if we knew how great a petition this is, no one of us would dare open his mouth; but Christ understood this petition when He said (Luke 12:32): "Fear not, little flock, for it is your Father's good pleasure to give you the kingdom," as though He meant to say: "Do not be afraid, and do not be concerned about the things of this life, as the heathen are. For it has pleased your Father to give you, not an earthly kingdom but one that is eternal. Think, therefore, of the heavenly kingdom and of the victory over death and sin; these are important and worthy to have you expect them from God, your Father."

[50] Cf. Augustine, *Confessions*, Book III, ch. 11.

Here Christ also points out that no one realizes what he is asking for and that God will not give those small things which we seek from Him but is eager and willing to give greater and grander things. In this the Holy Spirit helps us as He groans for us with groanings which we are unable to understand, much less to utter.

Therefore we must not despair amid these ragings of Satan and of the world against which our churches pray. The churches themselves are satisfied with an insignificant and small gift. But I hope that when God hears our small and narrowly defined prayers, He will not only defend our doctrine but will also propagate it and, in addition, will bring about marvelous things through it, so that the papists, however boastful they may now be, will be brought to naught. Thus the prayers of the church will destroy the Turk, and we shall find out that God gives greater things than we were able to ask for, yes, even to understand.

I am making these statements in order that we may be aroused, lest we despair because of our own unworthiness, because of the majesty of God, whom we address when we pray, or because of the magnitude of the things for which we pray or, to express it more correctly, do not understand as we pray for them, just as Abraham, an example for us, surely received more than he asked for, so that we may not cease praying or conclude that praying is fruitless. For God sees the innermost thoughts of the heart and understands those unutterable sighings which are in us and which are nevertheless not understood by us, who are like infants stammering at table.

The promise, which is here given to Ishmael, was without a doubt greatly exaggerated by the Saracens, who, through their teachers, laid stress on it against Moses and the prophets. For this promise began to be fulfilled at once and was not delayed as long as the one given to Isaac. Moreover, even though Sarah receives the promise that kings will come from her, nevertheless mention is made here of twelve kings.

But Isaac has the advantage because the Lord's covenant remains with him. Since the Ishmaelites are excluded from it, they are not, as I have stated several times above, for this reason excluded from grace and the promise of salvation. The only thing involved is the establishment of one definite line of blood in which the church is to be found and of which Christ is to be born in due time. This is denied to Ishmael and is left in the house of Abraham and Isaac.

Thus the exclusion — that the church must be sought neither in the house of Ishmael nor among the children of Keturah but in the line of Isaac — is temporal, just as we Gentiles do not have any utterances and promises of God given to us, and Christ was not born of our blood. Yet if we believe in Christ, we are not excluded from the church and the promise of salvation.

Only let us not pride ourselves on our wisdom, but let us go to wherever God has wanted the church to be at a given time. There we shall find the cornerstone which unites both, the Jews and the Gentiles. It is undoubtedly for this reason that the religion and knowledge of God remained among many of the descendants of Ishmael, as, for example, the priest of Midian and the Egyptian Potiphar, who were outstanding men, provided that they united through faith with the church of Isaac.

Today the descendants of Ishmael are intermingled with the Turks; and, like the Jews, they, too, have sunk into terrible darkness and into Mohammed's extreme blasphemy. Therefore you will find nothing similar today, nothing that could be compared to this promise.

But at this point it is proper to raise the question why in this passage God clearly distinguishes one covenant from the other, for He mentions two covenants. The first is the covenant of circumcision, to which Ishmael also is admitted, yes, the slaves too, whether born in the house of Abraham or purchased. It is for this reason that circumcision was retained also by Ishmael's descendants, who populated almost the entire East and the three parts of Arabia: Arabia Felix, Arabia Petraea, and Arabia Deserta. They all rejoiced in the name of their father Abraham.

The second covenant is here established with Isaac. Ishmael is clearly excluded from it. Hence this text proves that besides the covenant of circumcision there is another, which pertains to Isaac alone and not, like the covenant of circumcision, to Ishmael also.

What, then, shall we say was the nature of this covenant? It was obviously the promise concerning Christ, which Abraham understood well. And this is what I have stated, namely, that God always mixes and includes spiritual and eternal blessings with the physical blessings. The physical blessing is associated with a name, namely, that all the descendants of Abraham should be circumcised; but this second covenant is not associated with a name, nor is it marked by any definite work. Yet it is a spiritual covenant concerning the future Savior.

Hence this text gives the Jews clear proof concerning the twofold covenant. The covenant of circumcision, which they value so highly, is solely a covenant of the Law and is temporal. Not only Isaac but also Ishmael and the descendants of Ishmael rejoice in it; but the other covenant, which excludes Ishmael and is made with Isaac alone, is spiritual and eternal. The covenant of circumcision is given for our performance before the Law of Moses and is established for a definite people, in a definite land, and for a definite time, namely, while the generations of Abraham are in existence. The covenant of Isaac, however, is not given for our performance; it is entirely free, without a name, without a time, and yet from the seed of Isaac, lest one look for the blessing from another source.

From this passage the holy prophets drew their sermons concerning the kingdom of Christ, which, as they saw, had been withheld from the house of Ishmael, who nevertheless shared in the circumcision. In view of its extent and grandeur they openly dispensed with circumcision and the Law as inadequate for salvation and ascribed everything to the Son of God, who would be born from the house of Isaac.

Thus this passage deals with the promise concerning Christ, which goes beyond Abraham's wishes and request. But the Jews do wrong by clinging solely to the covenant of circumcision and not preferring to accept the other covenant. They are like the Ishmaelites, or even worse. The Ishmaelites did not seek salvation through circumcision, as the Jews did, but through the promise concerning Christ, which they accepted in faith. For it is sure that those who accepted circumcision together with faith in Christ were saved.

In this passage one should take note of the word מוֹעֵד, which we have generally translated with the German noun *Stifft*, while the Latin translation has "tabernacle of the testimony." But in this passage the word denotes a definite and fixed time, as, for instance, also in Gen. 1:14: "Let them be לְמוֹעֲדִים," "for certain times." Inasmuch as the moon has a definite time during which it is new and during which its brightness increases and decreases, it is a most convenient indicator of time.

Then מוֹעֵד also denotes a definite place in which the tabernacle of the covenant had been set up, where God had established a remembrance of Himself, that is, where He had commanded that His Word be taught and that He be worshiped. For remembrance of God is nothing else than preaching about God, and He wants men to be intent on this, as Christ says (Luke 22:19): "Do this in remembrance of Me." For where He Himself has His teachers who preach His name, there He wants to be found, to hear, and to bless.

But the Lord gives this command in order that the Jews may not go astray through various forms of idolatry and worship. He wants no assembly under every tree; He wants people to come together where He Himself has caused His name to dwell. This is a מוֹעֵד, a definite and specified place, *ein Stifft*, as we call it in German. Thus we read in Ps. 74:8: "Let us abolish all the festival days from the land." The Hebrew is: "We shall burn all מוֹעֵד of the land"; it denotes not only the festivals and the full moons but also the synagogs and schools. For the Law had prescribed that in every city the Levites should read and teach on certain days. The places devoted to this endeavor were called מוֹעֲדִים. But for the sacrifices a place has been appointed in Jerusalem, and there not only teaching took place, but also sacrifices were brought. In the same psalm (74:4) "They who hate Thee have boasted in the midst of Thy solemnities" would more correctly be rendered "in the midst of Thy churches," that is, Thy houses, where Thy Word is being taught. But in this passage it denotes a time, and a definite and specific one at that.

22. *When He had finished talking with him, God went up from Abraham.*

Moses added this closing statement in order to commend to us this account in which there is so long a conversation of God with Abraham. For it is of the highest importance when God speaks. The next thing, but separated by a great interval, is when everything is done by us in accordance with the Word of God.

This closing statement proves that God appeared in some visible form when He had this conversation with Abraham. God most commonly speaks through the patriarchs and those who are in the public ministry of the Word. Next in order, He is wont to appear in dreams, as at Bethel and Ai, and sometimes through a vision seen in an ecstatic state, when a human being seems to have been snatched outside himself, as above, when God brought Abraham out to count the stars. But in the present instance God appeared in some visible form and spoke personally with Abraham, not through a human being or an angel.

And this is the reason why Holy Scripture gives Abraham this glory and calls him a friend and intimate of God in Isaiah (41:8). Thus Christ does not call His apostles servants; He calls them friends

(Matt. 12:49). And it is indeed something very great to have God conversing and associating with us.

Nor are we ourselves deprived of this gift. Even though God does not appear to us in an extraordinary form, as He did to Abraham, yet His usual and most friendly and most intimate appearance is this, that He presents Himself to us in the Word, in the use of the Keys, in Baptism, and in the Lord's Supper. But we experience what the proverb says: Excessive familiarity breeds contempt. Likewise: Presence diminishes a reputation. Also: Everyday occurrences become worthless. And in Prov. 20:14 Solomon declares: "'It is bad, it is bad,' says every buyer, but when he has gone away, then he boasts."

No one of us would not heartily desire to see Moses, David, or even Augustine, Ambrose, and similar illustrious men. But if these men were here and lived with us for a year or two, they would surely be despised. Yes, if angels associated with us, the same thing would happen to them, not indeed because they would be lacking in glory but because our nature is inclined to disdain and despise.

Therefore we, too, could glory as the patriarch Abraham did. Indeed, if Abraham himself had seen the kindness God shows by speaking and associating with us daily through the ministry in Baptism and in the Lord's Supper, he would have died from wonderment and joy.

The monks extol the legends of their fathers Benedict and Bernard, but surely God generally speaks at far greater length and associates far more intimately with any Christian whatever than they boast about their fathers. Indeed, if I had the matter under my control, I would not want God to speak to me from heaven or to appear to me; but this I would want — and my daily prayers are directed to this end — that I might have the proper respect and true appreciation for the gift of Baptism, that I have been baptized, and that I see and hear brothers who have the grace and gift of the Holy Spirit and are able to comfort and encourage with the Word, to admonish, warn, and teach. For what better and more profitable appearance of God do you want?

But alas, the proud spirits despise these things, and we, too, do not assign to these common appearances in the Word, Baptism, the Lord's Supper, etc., the position we should give them. We would consider it as something glorious for us, however, if, as Münzer used to boast, God spoke with us visibly. But the outcome has shown what sort of God this was, namely, Satan, who feigns the glory of the Divine Majesty.

These facts must be impressed rather frequently, and it is not without reason that I am repeating them. If Abraham should be compared with us who live in the New Testament, he is, for the most part, less important than we are, provided that one considers the matter impartially. To be sure, in his case the personal gifts are greater; but God did not manifest Himself to him in a closer and more friendly manner than He does to us. Let it indeed be a great glory to have those appearances, but what greater or better advantage did Abraham have from them than the fact that God spoke with him? This happens to us too, however, and indeed daily, as often as and wherever we wish. It is true that you hear a human being when you are baptized and when you partake of the Holy Supper. But the Word which you hear is not that of a human being; it is the Word of the living God. It is He who baptizes you; it is He who absolves you from sins; and it is He who commands you to hope in His mercy.

It is great ingratitude to slight these faces of God, as Scripture calls them, and meanwhile to look for other appearances and revelations. Therefore under the papacy such people surely got the punishments they deserved when Satan made sport of them with foolish, silly, and laughable apparitions, which the monks nevertheless rant about and embellish, and which the popes, moreover, have acknowledged and confirmed by their testimony.

But such stories must be read with discernment, and one should not immediately believe what everybody says. All apparitions must be tested according to the norm of faith, and one must ask whether they are in harmony with faith, or indeed, as usually happens, conflict with the revealed Word. Moses wants even the prophets judged in this manner, so that if they proclaim anything contrary to the revealed Word, people will not listen to them even though they perform signs and wonders (Deut. 13).

I suppose, however, that some appearances, like those related about Dionysius and others,[51] are true. Yet they are of no concern to me. It is not that I utterly despise them; it is because I know that they are nothing in comparison with Baptism, the Lord's Supper, yes, even in comparison with a godly conversation which I can have

---

[51] Cf. Pseudo-Dionysius, *Epistolae*, VIII, 6, *Patrologia, Series Graeca*, III, 1097—1100.

with any godly brother. For these appearances are available to all and most reliable, and they cannot deceive.

Learn, therefore, that throughout one's life, in every work, and in every situation one must give attention above all to the Word of God. To the patriarchs and the prophets God appeared in an extraordinary manner, in dreams, in a vision, or through the words of the patriarchs and sometimes even of angels. We do not long for such revelations or appearances; we are satisfied, and we thank God to the best of our ability for our own appearances and faces of God, which we behold in Baptism and in the entire ministry of the Word. It is there that a brother becomes an angel for his brother. He absolves him from sins, comforts, instructs, strengthens, warns, admonishes, etc.

These are our own appearances, and we justly value them most highly. For through them we know God and obtain eternal life. Therefore one must note the differences in the legends or the lives of human beings. If God never appears to me visibly, as He did to Abraham, I do not even desire that He do so. What is more, I would not be willing to believe that it is God unless I were manifestly compelled to do so, because for eternal salvation it is enough for me that I have been baptized, that I hear the Gospel, and that by virtue of the Keys I am absolved.

But if God wants to speak to me in a dream and warn me about temporal matters, as He warned the Magi when they were about to return to Herod, well and good. For eternal life, however, I need no other revelation. Therefore I desire none. Even if one were given to me, I would distrust it because of the craftiness of Satan, who is in the habit of transforming himself into an angel of light (2 Cor. 11:14); for God amply reveals Himself to me in Baptism and in the ministry.

Paul says (Titus 3:4 ff.): "But when the goodness and lovingkindness of God our Savior appeared, He saved us, not because of deeds done by us in righteousness, but in virtue of His own mercy, by the washing of regeneration and renewal in the Holy Spirit, which He poured out upon us richly through Jesus Christ our Savior, so that we might be justified by His grace and become heirs in hope of eternal life."

This is a trustworthy saying. Hence if you read the accounts of the saints and find in them miraculous works and miraculous appearances, read them with discretion, and conclude with certainty that no appearance is more glorious, more magnificent, and more profitable to us than that most universal one among all Christians, through which the whole church has its existence, is sustained and preserved. This appearance is real and is shared by all, but the appearances to Abraham and to the prophets are incidental and concern the individuals.

I am saying nothing about the nonsensical statements of the monks. They are not worthy of attention and of being remembered. For the most part they are illusions of Satan devised to deceive and to do harm. Therefore they must be weighed according to the analogy of faith and the rule of the Scripture. Quite famous are the apparitions of Gregory. He himself believed that they were true, and by his example he filled the church with countless errors; for he believed that he saw the souls of the saints and heard them demand intercessory prayers — not those of Christ but those of people still living on earth — and likewise the help of their works: alms, Masses, and fasts.[52]

But let these claims be weighed according to the rule of Scripture. For what have all these things to do with the dead and with the future life? But Gregory disregarded this rule and believed that they were true and that they set an example for all monks, who were to conform to them and teach them in the church. Accordingly, the glory of the ministry of the Word and of the true and saving appearances was obscured, and special attention was paid to those nonsensical statements, yes, to those destructive deceptions of Satan.

It is a great gift that the divine mercy is again kindling for us this light of the Word, in order that we may know where God must be sought and truly found: not at Rome, not in the farthest parts of Spain, but in Baptism, in the words of the Gospel, in the use of the Keys, and indeed also with any brother who with me confesses and believes in the Son of God. These are the epiphanies or appearances that are common to all Christians. Moreover, in that special appearance which Moses is describing in this passage nothing is more magnificent and more important than that God is speaking with Abraham as with a most intimate friend.

Yet if we wish, we have the same thing. In fact, we have it more abundantly than Abraham did. Hence if he were living, he would undoubtedly be indignant because we so shamefully despise such great glories and such a great wealth of divine mercy.

[52] Gregory, *Dialogorum libri quatuor*, IV, chs. 11—36, *Patrologia, Series Latina*, LXXVII, 336—385.

Therefore in Deut. 4:7 Moses also has superb praise for this favor: "For what great nation is there that has a god so near to it as the Lord our God is to us whenever we call upon Him?" Isaiah (31:9) glories similarly in the fact that God has His seat and fire in Jerusalem.

Actually our glory in the New Testament is greater. We not only have God drawing near to us; we also have Him dwelling in us bodily. But if His Person is not manifest in such a way that we see Him face to face, yet His Word and works are manifest. Now there follows praise of Abraham's obedience, something that is set forth for us to imitate.

23. *Then Abraham took Ishmael his son and all the slaves born in his house or bought with his money, every male among the men of Abraham's house, and circumcised the flesh of their foreskins that very day, as God had said to him.*

24. *Abraham was ninety-nine years old when he was circumcised in the flesh of his foreskin.*

25. *And Ishmael his son was thirteen years old when he was circumcised in the flesh of his foreskin.*

26. *That very day Abraham and his son Ishmael were circumcised;*

27. *and all the men of his house, those born in the house and those bought with money from a foreigner, were circumcised with him.*

All these statements deal with the praise of Abraham's obedience, which must nevertheless be regarded in such a way that we do not maintain that Abraham was justified by it. For it is not works that justify a person, but a righteous person does righteous works. Yet the works show that faith is being put into practice and that through them it increases and becomes fat, as it were. For while Abraham carries out this act of obedience and is circumcised together with his household, faith thinks of God, who gives us His promises and accepts us.

Thus Peter (2 Peter 1:10) tells us to certify our election by doing good works, for they bear witness that grace is effective in us and that we have been called and elected. On the other hand, an inactive faith — a faith that is not put into practice — quickly dies and becomes extinct; but when faith has become extinct, it is doubtful whether we have been elected. But he who progresses in the unremitting exercise of his faith concludes: "I am not in the host that is against Christ; I am for Christ. I do not deny the Word, and I do not persecute the church. Hence I have been called to the kingdom of God and have been elected."

"But if I fall because of weakness, I rise again; I grieve over my sin and pray for forgiveness. Thus through the very works of repentance and love I realize that I am one of those who have been snatched from the conflagration of Babel or from the dregs of the world." Thus even though this obedience does not justify, it nevertheless gives evidence of faith and makes it manifest, as it were, so that it can be seen. Therefore Revelation (22:11) states: "He that is righteous, let him be righteous still." Just as those who occupy themselves with works of unbelief continually become more and more unbelieving, and through that continual effort sin gains strength, as it were, so, vice versa, faith increases in those who practice godliness. As a result, they conclude with certainty that they belong to the church.

Furthermore, an extraordinary example of obedience is set before us in this passage. What can be called more foolish, sillier, more senseless, and, I add, even more disgraceful and more disgusting than that Abraham, who is almost a hundred years old, is at once circumcised on this very day with his entire household? He does not debate with himself; nor does he ask anxious questions, as we all are wont to do. But as soon as God departs from him he calls his household together and carries out the Lord's command. It is proper for us to set this obedience before us as an example.

The monks have had various discussions about obedience. They have said that some obedience has something of its own and that some has little of its own; for we are frequently commanded to do things which we do with pleasure and without any annoyance, as, for example, when a monk is ordered to go out among the people. This obedience was not rated highly and was said to have something of its own. On the other hand, when either unreasonable or difficult and irksome tasks were commanded and yet were undertaken in a ready and cheerful spirit, this obedience was said to have nothing of its own and was given magnificent praise, even if it entailed foolish and childish works.

But if you ask to see a perfect example of obedience, look at the patriarch Abraham as he puts his faith into practice in circumcision. If he had wanted to act in accordance with reason and to argue, he would have said: "What is the use of being circumcised in this part of the body? Why did God not choose another part, one that is more honorable? This part cannot be touched without indecency, particularly in the case of adults."

This one way of thinking assuredly deceived Adam. Not satisfied with God's command, he sought also to learn the reason why God ordered him to keep away from only one tree. When people get into this way of thinking, either the work that was commanded is left undone, or it is objected to and becomes the opposite. Therefore it is ruinous and destructive to think about the *why*. This brings on certain ruin, especially when we soar too high and want to philosophize about predestination.

But let us keep in mind the example of Abraham. It teaches us that before God we must again become children and not argue about how or why God gives us a particular command, but that we must simply hold fast to what God has so commanded and obey. Did not Abraham, too, have a reason for arguing if he had wanted to follow his reason? What did circumcision have to commend it as a good work? There is not only no advantage in it, no glory, and no merit; but it is also shameful, disgraceful, unprofitable, and absurd.

Therefore reason concludes that God could have commanded something far more profitable, more suitable, showier, and better, so that through it Abraham might more properly put into practice both his faith and his obedience than by a work so foolish that the now hundred-year-old Abraham could not carry it out without manifest disgrace. But the saintly man puts up no argument whatever. It is enough for him to know that it pleases God to have him do this. Hence he obeys without delay and without regard for his own opinion and that of others. This is obedience which deserves praise and is set before us as an example — as obedience that has nothing of its own but simply cleaves to God's command.

Accordingly, after we have been justified through the mercy of God and have been called into the fellowship of the saints to carry on warfare under God, let us do without any argument what we have been commanded to do. According to Sirach (Ecclus. 3:22), "Let us not strive after things that are too high for us." But he who does not cease to investigate matters that are higher than he is and anxiously argues: "Why does He command this?" will be cast out of Paradise because of that *why*, just as Adam was; for the Divine Majesty simply cannot tolerate this, and it is beyond our ability.

When the Lord began to wash the feet of the disciples at the Last Supper and came to Peter, the latter refuses to allow it and says (John 13:6): "You are not going to wash my feet, are You?" This disobedience had its source in carnal wisdom, which did not see the purpose of the work which Christ had begun. But Christ does not want to argue with Peter any more about why He is doing this. He cuts off the question and admonishes Peter to be obedient: "Unless I wash you, you will have no part in My kingdom." Then Peter ceased to argue and requested that his entire body be washed rather than only his feet.

Let us, too, have the same way of thinking, so that we may obey God's commands without any argument. In this manner we shall make our calling sure. Inactivity or arguments and speculations do not make it sure; they cause us to lose it entirely.

But obedience is hindered by the schemes and stratagems of Satan; for because he has turned away from God, he would like to have us, too, turn away from God. For this reason he obstructs obedience and endeavors to torment us with unprofitable and most dangerous questions. From this source came the boundless sea of debates in the papacy, so that, if you should wish to sum up the entire doctrine of the papists in one word, you would be right in saying that it is nothing but a single *why*.

Against this temptation one must, therefore, adhere to this example, that Abraham, already a hundred years old, does not argue about the shameful, disgusting, and foolish work that is done on a disgusting member; but because he has heard that God wants it this way, he obeys without question or argument and compels his son as well as all his domestics to render the same obedience.

Saul is given the command to destroy all the Amalekites and all their booty. Because he begins to debate whether it is good to obey this command, his reason is offended by the senselessness, and he supposes that it can be dispensed with on the ground that mercy is more pleasing to God than tyranny. Therefore he spares the king's life and keeps the better part of the booty, with the intention, of course, that his worship of God might be more magnificent. But this showy disobedience results in the rejection of Saul and all his descendants. "For obedience is more pleasing to God than sacrifice" (1 Sam. 15:22).

Therefore let no one add this detestable and fatal little word "why" to God's commands. But when the command is certain, let us obey at once without any argument, and let us conclude that God is wiser than we are. He who argues about why God gives a particular command actually doubts that God is wise, just, and good. What sin can be more hideous and more intolerable to God? Therefore we must believe — this is part of our duty — and not argue, for these matters are too lofty for us to be able to argue about them.

If God followed our counsels, he would this very hour kill the Turk and the pope, and He would not allow Satan to give vent to his fury as he is doing and to rage without restraint. Everybody would regard this as a beneficial and good work. But God's wisdom makes it clear that this is a foolish thought; otherwise things would turn out this way. Therefore if you ask why God bears with the ungodly for so long a time, it is enough to say: "Thus it pleases Him, thus it is profitable, and thus it is beneficial; otherwise He would be doing something different." He who is not satisfied with this reason and searches into the reasons for God's counsel lays himself open to the danger by which Adam was overcome in Paradise.

Therefore let us crucify this baneful *why*, and let us say: "Glory to God, who alone is wise; but confusion to us!" Satan opened our eyes in Paradise, and now our every effort is directed toward closing them again and making them blind. The fact that Adam had his eyes opened is the occasion and cause of death and damnation for all his descendants.

Accordingly, Moses gives grand praise to Abraham's faith and obedience. For Abraham cuts off all hindrances and all causes of offense; he obeys God's command without arguing. He does not think, as we do: "Why does God command this? What profit is there in the disgraceful and shameful business? Can I not be saved without being circumcised at the age of a hundred?" He simply cuts the throat of this baneful *why* and tears it out of his heart by the roots. He takes reason captive and finds satisfaction in the one fact that He who gives the command is just, good, and wise; therefore He cannot command anything but what is just, good, and wise, no matter what the opinion of reason is, and no matter if reason does not understand. For God's judgments are beyond our comprehension. Reason cannot grasp them. Therefore if it argues about them, it not only deceives itself but also falls into blasphemy. Accordingly, let it be enough for us that we hear the Word and understand what it commands, even though we do not understand the reason for the command.

Hence this is a most beautiful and admirable example, not only because of Abraham's person but also because his influence was so great that he induced his entire household not to be offended by the disgraceful and shameful deed. Thus it is evident that Abraham's house was nothing else than the church instructed in the most saintly manner and accustomed to the worship of God and the obedience of the Word. Therefore it is not surprising that he performed very great deeds with his church and vanquished four very powerful kings.

If we had one leader like Abraham, do you have any doubt that we would overthrow the Turk? For it is a great thing to be so believing and simple in faith that without argument the entire household obeys God when He gives a command and complies, and is not offended by the disgrace but follows the example of the godly head of the household and its pastor.

Accordingly, let us, too, learn to put aside all questions and simply to go in the name of the Lord and do whatever God has commanded, whether it is foolish, offensive, or dangerous. If God's command is connected with it, even a work that is disgraceful and shameful in the sight of reason is most beautiful and holy; for there is no greater and better adornment than the Word of God. Inasmuch as circumcision had this adornment, it was a holy work and was most pleasing to God.

I have stated above that circumcision existed not for an unlimited but for a fixed time. Therefore it has come to an end in the New Testament, but its allegorical meaning has remained, namely, the mortification of the flesh and of sin; for the flesh is beset by sundry trials and scruples, in order that its smugness may be removed and occasion may not be lacking for occupying oneself with the Word and prayer.

But it is a source of offense that those who alone are the people of God and rightly rejoice in the possession of the truth are subjected to the cross, are killed by the pope and his followers, and are vexed in various ways, whereas the enemies of God and slaves of Satan triumph and are in glory.

Joined to these offenses are personal troubles which the saints carry about in their hearts and bodies. But so far as you are concerned, bear these, pray, do your work, and think: "Behold, Abraham let himself be circumcised without any argument and the eight-day-old infants were subjected to the same agony. Therefore let us, too, bear our little share." Thus Abraham gives us an example not only of justification but also of a seemingly senseless obedience.

Undoubtedly the heathen laughed at the aged patriarch, who could not undergo circumcision without pain. But Abraham does not feel ashamed; he does what God had commanded, and he is not offended because he has lived without circumcision for so long a time and must now submit to it when he is a hundred years old. Thirteen-year-old Ishmael likewise does not feel ashamed when he is stripped, and he does not object to the pain. In like manner, all the home-born and all the bought slaves bear that disgrace in a childlike and simple frame of mind and do not ask questions. Thus they please God and are saved through faith in the Blessed Seed. Because of this fatal and baneful *why* those who do not conform to this example by receiving the Word in simple and childlike obedience and obeying it will, in accordance with the example of Adam, be plunged into disobedience and death.

CHAPTER EIGHTEEN

1. *And the Lord appeared to him by the oaks of Mamre, as he sat at the door of his tent in the heat of the day.*

As has already been stated,[1] because of the importance of what took place when Abraham was ninety-nine years old, this year is particularly memorable. In fact, it is the most memorable year in his life. Within it fall circumcision and the two promises, the spiritual and the material; later on the journey to Palestine and the deliverance; also the overthrow of Sodom. And, what is most important, the Lord appeared to Abraham several times and conversed with him in a friendly manner.

The chief content of this chapter is that God wants to confirm the promise He had made concerning Isaac. In the preceding chapter Abraham is promised a son from Sarah, and the Lord calls this son Isaac because Abraham had laughed. But Sarah was not present at that time, and it seems that she did not believe Abraham when he told her about this. Therefore the promise is repeated here, in order that Sarah may hear it, not from the mouth of Abraham, as had been the case, but from the mouth of God Himself, of whom it is stated that He stood turned away; that is, He had turned His back, to indicate that Sarah did not believe until she was reproached.

Isaac is then promised a second time, and this passage about the children of the promise is treated in an admirable manner and at great length by St. Paul, who concludes from it (Rom. 4:1 ff.) that man is justified by faith and not by the Law or by works; and by means of this one argument he does away with all Jewish pride and presumption about their physical birth. For if physical birth is of any value, why is a difference made between Ishmael and Isaac? But just as Isaac was born as a result of the promise — and the promise demands faith — so not those who have Abraham as their natural father but those who believe according to the example of

---

[1] See p. 76.

faithful Abraham, no matter whether they are of the Gentiles or have been circumcised, are regarded as children of Abraham.

Inasmuch as this is the main passage, it is corroborated — in accordance with the practice of Scripture — by a twofold testimony, just as Joseph later sees two dreams involving cows, and both dreams have the same meaning.[2] Those who are without experience in spiritual matters will regard this as a thoughtless repetition and tautology. But there was an important reason for recording the same thing twice. For this removes a very great offense and puts an end to the otherwise never-ending debate about the prerogative of physical birth and about the presumption of human powers.

This repetition of the promise does not serve to untie this knot; it simply cuts it, in order that the Jews, who rely on their physical descent, as well as the Gentiles, who rely on their own powers, may see that the seed of the promise is the true seed of Abraham.

For even though Isaac was born from the flesh of Abraham, he was nevertheless born in a manner which was beyond the powers of the flesh, since both parents, so far as the flesh was concerned, were almost dead and, because of their age, were unfit for procreation. But the promise which they apprehend through faith revives their dead flesh, as it were. Consequently, you must maintain that Isaac was born not so much from the flesh as because of the promise. This is the chief passage of this chapter for the righteousness of faith over against the presumption and the righteousness of works.

In the second place, a very beautiful moral example of hospitality is presented here.

In the third place, note should be taken of the unique evidence concerning the Trinity, namely, that three men appear and that Moses continually speaks as though there were only one. But we shall defer the consideration of this evidence and speak first about the hospitality.

2. *He lifted up his eyes and looked, and behold, three men stood in front of him. When he saw them, he ran from the tent door to meet them, and bowed himself to the earth,*

[2] An allusion to the series of incidents reported in Gen. 41:1-7; 17-21. But it was Pharaoh, not Joseph, who saw the dreams; and in the dreams Pharaoh saw not two visions of cattle but one of cattle and one of ears of grain, both dreams signifying the same portent.

3. *and said: My lord, if I have found favor in your sight, do not pass by your servant.*

4. *Let a little water be brought, and wash your feet, and rest yourselves under the tree,*

5. *while I fetch a morsel of bread, that you may refresh yourselves, and after that you may pass on — since you have come to your servant. So they said: Do as you have said.*

That extraordinary praise of hospitality which appears in the Letter to the Hebrews (13:2) had its origin in this passage. "Do not neglect to show hospitality to strangers, for thereby some have entertained angels unawares." There is hospitality wherever the church is. For the church, if I may say so, always has a common treasury, inasmuch as it has the command (Matt. 5:42): "Give to him who begs from you." And we must all serve the church and take care of it, not only by teaching but also by showing kindness and giving assistance, so that at the same time both the spirit and the flesh may find refreshment in the church.

But especially the strangers whose lot is rather hard should be received in a kindly manner, for Christ's utterance on the Last Day against the inhospitable is clear (Matt. 25:35): "I was a foreigner or a stranger and you did not receive Me." Also (Matt. 25:40): "Whatever you did to the least of Mine, you did to Me." What greater praise can there be for this virtue than that those who are hospitable are not receiving a human being but are receiving the Son of God Himself? On the other hand, what is more hideous than inhospitality? By it you shut out from your house, not a human being but the Son of God, who suffered and died for you on the cross. Are you not willing to give Him the cost of one day's support or so much space of your dwelling that He may lie down with you? What punishments do you suppose will follow this inhumanity or cruelty? Therefore let those who want to be true members of the church remember to practice hospitality, to which we are encouraged not only by the example of the saintly patriarch but by very important testimonies of Scripture.

This appearance of the three men is an appearance of the Lord, and while Abraham receives them with hospitality, he is receiving the Lord Himself. They seem to have appeared in a lowly and wretched form: naked, hungry, tired from the journey, and as exiles, so to speak, who had just recently been released from some disagreeable prison. Abraham's words show that he regarded them as such.

Moreover, Abraham learned hospitality in a twofold way. In the first place he learned it from the instruction of the patriarchs and from the practice of the church; for they taught their children hospitality as a virtue of which the church stood in the greatest need. Since the Word is taught in the church, and since Satan hates the Word and has been a murderer and a liar from the beginning (John 8:44; 1 John 3:8), various perils and very many troubles are bound to arise.

Wherever God speaks, even in Paradise itself, Satan does not cease to rage by deceiving as well as killing, until he drives Adam out of Paradise and makes him a stranger and an exile. Outside Paradise he did the same thing in the church from the beginning. He subjected the godly to the hatred of the world. Whenever God's goodness did not allow him to rage against their hearts and bodies, he raged against their possessions, drove them out of their homes, and vexed them in exile by whatever means he could. For this reason the saintly patriarchs gave orders to receive wretched heads of households, together with their wives and their children, in a hospitable manner and to treat them generously, as though they were little birds cast out of their nest.

At all times the church has been like some refuge of the exiles and the poor. Just as Christ says (Luke 11:21) that a strong man guards his own palace in peace until a stronger man comes, so it has constantly been the lot of the godly that when the Word lets its light shine, persecutions and exiles were most common.

In our own age, too, there is the great light of the Word, kindled as the result of God's goodness. For this reason Satan rages and through the pope, the bishops, and tyrannical princes fills the entire world with poor people and exiles who roam about in misery, thirst, hunger, and are oppressed in various ways. Hence there should be some Lot, there should be an Abraham, and there should be some little domain of a godly prince in which there can be room for such people; for where there is no house, there can be no hospitality.

Here Abraham believes that he is seeing true strangers of this kind; for I am calling true strangers those who live in exile because of the Word, not those vagrants of whom there has been a very great supply under the papacy, who either out of wantonness and flippancy or because of hope in their own righteousness went into exile of their own accord without being compelled to do so by persecution. For it is characteristic of the Word of God that wherever it is heard, it provokes Satan to wrath. But this indignation of the powerful spirit does not depart without misfortune for those who believe. They are driven from their homes, despoiled of their means, and snatched away to be punished. In short, they are, as Paul calls them (1 Cor. 4:13), καθάρματα and περιψήματα.

The church can and must not be indifferent to these difficulties of the brethren. By God's command and by the instruction of the forefathers it is constrained to practice works of mercy, to feed the hungry and the thirsty, to receive exiles hospitably, to comfort prisoners, and to visit the sick.

The devil, too, has his beggars; but whenever these have nothing, they nevertheless have enough and have it in abundance, as we see in the case of the monks and the idle vagrants. But the true beggars are those who are beggars because of the promise of the Word. These the world hates and neither helps nor supports. But Abraham helps them, for he has learned from the instruction of his ancestors that these are necessary duties toward godly brethren. Therefore his house was open to all, and he joyfully received strangers, as we see.

Accordingly, let us bear this example in mind; for we know that, as Peter says (1 Peter 5:9), our brethren in the world are vexed and suffer in various ways. Hence if we want to be Christians, let our homes be open to exiles, and let us assist and refresh them.

In the second place, Abraham also learned hospitality from his own experience. For now about twenty-four years have passed since he lived in exile after his departure from Ur of the Chaldeans, wandered through the land of Canaan, and did not live in one definite place. From Ai he came to Bethel; from there to Hebron, to Palestine, to Beersheba, and other places. Furthermore, he was twice compelled to enter Egypt, not without great peril. He often endured the rigors of the weather in the open country and under the sky; he was often troubled by hunger, often by thirst. He was often beset by other perils — perils which Moses could not recount individually. But Moses indicates what they were by this one word, which means that Abraham was an exile; for the term "exile" includes countless hardships and perils.

These perils that he underwent enabled him to learn to be gentle, kind, and generous toward exiles. Therefore when these three men presented themselves in their simple and poor garb, they were regarded by him as exiled brethren who had fled from Chaldea itself, from Egypt, or from neighboring Damascus. Accordingly, he runs to meet them as men who were greatly in need of refreshment, asks them in a friendly manner to stay, offers them water with which to wash their feet, fetches food with which the tired men may refresh themselves, and by no means thinks that they are angels or God Himself.

This is a very beautiful picture of a man who is generous and bounteous toward brethren afflicted because of their profession of the Word, for Abraham believed that they were men of this kind. Therefore he does not wait until they knock at the door and ask for hospitality; but he sits at the entrance, and when he sees them from afar, he runs to meet them as though he wanted to prevent someone else from snatching these guests from him. So kindly is he disposed toward them.

Therefore Moses' statement that Abraham sat at the door is not without a purpose. It is a description of a kindly heart ready for the services that the brethren need, and it signifies not only a kindly heart but also a bounteous and beneficent hand toward strangers, whom he made a practice of [3] awaiting as he sat there in this manner. Similarly, Paul praises Philemon for refreshing the hearts of the saints who were either driven into exile or delivered from prison.[4] But, as I have said, this virtue exists solely in the church.

Consider what you will find like this in the papacy. The papists are like the people of Sodom, about whom the next chapter will speak. They in truth, as Ezek. 16:49 says, "have idleness and fullness of bread but do not extend their hand to the poor." Indeed, they rather oppress the poor, rage against the unfortunate churches, shed blood, carry off possessions, proscribe, and drive into exile. These monstrous sins and this more than inhuman cruelty which they employ against the ministers of the Word, against the heads of households, even against women and children, they try to cover with their hypocritical worship and by building and establishing hospitals on a grand scale, not so much for the benefit of the poor as for their own glory.

[3] The Weimar editors suggest the reading *solitus* instead of the *solicitus* in the original, and we have followed their suggestion; see also p. 198, note 24.

[4] This is probably a reference to Philem. 7.

Therefore they will hear a stern judgment on the Last Day, when Christ will accuse them of persecuting Him, casting Him out of His abode, driving Him into exile, etc.

By God's grace the wretched exiles now have a place under our most illustrious Prince.[5] Here they can flee for refuge, and here they are safe. But I am afraid that someone else will come — someone who does not know Joseph (Ex. 1:8); and I fear that this will happen because of the excessive cruelty, inhospitality, and greed of human beings. The nobles, the burghers, and the peasants do not help the churches with a single obol to be able to be generous toward exiles. Whatever we have, we have from the leavings of what was gathered and given under the pope.

Today nobody gives anything. Under the pope, however, there was no end of lavish giving. But now it would be proper to give all the more generously, because now there are more godly exiles than at any previous times. For men are being admonished by the Word of God; and it is especially the ministers of the churches who are in need, because they are now married and no longer live in impure celibacy. Therefore not single persons, as formerly, but entire families are now in exile because of their confession of the Word. It is a crime not to help these.

But we must have no doubt that the saintly patriarch often had the same experience that we have today. There is no lack of idle hypocrites who are accustomed to begging; and if you give them a handout, they at once spend it on gambling and carousing; and where they know of churches ready to assist the needy, they flock together as for prey and for a time simulate godliness solely in the hope of richer gain.

Thus Paul (1 Tim. 5:16) complains about the wanton widows who were being supported at public expense and were a burden to the churches. If this happened at that time, it is not remarkable if today many come to us too under the pretense of being exiles in distress, as though they had been deprived of their means because of their confession of the Word. So far as they are concerned, it is not hospitality but rapine and an unfair burden which is imposed on the churches. Therefore caution is needed here, so that we may beware of such vagrants.

---

[5] The prince to whom Luther is referring is Elector John Frederick the Magnanimous (1503—54); see also *Luther's Works*, 13, Introduction, p. x.

Undoubtedly idle men [6] frequently took advantage of Abraham by abusing his generosity and flocking to him, for they knew that a table was prepared for them where he lived and that everything was placed at their disposal. Such people are like the drones, which snatch the honey away from the busily toiling bees. But they do so without inconveniencing their benefactors; for those who are liberal in such a natural manner do not lose their reward, even though they do waste their kindness.[7]

Note must be taken of this account because Abraham is described as sitting at the door and running to meet his guests, whose appearance showed that they were not evil men and that they were in need of someone else's generosity. Let us also be generous in the same way, and let us open the door to poor brethren and receive them with a joyful countenance. If we are deceived now and then, well and good. In spite of this our good will is demonstrated to God, and the kind act which is lost on an evil and ungrateful person is not lost on Christ, in whose name we are generous. Hence just as we should not intentionally and knowingly support the idleness of slothful people, so, when we have been deceived, we should not give up this eagerness to do good to others.

Christ heals ten lepers, and He knew that only one would be grateful (Luke 17:11-19). This will also be our lot, and we should not on this account give up our eagerness to confer benefits on others.

Indeed, we should be generous not only toward the brethren and such as are exiled because of their confession but also toward those who are strangers in the state, provided that they are not manifestly evil, as, for example, if some Turk or Tartar were to come to us, not because of our doctrine, with which a stranger is not familiar, but as a beggar by nature, if I may use this expression. Even

---

[6] We have followed the conjectural emendation of the Weimar editors and read *otiosi* for *occisi*.

[7] Luther may well be reflecting his personal experience here. A contemporary account described the practice of hospitality in Luther's home as follows: "The home of Luther is occupied by a motley crowd of boys, students, girls, widows, old women, and youngsters. For this reason there is much disturbance in the place, and many regret it for the sake of the good man, the honorable father. If but the spirit of Doctor Luther lived in all of these, his house would offer you an agreeable, friendly quarter for a few days so that your Grace would be able to enjoy the hospitality of that man. But as the situation now stands and as circumstances exist in the household of Luther, I would not advise that your Grace stop there." Translated in E. G. Schwiebert, *Luther and His Times* (St. Louis, 1950), p. 597.

though he is not suffering because of the Word but is in distress in other respects, he should not be disregarded by us.

Nevertheless, this precept concerning hospitality pertains chiefly to those whom Christ (Matt. 25:40) calls "the least." For wherever the Word is, there Satan, the enemy, is stirring up physical and spiritual persecutions. In Paradise itself he was unable to rest until he drove Adam with his Eve into exile. Therefore we must be ready to give comfort to the brethren. Those who are afflicted by spiritual persecution should be comforted and strengthened with the Word; but those who are afflicted by physical persecution should be assisted with bread and water, that is, with love and hospitality, everyone according to his need.

This is what Abraham does here. He sees these three strangers. He does not know who they are; but he does know and see that they are poor and that they are tired from the journey. Therefore he quickly fetches water, washes the feet of the guests, orders a calf to be slaughtered, bread to be prepared, and drink to be fetched. But just as he unknowingly receives the Lord Himself in a hospitable manner, so we, too, when we show some kindness to the least in the kingdom of God, receive Christ Himself in a hospitable manner when He comes to us in the persons of His poor.

Why the place where Abraham is dwelling is called the Plain or Oak Wood of Mamre we stated above.[8] It has its name from its owner; for Mamre with his two brothers not only let Abraham have this place for a habitation; but he also allied himself with Abraham by a covenant, and it was without a doubt a saintly household which aided Abraham in the battle against the four kings.

Even though some call this place an oak wood and others a plain, it nevertheless seems more likely to me that it was a small grove or open wood, in the middle of which Abraham had a little hut. Hence he bids his guests sit down in the shade under an oak.

Nor is the description of the time without a purpose. It is stated that at that hour the sun was hot; that is, it was near noon. Those who are making a journey and have started out early begin to suffer from hunger and thirst at about that time, especially if they are poor. Therefore Abraham noted this time with special care, and he sat at the door with the intention of receiving hospitably anyone who happened to be on a journey and of refreshing a tired man.

[8] Cf. *Luther's Works*, 2, pp. 362—363.

Moses' additional statement that Abraham lifted up his eyes indicates that for some time he had been sitting in meditation. Perhaps he was thinking of the promise given to him, was praying, or was contending with some trial. But when he suddenly lifts up his eyes, behold, three seemingly pious and needy men are there. He runs to meet them, gives them an invitation, and treats them generously.

Therefore let us look upon Abraham not only as a father of faith and of believers because of his most extraordinary faith but also as a father of good works and as a most beautiful example of love, gentleness, kindness, and all virtues.

From Moses' words it appears that it was the custom of the patriarchs to sit at the entrance waiting for and receiving guests at the time of the noon and the evening meal, particularly at that time when Satan raged more cruelly against the godly, just as persecutions are sometimes harsher, sometimes milder.

If you place God and Satan in contrast with each other, the account will be much clearer. Satan hates teachers and hearers of the Word in the same way. In the first place, therefore, one must receive hospitably "those who are of the household of faith" (Gal. 6:10). For, as the apostles taught, this difference must always be observed: The first concern must be for the brethren, that is, for those who profess the same doctrine with us and for this reason suffer persecution. This virtue has a special name and is called "brotherly love." [9]

But it is not the brethren alone who experience misfortune, and Christ exhorts us with the example of the Heavenly Father to show kindness also to our enemies.

Thus in this passage praise is given chiefly to the hospitality we practice toward those strangers who are in exile because of the Word and their profession of the faith. These should not only be refreshed with bread and water in accord with Abraham's example, but they should also be treated with respect. For Moses thus describes Abraham that as soon as he sees the men approaching, he rises and joyfully runs to meet the guests. Then he bows down to the ground, as though he were about to worship God, and calls them אֲדֹנָי.

Surely the reverence with which Abraham treats the seemingly poor and distressed brethren, who appeared either as old men or

---

[9] The word appears in Greek in the original.

as youths — for Moses does not write in detail about this — is almost too great. How courteous, kind, and humble he is when he accosts them! Then how pleasantly he speaks! He implores, invites, and even importunes them to stay. It seems to him that he is all but in heaven; for guests like these have happened along, and he has been considered worthy of receiving them.

Abraham says: "If I have found favor in your eyes, do not pass by me." What else would he say, I ask, if they were bringing an immense amount of gold? But they are bringing nothing. They seem tired from the journey and have need of being refreshed, and Abraham does this so eagerly that he also asks them to remain as an act of the greatest kindness.

Thus this account is altogether without a parallel. A patriarch so great accosts the unknown guests with such reverence, falls to the ground, and receives them. He addresses them as אֲדֹנָי, namely, with a word that implies majesty. Then consider how he minimizes his possessions. He says: "Let a little water be brought" and "a morsel of bread." The courtesy he shows by not adorning his service with words is also very pleasing. For just as Sirach (Ecclus. 31:14) calls those who make kind deeds a matter of reproach "evil eyes," so it is by no means proper for you to praise and magnify your deeds. Such conceit makes the deed of kindness unwelcome.

Accordingly, this example of Abraham is altogether without any parallel. Therefore let him who wants to teach others about services to the brethren take an example from this. He will find far greater eloquence in these few words than it would be possible for him to imitate.

Moreover, the historical meaning shows that Abraham performed services of love toward the brethren and those who shared doctrine and faith with him. Christ, too, teaches us to do this when He says (John 13:20): "He who receives you receives Me; but he who receives Me receives Him who sent Me."

A great and wonderful statement indeed, provided that you ponder it carefully! Abraham did not have this promise so clearly. Yet how eagerly he invites the strangers, and how generously he treats them!

As I stated above,[10] Abraham learned this not only from the practice of his ancestors, who accustomed their people to show

[10] Cf. pp. 179 f.

hospitality — which the church needs most when the Word shines most brightly — but also from his own experience, because he encountered many troubles during his exile, and the services of pious people were most welcome to him. Thus from experience he learned this rule, that he who receives a brother who is in exile because of the Word receives God Himself in the person of such a brother.

Though Christ Himself has given us this rule, yes, though He has even promised that on the Last Day He will praise the deeds of kindness we have done for the poor (Matt. 25:31-46), we are nevertheless far more remiss and indifferent than the saintly fathers were.

Abraham thought that these three men had been driven from their homes because of their confession of the Word, and he saw that there would be no room for them in Sodom or in the neighboring places. Therefore he receives them and believes that in their persons he is receiving God, as his words prove, since he calls them אֲדֹנָי. His gesture proves the same thing, for he prostrates himself before them as though he were about to worship them. And he is not mistaken; he is receiving God Himself.

Therefore Abraham deserves to be held up to the churches as an example, in order that they may learn to receive the ministers of the Word as the Lord in heaven, as Paul says about the Galatians (Gal. 4:14) that they regarded him as an angel of God. Even though we do not have the custom of prostrating ourselves, yet we should prostrate ourselves in our hearts before brethren because of Christ, who dwells in them. For since He says (Matt. 25:40): "Whatever you have done to the least of Mine, this you have done to Me," He by that word establishes brotherhood between ourselves and Him.

But just as no one would hesitate to humble and prostrate himself before Christ if he saw Him, why would we not also prostrate ourselves before the brethren, at least in our hearts? Augustine has the excellent statement: "Mutually honor God in yourselves." [11] The Word of Christ does not lie. "You have done it to Me whatever you do to the least of Mine" (Matt. 25:35).

Therefore we justly complain about the unbelief of our hearts, which have become as hard as ice and are not softened by these most pleasing promises. Even though Abraham did not have so clear

---

[11] The exhortation of Augustine had become a familiar maxim: *Honorate Deum in vobis invicem.*

a word, he believed, as we see, that he was receiving God if he received these three guests. He had no doubt that they were human beings. Yet he had a loftier thought; for he had regard for the Lord, whom he is worshiping in the persons of these guests.

Even if they had been enemies, he would not have let them go but would have refreshed them first in accordance with love; but he would not have fallen down to the earth in accordance with brotherly love. For he knows that God dwells in the brethren and fellow believers, who are true temples of God, and not in the enemies of the faith or in those who have no knowledge of the true religion.

Nevertheless, I am not displeased with the opinion of those [12] who say that Abraham learned from instances that had happened both to him and to his ancestors, and that he experienced rather often that angels, coming in the form of human beings, enjoyed the hospitality of human beings, as we shall hear later about Lot in Sodom (Gen. 19:1 ff.). Because of this experience they treated all guests rather respectfully and hoped for occasions on which they themselves would associate with angels.

But even though this happened rather rarely, nevertheless, since they knew that one should honor God in the persons of the brethren, they considered themselves unworthy, so to speak, of giving lodging to weak, troubled, and poor brethren who were in exile because of the Word. For this reason they did so with such great joy and with such ready and willing hearts.

The world acts differently, for the King of Canaan did not receive Abraham in this manner. Far less did the people of Sodom do so in the case of Lot. Although there was a good king in Egypt, Abraham encountered a very great peril there because of Sarah; and we shall hear below in how friendly a manner the Philistines treated him. Thus the saints are not received in a kindly manner and treated generously anywhere except in the homes of Abraham and Lot, that is, in the church, which acknowledges that it is the servant of the servants of God [13] and — since God dwells in His saints — unworthy of so great an honor that it should give lodging to God in the persons of the brethren.

Because there are so many impostors and idle beggars today, I do

[12] Apparently drawn from Lyra *ad* Gen. 18:2.

[13] The papal title *servus servorum Dei* goes back to Gregory I (590—604) and came into common use about the time of Gregory VII (1073—85).

not know whether this physical reverence has to be shown; for "the whole world is in the power of the evil one" (1 John 5:19), and very many abuse the generosity of the godly.

Thus the foot washing has come down from the ancient fathers. It, too, is part of the reverence owed to guests.

This is the historical meaning of this passage and an outstanding praise of hospitality, in order that we may be sure that God Himself is in our home, is being fed at our house, is lying down and resting as often as some pious brother in exile because of the Gospel comes to us and is received hospitably by us. This is called brotherly love or Christian charity; it is greater than that general kindness which is extended even to strangers and enemies when they are in need of our aid.

Among our adversaries there is neither; for they hate us because of our confession, and for this reason they persecute, proscribe, and even kill us. Moreover, they have the utmost hatred for those who are their enemies in civil life. Therefore hospitality and brotherly love are found only among true Christians and in the church.

For the accounts of the friendships of the Gentiles, like those of Theseus and Hercules, of Pylades and Orestes,[14] are nothing in comparison with the brotherhood in the church; its bond is an association with God so close that the Son of God says that whatever is done to the least of His is done to Himself. Therefore their hearts go out without hypocrisy to the needs of their neighbor, and nothing is either so costly or so difficult that a Christian does not undertake it for the sake of the brethren.

But oh, what wretched and blind people we are! To us these facts are preached without fruit, for very few believe that they are true. But if anyone earnestly believed that he is receiving the Lord Himself when he receives a poor brother, there would be no need for such anxious, zealous, and solicitous exhortations to do works of love. Our coffers, storeroom, and compassion would be open at once for the benefit of the brethren. There would be no ill will, and together with godly Abraham we would run to meet the wretched people, invite them into our homes, and seize upon this honor and distinction ahead of others and say: "O Lord Jesus, come to me;

---

[14] Theseus aided Hercules in the latter's battles with the Amazons; and according to Pindar, *Pythian Odes*, 15, 35, Pylades, son of Strophis of Phocis, was a friend of Orestes.

enjoy my bread, wine, silver, and gold. How well it has been invested by me when I invest it in You!"

But because we do not do this, it is certain that we do not believe these facts. Hence we tell the story to deaf ears when we relate these examples of the patriarchs. But surely these examples have been recorded to put us to shame, and such stubborn unbelief will receive its punishment.

But what will those people answer on the Last Day — those people who even persecute the church, as the pope does? Nevertheless, the pope falsely declares that he is a servant of servants.[15] This title is appropriate for Abraham and for all who believe in Christ. If you want to call the pope by his true name, call him a tyrant and whatever is harsher and crueler than a tyrant. For he persecutes the church of God, drives faithful ministers from their stations, rages against them with sword and fire, and by no means receives them as brethren and friends. Hence he is like the people of Sodom and not like Abraham; and he deserves, not the land of Canaan, as Abraham does, but fire and brimstone from heaven and eternal flames.

Abraham nobly underrates his services. He says: "Let a little water be fetched. Meanwhile rest under this tree." The Hebrew verb is very graphic. It is הִשָּׁעֲנוּ, which means "recline," "lean on this tree as on a staff," the way those who are tired from a journey are wont to do.

Thus we read in Ps. 23:4: "Thy staff and Thy rod, they have comforted me." The psalmist calls the Word a staff; and if we lean on it when we are fatigued by perils and trials, we rest and receive strength.

It is also part of Abraham's underrating of his service that he does not say that he will set a table and get beds ready but bids them recline under the tree and promises them bread. This is an outstanding example and is described in such fitting words that unless you are a stone, you, too, wish that in this work of showing hospitality you could be like Abraham, whom we can call not so much a father of faith as a father of good works. Let this be enough about the account.

In addition to this, something must be said about the mystery of the Trinity; for the ungodly Jews laugh at us because our fathers wanted to prove the Trinity from this passage, inasmuch as three

---

[15] See p. 188, note 13.

men appear here, yet Abraham speaks with only one.[16] And it is indeed true that according to the historical meaning there is no other inference from this passage than that Abraham showed an admirable regard for afflicted brethren and received them generously, for he did not yet know that it was the Lord.

Since this is the historical meaning, they condemn us for making three Persons and one God in essence, and they boast that nothing of this sort is found either in Moses or in the prophets; for they think that he who wants to prove the Trinity from this passage is able to fashion from Scripture, as from wax, any shapes he pleases.[17]

Hence they regard this maxim as an undeniable proof, and on the basis of it they condemn our faith in its entirety. And, to tell the truth, if the Jews have read Cyprian or Hilary, they see that these men have cited many things with little aptness. But the saintly fathers wrote these things in a pious and godly spirit, and they were well aware that one should not deal with opponents in the same manner one deals with hearers who do not deny the foundations of the faith. For when you teach your own people, you are not beginning a war there but are providing training for war. You see, however, that in training it is not proper for us to use spears made of iron and swords that are sharp. No, then we use wooden sticks and swords fashioned of wood. In battle, however, iron is needed, and it must be firm and well sharpened for striking.

Thus when we argue against the enemies of the church, sound and strong arguments must be advanced; for if this is not done, the enemies not only laugh at us but are more strengthened in their error. Thus we have proved the Anabaptists and the Sacramentarians wrong, not only by proving our points with many sound reasons but also by taking note of the mistakes they make as the result of improper conclusions and quotations.

Therefore it is one thing to teach and another thing to exhort. Rhetoric, which is useful for exhorting, often plays games and often hands you a piece of wood which you suppose is a sword. But dialectic carries on war and busies itself with matters that are serious. Therefore it does not show the opponent pieces of wood; it shows iron. The fathers did not do this everywhere. Sometimes — for ex-

[16] This exegetical tradition is reflected, for example, in Augustine, *De Trinitate*, Book II, chs. 10—11.

[17] Luther usually phrased this simile to read that Scripture became a "waxen nose," which anyone could shape at will.

ample, among their own people — they made use of improper reasons to prove the doctrine of the Trinity, and sometimes their reasons were not strong enough. Consequently, the Jews adduce this maxim against us: "Since many passages are improperly cited by your teachers, this whole doctrine of yours is false." Now we do not deny that the antecedent is true, but in spite of this we give proof that the consequent is false.

So far as this passage is concerned, let us grant that its historical meaning is of no use against the Jews; but sometimes catachreses, too, are in place.[18] Thus after Paul has maintained the doctrine of faith dialectically and as though he were using a sword in battle, he then adds the allegory about Sarah and Hagar. Although this allegory is not forceful enough in battle — for it departs from the historical meaning — it nevertheless sheds light on the subject and adorns it.

The historical account does not teach that Abraham is God, that Sarah is the church, and that Hagar is the synagog. The historical account teaches that Abraham is the head of the household, that Sarah is the mother of the household, and that Hagar is the maid. But now that the foundation has been laid on the basis of other sure and clear passages of Scripture, what is there to prevent the additional use of an allegory, not only for the sake of adorning but also for the sake of teaching, in order that the subject may become clearer?

Thus Ishmael and Isaac, the natural sons of Abraham, denote two peoples: Ishmael, the people of the flesh; Isaac, the people of the Spirit or of the promise.

Therefore Augustine is right when he says that a figure proves nothing and should have no place in a disputation; for a disputation must lay sound foundations.[19] When these foundations have been laid, there is nothing to prevent clarifying and adorning the matter by means of an allegory or a figure.

Thus Augustine surely does not prove the Trinity from the fact that there are three powers in a human being. Nevertheless, it is a pleasing thought to look for signs of the Trinity both in the human being and in all the rest of the creatures and to take note of them.[20]

[18] On the meaning of "catachresis" cf. *Luther's Works*, 12, p. 346, note 16.

[19] Probably a reference to Augustine, *De doctrina Christiana*, Book III, chs. 5 ff.

[20] The outstanding discussion of the *vestigia Trinitatis* is in Books IX and following of Augustine's *De Trinitate*.

The Master of the Sentences, too, proceeds in the same way when he quotes the proposition that all things are based on weight, measure, and number, and when he states that a quantity has length, surface, and body; that in philosophy there is a single true something; that in the sun, there are substance, light, and heat.[21] Evidences of this sort do not convince the opponents of the Word, but for us they are welcome vestiges of a doctrine which has already been proved with certainty and is well known.

Thus we shall say to the Jews about this passage also: "Let them indeed laugh at us and at our teachers who have made use of this evidence; yet we have never said what they falsely accuse us of having said, namely, that those three men denote the three Persons of God."

Thus the papists, too, studiously distort our statements in order to enhance their own cause. When we declare that a man is not justified by works, they assert that we are forbidding and condemning good works. Such vipers are Cochlaeus, Witzel, and others.[22] These are satanic lies of venomous and very evil men who do not listen to our statements and do not want to listen. Yet they force them into having a different meaning — a meaning which they themselves want them to have.

Nowhere in the writings of the fathers will you find that Abraham regarded these three men as the three Persons of the Deity. Hence these are lies of venomous tongues that are like a sharp razor (cf. Ps. 52:2); and they speak nothing but rash words, which estrange and offend godly minds and cause them to fall. To be sure, the Jews hear in a physical sense; but since they are possessed by satanic malice, they do not listen to what we are saying, as Isaiah (6:10) prophesied concerning them.

The fathers did not speak so stupidly about the Trinity as to explain that these three men who were seen by Abraham with his physical eyes were regarded by him as the three Persons of the Deity.

At the baptism of Christ there are three distinct phenomena: Christ the human being, the voice of the Father from heaven, and the dove. But who will maintain for this reason that the humanity

---

[21] Cf. Peter Lombard, *Sententiae*, Book I, Dist. 3, *Patrologia, Series Latina*, CXCI, 529—530.

[22] A reference to two of his chief opponents: Johannes Cochlaeus (1479 to 1552) and a quondam Lutheran, Georg Witzel (1501—73). See also *Luther's Works*, 23, p. 212, note 12.

is the divinity, that this voice is the Father, or that this dove is the Holy Spirit?

It is correct to say that God is in Christ the human being, that the Holy Spirit is in the dove, and that the Father is in the voice. But we are not so stupid as to say that the outward phenomena or the physical object that is seen with the eyes and can be comprehended is God, for we know that the Trinity is invisible.

Therefore the fathers stated in different words and not in so stupid a manner why God wanted to reveal Himself to Abraham in three persons and not in four or in two, or why God chose to appear in just three persons.

Thus I have shown from the hidden meaning and not from the historical one that God is one and three, inasmuch as Abraham saw three and worshiped one. The saintly fathers expressed themselves in this manner, not as the venomous tongues of the Jews blaspheme; for God wanted to appear to Abraham in a trinity of angels. Inasmuch, then, as three appear and one speaks, and inasmuch as Abraham sees three and worships one, the fathers state that it is indicated that in God there is a trinity and not that those three forms or persons are the Trinity. But if there were no other proof of the Trinity than these three forms, I certainly would not believe in it. But we have other solid and sure foundations. Of these we shall speak elsewhere.

Against the venomous tongues let us, then, defend our teachers who say that Abraham saw the Trinity in a hidden sense, inasmuch as God appeared to him not in fewer or in more persons than three; for if he saw the day of Christ, as Christ clearly bears witness in the New Testament (John 8:56), he undoubtedly saw also His divine nature. But if he saw His divine nature, this could not have happened without a knowledge of the Trinity.

Hence the fathers were right in making use of this passage, for it is one thing to prove something and another thing to adorn it. Rhetorical arguments do not always give proof; but they provide strong adornment and contribute persuasiveness to those things which dialectics has proved.

After I know that we are justified by faith alone — for, like a dialectical argument, this has been abundantly proved and set forth in Holy Scripture — it pleases me very much that Augustine, Hilary, Cyril, and Ambrose say the same thing, even though they do not stress the foundations so much and at times express themselves less properly. I do not charge that this is an error on their part. It is enough for me that they say the same thing, even though they say it less properly; and I am strengthened by their testimony, in spite of the fact that it is more rhetorical than [23] dialectical.

Where the foundations have been properly laid, rhetorical statements, even though they are less sound, are nevertheless useful and pleasing. Nor are they fruitless. Concerning this testimony of the saintly fathers one must assuredly declare that they were right in stating that because God appeared in these three persons, Abraham had a knowledge of the Trinity from this appearance; for this argument is rhetorical and persuasive, yes, even profitable, after the foundations of the Trinity have been laid on the basis of other passages of Scripture.

So they said: Do as you have said.

6. *And Abraham hastened into the tent to Sarah and said: Make ready quickly three measures of fine meal, knead it, and make cakes.*

7. *And Abraham ran to the herd and took a calf, tender and good, and gave it to the servant, who hastened to prepare it.*

8. *Then he took curds, and milk, and the calf which he had prepared, and set it before them; and he stood by them under the tree while they ate.*

This is a description, not of a royal banquet but of one that is truly divine. And if one were a dialectician or a rhetorician, there would be rich material with which to occupy oneself. Nor must these words be glanced at indifferently, since it is certain that these events are not recorded by the Holy Spirit without a purpose; they are recorded for our sakes.

After Abraham realizes that these three guests want to stay, he joyfully hastens into the tent and prepares a banquet. For he is sure that in these three guests he is receiving God Himself. It is faith, therefore, that makes him so eager and ready.

Since we do not have this faith, we are not at all like Abraham,

[23] The Weimar edition, as well as earlier editions, have *et* here; we have conjectured the reading *quam* and have translated accordingly.

and we are very slow in performing these services of love. But if we were convinced by an unquestioning conscience that when we receive some brother or someone exiled because of the Word or otherwise in distress, we are receiving God Himself and that on the Last Day we shall have the Son of God Himself to bear witness to the service, we, too, would surely rejoice over the arrival of guests and would not think that we were being burdened.

But that physical appearance is a hindrance to us; and our physical eyes do not see the invisible yet truly present Guest. We must have inner eyes or faith. Since in Abraham this faith is most fervent, he makes haste for great joy and does not walk slowly. He delights in the opportunity given him to deserve well of brethren, and he does not make use of the service of his servants; but he himself starts to run and selects a calf. Furthermore, he orders to make haste and bake cakes.

All these details are recorded by Moses for the purpose of stressing that glorious faith of Abraham, whose undoubting conscience persuaded him that he had the God of heaven and earth as a guest. Not indeed that he recognized God as he recognized Him later on, but he is sure that God is coming to him in his brethren. This faith makes him so eager, ready, and zealous, so to speak, to do the good work.

The fact that we are slow to do these services and are either displeased or grumble when brethren arrive — these are signs of a faith which, if not altogether dead, is nevertheless asleep and very lazy.

Therefore these examples must be put before the churches and carefully impressed, lest we pay the penalties of ingratitude, as happened under the papacy, where we disregarded these sacred accounts and were occupied with the lies of the monks. But what are Antony, Francis, and Dominic in comparison with this patriarch, whose heart glows with faith like a fiery furnace? For this reason Abraham is so ready to do all services.

Above Abraham had said that he would fetch a little bread; now he brings out three measures of choice flour, not of that which the domestics used for inferior or ordinary bread. This is Moses' rhetoric. In this way he bestows praise on the love or hospitality of Abraham, or rather on his faith, by using grand and very splendid words. For this is what shines in these services.

I do not know what the content of the measure was. But it is certain that the Jews had small measures, for they were an exceedingly thrifty people.

Abraham computes the measures of flour on the basis of the number of his guests, and thus by his very action he now magnifies his kindness, which he had not extolled with words but had previously minimized. Generous people are in the habit of doing this, but the boastful do the opposite, for their words are bigger than their deed, since they exaggerate their kind of actions with high-sounding words and thereby render unwelcome their services, which by nature are welcome. Moreover, there is no doubt that Solomon has drawn maxims from the account of Abraham and has included them in his Proverbs.

It seems that bread baked in the ashes was a more delicate bread, such as among us either rolls or cakes which we serve at banquets. In the Hebrew it is called עֻגוֹת. The psalmist made use of this word in Ps. 35:16: לַעֲגֵי מָעוֹג, "mockers of bread baked under ashes," that is, flatterers who ridicule the godly because this is advantageous to them among the powerful by whom they are invited and sumptuously fed. Paul calls them brutes of the belly (cf. Rom. 16:18), such as are today the canons who do not teach, pray, or work in the church but merely consume finer bread and drink sweeter wine.

Hence the noun עוֹג denotes a baker, and in the books of Moses (Num. 21:35; Deut. 29:6) it is the name of the King of Bashan, that is, of fatness, because he dwelt in a fertile place and had most delicate bread. Thus Abraham wanted to treat his guests rather sumptuously when he gave orders to make bread from finer flour by the coals. But he himself hastens to the herds and selects a tender and fat calf.

What accounts for that profusion of words in Moses? Elsewhere, even in important matters, he is very sparing of words. In this manner he no doubt wants to commend to us the example of the saintly patriarch, in order that we, too, may glow with zeal for good works and, as Paul says (Rom. 12:10), may vie among ourselves in good works and try to outdo one another in services and welldoing toward poor and exiled brethren, in whom God Himself comes to us and seeks hospitality among us.

For this reason Moses says that Abraham himself runs to the herd and does not assign this task to a servant. He does not fetch a sickly or defective sheep. No, he fetches a very tender and well-fattened calf. Consequently, it is apparent that he was not an ungenerous or niggardly host; for niggardly people are disturbed by the arrival of guests and commonly set before them what they themselves loathe and is cheapest.

But Abraham does the opposite and arranges a sumptuous banquet, for he is convinced that in these three guests he has shown hospitality to God. To be sure, these facts are recorded only once by Moses, but there is no doubt that Abraham made a daily practice [24] of looking for guests in this manner at noon and of receiving them. For how would he, who firmly believes that God Himself is present in a brother who is in exile and has suffered persecution because of the Word, not display the utmost generosity toward guests?

Therefore you should keep in mind this host who is so occupied with pleasing unknown guests. What would he not do for acquaintances and friends? He addresses the unknown men courteously, and he begs them as though they would be doing a great favor if they stayed and enjoyed his hospitality. He promises a morsel of bread, but he brings out the most delicate flour and has cakes baked that are fit for a feast. To the bread he adds a fattened calf, to the calf butter and milk; and he does not sit down at the table, as was fitting for the head of a household. No, he stands near by like a waiter; and if somewhere anything should be lacking for the convenience of the guests, he is eager to set it right speedily.

From what source does this host get such zeal, attentiveness, and obliging good will toward unknown guests, whom he does not receive in the hope of gain or profit, as innkeepers [25] are in the habit of doing, but feeds free of charge? No doubt it is because he thinks that he is serving God while he is serving his needy neighbor.

Moses wants us to take careful note of this faith of Abraham and also to imitate it, not only toward those whose debtors we are, namely, parents, teachers, and magistrates, but also toward all fellow believers or brethren. But because few have this faith of Abraham and few believe that parents, teachers, and magistrates have been given us by God and have been ordained by Him, the services also are rather indifferent or almost nonexistent.

Thus Abraham's example deserves to be set before us by Moses as a mirror in which true services and virtues of every kind are clearly seen, especially, however, that extraordinary faith which is shown by

[24] Here the original has *solitum,* which supports the emendation made on p. 181, note 3.

[25] A reference to the Greek inns set aside for strangers who have no ξένος.

the fact that in these guests he recognizes, reveres, and worships God. This faith is the chief thing, but the flesh hampers it in us in various ways. Like an intervening wall, it obstructs our eyes and prevents us from recognizing God in our brethren, as Abraham did, and from worshiping Him so dutifully.

The place of the feast is a tree, and Jerome writes that it was a terebinth and that it continued in existence up to the time of Constantine.[26] If you prize the foolish pomp of the world, you do not see here an embroidered tapestry; nor do you see gold and silver goblets, as at the courts of kings. But what are these in comparison with the fact that God and angels are present?

We, too, could have such guests every day if our unbelief did not stand in the way. Therefore these events are recorded for our shame and reproach, because we do not do the same thing in faith and do not conclude that as often as we show hospitality to exiled brethren and to those who are in distress because of their confession, the Son of God Himself and His angels — not flesh and blood — are lodging with us.

If we had the faith that Abraham had, every tree and every hut, however small, would become a heaven and would excel all the palaces of all kings. Nor would the pomp, the gold, the silver, and the royal splendor be anything at all in comparison with the adornments of this poor abode in which God and His angels sit down as table companions.

But, as I have often said, because our hearts do not believe, we are so slow and reluctant in regard to these kindnesses and without any mutual regard among ourselves. We run about like swine and are forgetful of Paul's admonition: "Mutually honoring one another" (cf. Rom. 12:10 and Phil. 2:3) and of that of Augustine: "Brethren, honor God in yourselves."[27] For if he who has been baptized is a member of Christ, does not he who receives a baptized person receive Christ? But, as I have often said, our unbelieving flesh prevents us from seeing this glory and from deriving pleasure from it. Nevertheless, these examples are set before us for the purpose of counteracting this surliness of our nature and to incite our hearts to be hospitable and to perform other services.

[26] Cf. Jerome, *De situ et nominibus locorum Hebraicorum, Patrologia, Series Latina*, XXIII, 971.

[27] See p. 187, note 11.

9. They said to him: Where is Sarah your wife? And he said: She is in the tent.

After Moses has finished the description of the feast, than which the sun has never seen anything more sumptuous — for the table companions are God Himself with His angels — he appends the conversation or discourse that took place at the feast. He does so in order that this description may lack nothing and in order that it may become known to the entire world that this feast was not like one partaken of by monks upon whom silence is imposed.[28]

Nothing is more irksome and more senseless than a feast at which silence reigns; for discourses are the real condiments of foods [29] if, as Paul says (Col. 4:6), they are seasoned with salt. For word is whetted by word; and not only is the belly fed with food, but the heart is also fed with doctrine, since godly conversations refresh the hearts, arouse faith, kindle love, and instruct in many ways. Away, therefore, with the silly and silent monks who suppose that worship and saintliness consist in silence!

Sarah seems to have had some doubt concerning the promise that was given above in chapter seventeen, namely, that she herself would be the mother of the Promised Seed. Therefore the Lord calls her in order that He, in person, may strengthen her in faith. For it is the perpetual work of God to instruct, enlighten, and strengthen weak hearts through His Spirit, not to condemn them or to cast them aside because of their weakness.

Accordingly, God asks where Sarah is, and Abraham gives the short answer: "She is in the tent." An indifferent heart reads this and pays no attention to it; but by means of these few words the Holy Spirit wanted to set before all women an example to imitate, so that, just as Abraham is presented everywhere as a rule, so to speak, of faith and of good works, so Sarah might give instruction about the highest virtues of a saintly and praiseworthy housewife.

For the weakness or inborn levity of this sex is well known. Women are commonly in the habit of gadding and inquiring about everything with disgraceful curiosity. Or they stand idle at the door and look either for something to see or for fresh rumors. For this

---

[28] The monastic *Rule* of St. Benedict, ch. 38, had prescribed: "Complete silence shall be kept during meals. There shall be no whispering; no one is to say anything except the reader."

[29] The saying *sermones condimenta ciborum* is proverbial.

reason Proverbs (7:11) states about wicked women that they have "feet that do not tarry." This is due to their curiosity to see and hear things which nevertheless do not concern them at all. Therefore levity in morals as well as garrulousness and curiosity are censured in this sex.

In the case of Sarah, however, the opposite virtues are given praise in this passage, and this by means of Abraham's brief statement that she is in the tent. If she had been inquisitive after the fashion of other women, she would have rushed to the door, would have seen the guests, would have listened to their conversations, would have interrupted them, etc.; but she does none of these things. She busies herself with her own tasks, which the household demands, and is unconcerned about the other things.

Thus Paul prescribes (Titus 2:5) that a woman should be οἰκουρός, a domestic, so to speak, one who stays in her own home and looks after her own affairs. The heathen depicted Venus as standing on a tortoise; for just as a tortoise carries its house with it wherever it creeps, so a wife should be concerned with the affairs of her own home and not go too far away from it.[30] This is demanded not only by the tasks peculiar to this sex but also by the requirements of the children and of the domestics, who need careful supervision.

Hence it is great praise for Sarah that on this occasion she tends to her own affairs and does not offend by being curious but, like a tortoise, remains in her little shell and does not take the time required to get a brief look at the guests she has and at what kind of guests they are.

This modesty or restraint surpasses all the acts of worship and all the works of all the nuns, and these words, "Sarah is in the tent," should be inscribed on the veils of all matrons; for in this way they would be reminded of their duty to beware of inquisitiveness, gadding, and garrulousness, and to accustom themselves to managing the household with care. With this brief statement Moses has described all the virtues of a good housewife, one who gladly stays at home and takes care of the management of the household, in order that the things which her husband provides may be properly allotted and administered.

Our opponents, the papists, boast of their great and wonderful

---

[30] Perhaps a reference to the sacred tortoises on Mt. Parthenion, which were, however, sacred to Pan rather than to Aphrodite.

works; but they laugh at us when we bestow praise on such activities in the household and in civil life, for they regard these as insignificant and ordinary. But to fast on certain days, to dress in a particular color, to abstain from eating meat, to undertake pilgrimages to distant places, etc. — these things they extol with full cheeks, and for them they promise heaven and supreme blessedness.

But even though the papists are undeserving of our replies to their nonsense and their absurdities, it is useful for us to understand and appraise those domestic and civil works properly. Hospitality is a domestic and civic work; but it must certainly be preferred to all the works of the hermits, yes, even to the fasting of St. John the Baptist, even though he undertook this as a result of God's directive or order.

And this modesty or restraint of Sarah is a work that has to do with the home. What virgin or widow could be compared to her? But this union of male and female bothers the little saints so much that they not only do not believe that this kind of life is saintly but even think that it stands in the way of saintly religious exercises. It was for this reason that the pope imposed celibacy on his people. Furthermore, this kind of life is too [31] ordinary and common among all people; therefore it is devoid of all show and is especially looked down upon by those who want to be the saintliest.

Yet their eyes should have been fixed on Him who instituted the state and the household. If the popes did this, they surely would have a loftier opinion about both functions. "God created them male and female," and "He blessed them" (Gen. 1:27). You are not going to suppose, are you, that these are insignificant matters?

But if you consider the final cause, namely, that through marriage a church is brought into existence for God and that a hideous disease of the flesh is healed and the road is blocked to sin, lest it ensnare us, surely these facts also bestow grand praise on marriage.

Therefore let us maintain that those works in the household and in the state which the papists despise as ordinary and worthless are most excellent and also most pleasing to God. For, to mention hospitality, what work is there, I ask, among all acts of worship of the popes that can be compared to it?

It seems to be something insignificant to give a cup of cold water

---

[31] We have followed the suggestion of the Weimar editors and read *nimis* instead of the *minus* in the original.

to a thirsty person. But listen to Christ. What grand praise He bestows on this, and what rewards He promises (Matt. 10:42)!

But we shall reach the same conclusion about the other works in the household. If faithful parents bring up their children properly and accustom them to a godly conduct, and if through strict dicipline they keep the domestics at their duty, these are ordinary works, I admit, without any outward show and without any reputation for saintliness; but the verdict should have been reached on the basis of the Word, not on the basis of reason.

It would not have been difficult for Abraham to fast on certain days, something which he no doubt did; but Moses records nothing about his fasting, for he wanted to record his true virtues, not such works as hypocrites can and usually do imitate.

But the papists do not deserve a more extensive answer from us. Therefore let us give thanks to God that we, having been taught by the Word, know what are truly good works, namely, to obey our superiors, to honor our parents, to manage our domestics, and to render the ordinary services which the need of the brethren demands, etc. For we see that these works were so highly esteemed by Moses, by the prophets, by Christ Himself, and by the apostles that they were not ashamed to preach about them often and to prescribe them.

They saw what snares reason ties for itself. Entangled in these snares, it cannot arrive at a knowledge of the true forms of worship; for, because of their outward appearance, the works or the traditions of men are always wont to lead men away from true works and exercises of godliness.

Look at a monk. He shuns obedience to all authorities, even to parents. He does not bring up children, does not work, and is beneficent to no one; but he is filled with hatred and ill will toward his own people and grows fat on the sweat of the poor. Yet he takes pride in his vow of poverty.

But Abraham, the godly head of the household, is truly poor. For he obeys when God calls him into exile. Nowhere does he have a fixed place. Although God blessed him, he nevertheless looks among the unbelieving heathen for attacks, violence, and rapine at any hour. Sarah, his companion, willingly follows her husband into exile, looks after the domestics and the home, is obliging toward the neighbors, and is obedient to her husband.

These are the highest virtues. There is nothing like them in all human traditions. Learn, therefore, to regard them highly and, since they are ordinances of God, to prefer them to human traditions, however grand and showy. For these corrupt faith and the ordinances of God. Like innkeepers, they mix wine with water.

Therefore let us take note of this example. Sarah is praised for diligently performing her duty in her home. For if a mistress of the household desires to please and serve God, she should not, as is the custom in the papacy, run here and there to the churches, fast, count prayers, etc. No, she should take care of the domestics, bring up and teach the children, do her work in the kitchen, and the like. If she does these things in faith in the Son of God and hopes to please God for Christ's sake, she is saintly and blessed.

"What therefore God has joined together," says Christ (Matt. 19:6), "let no man put asunder." Therefore separation or celibacy, such as exists in the papacy, is not of God. On the contrary, the services which that divine union demands are holy and truly good works, no matter how insignificant and ordinary they are considered so far as outward appearance is concerned.

Where there is true obedience toward God in faith, there whatever the calling demands is holy and a worship pleasing to God. But if some prefer either widowhood or virginity and are able to forego marriage without sinning, let them do it, yet in such a way that they do not for this reason condemn domestic economy and the state. For these are kinds of life that have been ordained and instituted by God.

Let the monks and nuns glory in their works. For a husband let it be enough if he rules his house properly; for a wife let it be enough if she takes care of the children by feeding them, washing them, and putting them to sleep, if she is obedient to her husband and diligently takes care of the household affairs. These works far surpass those of all nuns. Nevertheless, nuns are exceedingly proud of what they do.

For from human traditions this bane results, that hearts become complacent and take their sanctity for granted. But a godly mistress of the household is not proud; for she is vexed and humbled in various ways when countless annoyances are put in her way by the domestics, by her husband, by the children, by the neighbors, etc. Thus opportunities are nowhere lacking for the practice both of faith and of prayer. But let this be enough about the example of Sarah, and let us go on to what follows.

10. *And He said: I shall surely return to you according to the time of life, and lo, your wife Sarah will have a son.*

This is the subject of the discourse or conversation at the feast. It is both very serious and very pleasant. But God by no means broke off after saying so little. Moses, however, mentions only the main points of the conversation. He has not covered it in its entirety. The evangelists follow a similar procedure. For what Christ says at the Last Supper — "I am going to the Father, and I send you the Comforter" (cf. John 16:5-7) — this He undoubtedly set forth in an eloquent and long sermon.

In the same way Abraham's guests thanked him for having fed them so generously and, since they intend to repay him they promise to return and that, when they return, Sarah will give birth to a son, to Isaac. Could anything greater, more joyful, or more welcome than this have happened to this couple?

The phrase כָּעֵת חַיָּה, "according to the time of life," has troubled nearly all interpreters. The Hebrews understand it in the sense that it promises Abraham and Sarah a fixed time of life, so that the meaning is: "When I return, both of you will still be living." [32] But if this is the meaning, it is nothing but a tautology and useless repetition. When God says (Gen. 1:28): "Be fruitful and multiply," life is taken for granted. Thus when he says: "Sarah will have a son," He at the same time promises Sarah a fixed time of life. Similarly, a dead Abraham will not beget children. But because procreation is promised to him, at the same time, by incontrovertible logic, life is promised to him.

Others think that the expression must be referred to the promised son rather than to the parents, so that the meaning is: "I shall return immediately after the time of life," that is, after as long a time as is required for an infant to live on earth. This is a better and more appropriate meaning if you think it over.

For the meaning is: "I say that a son will be born from Sarah in such a manner that he is her natural son, born as offspring is born from any young woman, lest anyone suspect that he had to be created from the mass of Sarah's flesh without a natural union. She will conceive from her husband, and for the natural and usual period of time she will carry the fetus in her womb. Consequently, he will be a true son."

[32] Luther had this information from Lyra *ad* Gen. 18:10.

Adam was created from earth, but he cannot for this reason be called a son of the earth; for it is one thing to be created from earth and another to be born from the earth. Similarly, even though Eve was created from Adam's rib, she nevertheless cannot be called a daughter of the rib. And if God were to make a human being from wood, the wood cannot be called the father of the human being.

Thus if God had created Isaac from the aged Sarah in a miraculous manner, Isaac would not have been a son according to the time of life. Therefore, when God says: "I shall return according to the time of life," it is the same as if He said: "In accordance with the manner in which an infant always receives life in the womb and is born, so Isaac, too, will receive life and be born."

Physicians say that the fetus begins to live and stir in the fifth month after conception and that during the remaining five months it matures for birth. The same thing, says the Lord, will happen to Isaac. And thus He eliminates an unusual and miraculous birth, such as the effete Sarah could have had in mind.

In order that the normal course of nature might be preserved, the Virgin Mary carried Christ in this manner up to the tenth month; and during the entire time He, like other embryos, received nourishment from the drops of blood of His mother, who was sanctified by the Holy Spirit.[33]

So far as the time is concerned, the statement under consideration can be understood to mean that the expectation of a miracle is excluded and that people will be convinced that Isaac is Sarah's true son, born to Abraham and Sarah in the normal manner of human procreation. For this reason the Letter to the Hebrews says (11:11) that it was through faith that Sarah obtained the power to conceive. This is said in order that you may understand that Abraham made her pregnant in accordance with the usual course of nature. She did not become pregnant by a miracle, as the Virgin Mary did. When the Holy Spirit overshadowed the Virgin Mary, she, too, conceived in her womb, but from her own seed, not from the seed of a man.

In our translation into German we have referred this phrase neither to the life of the child nor to that of the parents; there we

---

[33] Here, as elsewhere, Luther follows an earlier tradition, according to which Christ was preserved from the taint of original sin not only by His virginal conception but by a special sanctifying grace of the Holy Spirit between the moment of conception and the moment of birth.

have referred it to the angel who was speaking.³⁴ For inasmuch as the angels make use of these human characteristics — take on a body, speak, walk, sit, and eat — they are also in the habit of speaking in the manner of human beings. Therefore "according to the time of life" is the same as if one said: "If I am alive." For we are in the habit of speaking about the future in such a manner that we add: "If God grants life" or "If it is God's will."

Moreover, this example helps us to learn to speak reverently about God. Now the reader is free to follow whatever opinion he chooses, but to me the middle one appears most appropriate. But a great obstacle is put in our way by the fact that after the Hebrew language fell into disuse, its tropes and figures cannot be fully understood. Therefore the forbearing reader will pardon us to this extent.

And Sarah was listening at the tent door behind him.

11. *Now Abraham and Sarah were old, advanced in age; it had ceased to be with Sarah after the manner of women.*

12. *So Sarah laughed to herself, saying: After I have grown old, and my husband is old, shall I have pleasure?*

The table appears to have been so placed that the tent was behind the guests, and it was not closed by means of doors, as is customary among us, but was open. Sarah could easily overhear what was being said, since she was standing at the opening and was waiting to see whether her husband Abraham had any orders to give. Furthermore, the text states that she laughed when God predicted that a son would be born to her. For she could not believe that this would happen. This was not only because of a feeling of shame but also because of what follows, "They were both old, advanced in age"; that is, they had almost come to the end of their days; they were in their declining years.³⁵ They were already near death. Therefore Sarah did not believe; she laughed.

It had also ceased to be with Sarah after the manner of women. Young men do not understand this. Nevertheless, one should learn that God put seed for propagation into men and women — more into

---

³⁴ Luther and his colleagues on the "Biblical commission" had, in fact, struggled over the exact meaning of this phrase; the rendition of it in the various editions of Luther's Bible fluctuated considerably.

³⁵ The German expression is *Es war mit jnen auff die neige kommen.*

one, less into another; stronger into one, weaker into another. For procreation takes place by no other means than through insemination, since the woman has her own seed, and the male has his own seed. But from experience it is known that women who do not have menses are barren. When it was happening to Sarah after the manner of women, she was able to conceive. But when this had ceased to happen to her, she said: "Behold, God has closed my womb," and she handed Hagar over to her husband, lest the promise be hindered. The thought of this now stands in the way of her faith, with the result that she does not believe that she will give birth. But because of these most distinguished and grateful guests this sin of hers is venial. When Zacharias (Luke 1:18-22) does not believe the angel, he is punished with speechlessness for a definite time; but to Sarah nothing of this kind happens since the Lord overlooks her weakness.

But the very fact that it is recorded that Sarah laughed within herself is also proof of her extraordinary continence and chastity. You will find cadaverous old women who are more lascivious than young women. Sarah was not that kind. As long as hope of offspring remained, she had intercourse with her husband and waited for the blessing of the Lord; but after her age had put an end to this hope, she refrained from intercourse with her husband and looked for offspring from Hagar. This chastity is by no means an insignificant virtue when, on the contrary, the admirers of virginity and the celibates burn and are polluted day and night. But Sarah's chastity is without any show and without any glory before the world, for it is covered and concealed by a common cover because she is a married woman. This cover deceives the celibates. As a result they are unable to see such extraordinary chastity and cannot believe that what she says is true: "Shall I continue to have pleasure or delight?" But these are also words of extraordinary chasteness and shamefacedness. The Jews think and speak highly only about circumcision; but these examples were worthy to be set before all mistresses of households, since they were noted down by the Holy Spirit with a definite plan.

Nor should one overlook the fact that concerning her husband Sarah says most modestly and in a respectful manner that he has become old. She calls him lord, not man or husband. With these words she also praises the continence of her husband and lets it be known that she has respect for him.

St. Peter bestows extraordinary praise upon this passage in his list of duties (1 Peter 3:6), where he admonishes pious mistresses of households to be godly and respectable; for Sarah is a glorious example not of one or the other virtue but of all. She is described as carefully looking after her house and not running to and fro inquisitively and picking up new gossip about the neighbors. She diligently takes care of the household and lives chastely with her husband and not only considers him her husband but also honors and respects him as her lord.

If the mistress of a household does these things, what fault will a reasonable husband be able to find in her? But alas, few concern themselves with this; they are arrogant, proud, quarrelsome, abusive, rebellious, and puffed up by their supposed wisdom. Therefore they want to be regarded as rulers, not as wives.

But how far these women are removed from the example of Sarah! Peter justly praises her, makes a more proper application of this passage, and has a better understanding of it than all the rabbis, who pass over these words superficially, as though they were useless and unprofitable.

But Peter wants these words to be an example and like a mirror, in which all saintly and elect women who themselves also hope in God and please their husbands as Sarah did may look. Peter does not enumerate strange works like those of the nuns, who dress in a peculiar fashion and withdraw from the ordinary hardships and perils of this life. "Honor your husbands," he says (1 Peter 3:6), "as Sarah did. She calls her husband lord with the utmost respect." Accordingly, it is the true praise of a housewife that she hopes in God and respects her husband. No words can praise these virtues as they deserve.

But why does Peter add the statement about the hope in the Lord? Moses makes no mention of this here. Surely this hope shone throughout Sarah's entire life in various ways like a most brilliant star, for consider what the calling of Abraham involved. He is commanded to forsake his native country, and he wanders about in the land of Canaan like a beggar without a fixed dwelling place or home. One year he and his people tarry among the Gentiles at one place, another year they tarry somewhere else. Amid these great difficulties the chaste Sarah not only follows her husband but also respects him as a lord. You might find that another woman, displeased with her hardships and perils, would either compel her husband to pick out a fixed home or would leave him. But Sarah holds fast to her hope in God and obeys His word. Although hardships confront her in the course of so extended a migration, she nevertheless overcomes them through her confident hope in the help of God. Therefore she deserves to be held up to all housewives as an example. For here you observe no frivolity, and you hear no coarse jesting; everything is dignified, everything is proper, and everything is regulated in accordance with the norm of the Word.

These facts should be carefully noted and kept in mind because of the fanatical teachers, who not only teach works and forms of worship that are not required but even give preference to them over the works which God commands. You have never heard any papist either praise or admire accounts like this one. It has been the common saying of all that in this Book of Genesis nothing is recorded except the sexual relations of the Jews.[36] But do they not have pigs' eyes that blindly pass over the greatest virtues and are engrossed solely in the passion of lust?

Thus they reveal what sort of hearts they have. They revel in ease and abundance, and for this reason they cannot be otherwise than insane with lust. Yet they do not cease to praise celibacy, which is filthy and polluted in various ways. But virtues of this kind, which the Spirit wanted to praise with His own pen, they disregard or even disparage, just as matrimony was brought into ill repute and disparaged under the papacy in a variety of ways.

Therefore young people should be diligently reminded of these virtues of the home; and if some have the gift of continence and are able to live chastely without marriage, let them by all means have the benefit of continence and do without a wife. But let them be on their guard as against the worst poison lest because of their continence they either prefer themselves to those who are married or condemn them. For marriage was divinely instituted, and the life of married people, if they are in the faith, deserves to be rated higher than those who are famous through miracles.

This is the constant and unanimous judgment of Scripture. For apart from his faith you hear nothing about Abraham except that he is sitting in the tent and assists and receives strangers; then he tends to his own affairs.

[36] See p. 42, note 1.

Similarly, Sarah cooks, makes butter and cheese, feeds the cattle, etc. I agree that these are tasks of servants and maids. Yet they are presented by the Holy Spirit as an example.

But if the papists despise these works and choose for themselves other extravagant, difficult, and arduous performances of good works, let them take delight in their folly, and let them regard the duties of the household as filth. But let us maintain that if faith is joined to those menial works, they are regarded as more precious than all gold and as more excellent than any celibacy without faith.

Surely the Holy Spirit depicts the saintly mistress Sarah with these colors to make it clear that even though she is married, she surpasses virgins in chastity. Therefore it is a great sin for the papists to inveigh against the marriages of the patriarchs, which are most honorable workshops not only of chastity but of all other virtues. These facts should be carefully noted in order to shatter the opinions of the fanatics.

13. *The Lord said to Abraham: Why did Sarah laugh, and say: Shall I indeed bear a child, now that I am old?*

14. *Is anything too hard for the Lord? At the appointed time I will return to you, in the spring, and Sarah shall have a son.*

The Holy Spirit brings up these matters in order to strengthen the faith of this saintly and chaste matron; for inasmuch as she is hampered by the thoughts of her flesh, she does not yet believe, nor is she able to hope that she will have a son from her aged husband. She is satisfied to be the mother of an adopted son, but she is altogether dead so far as the hope of conceiving and bearing a child is concerned.

Therefore it is necessary for Sarah to hear a word by which she, as though brought back to life, may rise again to the hope of fruitfulness; for the word is truly a voice that raises from death. But it is death for Sarah to think that she is a corpse. This thought is corrected by the word, and the corpse, as though recalled from death, begins to live again. Thus all this takes place for the purpose of arousing faith.

But I have stated repeatedly above that in Sarah there is an outstanding example of extraordinary patience, because she was able to bear such a long exile and most willingly went along with her husband; likewise, that when she was barren, she was able to bear it that her husband lay with a maid. Because she sustains herself in these hardships by hope, she hears an unbelievable word, by which her heart is illumined and inflamed, so to speak, by a new light; and because of the countless troubles she has overcome in hope and patience her weakness is pardoned.

Sarah was now eighty-nine years old, and during so many years she had been hoping for the blessing of the Lord. When she sees that her hope is futile, she submits everything to God. Yet she does not utterly despair. For this reason the Lord puts up with her weakness and is not offended by her laughter, which has its origin in her thinking about something that is impossible. For what further hope could there be for a barren and exhausted woman? Therefore the Lord brings her to faith with a very friendly reproof.

Furthermore, I stated above that not only Sarah but also Abraham himself supposed that these guests of his were foreigners and that he had no thought either of angels or of prophets. Therefore when they promise a child, Sarah thought: "Who would be telling them this? They are not speaking from the heart; they want to ingratiate themselves, because they suppose that women hear such things with pleasure."

These were Sarah's thoughts when she laughed. But after she has heard Him who sees and has before Him all things, new thoughts arise in her; for she notices that these are not ordinary men, but that they are men full of the Holy Spirit, who sees the secrets of the hearts and reveals them.

Therefore this is a cheerful and very friendly reproof. From it Sarah concluded that these were men of God and prophets, because they are aware of her laughter and her thoughts even though she is not in their presence. After Sarah has been so earnestly reminded of God's power, namely, that nothing is either extraordinary or, as Luke (1:37) puts it, impossible with Him, she can no longer regard lightly the prophecy about the son who is to be born. For here her thoughts are held captive and come to an end when she hears that the event is miraculous and altogether impossible before the world yet not miraculous but very easy, yes, even common, ordinary, and an everyday occurrence for God if similar works of His are considered.

I am very fond of these powerful arguments. With one blow, so to speak, they refute every objection it is possible to present. But

I am not fond of those rhetorical arguments which we see the ignorant papists using. For example, when they discuss the Eucharist, they declare that the church has the power to make regulations about such things and to say that the laity should receive the Sacrament in only one kind.[37] Such reasons are puny and feeble. As Paul says, they evince "a morbid craving for controversy and for disputes about words" (1 Tim. 6:4).

But those axioms which overwhelm an opponent with one assault and shut off his breath, so to speak, when he tries to make many statements are powerful and instruct those who are really well informed, as when I say to a papist: "You babbler, why do you mention the dangers and inconveniences in case the cup is given to the laity too? Look at the text regarding the Lord's Supper, and listen to Christ, who instituted the Supper." Like a battering ram, this one argument demolishes whatever reasons the papists can advance concerning this matter.

Therefore it is not enough to be a rhetorician. A rhetorician must be a dialectician in order to pass judgment on recognized truths or axioms (for this is the name given to sound, sure, and true statements) and on what is worthless.[38] When this rock of a sure and sound axiom stands, it is proper later on to make those familiar rhetorical additions, such as what is easy, difficult, convenient, inconvenient, honorable, disgraceful, etc.

All the discussions of the papists move within the limits of what is allowable, what is expedient, and what is proper. From these they construct not only dangerous but even blasphemous propositions about the authority of the church, namely, that it is above the Word, etc. But as for you, apply the axiom that Christ is the Head of the church, and whatever the opponents have built up with great effort will immediately collapse.

One should look for axioms even in matters of morals. When the well-known Censorinus — in the sixth chapter of the first book of Gellius — tries to persuade the young men to marry, he does not urge those commonplace and familiar arguments. No, he looks higher than this and says: "If we were able to live without wives, we would

---

[37] During this time Luther was reflecting on the problem of the authority of the church to alter divine ordinances — an issue that was sure to be central to any "free and general council" that might be called to deal with the Reformation.

[38] Here the original has the Greek word εἰκαῖα; a cognate appears in Gal. 3:4.

spare ourselves great trouble." He admits that the life of married people is full of troubles, hardships, and various and countless dangers; but he cuts all this short with the axiom which declares: "We cannot do without women." [39]

All other reasons are puny and weak. Only the one which states that we cannot do without marriage is sound; it is the only one that appeals to an open-minded hearer. For how will states exist if there are no marriages? Human beings are needed for the defense of married people and children, and they are not born of wood or of stone; they are born of women.

But we must make use of such sound and sure reasons especially in theological matters. Your heart is assailed by unbelief, and you doubt that you can be saved; for you know that you are a sinner. In this situation a godly brother who will really comfort you will not make use of the popish and worthless arguments that you should seek relief for your conscience in this or that work; but he will place the Word of God before you. He will say: "God is truthful; He promises to be gracious to you for His Son's sake. Moreover, the Son of God has absolved you from all your sins by His Word, has baptized you, and has promised you eternal life if you believe, that is, if you conclude that His death is your redemption. Hence either God is truthful in His Word, or you are a liar when you have doubts about the forgiveness of your sins after these promises have been given to you through the Son of God." By means of this axiom doubt is dispelled.

Moreover, we must be well fortified against our adversary Satan, for he is a very shrewd debater and a very good rhetorician. He exaggerates your sins, magnifies God's wrath beyond measure, and adduces countless instances of God's wrath, even in the case of those who had the right faith in the beginning and eventually fell. Unless you confront him with the true axiom that the Son of God died for sinners and that those who believe in Him will live the life which He Himself is living, all other reasons that can either be mentioned or thought of are rhetorical, weak, and puny. But this is the axiom and recognized truth (Rom. 3:4): "God is truthful, but every human being is a liar."

Therefore call upon God, take hold of His Word, and cling to the sacrificial victim Christ, who has rendered satisfaction for your

---

[39] Gellius, *Noctes Atticae*, I, 6.

sins and has transferred your death to Himself and overcome it; and do not let it bother you that you are a sinner. Consider God's command. He wants you to cling to His Son and tells you to believe. Direct your eyes to this, and do not inquire into what has been done or will be done about others; but think about yourself, so that you may comply with this command.

These thoughts refresh and strengthen a sick heart. Those popish commands about alms, about buying Masses and calling upon the saints are sophistic reasons and worthless arguments. He who relies on them is deceived.

I once heard the jurist Dr. Henning debate about an important case with a learned, eloquent, and keen opponent.[40] When his opponent had cited a great mass of laws and had strengthened his case as best he could, Henning chided him in a moderate and friendly manner and said that he was at liberty to adduce whole volumes of laws. "But," he added, "even if you were able to fly across mountains and walk on the bottom of waters, nevertheless, if you want to deal with me about the case in point, you must come down to this matter." And he pointed out what the scope of the matter was, and by this single statement he curbed the eloquent and learned man and, as it were, floored him.

But — to compare great things with those that are small, and divine things with those that are human — Sarah, too, is likewise so affected by a powerful argument that she can turn nowhere. To be sure, she thinks: "I am a barren old woman, and it is altogether impossible for me at this very advanced age to bear a child." But this thought is not so firmly fixed that it is not driven out by this thunderbolt: "What is miraculous or impossible with God? For [41] He who created man of dust from the ground, could He not produce natural offspring from the seed of the male and the female?" Thus these words are spoken to strengthen Sarah's faith, in order that she may hear, realize, and know that these guests of hers are not merely human beings but are men of God and prophets in whom the Spirit of God dwells. This Sarah had not known until now.

In conclusion, the angel repeats the words about the time of life, the words which were explained above.[42] This is not a purposeless

---

[40] On Henning Goede see *Luther's Works*, 13, p. 158, note 21.

[41] We have followed the Erlangen edition and read *enim* rather than *eum*.

[42] Cf. p. 205.

tautology, as the unlearned think. No, it serves to confirm the promise and the faith of the hearers, and it is just as if you heard two witnesses giving testimony about one thing.

15. *But Sarah denied, saying: I did not laugh. For she was afraid. He said: No, but you did laugh.*

When Sarah recognizes the prophet of God from the fact that he knew the secrets of the heart, she no longer laughs but is thoroughly frightened; and the saintly mother adds a little sin and says that she did not laugh, even though she had laughed. But this sin itself is pardonable, because she fears God, obeys the prophets, and is subject to her husband. It is fear of Abraham, her master, that causes her to be thoroughly frightened and to deny that she has laughed. Furthermore, she is now sincerely sorry that she had received the words of God's prophet with laughter. She is sorry because of fear, and in this fear she commits another sin. But she is seriously refuted with only a few words: "No, but you did laugh." It is as if the prophet were saying: "First you sin by laughing; now you sin by lying."

Concerning domestic and civil works I have repeatedly stated that young people must be carefully habituated to take note of the works that have been commanded by God and to distinguish them to the utmost from self-appointed or human works.[43] For unless this is done — and most carefully at that — the distinction between good and evil is not only eliminated, but we shall cherish things that are most harmful and are truly an abomination before God as the things that are holiest.

Ahaz sacrifices his son to an idol (2 Kings 16:3) and, though he is a most infamous murderer, considers himself like Abraham in saintliness. For inasmuch as he gives no consideration to the Word and command of God, which alone is the true and eternal criterion of works, he accepts death as life and deadly poison as helpful medicine.

Therefore shut out from your heart and eyes the outward appearance, and see what God has commanded; do this, and you will not go wrong, even if in outward appearance it is small, ordinary, and insignificant. Antony withdraws into the desert, and Jerome makes a pilgrimage to sacred places and advocates devotion to chastity.[44]

[43] So, for example, *Luther's Works*, 23, pp. 357—360.

[44] On Antony cf. p. 217, note 46; Luther is referring to Jerome's stay at Bethlehem.

These works the world regards as great. But the fact that Sarah stands at the hearth and busily prepares food for the guests — this not only has no outward appearance of a good work but seems to stand in the way of good works. Yet to one who has regard for the Word it will be evident that Sarah did a holier work than all the hermits did.

This life is profitably divided into three orders: (1) life in the home; (2) life in the state; (3) life in the church.[45] To whatever order you belong — whether you are a husband, an officer of the state, or a teacher of the church — look about you, and see whether you have done full justice to your calling and there is no need of asking to be pardoned for negligence, dissatisfaction, or impatience. But if you have conducted your affairs in such a manner that there is no need of saying: "Forgive us our trespasses," then by all means go out into the desert, and occupy yourself with those showy and difficult works.

Thus the entire error of the papists lies in the fact that they consider the ordinary duties of this life which are commanded in the Decalog easy for them to perform perfectly. Therefore they ascend from the Decalog to their schemes, as though they were going up to a higher level. They praise the anchorites; but Abraham, who sits at the door and waits for guests — him they do not regard as worth mentioning or being held up as one to imitate.

Thus it is not enough for the papists if one has been baptized in the name of the Father and of the Son and of the Holy Spirit; they think that something more perfect and, if I may say so, closer to heaven should be attempted. For this reason they hide in monasteries, read Masses, etc. But how do these things agree with Scripture? Was not the hermit Antony called back to Alexandria to a tanner in order that he might learn what place he would occupy in heaven?[46] If this is fiction, I have nothing against it, provided that the papists admit that it originated in their church and was preached and believed there. But however this may be, it is certain that this baptized tanner was just as pleasing to God when he did his work in faith as Antony was when he tormented himself and prayed.

To bring this account to a close, I have considered it necessary

---

[45] See, among many other places, *Luther's Works*, 2, p. 83.

[46] The source of this story is the *Vitae patrum*, Book III, ch. 130, *Patrologia, Series Latina*, LXXIII, 785.

to add these things in order that young people may learn to shun self-chosen works and may devote themselves with the utmost zeal to those tasks which their calling brings with it and demands. For these works have been commanded by God, and for this reason they are truly divine works, whether you are a pupil and learn letters, a maid and sweep the house with brooms, or a servant and tend horses or do other things. A monk, of course, leads a more burdensome life and wears more sordid garments; but that he serves God — this he will nevermore be able to say truthfully, as can those who serve the household, the state, or the church.

16. *Then the men set out from there, and they looked toward Sodom; and Abraham went with them to set them on their way.*

We have heard a most delightful account. Angels were sent to Abraham, and the promise was made to him anew — without any roundabout or indirect talk — that he would have a son from his wife Sarah. Abraham received them generously, and Sarah, too, was brought to faith, with the result that she believed that she would become a mother. To the description of God's inexpressible friendliness toward Abraham there is now added a greater indication of God's kindness, in order that we may learn how pleasing a service and sacrifice to God it is to hear the Word and to receive it with reverence. For, as we see in this passage, God draws near to such people not as a Judge and Lord but as a Friend and Guest at table. But the sad and horrible account which follows shows God's attitude toward those who despise the Word.

Here Moses calls the angels three men, for it was the opinion of Sarah and Abraham that they were prophets of God driven into exile because of the Word. Moreover, in order to show his reverence for the Word, Abraham not only entertains these guests sumptuously and generously; but after he has entertained them, he accompanies them because of his love of the Word and his fear of God, and escorts them to the road which leads to Sodom.

But these things are also set before us as an example, in order that we may learn to revere the prophets of God or ministers of the Word and to honor them with services of every kind. But how the world does this and what punishments follow this ingratitude we have long since come to know in these wretched times. And the end is not yet.

17. *The Lord said: Shall I hide from Abraham what I am about to do,*

18. *seeing that Abraham shall become a great and mighty nation, and all the nations of the earth shall bless themselves by him?*

The passages must be compared. Before this Moses has said that three men arose; but here he says that the Lord, יְהֹוָה, spoke. He calls them three men in accordance with Abraham's understanding; for Abraham supposed that they were men, but men of God and holy. He did not think that they were angels. But Moses employs a way of speaking that is common in Scripture and says that God spoke. For the angels who were sent by God did not bring their own word; they brought the Word of God.

I have replied above to the scoffing of the Jews, who ridicule our people because they make use of this evidence to prove the doctrine of the Trinity.[47]

We are not so foolish or unlearned as to say that these three men are God the Father, God the Son, and God the Holy Spirit in Their essence, just as we do not maintain that the humanity of Christ is God in His essence. It is enough for us to have said that these three men signified the Deity which Abraham recognized and believed; for enlightened by the Holy Spirit and full of faith, he saw the day of Christ (John 8:56). But just as Abraham believed the Trinity, so this is represented to him outwardly in the appearance of the three men. Of course, these three men are not the three Persons of the Deity; they are signs or an appearance of the Deity in the Trinity, although so far Abraham is of the opinion that they are saintly men who are in exile because of their profession of the true religion.

But even though Abraham does not know that they are angels, he nevertheless has the conviction that in these three, among whom one was speaking while the rest were in accord, he was hearing God, who is one in His essence and trine in Persons. This is my opinion about this passage. Let him who is so inclined treat it with greater subtlety, provided that he does not do violence to it; for these matters must be given sober consideration.

In the first place, I follow the authority of Scripture, which says that God is speaking when either angels or saintly men speak as a result either of the command or of the revelation of God. In the

---

[47] Cf. pp. 190 f.

second place, I hold that the testimony of the Letter to the Hebrews should not be disregarded. It states clearly that "some have entertained angels unawares" (13:2). Nor does the fact that Abraham bestows divine honors on them present any difficulty, for he recognizes God in them and listens to their words just as though God Himself were speaking. He is following the general rule that one should not consider who is speaking but what he is saying; for if it is the Word of God, how would God Himself not be present?

Thus God is present in Baptism, in the Lord's Supper, and in the use of the Keys because His own Word is present there. Therefore even though we do not see or hear Him but see and hear the minister, God Himself is nevertheless truly present, baptizes, and absolves. And in the Lord's Supper He is present in such an extraordinary way that the Son of God Himself gives us His body with the bread and His blood with the wine.

The words which the Lord prefixes as a sort of preface — "Shall I hide from Abraham what I am about to do?" — carry with them a delightful indication of His extraordinary good will. Moreover, there was need of these words in order to strengthen Abraham; otherwise the announcement of the divine wrath would have overwhelmed him. The repetition of the promise concerning the Seed and the blessing of all the nations of the earth pertains to the same thing. For if Abraham had not heard this promise from God first, he would have cast away the hope of offspring as well as of his own salvation in so horrible a display.

Therefore it is an extraordinary proof of God's benevolence when the Lord declares that He cannot conceal anything from Abraham. In accordance with the usage of Scripture, Moses states that it was God who spoke these words even though the angel spoke them. In their sermons the prophets, too, speak in the same manner. They say: "This is what the Lord says." But another reason is added.

19. *No, for I have chosen him, that he may charge his children and his household after him to keep the way of the Lord by doing righteousness and justice; so that the Lord may bring to Abraham what He has promised him.*

God did not want to bring this awful judgment upon the five cities without first revealing the entire matter to Abraham. This is something worthy of the greatest admiration. When examples of cities destroyed by fire, earthquakes, or other causes are found in the books of the heathen, we observe what wise men conclude about such examples. Nearly all are assigned to natural causes, and reason is not in the habit of rising any higher. But the destruction of the five cities by fire is revealed to Abraham in this passage in order that you may understand that this extraordinary disaster was a punishment inflicted by an angry God because of the sins of the people.

So much importance is attached to this knowledge that the Lord wants this report spread abroad among the descendants and made known forever as an example for others, in order that they may learn to fear God and to shun the kind of sins that were the cause of such a great evil. Similarly, the Lord also wants the examples of His mercy, such as the deliverance at the Red Sea, made known; for there is need of such reminders in this life.

The godly who are burdened with a cross and in various ways are hard pressed and sigh have need of promises in order to be buoyed up by them. On the other hand, those who are callous, obdurate, and smug should be frightened by the examples of wrath, to the end that, as is stated in this passage, they may learn to fear God.

Furthermore, our hearts are inclined by nature to object to reproval. We all receive promises with joy and are not annoyed by them; but the preaching of the Law frightens men and almost drives them to fury. It is for this reason that the prophets were killed, not because they preached the blessings promised to Abraham but because they condemned evil ways and idolatry, and asked the people to return to sobriety and the fear of God.

Similarly, the world does not hate us for teaching the Gospel and the benefits of Christ in pure form. All accept this and approve of it, unless they are manifestly ungodly. But the mischief results from our attachment of a comparison with the doctrine of our opponents, from our statement that the pope is the Antichrist, and from our disapproval of the teachings and the wicked deeds of the adherents of the pope.

Thus Christ says (John 7:7): "The world hates Me because I testify of it that its works are evil." But this wrath and displeasure of the world should not bother preachers at all. For in this passage you hear God's command that such awful judgments of God should be impressed especially on those whose hearts are still weak and inclined to sin.

God says: "Abraham will command these things to his children"; that is, in the church of the saints accounts of this kind must be made known and be preserved, just as in 1 Cor. 10 St. Paul mentions the punishments that were inflicted on the people before they entered the land of Canaan and adds that these things happened to them as types and should be an example for us, as though he meant to say: "In this manner God punished the sins of that people; but the example concerns us, in order that we may learn to shun similar sins." And in Rom. 15:4 Paul states: "The things that were written were written for our instruction."

Grace and the remission of sins must indeed be preached, but to those whose hearts are blameless and whose consciences are troubled. But to those who are smug and have altogether discarded the fear of God God's blows and wrath must be presented in order that they may be warned by the example of others and cease to sin. For this is what is meant by saying that everything was written for our instruction.

Therefore those who, influenced by I know not what reasons, maintain that the Law should not be preached in the church are pernicious teachers.[48] Would you actually not teach the Law where there is a real people of the Law, namely, the greedy, the proud, adulterers, usurers, idolaters, etc.? Would you use the promises of the New Testament to increase the smugness of those who were smug before? Indeed, God wants the destruction of Sodom by fire and that lake of asphalt to be conspicuous to this day and to be spoken of in sermons and made known among all posterity, in order that at least some may be reformed and may learn to fear God.

St. Paul (2 Tim. 2:15) gives better instruction about rightly dividing the Word; for just as all foods do not agree alike with all bodies, so there is the one kind of doctrine by which the weak, the fainthearted, the bruised, and the penitent must be buoyed up, and another by which the obdurate, the callous, the smug, and the shamefully wicked must be called back to the right way. In Isaiah (61:1) the Son of God says: "The Spirit of the Lord is upon Me; He has sent Me to preach to the humble, in order that I may heal those who have a contrite heart."

But the pope and the bishops do not have a heart of this kind; they persecute the Word and seek to destroy our churches. Should

---

[48] Cf. *Luther's Works*, 22, p. 39, note 36.

the Gospel be preached to these too — the Gospel which tells them that they have a God who has been appeased by Christ? This will make them more obdurate, and they will sin with greater smugness. Therefore they must be crushed with the hammer of the Law. To such people one must show the lightning and thunder of Sinai.

On the other hand, let those who are struggling with death and are troubled by other perils hear (Ps. 27:14): "Let your heart be comforted. Be of good courage; wait for the Lord"; (Ps. 91:7): "If a thousand fall at your right, evil will not come near to you. I am with him in trouble"; and (Matt. 11:28): "Come unto Me. I shall refresh you." This is medicine for thankful hearts that are not like those hard crags and adamantine rocks which require a hammer.

Ezekiel (34:3-4) is right when he says that the prophets who frighten the heart of a righteous person with lies commit sin, for these are the smoking flax that should be tended and not altogether extinguished. And they sin in the other direction too, because they strengthen the hands of the wicked and do not rather accuse and condemn them.

Today you may encounter many who are offended by the necessary preaching of the Law and shun it, for they maintain that their consciences are burdened when they hear that sort of thing. But are they not fine Christians? They do not give up sinning; they are addicted to greed, to wrath, to lust, to reveling, etc. When they hear these sins censured, they are offended and do not want their consciences burdened. Shall we for this reason let everyone do what he pleases and declare him blessed? Not at all; for you hear that the destruction of Sodom by fire is to be set before all succeeding generations and indeed before the very church of God, in order that men may learn to fear God.

In the doctrine of the antinomians there was this statement: "If somebody were an adulterer, provided only that he believed, he would have a gracious God." [49] But what kind of church will it be, I ask, in which so awful a statement is heard? A distinction is necessary, and it should be taught that adulterers or sinners are of two kinds: some who become aware of their adultery or sin to such an extent that they shudder with their whole heart and begin to

[49] This quotation is contained in a catalog of citations from the antinomians condemned in the *Theses of the Disputations against the Antinomians* (W, XXXIX-1, 344).

repent earnestly, and not only feel sorry for what they have done but also sincerely desire and endeavor never again to commit anything like it. These are not smug in their sin; they are thoroughly frightened, and they dread God's wrath. If they take hold of the Word of the Gospel and trust in the mercy of God for Christ's sake, they are saved and have forgiveness of sins through faith in Christ.

Even though the others, whether adulterers or sinners, are unable to excuse their sin, they nevertheless feel no sorrow about it. On the contrary, they are glad that they have achieved their desire. They look for opportunities to commit sins and smugly indulge in them. Because these people do not have the Holy Spirit, they cannot believe; and he who preaches to such people about faith deceives them.

This sickness demands a different medicine, namely, that you say with Paul: "God will judge the adulterous" (Heb. 13:4); "They will not see the kingdom of God" (cf. 1 Cor. 6:9-10); and "Without chastity no one can please God" (Rom. 8:8). Hence they are defiled and under the wrath of God.

Such sledges are needed to crush these rocks. Abraham does not indulge in sins, but long before this he was truly humbled in spirit. Therefore the Lord comforts him, for He takes pleasure in a smoking flax. Therefore He tends its carefully, in order that it may burst into flames.

But the people of Sodom are like crags and very hard rocks. In their case brimstone, lightning from heaven, and thunder are needed. Those foolish and lying prophets who maintain that the Law should not be taught in the church and that, in general, no one should be rebuked too severely or burdened in his conscience are not aware of this.

If this is true, however, why does the Lord want the example of Sodom preserved in His very church and taught by Abraham? Moreover, in view of the fact that He adds "in order that they may fear the Lord," do not those who want only the promises to be taught exclude the doctrine of the fear of the Lord entirely from the church? Hence the fanatical spirits who confound the entire system of heavenly doctrine in a pernicious manner must be shunned.

But this doctrine of the Law is profitable not only for teaching the fear of the Lord; but, as the Lord adds, it also produces this fruit, that those who are frightened in this way by the judgment and wrath of God practice justice and discernment.

If you divide all Scripture, it contains two topics: promises and threats or benefits and punishments. And, as Bernard states, hearts that are neither softened by kindnesses nor improved by blows are properly called hard.[50] Thus the works of God are also twofold. Works of mercy are those which Paul mentions in Acts 14:17: "He gives rain from heaven, fruitfulness," etc. He does works of wrath when He also sends a plague, war, and famine in order to frighten and humble the obdurate. Thus in Christ salvation is promised to all who are baptized and believe. On the other hand, judgment and eternal death are threatened to those who do not believe in Christ.

In these circumstances how can or should the preaching of the Law be excluded from the church? Do you not at the same time exclude the fear of God and the majority of the works of God? God certainly does not perform these in order that they may remain hidden, but He wants us to see them and in this way to be led to fear Him. If there were no perils of fire and water, no sudden death and similar evils, I myself would surely not say anything about them and would speak only of God's kindness and of His benefits. But experience teaches otherwise.

Hence to declare that the Law should not be taught in the church is characteristic of men who do not know Christ and are blinded by their pride and wickedness. Previously Moses has set forth many examples of God's graciousness: when God promised Abraham the Blessed Seed, when He honored him with an outstanding victory, and when He came to him as a guest and ate bread at his home. These events are related by Moses, and nothing else is added to them; but in this passage there is added the command to preach: "He will relate them," says God, "to his children"; that is: "I want the destruction of Sodom by fire preached in the church." What is the reason for this? Because the church is never altogether pure; the greater part is always wicked, as the parable of the seed teaches (Matt. 13:3 ff). In fact, the true saints themselves, who are righteous through faith in the Son of God, have the sinful flesh, which must be mortified by constant chastening, as Paul says (1 Cor. 11:31): "If we would judge ourselves, we would not be chastened by the Lord." Therefore keep this passage in mind. It is adequate by itself to refute the antinomians.

[50] Cf. Bernard of Clairvaux, *De consideratione,* Book I, ch. 2, *Patrologia, Series Latina,* CLXXXII, 730—731.

20. *Then the Lord said: Because the outcry against Sodom and Gomorrah is great and their sin is very grave,*

21. *I will go down to see whether they have done altogether according to the outcry which has come to Me; and if not, I will know.*

The situation is altogether awful. Fifteen years had not yet gone by since the people of Sodom and their neighbors were defeated by the four kings and led away captive but were later freed by Abraham through a marvelous victory and were returned to their homes. Thus God revealed Himself to them in a twofold manner. By the captivity He showed that He hates sin and surely wants to punish it, but by the deliverance He showed that He wants to forgive and help the penitent. But neither the punishment nor the benefit had any effect. The very people who had seen these events with their own eyes forgot and relapsed into the awful abyss of sins, since they had completely discarded their fears of God.

This is surely an astonishing situation and a remarkable picture of human hearts, which in their nature are so corrupted by sin that they can neither be improved by threats nor moved by kindnesses. When they returned to their homes from captivity, they no doubt gave thanks to the God of Abraham who set them free. But this piety was of short duration; gradually they slipped back into smugness and indulged their desires, until eventually, as happens when there is great abundance, everyone did without any shame what he wanted and was utterly beyond reform. For here, too, applies the statement in the writings of the natural philosophers that when motion approaches its end, it has its greatest force.[51]

They not only forgot the disaster and the marvelous deliverance and not only had no respect for the Word, the household, and the government; but they became even worse than beasts. This is an awful example, that a land which was freed through such great miracles degenerates so disgracefully and bestially within fourteen years.

Abraham's kind deed was completely lost sight of, and they imagined that they were delivered, not by his valor but by their own good fortune. Moreover, they even spoke irreverently of the doctrine of Abraham and Lot, because it was against their lusts; and with these sins they combined the presumption of wisdom and pride.

---

[51] This is perhaps a reference to Aristotle, *Physics*, Book V, ch. 6, or some similar passage.

This was the beginning of their downfall, as Solomon says (Prov. 16:18): "The beginning of one's downfall is to be proud and fall away from the Lord." Where there is contempt for the Word and ingratitude toward God, there order also and good manners break down. These fruits result only from the seed of the Word of God. After the downfall of the church came the downfall of the government.

When the fear of the Lord had been discarded, conjugal faithfulness vanished. Not satisfied with their own wives, they desired others but made prostitutes of their own, until they finally engaged in practices which are contrary to nature and more than bestial. This is Satan's procedure after he has turned people away from God and has made them ungrateful toward Him.

Among ourselves, alas, the beginnings of such evils are overmuch in evidence. Look at the evangelicals in the cities. Consider the morals of the officers of the state and of the nobles, then of the burghers and the peasants. Should they not all alike give thanks to God day and night that they have been delivered from the iron furnace of the pope and from that most wretched darkness of ignorance? Yet this is not done. Nowhere is there sacrifice of praise and gratitude. On the contrary, all exert themselves for the sole purpose of accumulating wealth and oppressing others through deception, frauds, and wrongs. They do so in order that they themselves may become rich. Must not the administration of the household eventually collapse because of this conduct? When this happens, universal [52] ruin necessarily follows.

But we shall begin the discussion of this account somewhat farther back because of the less learned; for even though the heart dreads such an awful display of wrath, these examples of divine wrath must nevertheless be impressed well, because the world is full of Pharaonic and pharisaical doctrine.

From the beginning of the Book of Genesis we have seen that two generations of human beings are being dealt with:[53] the one of the righteous, which was the true church; the other of the unrighteous, which has always been the school of Satan (Rev. 2:9), in which human beings are not only trained for sins against the Second Table — so that they commit murders, adulteries, etc. — but also speak irrever-

---

[52] We have followed the Erlangen edition and added the word "universal" here.

[53] Cf. *Luther the Expositor*, pp. 95—97.

ently of the Word and persecute and kill the godly. Eventually, however, God always intervened as Judge and brought about an evil end of the wicked.

The same thing happened in this instance. Abraham's house is the true church; for even if other patriarchs were living at that time, nevertheless by the divine Word the church had been attached to Abraham's house, descendants, and line.

Accordingly, if you draw a comparison between the house of Abraham and the people of Sodom, you will find everything most pleasant and friendly in the house of Abraham — to such an extent that the very angels of God seem to jest jovially with Sarah when she laughs and denies that she has laughed. Consequently the Word of God is continually heard there, and Abraham's home is nothing else than a kingdom of the forgiveness of sins and of grace, yes, a very heaven in which dwell the angels of God, whom he receives reverently. In them he worships God, whom He knows and believes in as One in Three. In short, in Abraham's home there is nothing but grace and life.

On the other hand, in the generation of the wicked among the people of Sodom one finds nothing but awful threats. Angels do not come to them; but when they do come, they are not only not received with any reverence but are treated most outrageously, and the ungodly people do not grant them food or a place to stay. On the contrary, they attempt to inflict on them the most shameful disgrace that can happen to a male. Therefore it is clear that they sinned not so much from lust as from malice.

Thus when the men who were besieged in Jabesh Gilead declared that they were ready to come to an agreement (1 Sam. 11:2), Nahash, the king of the Ammonites, refused to make a covenant with them unless he had plucked out an eye from each one. He did not have in mind any gain or pleasure, but he simply wanted to satisfy his malice. Men are for the most part induced to sin for the sake of either some pleasure or advantage. In so hideous a display, however, there was no pleasure or advantage; here there was the utmost malice.

Thus the Jews killed Christ out of pure malice. Similarly, an ungodly soldier does many things solely for the sake of contumely and to increase annoyances and grief, not to enrich himself. For **what advantage does he derive from cutting off the legs of cattle,** from breaking down the doors of houses, and from setting villages on fire? These sins are acts of malice and in its extreme form at that.

Therefore it is the endeavor of the generation of the wicked to hate the saints. Nor is it satisfied if it maltreats them in various ways, but its utmost delight is to subject them to abuse. This is shocking malice and deserves such a judgment. But it is astonishing that in so short a time this people was corrupted to such an extent that there remained not ten men who feared God and preserved some discipline.

It is recorded (Gen. 6:15) that before the Flood God saw that the malice on earth was great. But here Moses says that God heard the outcry, and this appears to be something more serious. Both figures, however, are intended to depict the smugness of the people; for they lived as though God did not see or hear, yes, even as though He did not exist, as the psalm (14:1) has it: "The fool says in his heart: 'There is no God.'"

But the godly also experience this trial, yet in a different manner, inasmuch as they sometimes suppose that God is sleeping and does not hear or see. Though this has happened since the beginning of the world, it happens much more now in this madness and extreme old age of the world. What awful blasphemies the Turkish kingdom and the papacy are! Yet for nearly 800 years the Lord has been keeping silence; and both the Turk and the pope flourish, strengthen their wealth and power, and in every respect live as though there were no hereafter and no God.

Blessed was the age in which Christ lived, for then He not only heard and saw but was actually present, as John says (1 John 1:1): "which our hands touched." Now, however, we cry from afar and think that we are crying to Him who does not hear but is sound asleep. Meanwhile the devil and the pope make progress and arbitrarily throw everything into confusion, sects arise, etc.

Hence this is stated in human fashion, in accordance with Scripture's usual way of speaking; for what Moses reports about God in this passage was the case in the thoughts and unbelief of the people. For God does not sleep, since a spirit is free from such proclivities. But people who sin in a smug manner think that He is sleeping. Indeed, they dream that they are also being regarded and heard by God. Thus the Turk, puffed up by his good fortune, believes that he is the people of God. He believes that there is no wrath of God and supposes that hell has been destroyed and judgment done away with; for so it seems in effect.

Hence there are passages in the Scriptures like this: "O God, be not silent to me" (Ps. 28:1). For the godly, who are struggling under the flesh and are near desperation because God puts off hearing them, think that God is sleeping, is unable to speak, etc. This is the sentiment of faith or of the spirit in the godly. But we have stated this at greater length above in the sixth chapter.[54] At this point it is sufficient to have pointed out that Scripture accommodates its way of speaking to human custom, not because God has undergone this change, but because this is the way it takes place in the hearts of the godly. Thus Abraham, Lot, and the other patriarchs heard and were aware of this outcry and concluded that God was angry and was making haste to inflict punishment on the incorrigible people.

Moreover, in this passage one must not disregard the moral teaching for the benefit of officers of the state and those who preside as judges. Above, in the eleventh chapter, when the tower was being built at Babel, the Lord said (Gen. 11:7): "I shall go down and see." Hence the Divine Majesty teaches that verdicts should not be reached in haste; nor should only one side be heard, but there should be a full investigation of a case. For if Scripture says of God, who knows all things and from whom nothing is hidden, that He came down, how much more we human beings stand in need of this endeavor, we who are influenced by emotions, prevailed upon by the remarks of friends, deceived by flattery, etc.!

At this point there are debates about the sins that cry to heaven. Some put their number at four, others at five.[55] Even though this was done without good reason, I nevertheless do not condemn the effort of godly men. But if we want to speak properly, the outcry in Scripture does not denote those four or five sins but refers in a general way to all sins with which impenitence and malice are connected. Such is the case in Is. 5:7: "I waited for them to do justice, and behold, a cry"; that is, they sin shamelessly, and there is no one who punishes; nor is there any redress with the officers of the state or judges, and nothing remains but an outcry. Everybody raises a hue and cry over the disgrace.

Hence where there is still some fear of God, there the officers of

---

[54] A reference to *Luther's Works*, 2, pp. 43—50.
[55] Apparently a reference to Lyra *ad* Gen. 18:21.

the state do their duty and proceed against malefactors. The result is that men do not cry out but thank God and the officers of the state that they are safe with their wives, children, and possessions, and are not subjected to the wantonness of anyone you please. On the other hand, where the Word is not, where the officers of the state neglect their duty and no discipline is maintained in the households, where the parents are treated disrespectfully by their children, the master by the domestics, etc., there the outcry must necessarily follow.

Similarly, greed and usury are excessive today. The officers of the state wink at these sins and do not punish them as they should. Then what happens? Do not those cry out who suffer wrong and see that the officers of the state do nothing to protect them? Peter (2 Peter 2:14) calls such people "insatiable for sin," namely, such as do not want to be restrained and, after they have been admonished, proceed to sin with greater madness and thus heap sin upon sin, after the example of Pharaoh, who carried on so much the more like a madman the more Aaron and Moses preached to him.

The holy fathers saw this; and when they beheld such great malice, they were deeply troubled in their heart. For it is easier to die than to behold the exceedingly great and unrestrained malice of the world. Therefore in these men was fulfilled what the text says: "The outcry against Sodom is great." Nevertheless, Abraham was not influenced by this outcry and by the gravity of such great sins; but he is averse to it and makes himself the intermediary for these very wicked people when he intercedes for them, as we shall hear. Just as his faith has thus far been praised, so now his love toward his enemies will be praised; for there is no greater love than to intercede with God for bloodthirsty enemies.

22. *So the men turned from there and went toward Sodom, but Abraham still stood before the Lord.*

23. *Then Abraham drew near and said: Wilt Thou indeed destroy the righteous with the wicked?*

24. *Suppose there are fifty righteous within the city; wilt Thou then destroy the place and not spare it for the fifty righteous who are in it?*

25. *Far be it from Thee to do such a thing, to slay the righteous with the wicked, so that the righteous fare as the wicked! Far be that from Thee! Shall not the Judge of all the earth do right?*

26. *And the Lord said: If I find at Sodom fifty righteous in the city, I will spare the whole place for their sake.*

Here there is a new question about the appearance of God and of the angels. It is my opinion that these angels had assumed the form of men and were not the Trinity in essence. Some give the names of these angels as Michael, who was the spokesman and spoke while the rest were silent; as Gabriel, the divine power needed to destroy Sodom; and as Raphael, the medicine of God who came to deliver and heal Lot. Whatever these ideas may be worth, they are sinless thoughts and are not hurtful. Yet I myself do not believe that they are true. Furthermore, the Jews say that when Raphael and Gabriel went away, Michael disappeared, but that the Lord appeared in a special apparition apart from those three and that Abraham conversed with Him. But I adhere to my opinion, which is simpler and is in harmony with Scripture.[56]

The third angel remained. Him, like the other two, Abraham regarded as a human being, but as such a one in whom was the Spirit of God. For he saw that this angel had the Word of God, and he concluded that this angel was speaking the Word of God, not that of a human being. For this reason Abraham also worshiped him as God. Therefore the statement of the text — "He still stood before the Lord" — is the same as if it stated: "Abraham listened to and looked upon this third angel as upon God, because he knew that this angel had the Word of God."

These words have reference to the high office of the ministry, which, although it was still unclear, so to speak, the holy patriarchs supported with such great zeal. But we, who have the light at its brightest, add even insults, yes, also the sword and hunger. In this way we kill off the ministers of the Gospel. Now let us hear Abraham's prayer, which is indeed an awful one if you consider the outcome.

Abraham formulated his prayer with the utmost prudence. He is satisfied with a small number because he thinks that he will all the more easily get what he wanted. But it is horrible that not ten righteous men are found in these five cities. Here we are saying nothing about the children. They are being preserved in a manner which is unknown to us, as is proved by the passage in Jonah about those who

[56] This material from the Jewish exegetical traditions comes from Lyra *ad* Gen. 18:22.

do not know the difference between the right and the left (Jonah 4:11). But the adults were all so corrupt that not ten were righteous. Nor did they pollute themselves solely with those ordinary sins: drunkenness, thieving, adultery, and avarice. The chief sins were contempt of the Word, of the officials of the state, and of parents; then abuse of the saints and exultation in most wicked enterprises.

Therefore consider these three facts — the short time during which they deteriorated to such an extent, the large number of those who were sinning, and the seriousness of the sins — and you will declare that God's judgment, even though most awful, nevertheless was just. For Abraham it is indeed impossible to believe that all are corrupt to the same extent. He thought that at least among the officials of the government and in the council of the kings there could be found some honorable and God-fearing men. For the individual cities had their own kings. Moreover, each king had his own senate. It is unbelievable that not ten pious men are found among these. Accordingly, Abraham pleads with such great confidence; and although he is disappointed once, he does not stop. So ardent is his love for very wicked people.

The eleventh chapter of Genesis informs us about the church of this time at which Sodom perished.[57] Six patriarchs were then living: Shem, Arphaxad, Salah, Eber, and Serug. And because Abraham lived almost fifty years together with Noah and saw nine patriarchs, he had most excellent teachers. But Noah died about forty years before the destruction of Sodom. Since he had seen the previous age — the age before the Flood — he was also known to the people of Sodom, who saw and heard him as he, together with his descendants, preached and cried out concerning the Flood and the wrath of God. Nevertheless, they despised him and his offspring. For this reason I believe that at this time there was a church the like of which did not subsequently exist on earth up to the time of Christ.

But it is terrible that in this golden age — when so many patriarchs were living and teaching, and when Shem himself was upholding the ministry of the Word in the neighborhood at Jerusalem — the people of Sodom degenerated to such an extent and abandoned all fear and knowledge of God. Why, then, are we complaining about our own age, when this has happened to so many and to such distinguished patriarchs? Therefore let us put up with these dregs of the world

---

[57] Cf. *Luther's Works*, 1, pp. 333—335, and *Luther the Expositor*, pp. 103 to 105.

and with such extraordinary ingratitude and contempt; for we are not worthy of being compared to the saintly patriarchs. Yet they, too, were compelled to see so awful and hideous an example of the wrath of God, and their persistent prayers had no effect whatever.

But who will doubt that those six patriarchs tried most zealously to call back to the right way the multitude that was rushing to its destruction? Lot lived in Sodom itself; Shem or Melchizedek lived in neighboring Jerusalem; Abraham lived in Mamre; and the others lived in other places, but those places were in the neighborhood. These men undoubtedly sent preachers to the people of Sodom, preachers who exhorted them to repent and reproved them. But everything was in vain. For where the Word is not held in reverence but is despised, there Shem and Abraham teach in vain, and nothing else is to be expected than destruction and a flood.

From this one can gauge the greatness of God's wrath against sin. If these saintly and God-pleasing men were unable to avert the punishment by means of their intercessions, what could we hope for at this advanced age of the world? Remember, therefore, that at this very time, when the church was in a most flourishing state and had the saintliest and the most faithful teachers, the world was at its worst. Satan is in the habit of marring the church in this manner by scandals which the uninformed attribute to the Word. By the same reasoning, however, the destruction of Sodom should be attributed to Lot, Abraham, and Melchizedek; for these men were the outstanding teachers of that age. But I return to Abraham's prayer.

Abraham's prayer has six parts; for he makes his request six times with such fervor and driving emotion that because of his excessive anxiety — since he desires advice for the wretched cities — he seems to be speaking foolishly. The verb תִּסְפֶּה is very significant and forceful, if I may express it this way; for it means to snatch away in such a manner that you let nothing remain. Hence if you were to weigh the words, it is a foolish prayer, as though God did not know how to make a distinction between the just and the unjust. "Do You want to snatch away a righteous man together with one who is godless," he asks, "and rage indiscriminately against all after the fashion of brigands?"

It seems to be a stern prayer, but it is a most praiseworthy one if it is judged according to Abraham's heart; for he sees that it is impossible for God not to have regard for the righteous. Therefore

Abraham prays as David did (Ps. 26:9): "O God, do not destroy my soul together with the ungodly." For this is characteristic of tyrants: in order to indulge their wrath, they burn houses, villages, and towns without caring whether the just or the unjust perish. "Such cruelty," says Abraham, "I know, does not befit God. Therefore He will spare the entire people because of fifty pious men." It is Abraham's very great emotion and his consternation, so to speak, which impel him to say foolish things. For the emotion of his heart is greater than the heart can hold, because the saintly man sees that the entire people is to be destroyed.

It is a forceful and impulsive prayer, as if Abraham wanted to compel God to forgive. Surely it is well known that because of one righteous man God spares, and shows kindness to, an entire house, city, and region. Thus Syria flourished while Naaman was living. Egypt is blessed because of Joseph, and Laban is blessed because of Jacob. And would God really forget Himself to such an extent that He would have no regard for fifty righteous men? "O Lord, Lord, do not do it!" These are words indicative of the vastness of Abraham's emotion. At the same time tears streamed from his eyes, and his heart overflowed with unutterable sighs. "Far be this from Thee!" he says, as though he wanted to tell God what He should do, just as he adds: "Will not He who judges the entire earth do what is right?"

To do what is right means to punish evildoers and to spare the innocent. "And this," says he, "behooves Thee especially. Thou judgest the entire earth. But what sort of right is it to bring even innocent people to trial?" This is surely a bold and impulsive request. Abraham reminds God of His duty to spare the righteous and, because of the righteous, even the wicked. Accordingly, the Lord answers and promises that He will have mercy if there are fifty righteous men. For He is pleased with the fervent prayer in which faith and love are so manifest. But when Abraham hears that fifty are not found, he is somewhat frightened. Nevertheless, he continues to pray.

27. *Abraham answered: Behold, I have taken upon myself to speak to the Lord, I who am but dust and ashes.*

28. *Suppose five of the fifty righteous are lacking? Wilt Thou destroy the whole city for lack of five? And He said: I will not destroy it if I find forty-five there.*

Prayer must be bold. Therefore Abraham continues to pray. But in this instance he adds outstanding humility, which is indispensable in every prayer. He says: "I am but dust and ashes. Yet, because I have begun to pray, I shall continue. Wilt Thou be merciful if five are lacking?" The Lord says: "I will be merciful."

29. *Again he spoke to Him and said: Suppose forty are found there. He answered: For the sake of forty I will not do it.*

30. *Then he said: Oh, let not the Lord be angry, and I will speak. Suppose thirty are found there. He answered: I will not do it if I find thirty there.*

31. *He said: Behold, I have taken upon myself to speak to the Lord. Suppose twenty are found there. He answered: For the sake of twenty I will not destroy it.*

32. *Then he said: Oh, let not the Lord be angry, and I will speak again but this once. Suppose ten are found there. He answered: For the sake of ten I will not destroy it.*

33. *And the Lord went His way when He had finished speaking to Abraham; and Abraham returned to his place.*

From fifty the number drops to ten, and Abraham is sure that he will get his wish. He thinks: "How, since Lot, the godly teacher, is there, is it possible that there should be no fruit of the Word to such an extent that not ten are found?" Therefore it is a deep sigh of Abraham that he promises to pray this last time and not to weary the Lord any more. Consider this example whenever you pray, and learn that persistence is needed in praying. It does not offend God; it pleases Him. But Abraham undoubtedly comforted himself with the account of the Flood, when eight souls were preserved. Even though he was unable to ensure the preservation of the others, he was nevertheless sure about his nephew Lot that God would take care of him and that he would be delivered. So he returns home and leaves everything to the just judgment of God. For he realizes that where there is such great malice of human beings, it is necessary for God to reveal His wrath against sin, lest the godly be offended and themselves also begin to turn away.

And this is the reason why God commands that this account be committed to Abraham's descendants. God wants to be feared, but the smug He detests and hates. In Is. 66:2 He promises that He will dwell with those who have a contrite heart, and in Ps. 51:17 He states that the sacrifice most pleasing to Him is a greatly troubled spirit. Nevertheless, He does not want fear alone to dominate; He also wants the hope of mercy to be retained in that anxiety of heart.

God teaches the same thing in the books of Moses by means of a figure when He forbids (Deut. 24:6) taking the lower and the upper millstone from the needy at the same time. The upper millstone is the fear and judgment of God. This the lower millstone supports; it signifies the hope and feeling of mercy. Thus the ministry should connect the Law and the Gospel, penitence and the remission of sins.[58]

The pope has preached nothing but terrors. Our false prophets today, on the contrary, want nothing taught except the Gospel and the promises; and this error is almost more harmful. Grace and the remission of sins should be preached, but among those who have sins, that is, who acknowledge that they have sins and sincerely desire to be freed from them. But those who smugly continue in sins are as though they were without sins — to these the Law should be presented. They should be frightened by the destruction of Sodom and in this manner be brought to the fear of God.

And this, as we have also said above,[59] is dividing the Word of God rightly. Just as in the case of the sacrifices there was a definite procedure of dividing the victim, so in teaching a definite order should be maintained to the end that God may eventually be known both as gracious to those who believe and as angry with those who are smug, and also that we individually may learn to fear God and to rely on His mercy, which He has revealed in His Son, whom He sent. Thus the First Commandment says (Ex. 20:2, 6): "I am God who shows mercy to thousands of them who love Me but who punishes to the third and fourth generation those who hate Me, that is, do not obey My Word."

The world does not allow itself to be persuaded to believe that this wrath is real. Consider Micah and Jeremiah. When they threatened the wrath of God, they were regarded as false prophets and were ordered to keep silence. But what does the Holy Spirit say? "My words are good for those who walk in My ways." [60] Thus since

---

[58] Luther develops this allegory in his *Lectures on Deuteronomy* of 1525, *Luther's Works*, 9, p. 244.

[59] Cf. pp. 222 ff.

[60] Luther seems not to be quoting a specific passage of Scripture but paraphrasing passages like Jer. 26:9 and 26:18.

the people of Sodom were sinning with the utmost smugness, they perished. And so great a multitude, so many distinguished persons of great mental capacity, yes, even the little children do not influence God; but He snatches everything away at the same time, in order that His wrath against sin may become well known.

Therefore I believe that Abraham went home full of sorrow and spent that night without sleep and in tears and sighs because of the destruction of so great a multitude. But while godly Abraham is so concerned about the people of Sodom, they live in luxury and do violence to their guests, altogether unconcerned about their own destruction. This is a picture of the world and of the church, as Christ, too, says (John 16:20): "You will lament, but they will rejoice."

CHAPTER NINETEEN

1. *The two angels came to Sodom in the evening; and Lot was sitting in the gate of Sodom. When Lot saw them, he rose to meet them, and bowed himself with his face to the earth.*

This chapter contains a description of that punishment for sins which has been mentioned in the previous chapter, namely, that the outcry against Sodom came up to heaven. Now I do not discuss this awful account with pleasure, any more than I did the account of the Flood. For it is something awful to feel and experience the wrath of God raging almost beyond measure against the wretched human race. Therefore I am profoundly affected whenever I either read about or discuss these events. Even though I am a human being who is prone to anger, I am nevertheless deeply moved by such an extraordinary disaster; and I am aware of the trial which Abraham underwent when, through his intercession, he tried with all his power to turn away such great wrath from the impenitent sinners.

The antinomians, those modern prophets, maintain that people must be dealt with gently and must not be frightened by examples of God's wrath.[1] But Paul states the opposite in 2 Tim. 3:16-17. He says there that Scripture is also "profitable for reproof and correction, that the man of God may be complete, equipped for every good work." Well known is also the command about rightly dividing the Word of God. And in 1 Cor. 10:6,[2] after diverse evidences of God's wrath against sinners, he states plainly that those things were written for our sakes, lest we sin through lust in conformity with their example.

Therefore the examples of the wrath of God, such as the one before us, must be dealt with in such a manner that they serve for our instruction and learning. Thus the Lord commands Abraham, who was far saintlier than we are, to relate these events to his children. For you will always find two kinds of human beings. One of these is haughty and obstinate, despises the Word and godly

[1] On the antinomians see also p. 222, note 48.
[2] The original has "1 Cor. 15." Cf. 2 Tim. 2:15.

admonitions, and is smug beyond measure. If you treat these people gently and proclaim the mercy of God to them, you will make them worse. This, of course, is the fruit which the error of the antinomians produces. But I warn you to be on your guard against them. For they are not satisfied that they themselves perish; but they want to drag us, too, to destruction with them and to burden us with their sins, since they, like the people of Sodom, do not want them checked.

But God has put the ministry of the Word into this world, not that the ministers should be silent, but that they should reprove, teach, comfort, terrify, and in this manner save whomever they can. The antinomians do away with this ministry entirely when they refuse to tolerate reproofs and order us to acquiesce in their sins, contrary to the statement of Paul, who in Rom. 2:1 condemns not only those who commit sins but also those who acquiesce in them. But those who do not reprove sins acquiesce in them. That is what I would be doing if I were to conceal the sins, blasphemies, and tyranny of the cardinals, the pope, and the bishops. But the Lord says in the book of the prophet (Ezek. 3:19): "You will deliver your soul if you reprove the sins of your people." Even the most wicked human beings must be borne [3] with compassion; but when they want to snatch us with them to destruction, compassion must cease. Neither the authority of parents nor the love for our children must mean so much to us that we are willing to perish with them. Then all compassion must be forgotten, in accordance with the example of Lot, who abandons his wife when, contrary to the Lord's command, she looks back while she is on the way. Because such people have become hardened and accept no admonition, they must be abandoned.

But toward those who are not so obstinate but can be guided God wants us to show compassion, as the parable about the lost sheep teaches (Luke 15:4 ff.). For they are not impenitent Sodomites, for whom God's rock-crushing hammer is appropriate. From these the judgment of the Lord should not be concealed; otherwise it will happen that we pollute ourselves with their sins by acquiescing in them. All Christians have been placed into the world for the purpose of serving their neighbors, not only so far as the Second Table is concerned but rather so far as the First Table is concerned, in order that they all may learn to fear God and to trust in His mercy. The other kind have already been humbled and are terrified.

---

[3] Although the original has *sicut* here, we have followed the Erlangen edition and read *sunt*.

Christ (Luke 12:32) calls them a little flock and tells them not to fear. Even though they are weak and sin in various ways, they are not inflexible or callous. Toward such the minister should be prudent and faithful. He should divide the Word of God rightly (2 Tim. 2:15) and not mix anything foreign with the sound doctrine. Nor should he further frighten those who are frightened by the wrath and judgment of God; he should encourage them. This is great wisdom and is very necessary in the ministry. The two kinds of hearers should be properly distinguished, and everyone should hear the words that are intended for him — the obstinate, the awful examples of God's wrath; but the fearful, the sweet words of comfort. For Christ is set for the rising of some and for the fall of others (cf. Luke 2:34). Those who have been humbled must, therefore, be buoyed up. On the other hand, those who have exalted themselves in their smugness must be crushed, as St. Mary teaches in her song (Luke 1:52). This is the right division, for the fearful are unavoidably mingled with the smug. Therefore this moderation is needed in order that those who are obdurate may know that these awful examples are aimed at them. But those who have been frightened should apply the words of comfort and promise to themselves.

After this it is the work of the Holy Spirit to direct the hearts of men by means of the Word and confession, with the result that the fearful apprehend the comforts but the obstinate are either converted after they have been frightened by the words of the Law or perish utterly. Not all people should be condemned without distinction. Just as the Flood and the destruction of the Sodomites are like thunderbolts by which the hearts are frightened, so there is added to these examples of wrath the comforting knowledge that Noah and Lot were preserved. In this way the fearful will be kept from despairing.

This is why I read awful accounts of this kind. Yet I read them reluctantly, because I am frightened by the greatness of God's wrath. Still I see that this doctrine is useful not only to frighten the proud but also to keep the godly in the fear of God, lest they sin and perish in accordance with the example of the ungodly. Furthermore, in these examples the wrath of God is presented in such a way that at the same time the goodness of God, who mercifully preserves the faithful, still shines forth.

Thus Christ says in Is. 61:1 ff.: "The Spirit of the Lord God is upon Me, because the Lord has anointed Me to bring good tidings to the afflicted; He has sent Me to bind up the brokenhearted, to proclaim liberty to the captives, and the opening of the prison to those who are bound; to proclaim the year of the Lord's favor and the day of vengeance of our God; to comfort all who mourn." Behold, the poor, the brokenhearted, the prisoners, the confined, and the mourning are promised pardon, freedom, and a "year," or a time, when God has been placated. Therefore those who are not poor and brokenhearted — to them the day of vengeance, that is, the wrath of God, is proclaimed.

Therefore if Christ teaches in such a way that He connects the doctrine of wrath with mercy, why should we not follow Him? Accordingly, it is the highest wisdom properly to combine the mercy revealed in the preservation of Lot and the wrath revealed in the destruction of the people of Sodom. Frightened and fearful hearts undoubtedly please God; for He promises (Is. 42:3) that "a bruised reed He will not break, and a dimly burning wick He will not quench."

Even though these examples of wrath bring about contrition, one must nevertheless cease mentioning them when hearts have been broken; the grief must be lessened, and the wound must be healed. In Ps. 51:19 Scripture calls fear a sacrifice to God and worship. But since these accounts were written through the Holy Spirit for the purpose of impelling hearts to fear God, to shun sins, and to do justice and righteousness, it is proper to present them in the church, which, just as it has two kinds of people, also presents a twofold Word: the accounts of wrath and the threats against the obdurate, the smug, and the impenitent; and the promises for the benefit of the contrite and the humbled. But it is the highest wisdom to dispense these rightly.

The pope has the thunderbolt of excommunication, but against whom does he employ it? Does he not use it against us, who are not smug but are contrite and humble? But men of his own kind — Epicureans, smug canons, cardinals, bishops, and tyrants — he declares blessed and elevates to heaven. In this way he lives up to his title by comforting the poor of the church and condemning the recalcitrant.[4]

But this is nothing new, for consider Ezek. 13:19: "You have profaned Me among My people for handfuls of barley"; that is, for the sake of acquiring temporal possessions you have corrupted the doctrine and have condemned the pious. But you have emboldened the

---

[4] Luther is referring to the papal slogan: *Comfortat pauperes ecclesiae, et damnat rebelles.*

wicked. This is the meaning of what follows: "For pieces of bread you have killed souls that should not have died, and you have kept alive souls which should not have lived, when you lied to My people, who listen to lies." And in another passage (Ezek. 13:22): "You have made sad the heart of the righteous whom I have not made sad." Thus the entire papacy lacks that wisdom of rightly dividing the Word. Therefore it cannot build. On the contrary, it destroys and overthrows everything by its doctrine.

But the Holy Spirit presents these accounts of God's wrath and judgment also in such a manner that at the same time He points out the solid comfort that God will deliver from certain destruction those who fear Him, as He delivered Lot. Hence not only do the people of Sodom perish, but Lot gives thanks to God after he has been saved. You who are fearful and have been humbled, think of Lot, who was saved, and hope that God will do the same thing for you. On the other hand, you who live smugly in whoredom, that is, heap up riches, sumptuously take care of your own skin, and are a sow from the herd of Epicurus, turn your eyes toward the people of Sodom! See what severe punishment followed their disgraceful crimes! Consider that suddenly five cities were consumed by fire from heaven, that the earth sank down, and that an awful lake of bitumen took its place, as in one single moment the sinners were destroyed and perished eternally!

A careful consideration of these events will induce you to think of your own peril, to cease sinning, and to implore pardon for your sins. This our foolish and blind antinomians, Agricola and Schenk, do not know.[5] Consequently, they do away with the preaching of God's wrath in the church, to its great and certain detriment. Therefore I warn you to beware of such men, for they are fanatical spirits and are ignorant of spiritual matters. Yet they are puffed up with a vain notion of their erudition and wisdom. But I return to the account.

In the preceding chapter Moses designates as men those whom in this passage he clearly calls angels. In both instances, however, the designation must be understood in such a way as to lead you to the conclusion that the Lord appeared in them. But why Moses altered the designation in this way I do not know, unless perhaps

[5] By the nicknames *Grikel* and *Iekel* Luther is referring to Johann Agricola and Jacob Schenk, spokesmen for the antinomian movement.

the Holy Spirit wanted to indicate that they were not natural human beings.

The evening Moses mentions was, I think, the next evening after the noon at which they dined with Abraham. But the journey from Mamre to Sodom is too long to be completed in so few hours by a human being; and for this reason the Psalm [6] states in this passage that they were angels, lest anyone suspect that fiction is being related.

Furthermore, to this account should be applied what we have said above concerning hospitality.[7] For just as you heard about Abraham, so you hear also about Lot that he longed for guests, received them with open arms, and all but compelled them to enjoy his hospitality. I have also stated that there is no greater praise of hospitality than that in Matt. 25:35: "I was hungry, and you gave Me bread."

Lot's sitting in the gate of Sodom is something different from sitting in the gate of the city, for the gate of the city denotes the place of the court. It was the custom of Oriental peoples to place the court in the gates, for there they had a citadel or ramparts and came together whenever they were about to deliberate on matters of state. Lot, however, is sitting in the entrance to the city.

This, however, is praise of his hospitality, for the circumstances reveal why he did not remain at home. He is looking for guests and is aware of the raging of the citizens and of their deeds of violence. Therefore if some strangers should come, he wants them to stay with him, where they can spend the night free from abuse and violence. And perhaps there was at that time a great persecution in Ur of the Chaldeans. For this reason large numbers of the godly preferred to follow the exile Abraham, to live with him in exile rather than with the ungodly in their native land. Accordingly, since Abraham and Lot have been cautioned against the perils of the brethren, they sit either at the house door or in the gate, so that any who come will find guest rooms ready.

Therefore when Lot sees the angels, he worships them with his face down to the earth. This was not recorded about Abraham, who merely bowed or genuflected. Lot falls down on his face on the earth; so great was his respect at that time toward guests.

---

[6] The original has the word *Psalmus* here, but the closest Biblical parallel to what Luther is saying appears in Heb. 13:2. Could *Psalmus* be a misreading of *Paulus* in the manuscript or notes?

[7] Cf. p. 183, note 7.

From this it is apparent what discipline there was in the households of the godly and how they accustomed their descendants to receive strangers as reverently as if God Himself were coming; for in them they revered and honored God.

In our age, in these dregs of the world, there is such great wickedness, and there are such manifold instances of fraud and deceit that you do not know what to do for anyone. Yet we must at least treat with respect those whom we know and aid them by means of our service. But hear how Lot talks with his unknown guests.

2. *And he said: My lords, turn aside, I pray you, to your servant's house and spend the night, and wash your feet; then you may rise up early and go on your way. They said: No; we will spend the night in the street.*

3. *But he urged them strongly; so they turned aside to him and entered his house; and he made them a feast and baked unleavened bread, and they ate.*

The word "lords" is not the usual אֲדֹנִים or אֲדֹנִי but אֲדֹנָי, which is appropriate for God alone. How it is to be understood has been adequately stated above at great length;[8] and the account shows that Lot, too, had been properly instructed about the doctrine of the Trinity, either by Abraham himself or by another of the patriarchs. Therefore since two guests are present, he does not endeavor to show honor to lords but to the Lord in them. The books of the heathen contain no such examples of hospitality. Therefore we should give them careful consideration.

Lot offers them hospitality in a very generous manner, makes himself their servant but calls them lords, and also bids them act as such, in order that they may do everything as though they were the masters of the house. He offers them water for their feet, which was a customary service to strangers, not only for washing off the dirt gathered on the journey but also to revive their tired feet and to restore their vigor.

Christ, too, instituted a washing of the feet (John 13:1 ff.), but one far different from the one which is practiced today by the monks and bishops, the pope, kings, and princes, who have kept only the show.[9] Christ wants us to humble ourselves at the feet of others;

---

[8] See pp. 190 ff.

[9] A reference to the medieval practice of obeying the *mandatum* of John 13:4-17. The rite was observed in cathedrals and in monastic churches.

He wants us to serve the needs of others. But these facts all of them disregard. Meanwhile they suppose that by means of this empty show they are imitating Christ. But it is very well known what kind of example He has given us and how much the hypocrites differ from Him.

Here the angels do something they did not do at Abraham's house. When Lot invites them to his house, they refuse and want to spend the night in the street. But when Abraham offers them hospitality, they immediately assent and say: "Do as you have said." So Lot does something which Abraham did not do. He insists when they decline, for he feared for them because of the citizens.

The Hebrews say that the reason why the angels pretended to be unwilling to enter Lot's house was to make more apparent the zeal and ready willingness of Lot, who could not be satisfied but even forced them to enter into his house.[10] But it is futile and useless for us to investigate these matters more closely. In the world, of course, it is exceedingly common to be generous with words. Thus the invitations extended to people whom we nevertheless would not want to come are termed polite words. One encounters these deceptions at court, but the words of the pious fathers were not in disagreement with their hearts. Therefore I do not believe that this refusal was made in order to test Lot.

Solomon earnestly warns in Prov. 23:6-7: "Do not eat bread with an envious person; for he tells you: 'Eat and drink,' but his heart is not with you." Many strive for applause and want to appear hospitable even though they are very stingy and are angry for three whole days because of a single penny. This failing is especially prevalent among the mighty. In people who bestow a favor there should be a sincere heart, but in those who receive a favor there should be reasonableness and modesty.

And this, it seems to me, is the reason why the angels declined the favor; for, as modest people are wont to do, they decline as though they did not intend to burden Lot — not deceitfully, of course, but truthfully. But when they modestly refuse, Lot generously and sincerely offers them hospitality. He is not one of those who, when they are about to give something, first ask a question and subject modesty to a test. For it is true what a familiar little verse states: "He who wants to give to others should not say: 'Do you want it?'"[11]

---

[10] Cf. Lyra *ad* Gen. 19:2.

[11] The Latin of the verse is *Qui dare vult aliis, non debet dicere, vultis?*

[W, XLIII, 51, 52]

It is impolite to subject modesty to a test and to force one, as it were, to beg.

Even under the stress of need modest people nevertheless almost want to be forced to accept a favor. On the other hand, you may find others, who are impudent and do not wait until you bid them but obtrude themselves of their own accord, take a seat at the table, and want this and that given to them. Such people deserve to be disliked.

Thus this passage deals principally with the fact that those who bestow a favor should bestow it with sincerity. Those who accept it should accept it with modesty. I think that this maxim is rightly taught on the basis of this passage. But one must not stop here, for the Holy Spirit also reveals something else.

We observe that Holy Scripture is in excellent agreement with itself and is uniformly consistent everywhere. Above, when Abraham interceded for the people of Sodom, he hears the awful and unexpected verdict that not ten righteous men are found in the five cities. The circumstances before us serve to lend support to this statement. The angels themselves, like exiles who are unfamiliar with the ways of the people (for so they pretend to be), consider it just as safe to sleep in the streets as it is in other well-behaved cities. But Lot, who is familiar with everything, entreats them all the more earnestly to stay with him, because he knows for sure that harm will be done to them if they spend the night in the street. He knew that the people of Sodom not only were inhospitable but also persecuted strangers and treated them outrageously.

This is what Moses wanted to point out, just as Ezekiel also says: "Behold, this was the guilt of your sister Sodom: she and her daughters had pride, surfeit of food, and prosperous ease, but did not aid the poor and needy. They were haughty and did abominable things before Me" (16:49-50). These are very harsh words. He calls them proud despisers of the Word, that is, of God and of men; for they were practicing no reverence toward God and no love toward human beings. They had forgotten the kindness with which they had been treated by Abraham, and they assumed that they were the only ones whom God loved and who could not offend God, inasmuch as He was blessing them in this manner.

Today, too, the world allows itself to be deceived by this foolish conclusion. Because it sees that it is being made rich through prosperity, wealth, and health, it concludes that it has a gracious God and proclaims: "Behold, God is dwelling among us." [12]

Similarly, the Jews say (Zech. 11:5): "Blessed be the Lord, we have become rich." In the schools they called this conclusion "from the staff to the corner." [13] God does not grant wealth in order to cause you to conclude from it that He is gracious; He has bestowed another greater benefit, and from it you may properly reach this conclusion. He wants to put you to the test, to see whether you are willing to abide in His fear, to humble yourself before Him, and also to render the obedience that is due Him. For very few do do this; they become haughty because of their good fortune. Hence there is the proverb: "Gold makes bold." [14] "Good fortune commonly induces hearts to be unrestrained." [15] Also: "It takes strong legs to carry good days." Unless hearts are enlightened and ruled by the Holy Spirit — as in the case of David, Abraham, and others — it is impossible for them not to be corrupted by favorable circumstances, as has been elegantly stated: "Those whom fortune favors it makes foolish." [16] Therefore the psalm (62:10) warns: "If riches increase, set not your heart on them."

But the world does not believe this. Together with the people of Sodom it holds fast to this firm conclusion: "Behold, we have a very fertile land, a very powerful city; we have been weighed down with gifts and with good fortune of many kinds. How, then, could God hate us; or how could any misfortune befall us?"

In addition to this, there was an abundance of food. They indulged in drunkenness and gluttony, just as we Germans, too, are in the habit of doing. But it is also well known what usually results from drunkenness. On the evening when they wanted to perpetrate this crime against the angels who were guests there may have been a public feast at which they swilled wine.

Furthermore, Ezekiel mentions ease or the good fortune of a quiet life. Everything was serene, and they experienced no famine, no plague, and no diseases; but, as Moses says of his own people (Deut.

---

[12] Here Luther breaks into German: *Hie wonet Gott.*

[13] Cf. *Luther's Works,* 2, p. 271, note 29.

[14] The proverb *Gut macht Mut* appears frequently in Luther; its Latin form is *Ubi uber, ibi tuber.*

[15] Ovid, *Ars amandi,* II, 437.

[16] The customary form of this saying is *Fortuna nimium quem fovet stultum facit.*

32:15), they became as fat and thick as pigs. Therefore there also followed what pertains to the situation before us; they did not stretch out their hand to the poor, and they were inhospitable. Similarly, today in Germany many pastors of churches almost starve. Poor Christ is hungry. Everywhere He all but perishes from His afflictions. Indeed, there is no compassion among human beings.

Since this was the state of affairs in Sodom and in the neighboring cities, the report about them spread to other cities and places close by. For a city gets its reputation from its morals. Similarly, in Germany today some cities are notorious for usury,[17] which is also a sin of Sodom and is not only not concealed but is even publicized. They are also notorious for excessive eating and drinking. When these sins are committed publicly and are customarily excused by men so that they are not only not infamous but even give rise to laughter — just as we see our nobles and burghers boast of their association with prostitutes — then they are indeed sins like those of Sodom.

Thus Isaiah (3:9) declares concerning his people: "They proclaim their sin like Sodom; they do not hide it." Where shame and modesty are found, and you blush at your sin and are afraid that it may be made public, there sin is still not serious; but when it is publicized, and criminals, as Solomon says (Prov. 2:14), rejoice in the most evil deeds and delight in wickedness, there nothing is left but hell-fire.

Scripture itself gives evidence that the Sodomites were most corrupt and that in such a great multitude there are not ten men who are good. Accordingly, this is the main purpose served when it states that Lot compels the angels to enter his house when they want to spend the night in the street and decline his hospitality. Therefore Lot intends to protect them from harm and almost forces them into his house. But what happens? What he eagerly seeks to avoid takes place. Because he protects his guests and takes them into his house, the Sodomites are stirred up to attempt a horrible crime.

Thus the circumstances make the villainy greater. The angels, as strangers, walk along barefoot and with uncovered heads, as though they were weary from the journey. But at that place, among so many rich citizens, there is none who offers them a drop of water; indeed, they even seek to kill them and subject them to the utmost contumely. But godly Lot not only gives them lodging but also prepares a feast.

---

[17] In his treatise of 1524 *On Commerce and Usury* Luther mentioned Lüneberg and Holstein by name as cities noted for the practice of usury (W, XV, 321). Later in these *Lectures on Genesis* he added the name of Leipzig (W, XLIV, 418).

Scripture does not mention whether he invited some of his sons-in-law. His other actions prove that he certainly attempted to do so in order to put his guests in a cheerful mood. After the rich meal he also serves them unleavened cakes, lest anything be lacking either to meet the needs of his guests or to show his generosity.

Inasmuch as the text mentions unleavened bread, the question arises here whether anything of the Mosaic laws was in existence at that time. Furthermore, the Jews maintain that Sodom was destroyed on the day of the Passover, which is the most joyful festival of all during the year, and that for this reason the people of Sodom had given themselves up to drinking. Lyra vehemently opposes this idea, but to no great advantage.[18] For what good or evil results from it? At all events, however, it is profitable for students to learn to distinguish the Law of Moses from all other laws; but whether the Feast of Passover or Pentecost was then in existence I neither deny nor assert.

Nevertheless, I think that it can be stated with assurance that Moses kept in his laws many things which had previously been observed by the fathers. He commands sacrifices, but Abel sacrificed a lamb and Cain sacrificed the fruits of the field long before the time of Moses. Thus Noah distinguished between clean and unclean animals. Who would deny that at God's command Moses retained in his laws other similar things that had previously been observed by the godly? He had to establish a new people and to found a new kingdom. This could not be done without laws, and these laws had to be written with care.

Moreover, because the church was in this kingdom, there had to be worship and ceremonies. Since the age of the patriarchs had preserved some of these, Moses, by divine command, retained them, just as he retained circumcision. Judicial procedures were also laid down concerning the punishment of criminals. But who would doubt that most of the judicial procedures were also taken over from the practice of earlier times and from the tradition of the fathers? But Moses, as the lawgiver with a pious regard for his own times, added others, as the Lord commanded.

But whether Moses transferred to his own people some things either from the tradition and practice of the fathers or from the custom of neighboring nations, the whole is nevertheless called the

---

[18] Lyra *ad* Gen. 19:3.

Law of Moses. And the passage before us gives evidence that the use of unleavened bread was in existence before the Law and that it was made use of either at a definite time, as later on in the Law, or at feasts.

The Jews do wrong when they praise their laws so highly at the present time and maintain that these laws are indispensable. Like the tribes of Levi and of Judah, these laws were meant for a definite place and for a definite time, that is, up to the time of Christ; the place was the land of Canaan, in which the twelve tribes dwelt. This was the boundary and limit, so to speak, of the Mosaic kingdom. Since today the Jews have lost their land or place, they are certainly bound to disregard the Law too; for the time has expired, and the locale has been shifted. The persons, too — that is, the royal and the priestly tribe — have become mixed.

Before the Law the practice of eating unleavened bread was in existence among the Orientals, but in such a way that it was served at all banquets, at weddings, and at festivities. But at the Lord's command Moses placed a restriction on this custom and wanted his people to eat unleavened bread at the Passover. Hence the Law of Moses must be distinguished from other laws. In the Law the use of unleavened bread took place at a definite time; before the Law its use was unrestricted at all times. Similarly, Moses commanded to sacrifice a lamb at the Passover; but before Moses it was permitted to sacrifice a lamb whenever one wished. Therefore the use of unleavened bread is of no concern to Moses, although later on he wanted it to be part of a specific occasion. Because of Lyra's discussion I wanted to call attention to these facts in passing. Now let us explain the remaining matters in the account.

4. *But before they lay down, the men of the city, the men of Sodom, both young and old, all the people to the last man, surrounded the house;*

5. *and they called to Lot: Where are the men who came to you tonight? Bring them out to us, that we may know them.*

Moses proceeds with a description of a terrible sin. I for my part do not enjoy dealing with this passage, because so far the ears of the Germans are innocent of and uncontaminated by this monstrous depravity; for even though this disgrace, like other sins, has crept in through an ungodly soldier and a lewd merchant, still the rest of the people are unaware of what is being done in secret. The Carthusian monks deserve to be hated because they were the first to bring this terrible pollution into Germany from the monasteries of Italy. Of course, they were trained and educated in such a praiseworthy manner at Rome.[19]

But this passage contains a necessary and profitable doctrine. We see that when sins become the fashion and human beings smugly indulge in them, the punishment of God follows immediately. Therefore let us learn to fear God and to arm ourselves against the flesh and the devil, in order that we may not fall into similar disgraceful sins which God cannot allow to go unpunished. Moses describes the wretchedness and misfortune of the human race in strong enough terms. After the angels had eaten, he says, they undoubtedly talked about various things at table — about the fear of God, about righteousness, and about the corruption of morals and the collapse of discipline; for perhaps saintly Lot complained about these matters. Peter does not state without cause (2 Peter 2:8) that the soul of righteous Lot was tortured day [20] and night because he was compelled both to see and to hear shameful things. Therefore Lot's mouth spoke out of the abundance of his heart (Matt. 12:35), and he could not control his grief when such saintly guests had arrived at such an opportune time.

After they had finished the meal and the time called for sleep, what happens? The men of the city, the men of Sodom (this repetition serves to aggravate the sin), are in such a frenzy that they not only showed no courtesy toward the guests but did not allow the tired men to rest even for an hour in someone else's house. They vent their rage upon the weary men before these men go to bed, and they begrudge them their sleep. Is not this extraordinary rudeness and cruelty? But it is more serious and altogether unheard of for them to demand the men for their sensual desire. It is the men of the city who do this, not the unimportant people of the populace — hirelings, slaves, and sojourners — but the foremost citizens, whose obligation it was to protect others and to punish similar crimes in the case of others.

Accordingly, this, too, serves to make you realize that there were not ten righteous men in the city. These were the foremost citizens.

[19] Cf. Luther's *Warning to His Dear Germans* of 1531 (W, XXX-3, 304—305).

[20] Although all the editions have *diu* here, we have followed the conjecture of the Weimar editors and read *die*.

They had wives. They had children and domestics, and they should have ruled these and accustomed them to discipline and modesty. But what are they themselves perpetrating? What are they attempting to do? And that in public and against innocent guests!

Moreover, Moses repeats and says that this was done by the men of Sodom, which is the chief city of the entire region and for this reason should have been an example for the neighboring cities. It usually happens that smaller states conform to the example of larger ones. But what shall be our opinion about those four lesser states, when so much vice is in evidence in the chief one, which was the leader, so to speak, of the others? But listen further to Moses.

They surround the house; they do not send servants or attendants to Lot's house to learn the identity of the guests who have arrived. Nor do they themselves come to find out. No, they surround the house and threaten some hostile act. The Hebrew verb in this passage is "passive," [21] but its meaning is well known from Jer. 31:22: "At that time a woman will compass a man." It means to encircle, just as a hoop surrounds a container on all sides. In this manner they encircled Lot's house; they run toward it from all corners and streets.

This situation causes me to think that at that time there was a feast day and that banquets were held throughout the city, for the entire city was in a frenzy. Even though they did not all want to perpetrate the crime, they were nevertheless all involved in the endeavor and took pleasure in this raging of the citizens against the strangers. But he who commits a deed and he who gives his consent are in the same position.

Furthermore, among the four parts the most distressing is "young and old." נַעַר is a term for an age, and the Hebrews commonly use it when they speak of servants and maids. It denotes those who have reached the twentieth, twenty-fourth, or twenty-sixth year, are now qualified by age to perform services, and now feel the passion of the flesh. All these join the citizens, the king, the counselors, the senators, and the aristocrats; even old men are there, among whom sexual desire is dead or who at least would have been able to check the frenzy of the rest because of their gray hair and their influence. And in order that you may understand the situation more clearly, the entire populace comes running at the same time from every corner

---

[21] Actually the verb is in the Niphal, which corresponds more closely perhaps to the Greek middle than to the passive.

of the city. To be sure, they could not all perpetrate this crime; but they were both delighted by the deed and gave their consent.

But what shall we suppose was in the mind of godly Lot, toward whose house everybody was going during this uproar in the whole city? He alone feared God, and in his house he maintained discipline and chastity to the utmost of his ability, while the others indulged freely and without shame in adultery, fornication, effeminacy, and even incest to such an extent that these were not regarded as sins but as some pastime, just as today among the nobility and the lower classes of Germany fornication is regarded as a pastime, not as a sin, and for this reason is also entirely unpunished.

First in Italy and then by some canons in Germany it was argued that simple fornication of an unattached man with an unattached woman is not a sin but is a cleansing of nature, which seeks an outlet.[22] Let this be said with due respect for innocent ears, for I do not relish dealing with these matters. Yet we must be on our guard lest such shocking utterances carry away and ruin the age that is rash and in general is inclined toward sin. For where people live and teach in such a way and vices become customary, there, says Seneca sternly, there is no room for a cure.[23]

As for you, set before yourselves the statements of Paul, and on the basis of them reach the decision that "God will judge the immoral and adulterous" (Heb. 13:4); "Be not deceived; neither the immoral nor adulterers will inherit the kingdom of God" (1 Cor. 6:9); and Rom. 8:8: "Without chastity no one will please God."

In Rome I myself saw some cardinals who were esteemed highly as saints because they were content to associate with women.[24] Hence unspeakable infamies are committed there, not in secret or in privacy but openly, because of the example and the influence of the leading men and of the entire city. What room can there be here for a cure? Or who will rebuke such people? They regard sins as praiseworthy morals and suppose that they can be practiced with commendation. If you compare these people with those who, although they sin, nevertheless keep their sin secret and blush with shame, you will say that they are sinners who can be tolerated, just as the German

[22] Cf. *Luther's Works*, 1, pp. 166—167.

[23] Seneca, *Epistolae*, 39.

[24] Luther had visited Rome in 1510—11. There is much controversy among scholars about what he saw there and what effect it may have had on his further development.

proverb says about Nobody: "Even though Nobody sins, yet he sins tolerably." For he has fear and at least a crude and slavish sense of shame, because he would not want his sin to become public. The people of Sodom were not of this kind. Therefore among them everything was beyond hope, and no room remained for a cure; the Lord had to come down from heaven and punish them.

Even though it is awful to experience and to observe how great Satan's power is after a person has once turned away from the fear of God — for Satan does not cease to drive on from sin to sin — it is still profitable to ponder these facts; for they encourage us to pray. Yes, they even commend to us the concern which our heavenly Father has for us when He warns us and calls us back, so to speak, to the right way by means of His fatherly rod, which thus becomes sweet when you reflect what a human being is wont to do when he is left to himself and indulges freely in sin.

The heinous conduct of the people of Sodom is extraordinary, inasmuch as they departed from the natural passion and longing of the male for the female, which was implanted into nature by God, and desired what is altogether contrary to nature. Whence comes this perversity? Undoubtedly from Satan, who, after people have once turned away from the fear of God, so powerfully suppresses nature that he blots out the natural desire and stirs up a desire that is contrary to nature.

Moses emphasizes this sin very much when he adds those awful words which are unbearable in the ears of all sane human beings: "Bring out those men, that we may know them." It is not one or the other who is crying this. No, it is the entire city, young and old, even the officers of the state. Learn, therefore, what the prophet Isaiah (3:9) means when he says about his people: "They proclaim their sin like Sodom." It is not in the house that they utter such unspeakable words; but they are standing outside in the open, and by authority of the officers of the state they publicly demand that the two angels be brought out. Therefore this was not a sin of such a kind that they desired it to be secret and to remain hidden; it is clear that it was an open practice of which no one was ashamed.

What makes their disgraceful action worse is that they have the audacity to do these things to strangers. Moreover, what did the other four lesser cities and, as it were, pupils do when Sodom, their leading city, was doing this? Therefore if the Lord had not brought on the punishment which they deserved, the government would gradually have collapsed and could not have continued to exist. For if you do away with the marriage bond and permit promiscuous passions, the laws and all decency go to ruin together with discipline. But when these are destroyed, no government remains; only beastliness and savagery are left. Therefore as an example for others the Lord was compelled to inflict punishment and to check the madness that was raging beyond measure.

6. *Lot went out of the door to the men, shut the door after him,*

7. *and said: I beg you, my brothers, do not act so wickedly.*

8. *Behold, I have two daughters who have not known man; let me bring them out to you, and do to them as you please; only do nothing to these men, for they have come under the shelter of my roof.*

All this is intended to describe incorrigible madness and an utterly incurable sin. To be sure, pious Lot tries to resist the madness of his fellow citizens with sound instruction and a godly and friendly admonition; but he does so in vain, for they are inflamed all the more. He calls them brothers and not, as they had deserved, tyrants or rascals; and he begs them in a most friendly manner to desist from their design and to do no harm to his guests. But they are irritated all the more. What, then, would they have done if he had roundly condemned them and had called them slaves of Satan, as they actually were, and enemies of God?

"A soft answer," says Solomon (Prov. 15:1), "turns away wrath"; but the madness of these people is so great that they are inflamed all the more. Nor is it enough for Lot to have tried to gain his end by means of soft words, but he makes a final effort and offers them his two daughters merely to have regard for the decency of his guests and to save them from harm. Nor does he take into consideration the most certain danger to which he was exposing his daughters, who were already betrothed.[25]

Accordingly, you see the magnitude of the sin of the people of Sodom, which could not be cured by any method. They utterly despised the Word. Moreover, the two remedies — and very important ones at that — which Lot applies in such great danger, namely, very friendly words and his offer to surrender his daughters to the lust of the raving people of Sodom to misuse them as they please, are not

---

[25] The Weimar editors suggest that *desponsae* here should be *desponsatae*.

only futile but even increase their frenzy. They make no reply to his proposal concerning his daughters. Instead, as frenzied men are wont to do, they spurn women, as though they wanted to say that the ravishing of girls is an everyday sport. Therefore they turn to Lot and reply to his speech.

9. *But they said: "Draw near to that place!"*

Jerome has translated this with "Stand back!" as though they were ordering him to depart from the city;[26] but it is more likely that they ordered him to return to the house and to bring out his guests.

And they said: This fellow came to sojourn, and he would play the judge! Now we will deal worse with you than with them. Then they pressed hard against the man Lot.

In short, they do not want to be corrected, and they do not want to be rebuked. They rely on their power and on their large number, and they look down upon Lot as a sojourner. They do not want to be either judged or admonished by him. Today the pope is accustomed to deal with his people in the same way. Because he is sitting on that summit of authority, he thinks that he may do what he pleases, is impatient of all reproof, and calls those seditious whom he sees offering resistance to his whims. He is altogether like the people of Sodom. But where no room is left for remedies, there ruin and destruction must ensue. So far Moses has described the sin of Sodom; now he proceeds to describe the punishment. But first we shall occupy ourselves with the usual questions.

In the first place, it is customarily asked whether all the people in the five cities were so perverse and wicked, what our opinion of the women and the virgins should be, likewise what we should think about the little children, who do not yet have the use of reason. But we shall put off these questions until the end, and we shall now concern ourselves with that familiar one with which Lyra, and before him Augustine, have dealt.[27]

Did Lot do right when, for the sake of saving his guests, he offered his daughters — and betrothed daughters at that — for defilement? For it is a great disgrace for a parent to expose his daughters — and betrothed daughters at that — to prostitution, and not to simple prosti-

---

[26] The Latin version of this verse has *Recede*.
[27] Cf. the discussion of this verse in Lyra *ad* Gen. 19:9.

tution but to adultery, yes, even to death. Yet we see that Lot, who does this, is the kind of man who is worthy to show hospitality to angels, something which is a distinct proof of his sanctity and godliness.

But just as the loyalty toward his guests deserves praise, so his extreme disloyalty toward his daughters, whose respectability the parent should defend at the risk of his own life, is execrable.

These facts cause Augustine to waver. Consequently, he does not come to a definite conclusion. It seems to be true that between two evils the lesser evil should be chosen. This he calls balancing one shameful deed with another. Since the respectability either of his guests or of his daughters had to be put in peril, the sin against his daughters seemed less grave; for the other sin was against nature. But the apostle overthrows this opinion when he says (Rom. 3:8) that evils should not be done in order that good may result. And Augustine himself leans toward a less harsh opinion and concludes that Lot resorted to this plan because of unusual perturbation of spirit, but that the perturbation of spirit was wicked and for this reason should not be expressed. In this manner Augustine extricates himself and leaves the hearer in doubt.

Lyra's discussion is somewhat more outspoken. Although he does not approve of Augustine's idea about balancing one shameful deed with another — just as it should not be approved — he nevertheless adduces two examples which seem to support Augustine's view.

In the first place, divorce was permitted to the Jews in order to avoid greater sin. In the second place, in the more populous and crowded cities houses of ill fame are tolerated in order that because of this opportunity fewer acts of debauchery and adultery may be committed. Thus in this instance, too, Lot was at liberty to avoid a greater sin by permitting a lesser one. But Lyra is correct when he submits that this may be done in material situations; for it is right if you lose ten guldens in order to save a hundred, and it is also right for you to cut off a finger or a hand in order to preserve the entire body. In material situations the general rule holds good that in order to avoid a greater evil you should choose the lesser evil; but in spiritual affairs the situation is different, and evils should not be done in order that good may result. It is a sin to kill one's wife; but if by adultery you could save her from being killed, this should by no means be done. Similarly, Augustine does not even want a lie to be told in order to forestall a murder.

So far as the Jewish divorce is concerned, Lyra is right when he cites those who maintain that Moses, as a lawgiver, allowed this by divine authority, not on his own authority; for God, he says, is able to join people in marriage and to dissolve marriages. Similarly, the Jews carried off the property of the Egyptians by divine authority. Yet they were not sinning (Ex. 12:36).

The example concerning the houses of ill fame which are tolerated in large cities does not deserve to be discussed; for it is clearly in conflict with the Law of God, and those who publicly tolerate this disgrace should be regarded as heathen. It is silly for them to suppose that outcroppings of debauchery and adultery are reduced by this means. Once a young man who associates with prostitutes has surrendered his modesty, he will, when the opportunity arises, keep away neither from married women nor from virgins. Therefore lust is increased rather than cured by this means, and it becomes a warrant to sin for those who otherwise would be continent if this opportunity had been denied them. Other and better remedies have been pointed out and commanded by God, namely, marriage. Therefore a government which tolerates houses of ill fame should be regarded as heathenish. For a godly government should not tolerate fornication, especially manifest licentiousness. Even against the will of the officers of the state and in spite of their prohibition this evil nevertheless prevails and cannot be completely abolished.

But I return to the main question: whether Lot can be excused. Lyra reaches the conclusion that he indeed committed a mortal sin; yet, inasmuch as this sin resulted from perturbation of spirit, he should be exonerated to that extent, but not entirely. This is how they spoke in the schools when they wanted to indicate a somewhat lighter sin. We shall act more correctly if we discuss such cases soberly. What reason have we for exerting ourselves so diligently to excuse the sins of the saints? They were human. Therefore when they were perturbed by dangers, they could be deceived at times and err. Yet so far as the account before us is concerned, I excuse Lot and think that he adopted this plan without sinning. He did not plan to expose his daughters to danger, for he knew that they were not desired by the frenzied men; but he hoped that this would be a way to soften their wrath. Therefore this speech should be regarded as a hyperbole.

Otherwise, whatever the case may be, one must adhere to the rule that the deeds of the saints should not be imitated or taken as examples. It is not logical to say that because Abraham, Augustine, and Peter did this, I, too, must do it. But this is a valid argument: God says and commands this; therefore it must be done. For the Word is a reliable rule which cannot deceive. Thus the jurists, too, say that an action is not a law, just as a law is not an action. But to pass judgment on the actions of others is all the more difficult because we see only what is seemingly being done; we do not see the heart.

It is certain that Lot was dear to God and that he was a saintly man; otherwise he would have had to perish with the people of Sodom. But he offers his daughters in the hope of saving his guests. Yet one does not see in what spirit he offered them. What if he, a man full of faith in God, was firmly convinced that God would dispel all danger of harm to his daughters and that at the same time there was hope of rescuing his guests? Surely you will not readily condemn a heart that looks to the goodness and the omnipotence of God when danger is very close at hand. Moreover, who will doubt that Lot added prayers and sighs for the protection of his family? Yet the danger at hand drove him to take this course.

Even though I am not defending Lot — for he was a human being and could be subject to something that was human; and merely the bare deed, not the heart itself, is open to our view — the circumstances compel me to conclude that his action is blameless. Nevertheless, it does not follow from this that he should be imitated or should be taken as an example, as though it were permitted to commit a lesser sin to avoid a sin that is greater. For what happens outside the law should not be taken as law but should be regarded as miracles, on the basis of which surely nobody should make a rule or a law. And especially in the church should the teachers try to teach what is certain. Therefore they should not present examples; they should present the rule. You are not Lot; you are not Abraham. Therefore you should not imitate what Lot and Abraham did.

The rebellious Münzer used to present to his peasants the example given by David when he fought against the Syrians; he ordered the peasants to fight in the same way against the nobility.[28] This is turning an example into a law and making a rule out of an action. The result of this is never without certain danger, for to depart from the rule and to rely on the bare deed is to tempt God. Therefore those who are not called by a specific command outside the rule, to be "wonder

[28] Cf. p. 31, note 25.

men"²⁹ (if I may use this expression), should keep within the rule. Then they will not transgress or err. But Lot, Abraham, and their like are "wonder men"; their spirit is carried away beyond the law, beyond example and consequence. For they have an extraordinary call and impulse. You do not.

Therefore when such accounts are presented, you must remember not to lay stress on the examples or deeds but to emphasize the law and the rule. What Lot did does not concern you at all. "For who are you to pass judgment on the servant of another?" (Rom. 14:4) But the Law does concern you, in order that you may instruct your wife and children in godliness and may beware of becoming a cause of sin to them. If danger threatens and you are able to protect their honor, do not expose them to dishonor or excuse yourself by citing the example of Lot; for you are not Lot, and because you depart from the rule, you are tempting God. It has not been given you to depart from the rule and to imitate the examples and the wonderful deeds of others.

Abraham kills four kings in Egypt, twice he exposes his wife to danger in regard to her honor, and Lot offers his daughters for defilement. Why they do this is none of your concern. For in this way God wanted to reveal His wisdom and power.

Therefore I can marvel at these deeds, but I cannot imitate them. In like manner, we marvel at Peter when he walks on the sea, and at Christ and Moses when they fast for forty days; but we do not imitate them. In the case of the saints the things that are in conflict with the law and the rule are extraordinary and cannot be done by us; but their deeds that cannot be excused — for instance, Lot's intercourse with his daughters — are sins and must not be done by us. Yet it is not rare that the saints stumble and fall. "A righteous man falls six times in the course of a day," says Scripture (cf. Prov. 24:16).³⁰ Because they have sinful flesh just as we do, it is not at all surprising if they sometimes fall. But where they can be excused, let us glorify God. Thus I believe that Lot is a divine miracle and that in him God wanted to reveal His wisdom and power.

Accordingly when Scripture presents deeds and rights, examples

---

²⁹ On these *Wundermänner*, who "have a special star before God" and who have appeared among both Jews and Gentiles, cf. *Luther's Works*, 13, pp. 154—156.

³⁰ Here Luther's memory is at fault. Prov. 24:16 says: "For a righteous man falls *seven* times."

and rules, miracles and commands or a law, the right, the rule, and the law must be taught and considered. If a grammarian lays down the rule that every noun ending in "a" is of the feminine gender, the word *poema* is a miracle, so to speak, when it is considered according to this rule; for it is a neuter noun. Thus in the case of a right, moderation [31] should be aimed at. This is a miracle of the jurists, because it deviates from the rule. For it is true that the height of right is the height of wrong.[32] In like manner, physicians have their canons. But how often unexpected happenings compel them to deviate from these canons and apply the opposite method of healing! Accordingly, inexperienced jurists and physicians who simply insist on the rule without considering unforeseen happenings are like the legalists in the field of theology, who rigidly rule the entire world but do enormous damage to property, bodies, and salvation.

To be sure, rules should be taught and observed. But in order to reveal His power and wisdom, God does many things contrary to the rule; He does so through heroes, whom He Himself calls in a special way, although these heroes are rare and few. The others must adhere to the norm and rule, because, if they want to imitate those heroes, who deviate from the rule, they will stumble disgracefully. Such deeds are praised because they are done by heroes and "wonder men," but nobody can successfully imitate them. The situation is similar when a strong and agile person leaps across a moat or a brook, but one who has neither strength nor agility employs skill and supports himself with a staff. Thus skill enables him to achieve what he cannot do by nature. But let us return to Moses.

And they drew near to break the door.

10. *But the men put forth their hands and brought Lot into the house to them, and shut the door.*

11. *And they struck with blindness the men who were at the door of the house, both small and great, so that they wearied themselves groping for the door.*

The raving people of Sodom were already trying to break open the door. Consequently, it was time for the guests to protect themselves and do a kind deed for so generous and faithful a host who was trying

---

[31] The Greek word used here is ἐπιείκεια, a favorite of Melanchthon's.

[32] Cicero, *De officiis*, I, 10, 33; cf. also *Luther's Works*, 13, p. 150, note 12.

everything that seemed useful for their safety. Lot did not know that they were angels; he thought that they were saintly men who were visiting the churches and were teaching the Word far and wide. Therefore he worshiped God in them and honored them solemnly as guests who had been sent by God. And he and his entire house receive a very rich reward for this godly conduct. In the first place, he is defended against the raving people. For — as Lyra, too, remarks — the angels do not [33] smite them with such blindness that they see nothing at all; but they smite them with confusion, so that even if they did see, they still could not make out what they were seeing,[34] just as a drunken person has his eyes open and sees but does so without being able to make out what he sees; for he does not recognize what he is seeing.

This the Hebrews properly call סַנְוֵרִים. The people of Sodom saw the door, but they erred in their judgment and thought that it was the wall. On the other hand, they thought that the walls were the door. This is not a natural blindness; it is a miraculous blindness. It involves the mind and is called ἀκρισία and also ἀορισία, the loss of a function, not of a faculty.[35] Thus the Syrians did not see Elisha and his servant (2 Kings 6:18), and the Jews did not see Christ in the temple (John 10:39). God often employs a miracle like this to rescue His own whom He wants to protect even while enemies are looking on. This is called being deprived of the function, not of the faculty, of sight. The actual seeing is taken away, as is stated in the Gospel (Luke 24:16): "Their eyes were kept from recognizing Him." Thus Magdalene thought that Christ was the gardener (John 20:15); and the Syrians did not see that they were being led aside into Samaria, even though they saw everything else. In like manner, the people of Sodom, who were about to break down the door, were stricken with blindness by the angels, so that the door and the windows disappeared from their sight. Thus at all times many have been delivered in a miraculous manner, so that they escaped while sport, so to speak, was being made of the eyes of their enemies.

[33] Following the suggestion of the Weimar editors, we have inserted the word *non* here.

[34] Lyra *ad* Gen. 19:11.

[35] The word in the text is ἀορισία. This may be meant as ἀορασία, "blindness," or as ἀοριστία, "indecision, indefiniteness"; in either case the influence of Melanchthon or of his pupils seems to have been at work.

But here one must note a difference. The Syrians who had been stricken with blindness by the prophet improve when they feel the hand of the Lord. But when the people of Sodom feel the hand of the Lord, they do not improve; for they are blind throughout the entire night and do not stop looking for the door until they are utterly fatigued and worn out. In what frame of mind do you suppose Lot was here, while sitting all night and expecting the citizens to burst in at any moment? But the angels undoubtedly cheered him with the assurance that this effort of the Sodomites would be in vain. So Lot, and particularly his wife and daughters, spent the whole sleepless night worrying and weeping.

But when the people of Sodom realize that they have been smitten with blindness, they do not at all accept this as a punishment inflicted by the Lord; they suspect that it is some magic and believe that they have been bewitched by Satan. This is the way it always happens; the ungodly are most obdurate and conclude that they are being caressed in God's bosom, while the godly, on the other hand, are terrified and fear God's wrath. They conclude that the scourge is being sent by an angry God, not by Satan. For this reason they are greatly terrified at the sound of a falling leaf (Lev. 26:36) and are afraid of everything that presents no danger. They cannot have the thoughts that the ungodly have: that the devil is the author of these misfortunes, as he actually is. For God does not afflict the godly; He permits the devil to do this, as we see in the case of Job, whose children are killed by fire and his cattle by storms, not because God was angry with him, but because Satan was.

Therefore when a plague and other misfortunes assail us, we, too, should say that these are the works of Satan, that Satan is raging and is angry, but that God is merciful and is kindly disposed toward us because we believe in His Son.

And in this manner the saintly martyrs overcame death and all dangers; for they were sure that God was kind to them. But they concluded that their tortures and afflictions were due to magic and the devil, and were permitted by God for the purpose of testing their faith. Therefore they even rejoiced in their adversities and scoffed at Satan. We should do the same thing; but we are very frequently overcome by weakness, as the examples even of great saints prove. For Paul, too, is filled with fears and regains his courage when he sees the brethren (Acts 28:15). Such fear is not felt by the ungodly, for they are sure of God's favor. Accordingly, even though some adversity befalls them, they smugly attribute this to Satan.

In like manner, when the people of Sodom have been smitten with blindness, they realize what has happened to them; but they do not accept this as a punishment inflicted by God. They imagine that a magic formula has been used against them and that they have been bewitched by Lot. If we were able to do this and to imitate the ungodly in this respect, we would be happy; yet countless most dependable promises invite us to this state of happiness.

Moreover, these truths should be carefully impressed and taught, lest we yield to the flesh when we are tried or to our reason when we disregard the Word. For it is not God who torments you if you believe in Christ; it is the devil. He hates you and looks for opportunities to trouble you. But you will say: "I realize that I am a sinner. Therefore I am not a Christian. Therefore if any evil befalls me, it is sent by an angry God." But this conclusion is false, for those who believe in the forgiveness of sins are Christians. Therefore if you believe in Christ, if you gladly hear His Word and receive it in faith, you are a true Christian, and your sins do not stand in the way. Hence if any misfortune befalls you, conclude boldly that it is from the devil and does not mean that God is unfriendly toward you, except insofar as He lets this happen as a trial, in order to put your faith to the test for your own good.

Learn from your own enemies and from the enemies of God that although the threats properly apply to them, they do not recognize this fact but appropriate, and comfort themselves with, the promises. You, too, must do this. For it is a disgrace for you to be ignorant of the true doctrine which you profess. You fear God and believe in God; therefore not the Law but the Gospel applies to you. But you forsake the Gospel and appropriate the Law, which concerns not you but the obdurate and the smug.

This is a spiritual weakness of which all the saints complain. Yet it is useful for repressing pride, in order that we may not put our trust in ourselves but may humble ourselves and learn to trust solely in the grace which God offers us in His Son. It is most certainly true that God is not angry with us; otherwise He would not give us the most excellent knowledge of His Son. Nor would He give us the Holy Spirit, whose first fruits we have received.[36] Therefore we also confess

---

[36] Cf. *Luther's Works*, 13, p. 90, note 24 on this concept of the first fruits.

the Son of God and do not blaspheme Him, as the papists do; and we resist sin to a degree. Therefore it would be desirable that we be like the people of Sodom in this respect, that we, following their example, laugh at, and consider as a jest, the ravings of Satan but steadfastly conclude that we who believe in Christ are loved and protected by God, as is truly the case.

Where our translation has "so that they were unable to find the door," the Hebrew is: "They wearied themselves groping for the door." יִלְאוּ is a familiar verb. From it is derived לֵאָה, a languid, feeble, deficient girl who, as it seemed, could not live for weakness.[37] Thus this expression serves to describe the incorrigible stubbornness. They did not stop when they were stricken with blindness; but they kept up the laborious search they had begun — kept it up until weariness compelled them to cease and, as usually happens in the case of tired people, they were overcome by sleep.

12. *Then the men said to Lot: Have you anyone else here? Sons-in-law, sons, daughters, or anyone you have in the city, bring them out of the place;*

13. *for we are about to destroy this place, because the outcry against its people has become great before the Lord, and the Lord has sent us to destroy it.*

For linguistic reasons it is debated at this point whether Lot had more children, both sons and daughters, since the angels say that if he had any others in the city, he should take them out with him. Later on only two daughters are mentioned. I agree with Lyra's opinion that the angels are speaking in human fashion or as human beings are accustomed to speak, as though they did not know whether Lot had any others who belonged to his household or family;[38] for above it was stated about Lot that he had so many cattle and herdsmen that he was unable to dwell with Abraham.

But here another question arises. Where had the cattle and the herdsmen remained? For the account that follows reveals nothing concerning them. I myself surely cannot reach a conclusion about this odd account, unless perhaps, as is likely, the herdsmen and the cattle were outside the city in the field and in some safe place. For

---

[37] Probably a reference to Gen. 29:16.
[38] Lyra *ad* Gen. 19:12.

the supposition of some that Lot, compelled by want, had sold his cattle and had dismissed his domestics is not only unlikely but also involves a reproach. If, however, they were in the city, it is exceedingly shocking that even the servants in Lot's house were against their master and were involved in the same smugness in which the whole ungodly city lived. But let us leave this undecided, since Scripture makes no mention of it and states clearly that only four souls were saved, although eventually Lot's wife also perished on the way, and only the father and his two daughters were saved.

But it is a notable example of extraordinary wickedness that the godly head of the household was unable to keep either a single herdsman or a single maidservant in their calling. The very great offense that the master alone had the entire city against him, deceived them all. Therefore they thought as follows: "Our master is a sincere and pious man; he indiscriminately receives whoever comes here as guests. Yet, as is the habit of the world, he is often poorly thanked for this. Thus he has now brought harm upon himself by putting up these guests in his home against their will." It is usual for the world to think that the saints are foolish and do many foolish things. Accordingly, when Lot preached about the coming punishment and wanted to save his household, they spurned him as a doting and ridiculously credulous old man. This idea pleases me more; and the examples show that domestics are usually wont to conduct themselves in this manner, especially in dangers, which reveal who are true friends and who are false.

In this passage you should note the verb יֹצֵא, which the translator renders: "Bring out." It is the same verb that Moses employed above (Gen. 14:18) concerning Melchizedek in the story of Abraham, namely, that he brought out bread and wine. The papists distort this passage and explain it as referring to an offering or the Mass, although this word denotes nothing else than that Melchizedek brought out bread and wine to be shared in common when he was about to welcome his victorious guest with this gift.[39] Accordingly, the stubborn advocates of the ungodly Mass are refuted not only by the theologian who treats these events but also by the philologian; for it is absurd if in the account of Melchizedek you explain the verb יֹצֵא to mean "to sacrifice" and in this passage maintain that Lot was ordered by the angels to sacrifice all his possessions.

[39] Cf. *Luther's Works*, 2, pp. 383—388 on the interpretation of Melchizedek.

14. *So Lot went out and said to his sons-in-law, who were to marry his daughters: Up, get out of this place; for the Lord is about to destroy the city. But he seemed to his sons-in-law to be jesting.*

After the people of Sodom were exhausted by their searching and were overcome by sleep, Lot, having been commanded by the angels to do so, goes out to warn his sons-in-law, to whom he was about to give his daughters, that they should be on their guard and escape from the impending destruction. But they, too, seem to be suffering from the effects of their intoxication on the previous day, since they even laugh at the pious old man. They thought: "What? Would the Lord so suddenly destroy this place? How foolishly credulous you are to believe those guests, or rather impostors! If anything like this were impending, there would surely be some evidences of the disaster which is about to happen. Now, however, everything is gay and serene, and you dream of destruction!"

It always happens this way. The nearer the world is to destruction, the smugger it is. It not only laughs at threats but believes that it is altogether impossible that it should perish so suddenly. Noah warns of the Flood that is to come and calls his fellow citizens to repentance, but he is laughed at and is believed to be out of his wits because of senility. We, too, preach about the Son of God, who will come to pronounce judgment and will consign the ungodly to eternal fire; but when the pope and his cardinals either read or hear this, they laugh at it as at an impossible event and say: "What if heaven should fall down?"

Thus the story is told about Pope Leo [40] that he once invited two philosophers to dinner. One of them discussed the immortality of the soul; the other discussed its mortality. When, after a long, hot debate, the pope had to decide which of the two had spoken more correctly, he said to him who had defended the immortality of souls: "To be sure, you seem to be stating facts; but your opponent's discourse creates a cheerful countenance." Epicureans are in the habit of doing this; over against the clear truth they draw conclusions that suit the flesh and reason.

But let us not disregard the threats or disdain them. For Lyra is correct when he states that Lot's sons-in-law represent those who,

[40] On the significance of this argument for immortality cf. *Luther's Works,* 1, Introduction, p. xi.

when they hear the threat of God's judgment, laugh and declare that it is a delusion.[41]

"But," you will say, "If Lot's sons-in-law were such men, why did the godly old man let them have his daughters? It should be a parent's first concern to seek a relationship by marriage with the godly and not to join his children with the ungodly." My answer is: Lot had a little church in which he taught and propagated the true knowledge of God. Undoubtedly his sons-in-law were also in this church. For this reason Lot thought that they were pious and saintly, for he could not look into their hearts. But they were hypocrites; they feigned godliness for a time, but now they revealed their true character when they laughed at the Word. Because they laugh, they perish, for they do not believe that the aged Lot is speaking in earnest; they make sport of and laugh at him as if he were insane.

This is surely a notable account. No matter how righteous we may be, it should be proclaimed in the church frequently, lest we fall into the madness of the antinomians, who remove the Law from the church, as if everybody in the church were actually a saint and there were no need for such examples of God's wrath. The world, of course, is fond of such teachers, as in the Book of Jeremiah the people say: "Speak the things that please us." [42] But St. Paul (Rom. 16:18) does not want the church to be led astray by pleasing speeches; for sins should be denounced, and God's wrath should be exhibited for the sake of the unbelievers who are in the church, yes, also for the sake of the believers, lest they yield to sin, which still adheres to them, and to their natural weakness. Thus even though Christ Himself most pleasantly invites sinners to come to Him, He nevertheless repeatedly cries out the awful "Woe!" over the impenitent Pharisees.

But I had almost forgotten that at this point something should also be said about the angels who boast, as it were, that they have been sent to destroy the cities. They say: "We are about to destroy this place," and likewise: "The Lord has sent us to destroy it." This is just as if they were boasting of being executioners and God's destroyers and ravagers.

This, however, serves to describe the duty and the power of the angels. Elijah, Elisha, and others — as is stated in the eleventh chap-

[41] Lyra *ad* Gen. 19:14.

[42] Despite the reference to "Jeremiah" in the original the passage being referred to is actually Is. 30:10.

ter of Hebrews — also performed great miracles, but not by their own strength. Prayer and faith must be added; and from these, as from a *causa sine qua non,* as the philosophers call it, miracles result. Thus Peter (Acts 3:6) prays, and in faith in Christ he bids the lame man rise; but the angels are powerful. Consequently they perform miracles by reason of the strength given to them when they were created.

It is certainly true that God governs this visible world not only through men but also through angels. Of course, He could kill thieves without the services of an executioner and without the verdict of an officer of the state, as He sometimes does, especially in the case of murderers. He could also create human beings without the union of a male and a female, just as He created Adam and Eve. But it has pleased the Divine Majesty to make use of the help and services of human beings, evidently in order to reveal His marvelous divine power in His creatures, whom He did not want to be idle. Therefore Paul (1 Cor. 3:9) calls us all God's fellow workers; for He makes use of our help for various purposes, just as He makes use of the help of the angels, whom He endowed with such great might that by their own or innate power they are able to destroy lands and peoples if God is with them.

Moreover, it is a great glory to be endowed with such great might; for it is well known that at the time of King Hezekiah the angel of the Lord killed 185,000 Assyrians in a single night and by a single assault (2 Kings 19:35). And Christ praises the might of the angels when He tells Peter (Matt. 26:53) about the twelve legions, although a single angel would have been enough to turn back and destroy the enemies of Christ. Indeed, the story of Job proves that even the wicked angels are endowed with great power.

It is profitable to know these facts; they serve to comfort the godly but to frighten the ungodly. For we who believe must be certain that the princes of heaven are with us, not one or two, but a great multitude of them, as is recorded in Luke that the heavenly hosts were with the shepherds (Luke 2:13). But if we were without this protection, and the Lord did not restrain the fury of Satan in this manner, we would not remain alive for a single moment. From the account of Job one can gather sure enough proof of what Satan is able to do and of what he desires most. He stirs up storms, hurls thunderbolts, or, in the language of Scripture, lets fire fall from heaven. He sends enemies; he even infects the body and covers it with boils. Therefore the good angels are busy in order that the fierce enemy may not inflict harm. Neither medicine nor other means would be effective by themselves if the angels were not present. And the fact that new remedies become known when new diseases make their appearance — this is not a matter of the diligence of human beings; it is a service of the angels, who direct and urge on the hearts of the physicians, just as Satan directs and urges on his own, as Paul bears witness (Eph. 2:2).

Accordingly, what Moses states in this passage about the good angels who lay waste and destroy the earth serves, in the first place, to teach us to fear God, since we have such a powerful opponent in Satan. In the second place, it teaches us to trust in the goodness of God, who has appointed such excellent princes and leaders through whom He so mightily defends His people. Everybody is aware of what Satan achieves through the Turk, the Roman pope, and the fanatical spirits, not only by attacking bodies but also by seizing souls and holding them captive (2 Tim. 2:26). But this protection of the angels, which God wanted to be more powerful than Satan, gives us comfort.

This government of God through His creatures is wonderful, because the angels, who support the godly, defend the entire human race, even though it is exposed to lions, wolves, dragons, and all the horrible leaders of Satan who have been trained to inflict harm not only with the sword, plagues, and countless diseases but also with heresies of every kind. Thus it evidently pleased God to reveal His glory through His creatures, but in a different way. Elijah commanded fire to fall from heaven, and the fire obeyed his word and faith. Similarly, he commanded heaven to rain, but not by the power of the angels, who do such things by their own power or by means of a gift given them at their creation. If the saints do anything like this, they bring it about through faith and prayer.

Above we dealt with the question whether Lot did not sin when he worshiped the angels.[43] What the angels state in this passage — that they were sent by the Lord — pertains to this question. Accordingly, he is not speaking as with angels, but as with the Lord, just as the works done at God's behest and command are also correctly called God's works. Therefore Christ, too, says (Luke 10:16): "He who hears you hears Me." Likewise (Matt. 25:40): "Whatever you have done to the least of Mine you have done to Me." It is a general

[43] Cf. pp. 243 f.

rule that whether something good is done through human beings or through angels, you must conclude that it has been done by the Lord and give Him the credit for it.

This rule is necessary, lest we make Moses a heretic and Lot an idolater who speaks of a creature as of the Creator. "The Lord," he says to his sons-in-law, "will destroy this place," although the angels had said that they would destroy this place. Therefore Lot does not consider the person of the angels; he considers God, who gives them the command.

Christ's statement in the Gospel (Matt. 19:4-5) is similar: "Have you not read that He who made them from the beginning made them male and female, and said: 'For this reason a man shall leave his father and mother'?" How shall we in this instance bring Moses into agreement with Christ? For Moses testifies in very clear words that this is Adam's statement, yet Christ asserts that God spoke in this manner.

My answer is: What Adam says, he says by divine authority. Therefore these words are not his own; they are God's. This, then, is the great glory with which the Divine Majesty honors us: It works through us in such a manner that It says that our words are Its words and that our actions are Its actions, so that one can truthfully say that the mouth of a godly teacher is God's mouth and that the hand which you extend to alleviate the want of a brother is God's hand. Thus when Adam says to Cain (Gen. 4:6): "Why has your countenance fallen?" it is correct to say that these words are God's words, even though they were spoken by the mouth of Adam.[44]

In this respect the heretics err greatly and associate things that have no connection when they argue about the spoken Word and the Sacrament and divest God altogether of the ministry; for he who does away with the Word and does not accept it as spoken by God does away with everything. Separate the Word from Baptism, from absolution, and from the Lord's Supper, and they will be nothing.

Therefore it is not only a foolish but also an ungodly argument of the Sacramentarians to maintain that externals are of no profit for salvation and then heap up examples and statements of Scripture such as (John 6:63): "The flesh is of no avail," etc. A distinction must be made among externals, and not all externals should thus be cast aside in general. Externals are rightly condemned as profiting

---

[44] See *Luther's Works*, 1, p. 262, and *Luther the Expositor*, pp. 103—105.

nothing for salvation when they have been instituted by the will of man or, more correctly, rashly, without the Word of God. In other respects God wants to work through the service of His creatures. For this reason one must consider above all whether these externals are performed in accordance with the institution and will of God or not. If there is no Word or institution of God, then you are correct in saying that the externals profit nothing for salvation but even do harm. Thus Christ says (Matt. 15:9): "In vain do they worship Me with the precepts of men."

But if you see that the externals rest on the Word and were instituted by God's command, then worship those externals silently on bended knee, and say: "Not my pastor, not Peter, not Paul, commands this to be done; it is my Father in heaven who gives the command. Therefore I shall obey in humility, and I shall believe that this obedience will be profitable for salvation."

This distinction is very necessary; for the heretics — either because they have no knowledge of it or disregard it — fall into ugly errors. The conclusion at which Schwenkfeld arrives in the following manner is not universally and unqualifiedly true: Nothing external is profitable for salvation. Baptism, the preaching of the Gospel, and the Lord's Supper are externals; hence they are of no avail for salvation.[45] The major premise is clearly false, for one must make a distinction among externals. Some are wholly human and have been invented by human beings. Of these the major premise is true. But concerning those that have been instituted and commanded by God the major premise is not true; for they have been instituted for our salvation, as Christ says about Baptism (Mark 16:16): "He who believes and is baptized will be saved," and Paul (Rom. 10:10): "With the mouth confession is made unto salvation."

Thus the spoken Word is indeed the word of a human being, but it has been instituted by divine authority for salvation. For God wants to govern the world through angels and through human beings, His creatures, as through His servants, just as He gives light through the sun, the moon, and even through fire and candles. Here, too, you could say: "No external thing profits. The sun is an external thing. Hence it profits nothing; that is, it does not give light, it does not warm, etc." Who would put up with one who argues in such a silly way?

[45] Cf. *Luther the Expositor*, pp. 99—100, 105—107.

Therefore the rule of which I have also spoken above stands. It states that God no longer wants to act in accordance with His extraordinary or, as the scholastics express it, absolute [46] power but wants to act through His creatures, whom He does not want to be idle. Thus He gives food, not as He did to the Jews in the desert, when He gave manna from heaven, but through labor, when we diligently perform the work of our calling. Furthermore, He no longer wants to form human beings from a clod, as He formed Adam, but He makes use of the union of a male and a female, on whom He bestows His blessing. This they call God's "ordered" power, namely, when He makes use of the service either of angels or of human beings. Thus in the prophet Amos (3:7) there is the noteworthy statement that God does nothing that He does not first reveal to His prophets.

But if at times some things happen without the service either of angels or of human beings, you would be right in saying: "What is beyond us does not concern us." We must keep the ordered power in mind and form our opinion on the basis of it. God is able to save without Baptism, just as we believe that infants who, as sometimes happens through the neglect of their parents or through some other mishap, do not receive Baptism are not damned on this account. But in the church we must judge and teach, in accordance with God's ordered power, that without that outward Baptism no one is saved. Thus it is due to God's ordered power that water makes wet, that fire burns, etc. But in Babylon Daniel's companions continued to live unharmed in the midst of the fire (Dan. 3:25). This took place through God's absolute power, in accordance with which He acted at that time; but He does not command us to act in accordance with this absolute power, for He wants us to act in accordance with the ordered power.

In the schools they recite the statement of Dionysius that God works through His essence but that we work through a quality that has flowed down.[47] But who will understand this? He, however, who properly adheres to the canon we have set up can judge the pope and the world in all their wisdom, namely, that God regularly does everything through the ministry of human beings. Therefore nobody

---

[46] See the discussion of this question in *Luther's Works*, 1, pp. 74—79.

[47] The distinction is between the divine operation *per essentiam* and the operation of creatures *per qualitatem defluxam*. The problem is discussed, for example, in Pseudo-Dionysius, *De divinis nominibus*, V, 3, *Patrologia, Series Graeca*, III, 817.

will obtain salvation through so-called spiritual speculations, without external things. Attention must be paid to the Word, and Baptism must be sought. The Eucharist must be received, and absolution must be required. All these are indeed externals, but they are included in the Word. Hence the Holy Spirit works nothing without them.

Formerly — before God revealed the light of the Gospel — much was written and said about the contemplative and the active life;[48] and in the monasteries and convents monks and nuns who, on the whole, were very pious eagerly strove to have visions and revelations presented to them. Consequently, some even noted down all their dreams. Evidently they all waited for extraordinary illuminations without external means. What else is this than a desire to ascend into heaven without ladders? Consequently, these monks and nuns were very frequently deceived by delusions of the devil.

Hence a certain father in the desert was correct in his judgment; for when he saw that his monks were given to such speculations, he warned them to refrain. He said: "If you think you are ascending into heaven and already setting one foot on the threshold of heaven, draw it back immediately, and do not follow with the other foot."[49] This man condemned speculations, or the contemplative life, which the unlearned and ignorant later on exalted with such great praises. Let him who wants to contemplate in the right way reflect on his Baptism; let him read his Bible, hear sermons, honor father and mother, and come to the aid of a brother in distress. But let him not shut himself up in a nook, as the sordid mob of monks and nuns is in the habit of doing, and there entertain himself with his devotions and thus suppose that he is sitting in God's bosom and has fellowship with God without Christ, without the Word, without the sacraments, etc.

People of this kind speak most contemptuously of the active life, and I certainly had to pay a high price before I was freed from this error, for it pleases reason and seems to be a worship of angels, as Paul calls it (Col. 2:18). The hypocrite and blasphemous apostate Witzel once reproached me by saying that we teach externals too

[48] When Luther speaks of God revealing the light of the Gospel here, he is referring to the beginning of his Reformation; cf. also p. 6, note 4.

[49] On this story from the medieval tradition about St. Antony see also *Luther's Works*, 24, p. 65.

much and should place emphasis on spiritual things.⁵⁰ For reason wants to move about among wonderful things that are beyond it. But beware of these snares of Satan, and set up a definition of the contemplative life different from the one they taught in the monasteries, namely, that it is the true contemplative life to hear and believe the spoken Word and to want to know nothing "except Christ and Him crucified" (1 Cor. 2:2). He alone, with His Word, is the profitable and salutary object of contemplation. Beware of forsaking Him; for those who have given up or disregarded the human nature or the flesh of Christ and speculate about God as the monks used to do and now Schwenkfeld and others are in the habit of doing are either driven to despair when they are overwhelmed by the clarity of the Majesty, or they foolishly exult and dream that they have been placed into heaven. But they have been deceived by Satan, who makes sport of hearts by means of such deceptions. Those who despair can indeed be helped; but the same thing does not hold true of those who, like people drunk with joy, think that they are sitting in God's bosom.

Gerson, too, has written about the contemplative life. He gives it high praise.⁵¹ When the unlearned read such statements, they accept them as oracles of God; but actually, as the proverb says, they accept coals as treasure.⁵² Hence if these good-for-nothing contemplators should call you either an externalist or a worldling, do not let this bother you. Give thanks to God for the Word and these externals, and leave these high-sounding speculations to others.

I once read books of that sort with great zeal, and I urge you, too, to read them, but with discretion. I have good reason to stress these things in this manner. You should direct your attention to the ordered power of God and the ministrations of God; for we do not want to deal with the uncovered God, whose ways are inscrutable and whose judgments are unsearchable (Rom. 11:33).

We must reflect on God's ordered power, that is, on the incarnate Son, in whom are hidden all the treasures of the Godhead (Col. 2:3). Let us go to the child lying in the lap of His mother Mary and to

---

⁵⁰ See p. 193, note 22.

⁵¹ John Gerson (1363—1429) wrote a mystical work in 1397 entitled *The Mountain of Contemplation*. Luther is probably referring to this and other mystical works of Gerson, contained in the third volume of his *Opera*, edited by Louis E. Dupin (Antwerp, 1706 ff.).

⁵² Phaedrus, V, 6, 6.

the sacrificial victim suspended on the cross; there we shall really behold God, and there we shall look into His very heart. We shall see that He is compassionate and does not desire the death of the sinner, but that the sinner should "turn from his way and live" (Ezek. 33:11). From such speculation or contemplation spring true peace and true joy of heart. Therefore Paul says (1 Cor. 2:2): "I determine to know nothing except Christ." We have leisure to speculate on this with profit.

But that union of the soul and the body about which Gerson discourses in a grand manner is often fraught with great peril and pure mockery of Satan, who stirs up such devotions in the heart.

A story is told about a certain nun who took delight in her contemplations and carefully kept away from the other nuns, lest her thoughts be hampered.[53] When she thought she was dressed in a golden robe and adorned with a golden crown and thus, like a bride at her marriage, sat there delighted and rejoiced, the rest of the nuns discovered the mockery; for instead of a crown on her head they saw cow dung. She dreamed that this was a golden crown. Whether this actually happened or not, it nevertheless shows that people have been shamefully deceived by their contemplations. Therefore let him who wants to be safe in this respect shun such contemplations and have a high opinion of the ministry, through which God deals with us and presents Himself to us, so to speak, to be observed. But let us finally get back to the account.

15. *When morning dawned, the angel urged Lot, saying: Arise, take your wife and your two daughters who are here, lest you be consumed in the punishment of the city.*

This is a moral example by which we are given instruction concerning love, of which Lot personally presents an extraordinary example. He is unwilling to leave the city, not so much for his own sake as for the sake of the citizens; for he desired that the punishment should at least be put off if he could not avert it altogether. For this reason he delays and lingers; he follows the example of Abraham, who also left no stone unturned in his effort to save his neighbors in the city. For his love is such that he grieves even when his enemies are in danger and suffer harm. So far as he himself is concerned, he does not doubt the words of the angels; but he

[53] For a similar discussion cf. *Luther's Works*, 21, pp. 33—39.

already has before his eyes, so to speak, the sight of the burning city after fire has been sent down from heaven. For faith apprehends the Word and believes the Word; to it then comes love. Consequently, he also thinks about delivering his neighbor and forgets all wrongs. But since he was unable to avert the calamity, he seeks a postponement by delaying. He is an example for us; we should be concerned for the welfare even of our adversaries and should consider not only our advantage but also the advantage of others.

At the present time we see that a great and certain catastrophe is threatening Germany, and the more we cry out and the more earnestly we exhort people to repent, the worse our opponents become. If we reprove them, as we should do, they blaspheme, and they rage against the members of our church and kill whom they can; they are utterly uncontrollable and are intent on their own destruction and that of all Germany. In these circumstances faith does what is its duty, for we believe that it is impossible for God to put up with such great blasphemy any longer. Yet since the punishment cannot be averted, love prays that God may delay it, if perhaps some may still be converted.

Thus when Hezekiah hears the prophecy about the Babylonians, who will lay Judea waste, he prays that there may be peace at least in his days. And in the letter of Jude (22—23) we are instructed to snatch others from the conflagration, so to speak. Therefore let us, too, pray the Lord at this time not to lead us into temptation and that if we cannot restrain His wrath, we may nevertheless be able to put it off, in order that at least some may be snatched from the coming conflagration which threatens all Germany because of our sins.

About Lot's daughters the question is raised whether they were married. But this is immaterial. It is the general opinion that they were betrothed. Accordingly, one should rather consider that the saintly girls, who were not at all disturbed by the offense of the men to whom they were betrothed, followed their father rather than their fiancés, who smugly laughed at the godly warning and concern of the old man.

But here one should note the unusual expression which Moses employs. By God's decree the angels order Lot himself to leave the city and add the grave threat: "Lest you, too, be snatched away in the sin, or because of the sin, of the city." He expressly calls it the sin of the city — not the sin of some people but the sin of the entire place. But this is a harsh statement; by it he represents the sin as so general and widely known that it is designated, not as the sin of adolescence or youth, not of men or women, not of the common people or the officers of the state, but of the entire city. Therefore it must have been the kind of sin that was committed with the consent of the officers of the state and all classes of people in that city and was tolerated by public consent, something which involved all alike, not only those who committed it but also those who consented to it. Such a sin was that of the Benjamites, who not only did not punish the hideous crime of rape by bringing the perpetrators to trial but even forced the entire tribe to defend it. Sins of this kind which are defended by the very officers of the state who ought to punish them accelerate the punishment. Therefore the Benjamites were completely cut down, so that only 600 remained of the entire tribe (Judges 19—20).

God has appointed three social classes to which he has given the command not to let sins go unpunished. The first is that of the parents, who should maintain strict discipline in their house when ruling the domestics and the children. The second is the government, for the officers of the state bear the sword for the purpose of coercing the obstinate and remiss by means of their power of discipline. The third is that of the church, which governs by the Word. By this threefold authority God has protected the human race against the devil, the flesh, and the world, to the end that offenses may not increase but may be cut off. Parents are the children's tutors, as it were. Those who are grown up and are remiss the government curbs through the executioner. In the church those who are obstinate are excommunicated.

Thus the Divine Majesty, as It makes use of the service of human beings in accordance with Its manifold wisdom and unlimited insight, is everywhere discernible. If some are remiss in their calling and either connive at offenses or do not punish them in earnest, they take the sin of others upon themselves.

If a father does not censure the sin of his children, it becomes the father's own sin. To be sure, the sins of adulterers, murderers, and usurers are the sins of the citizens who commit them; but if the government does not punish them, as happens here and there at the present time, those personal sins of the individuals become the sins of the city or public sins, and public disasters are always wont to result from them. For the laws are right in stipulating that like punishment should be inflicted on him who commits an offense and on him who consents to it. Thus if a bishop is aware of errors, heresies, and evil conduct in the church and does not resort to reproof and excommunicate the unrepentant, he makes himself guilty of all those sins. Thus Lot hears the terrible sentence that if he does not leave, he will have a share in the sin of the city and will perish with the unbelieving citizens.

Similarly in Num. 16:24, when the Lord was about to punish the rebellious Dathan, Abiram, and Korah, Moses cried aloud to the others: "Separate yourselves from the ungodly men, lest you, too, be swallowed up." And when they sacrificed to the calves (Ex. 32:28), 23,000 were slain by the Levites; otherwise, if this had not been done, the entire people would have been destroyed, and that sin would have been charged to the people. And in Joshua, after the Reubenites had built an altar, the entire people, since they feared punishment, sent ambassadors and said: "We have not yet been cleansed from the sin of Balaam, and you are bringing a new sin upon us" (22:10 ff.). For they realize and see that the statement of Ezekiel is true: "If I say to the wicked: 'You shall surely die,' and you give him no warning, nor speak to warn the wicked from his wicked way, in order to save his life, that wicked man shall die in his iniquity; but his blood I will require at your hand" (3:18).

Furthermore, this command about censuring sins concerns not only the teachers in the church and the officers in the state but also every citizen and every member of a household. Joseph reported his brothers' sins to his father and accused his brothers (Gen. 37:2). Thus citizens should not disregard the sins of others among themselves, and in the church a brother should reprove a brother in accordance with Christ's command, lest he have a part in the sins of others. And in the state it is not rare to find examples which show that ruin and terrible disasters of the people have followed whenever the government has either supported or defended manifest sins. Then, of course, one must flee, unless one wants to become a partaker of the sin of others and bring down upon one's own head punishment for the sin of others. Thus we are warned in Revelation (18:4) to depart from Babylon and forsake her; that is, we should completely separate ourselves from the pope's church, unless we want to perish with it.

So far as Lot is concerned, he is a saintly and guiltless man; he is beyond reproach. Yet he hears this threat: "'Lest you be consumed' — not, of course, because of your own sins, for the angels have been sent to you to save you, but because of the sin of the city." Therefore whether we are officers of the state or private citizens, we should of one accord oppose sins, lest the wrath of God come upon us and we all be consumed together.

In the accounts of the Greeks there is a story about a certain Amyris, a citizen of Sybaris.[54] He had seen that a slave, who had been dragged away from an altar by his owner, sought refuge at the tomb of the latter's father. There the owner, moved by reverence for his father's tomb, spared the slave. Since Amyris considered it disgraceful that reverence for the tomb was greater than for the altar, he sold everything he had and went away to the Peloponnesus from the then rich and flourishing city of Sybaris, because he concluded that certain punishment would result from such practices. Because of this action he seemed mad to his fellow citizens; but he himself obtained a most excellent return from this madness of his, for Sybaris was shortly thereafter destroyed. Hence one should note that when sins are continually prevalent, the wrath of God must come. Therefore let those who hold an office or are officers of the state do their duty, and let them not wink at any offense, however small. But if iniquity prevails, let them flee, lest they become partakers of the sins of others.

Therefore we justly censure the antinomians, who assert that the threats of the Law have no place in the church. But there is a definite command of God that sins should be rebuked. Therefore let no one be troubled by the fact that truth begets hatred. Let him who bears the sword punish with severity those who give rise to offenses, and let him pay no heed to whether or not the citizens are offended. In like manner, a teacher in the church should censure without restraint the things that are done with offense, and he should keep the impenitent from Communion and other sacred ceremonies. For the Gospel should not be preached to ungodly despisers; it should be preached to the afflicted, the wretched, and the ailing, as is stated in Is. 61:1: "The Holy Spirit is upon Me; He sent Me to preach to the afflicted, to heal the brokenhearted" — not to comfort the proud and stubborn despisers, of whom there is always a very large multitude, as Christ points out in the parable of the seed (Luke 8:5-15). And in this passage we hear the rule that one should not participate in the sins of others. For even

---

[54] The story of Amyris appears originally in Herodotus, *History*, VI, 127; it is then expanded by writers like Athenaeus to include such anecdotes as this.

though Lot was not an officer of the state but was a private citizen beyond reproach, nevertheless, if he had not fled, the sin of the city would have become his own, and he would have perished together with the rest.

16. *But he lingered; so the men seized him and his wife and his two daughters by the hand, the Lord being merciful to him, and they brought him forth and set him outside the city.*

Lot had God's command to leave the city and abandon it. This command he should have obeyed. For when God speaks, He speaks in earnest and is not jesting or making fun, as we human beings are in the habit of doing. We often say one thing and have something else in mind. But the pious old man is troubled by the trial which plagues all of us too; for just as Satan disturbed Eve in Paradise by injecting the question (Gen. 3:2) why and with what intention God forbade the eating of the fruit, so our reason hampers and deceives us too. Consequently, we are not satisfied with knowing that God has given a command; but in our foolish anxiety we also want to inquire into the reasons for the command. God hates this inquisitiveness and does not want us to make it our business to ask why and wherefore, if I may use this expression; He wants us simply to obey His command and to be satisfied with this one reason, that He Himself has given the command.

Hence in this passage Lot suffers from a human failing, inasmuch as he acts slowly and delays too long because of his good intention, as he thought. Perhaps he thought that God would act more mildly and would at least spare those who were still in the innocent years. But God did not want such thoughts; He wanted Lot simply to obey His command and to get out of the city. Therefore in this passage Moses employs the squared or reduplicated verb מָהְמַהּ, which, in my opinion, means "to delay" or "to act slowly," because those who delay debate or deliberate with themselves. But God cannot put up with this מָהְמַהּ or permit it, for he who deliberates and hesitates after he has received a command regards God either as a liar or as a joking God. If He were to say to you: "Go submerge yourself in the Elbe," you should do this without any hesitation, just as Abraham obeys at once when he is commanded to be circumcised with his people; and when he hears that he should sacrifice his son, he does not debate with himself why God has given this command but goes immediately to the designated place. Lot should have done the same thing, but he hesitates and, without saying anything, wishes that God's plan can be changed while he is waiting to see if perhaps his sons-in-law and the domestics will still come.

For this reason there follows the stern text that Lot and his family were seized and dragged forth outside the city from the house; for God could not bear this delay or questioning, if I may use this expression. If His mercy toward the saints were not as great as the psalm (103:8) states, Lot would have perished with the rest when he delayed in this manner.

Therefore let him who likes to jest, jest with human beings — with his wife, his children, and his money — for God does not begrudge us a gay life. But when you hear God's Word, see to it that you obey directly, without discussion. And if you either lack the capability or some other hindrances are put in your way, let at least your will be ready. God does not want any delay when He gives a command; He wants you to say with David (Ps. 108:1): "Lord, my heart is ready." That is the kind of man David was, and for that reason he also prospered and was successful. But Saul, who became engrossed with the wherefore after he had received the command to exterminate the Amalekites completely, was utterly rooted out of the kingdom together with his family; and the good intention with which he designated the best booty for sacred uses did not benefit him (1 Sam. 15). Obedience to His Word was more important and more pleasing to God. Therefore if you are unable to obey with a deed, let at least your heart be ready; otherwise God is deeply offended.

Thus in the Song of Solomon (5:2-5) the bride complains that she rose to open to her beloved, but that her hands dripped with myrrh, and her fingers were full of myrrh; that is, she had become weary and exhausted by her cross. Therefore after she had unbolted the door, her suitor had gone elsewhere; but she was troubled in her mind. For this reason St. Paul (2 Cor. 6:2) exhorts the Corinthians not to disregard the time and the opportunity, and he quotes from Isaiah (49:8): "In the day of salvation I heard you." And Christ says (John 12:36): "While you have the light, believe in the light." So we Germans say that one must buy when there is a market, lest we be מַהְמָהּ or hesitate — unless our capability prevents us.

Hence Lot sins here by putting off his departure and not leaving at once. In affairs of the state the heathen, too, condemn delay; and Sallust was right when he said: "After you have taken counsel, you must act swiftly." ⁵⁵ Wise men have realized that delay is fraught with danger, and they were right in depicting opportunity as being bald; once it has been lost, it cannot be pulled back. Yet how much better it is not to delay when God has given a command, but to obey promptly, without any deliberation! The thought which hinders Lot is good and most honorable; for he is moved by his concern for his sons-in-law and his domestics, and he deplores losing these. But no reasons should be put ahead of the Word. Abraham had weighty reasons for putting off the sacrificing of his son, but he places God's command ahead of his own thoughts. This obedience is a worship most welcome to God and brings with it a rich blessing, as examples before our eyes show.

Before the light of the Gospel was revealed, the monkish way of life used to be considered the saintliest; but as many of us as lived in monasteries certainly led a corrupt life. Now, when the Word is shining forth, we do more good in one hour than we did during the entire time of our life in cloisters. For it is the Word of God alone that makes learned, ready, and courageous men — men who without any strenuous effort accomplish many things in an admirable manner, while the ungodly, on the other hand, deliberate a long time and yet do nothing right. Therefore young people should be accustomed to show obedience both to their parents and to their teachers; and this obedience should be quick and not slow, for God hates obedience when it is slow but is fond of it when it is prompt and ready. Similarly, among ourselves, too, those services are pleasing which we see are prompt and spontaneous, in accordance with the old saying: "He who gives quickly gives twice." ⁵⁶

Therefore Lot sins by resisting God's command and not obeying God's command at once; and he would have paid the penalty for this disobedience if the angels had not snatched him away by force. For the Lord was sparing him. Otherwise Lot would have deserved to perish because of the sin of others. Therefore one should note this example of mercy.

Because Zacharias, the father of John the Baptist, did not believe the angel, he became dumb (Luke 1:20). The man of God in the Book of Kings is killed by a lion because of his disobedience (1 Kings 13:24). The sons of Aaron are killed by the Lord because they kindle

---

⁵⁵ Sallust, *Bellum Catilinarium*, 1.

⁵⁶ The proverb reads: *Bis dat, qui cito dat.*

a strange fire (Lev. 10:2). But the Lord does not employ such severity against Lot. He spares and forgives him and saves him against his will, so to speak. Although He is offended by Lot's disobedience, He is nevertheless pleased by his artlessness; for Lot had some reason for delaying, and he was sad. He was hoping for some mitigation and would gladly have saved at least his domestics and shepherds in addition to other things.

17. *And when they had brought them forth, they said: Flee for your life; do not look back or stop anywhere in the valley; flee to the hills, lest you be consumed.*

The angel gives Lot and his family four commands. In the first place, he tells him to save his soul. It is as though he were saying: "What is it to you if the others do not want to be saved? You do not intend to perish with them on this account, do you?" In the second place, the angel tells Lot not to look behind him. In the third place, Lot should not stop in any part of this region. The fourth command is that he should stop in the neighboring hills. These commands of the angel indicate sufficiently how Lot thought and felt. He leaves the city against his will. After leaving it he desires to stay in the neighborhood, evidently because he is moved by compassion for the city that is going to ruin and perishing. But the angels command: "Save your life." It is as though they were saying: "The people of Sodom are incorrigible; their hour has come. Therefore leave behind those people who so wretchedly disregard their soul or life, and save your own life, lest you become involved in the same danger. God has definitely decided to destroy this place. Therefore go farther away."

But this, too, serves for our instruction; for whenever you see that some, like the people of Sodom, have the Word and despise both its threats and its promises, then keep in mind that you should save your soul, lest you perish together with such people; for such people are like those whom Solomon describes as saying (Prov. 23:35): "They struck me, but I was not hurt," and their destruction cannot be too far off. Hardened Pharaoh perishes in the sea, and Samuel sheds tears in vain over King Saul. We must be on our guard against those who are thus given over to a wicked disposition, lest we share in their sin and perish together with them. Therefore in Revelation (18:4) the church is commanded to come out of Babylon; that is, we are commanded to leave the ungodly church of the pope. And Paul (2 Cor. 6:17) enjoins: "Go out from their midst," keeping in mind the angel's command to save your own soul, as though he were saying: "Give thought to your own salvation, for your anxiety about the salvation of others is in vain."

The emphasis lies on the pronoun "you." Thus Paul says (Titus 3:10-11): "As for a man who is factious, after admonishing him once or twice, have nothing more to do with him, knowing that such a person is perverted." And in Rom. 12:19 Paul says: "Give place to wrath," as though he were saying: "If the unbelievers want to perish, let them perish indeed." Our opponents, the papists, have been brought to the point of being compelled to admit that our doctrine is true.[57] Therefore they no longer sin because of weakness or a lack of knowledge; they sin because of stubbornness and wickedness. Therefore let us separate from them and depart from their midst, for they have recognized the truth and nevertheless persecute it after recognizing it. Who, then, could have any doubt about their impending destruction?

The second command — about not looking back — depicts also the emotion of Lot when he was concerned about the salvation of the city, for departing friends are wont to act in this manner; and they look back toward their people rather frequently. Therefore the angel commands Lot to separate himself so completely from the city that he does not even look back at it and is entirely without any desire to save, and feel compassion for, it. This is a difficult and serious command. Consequently, Lot's wife was unable to keep it. For consider this: "If you should hear a storm behind you and the cries of those who are perishing, especially of those whom you had held dear, how could you restrain yourself from at least looking back toward them?" But the angel looks askance at Lot's disobedience, as though he were saying: "So far you have sinned enough by delaying to obey; henceforth, therefore, learn to obey, and beware of looking back."

It is the purpose of the third command — "Do not stop anywhere in the valley" — to urge Lot to hasten and to proceed straightway to the place of safety and not to devise delays anywhere or look back. This, too, serves to describe the thoughts of Lot, who was looking for various subterfuges, just as Moses invents many reasons for declining his call but is pressed to the point of not being able to refuse. For since we have God's Word and command, we are bound to obey it.

[57] For quotation on this cf. *Luther's Works*, 13, p. 352, notes 2—3.

Seneca indeed has beautifully said: "Do not consider who is speaking, but consider what is being said."[58] It is correct to apply this rule to human beings; and it has a place in civil affairs, but not in the church, for there one must look only at who is speaking. When Eve did not do this in Paradise, wanted to investigate what was said, and forgot Him who had spoken, she fell. In the case of human beings it can happen that they are foolish and say things that should not be said. But God is not that kind. He is good and wise. Therefore He cannot err. Consequently, one must consider who is speaking, not what is said.

The fourth command — "Flee to the hills" — suggests the location of the place; for Sodom and the neighboring cities were situated in a valley near the hills of Abarim, toward the East. Moreover, this valley has received high praise for its extraordinary fertility, and by nature fields located in a plain are more fertile than those that are on the hills. Accordingly, Lot is commanded to get out of that place and go to one that is more barren.

18. *And Lot said to them: Oh, no, my lords;*

19. *behold, your servant has found favor in your sight, and you have shown me great kindness in saving my life; but I cannot flee to the hills, lest the disaster overtake me, and I die.*

20. *Behold, yonder city is near enough to flee to, and it is a little one. Let me escape there — is it not a little one? — and my life will be saved!*

This is an excellent example. Here one can see how great the power of prayer is, inasmuch as Lot rejects that last command — about ascending the hills — when he pleads his exigency, namely, that he cannot save himself in the hills; for he could have been tempted, and from the high place he could have looked back into the valley and thus perished. Moreover, this seemingly brief prayer has all the requirements of a good prayer. To be sure, God gives all things out of free mercy; yet He wants to be entreated, for there is a plain command by which we are directed to pray. Besides, there is joined to the command the promise that He will hear. Finally, the form for a prayer has been prescribed by the Son of God Himself.

---

[58] Seneca's advice, which had become proverbial, was *Non attendas, quis, sed quid dicatur.*

Therefore let us learn that prayer is highly necessary, and let us not allow ourselves to be deceived by this evil temptation, that we think that even without our prayer God will give us what we need, and that since He knows what benefits us most, there is no need of prayer. Augustine is right when he says: "He who made you without you does not want to save you without you." [59] Accordingly, we have been appointed to perform a variety of duties, in order that we may be helpers, as it were, or "workers together with God," as Paul terms it (2 Cor. 6:1). And I stated above that God is able to make a human being out of clay. But a different way pleases Him, namely, that you become a husband and take a lawful wife.[60] Thus He would be able to teach and enlighten hearts without the ministry of the Word, but He does not want to do so. For this reason He has established the external ministry and has instituted the sacraments. He is able to forgive sins without Baptism, but He does not do so; for He wants us human beings to have a share in His workings. Therefore it would be the height of ingratitude to despise these. You must have the same conviction about prayer. For this is God's ordered will: He wants to be entreated, and to those who entreat Him He wants to give the Holy Spirit and everything they need.

Now let us look at the parts of a prayer. The first requirement of a good prayer is that it give thanks to God and recall in the heart and in words the benefits you have received from God. Thus in the Lord's Prayer we indeed ask for daily bread; but since in its beginning we call God our Father, we confess by this very term that up to this time we have been supported and defended by God and have received every fatherly kindness from God. In the rules of rhetoric this is called gaining good will,[61] which is best brought about by praise and giving thanks.

In the second place, there is either the complaint or the mention of the need. Lot says: "I am in the greatest dangers if I go up into the hills in accordance with Your wish. I have already sinned by delaying, but a similar misfortune could happen to me. Therefore I pray You because of the mercy with which You have saved me to grant me what I am asking."

[59] Such aphorisms appear, for example, in Augustine, *Sermones,* LVI, ch. 5, *Patrologia, Series Latina,* XXXVIII, 380.

[60] See *Luther's Works,* 1, pp. 125—127, for a discussion of this aspect of the doctrine of creation.

[61] Luther is referring to the rhetorical device known as *captatio benevolentiae.*

In the third place, Lot states what he wants granted to him. He says: "I shall flee to the city which is close at hand, and there I shall be saved." Moreover, he enlarges on this request in an excellent manner by giving particulars. "The city is small," he says. "Furthermore, it is close by, and there I shall be able to be safe from every danger."

This is Lot's prayer, and in accordance with it God changes His plan and intention — something of which you should carefully take note — for at this point one should not debate about the secret change of God's will. On the contrary, one should learn what the psalm (145:19) also teaches: "The Lord fulfills the desire of all who fear Him." God's power had been so ordered that the sun retained its course and motion; but when Joshua prayed in his distress and commanded the sun to stand still, the sun stood still at Joshua's word. Ask the astronomers how great a miracle this is! But what is the reason? No other than that God does the will of those who fear Him and subordinates His will to ours, provided we continue to fear Him. Moreover, here the text states clearly enough that it is God's will that Lot should not remain in any part of the region. But God changes this will because Lot fears God and prays. This is God's ordered power, not His secret power. For God does not want to rule us in accordance with His secret will; He wants to do so in accordance with His will as it has been ordered and revealed by the Word.

Thus this account serves to rouse and spur us on to prayer in all our dangers, since God wants to do what we want, provided that we humbly prostrate ourselves before Him and pray. In this way the Ninevites, to whom the prophet had announced even the day of their destruction, were saved. And in Scripture there are more evidences of this kind; they prove that God allows Himself to be prevailed upon and subordinates His will to ours. Why, then, are we so remiss in regard to prayer? Why are we without faith to such an extent and so fainthearted, as though our prayer amounted to nothing? Let the monks despair of their praying; they have no knowledge of God and are altogether without faith. Their prayer is not a sincere request; it is arduous toil and actually an empty sound.

But as for ourselves, who have the knowledge of the Word, when we come together and bend our knees in true humility, we know — because we have been taught not only by the promises but also by examples — that God wants to disregard His own will and do ours. These facts must be earnestly impressed on the people and on us, lest the disposition to pray flag in us. To be sure, God does everything; but we, too, must do what belongs to our calling. He gives bread to nourish and preserve the body; but He gives it to him who labors, sows, reaps, etc. And when you sow the land, you must not think that nothing will result from your labor. For it is God's command that you should do your duty, and He wants to work through you. Therefore you must devote yourself to your work and duty with all your strength and attention, and leave the rest to God. Thus when it is necessary to fight against the Turk, God's command urges you in the first place to defend your subjects. Therefore you should equip yourself and provide weapons as well as the other things necessary for war and say: "I have done what I could; but supply, Lord, what is still lacking in me, in order that Thy will may be done." For this reason, Paul, too, admonishes us (Rom. 12:11) not to be slothful in our zeal or to relax our zeal; for those who are indolent and, like the servant in the Gospel, do not do their duty will hear (Luke 19:22): "I will condemn you out of your own mouth." But the diligent and godly the Lord will make rich, for "He fulfills the desire of all who fear Him." Undoubtedly because of such examples and because of his own experience David wrote many psalms.

21. *He said to him: Behold, I grant you this favor also, that I will not overthrow the city of which you have spoken.*

22. *Make haste, escape there; for I can do nothing till you arrive there. Therefore the name of the city was called Zoar.*

A surprising situation and an account decidedly worth noting! It was God's will that the city of Zoar should be destroyed together with the others; but because Lot intercedes for it, God changes His will and does what Lot wants. Similarly, because of Paul alone all who were sailing in the same ship were preserved in the shipwreck (Acts 27:43). But inasmuch as there follows: "I can do nothing till you arrive there," where you can be safe, someone may perhaps ask: "Then is Lot able to prevent God from doing immediately what He wants?" Moses' answer is: "Lot's prayer does this; it compels God not to carry out His wrathful will. God permits it to be broken and does the will of those who fear Him."

These are very strong statements, and they are hard to believe.

But we should note them carefully for our learning and comfort, so that we may pray cheerfully and, as Paul teaches, without hesitating and murmuring (cf. Phil. 2:14). It is murmuring, however, when we have been offended by a perplexing situation and ask God why He does this or that in such a manner. But, as I have said, we must not be inquirers into the wherefore and say to God: "Wherefore art Thou doing this in such a manner?" We must obey His will; and if anything in His actions offends us, we must pray. Paul calls hesitation doubt. This must be completely excluded from prayer, for it alone is what vitiates prayer.

Therefore Bernard admonishes his brothers not to esteem their prayers lightly but to know that their prayers are written in heaven before they themselves have finished them.[62] The holy man observed the faintheartedness in praying with which we all are commonly plagued; for since our weakness is great and we observe greater gifts in Paul, Peter, and others, we shrink back when we are about to pray, and we are terrified by our unworthiness, because we are unworthy to obtain anything from God. Because of these thoughts the faith and fervor of prayer not only become lukewarm but are altogether extinguished, and their place is taken by harmful hesitating and detestable murmuring. Why do we not rather think that Lot, too, was unworthy? For who is worthy to speak with the Lord? Therefore let it be enough for us that we have been called to faith through the Word, have been taught by the Word of God, and for this reason are part of the church, which has the definite command to pray. Consequently, you should not look at your unworthiness; you should look at God's command and not debate whether you are worthy or not. But you should hold fast the promise that the Lord wants to do the will of those who fear Him.

In this way we should gain the courage to pray, which men taught by spiritual discernment have called a labor above all other labors. Why is this? For no other reason than that a most violent conflict must be maintained against the hesitating and murmuring to which faintheartedness and a feeling of unworthiness give rise. Let us, therefore, learn to fortify ourselves against these plots of Satan, and let us direct our attention to promises and examples like those re-

---

[62] The passage Luther has in mind is probably Bernard's *Sermones de diversis*, XXV, 7—8, based on 1 Tim. 2:1, *Patrologia, Series Latina*, CLXXXIII, 608 to 609.

corded here about Lot. For these things were not written for Lot's sake; they were written for our sakes, in order that we may learn how to check God's angry will and to meet God when He shows the rod that is near by, just as the Lord Himself says in Ezekiel (22:30): "And I sought for a man among them . . . who should stand in the breach before Me . . . and I found none. Therefore I have poured out My indignation upon them." Furthermore, He severely chides the priests who were guiding the people with their teaching (Ezek. 13:5): "You have not built up a wall for the house of Israel in the day of My wrath."

Hence God is provoked to wrath if we neglect prayer, for His own command is being disregarded. Let us, therefore, pray boldly and with confidence. If He does not give what we are asking for, He will nevertheless give something else that is better; for prayer cannot be in vain, as James, too, states (5:16): "The prayer of a righteous man avails much if it is persistent," that is, earnest and ardent. For God cannot despise a righteous man and all his works. Even though the world persecutes him, God nevertheless respects his works and words, yes, even his sufferings. "Precious in the sight of the Lord is the death of His saints" (Ps. 116:15).

The reason for Moses' additional remark concerning the change of name of the little town of Zoar, which previously was called Bela, is God's purpose to distinguish it as an example for posterity by means of a new name, in order that it, too, may learn to fear God, who executes judgment on the ungodly, to place its hope in His mercy, and to seek His help; for this account includes both. The destruction of the people of Sodom serves to frighten the ungodly, but the deliverance of Lot with so generous a hearing of prayer comforts the godly. They should pray when they are in dangers, and they themselves should also hope for deliverance.

23. *The sun had risen on the earth when Lot came to Zoar.*

24. *Then the Lord rained on Sodom and Gomorrah brimstone and fire from the Lord out of heaven;*

25. *and He overthrew those cities, and all the valley, and all the inhabitants of the cities, and what grew on the ground.*

Here Moses' style is unusual. He says that the sun had risen on the earth. But his statement points out that Lot and his people had risen at daybreak and had gone forth under compulsion; had walked along with their little bundles, bread, drink, and other necessities; and had arrived at the town Zoar, which was perhaps an Italian mile [63] distant from Sodom. It is possible that by saying that the sun had risen Moses wanted to point to the deliverance of the human race through the Son of God, but we shall relegate these ideas to allegory.

Even though the statements which follow are brief, they nevertheless include events of such magnitude that human speech is unable to express them. Who would not shudder when five very rich and flourishing cities with all their inhabitants, animals, gardens, and fields are destroyed in one storm? How great the wailing at that place was! How great the outcry of the human beings and of the beasts of burden! They were all swallowed up at the same time. This is an altogether horrible example; it surpasses all the accounts of all the heathen. Troy was destroyed by war; but this is nothing in comparison with what happens here, when so many cities, in which there were many thousands of people who, because of their age, do not yet know the difference between right and wrong, are swallowed up by the earth in one moment. They all perish. Not even one person is saved. At the same time all the cattle and all the fruits of the earth perish. Not even a sprig remains.

These are terrible facts, yet they do not affect the ungodly; for when St. Peter, by the Holy Spirit, speaks of the last evil of the world, he adduces this example against the papists. He says (2 Peter 2:6) that God did not spare the five cities which were situated in God's Paradise, in the best place of the earth, which seemed to be like God's place of rest. Nor did He spare the original world, which came to an end by perishing in the waters of the Flood. The cities came to an end by perishing when fire was sent down from heaven. But why did God do this? Undoubtedly because He wanted to set a terrifying example for all the ungodly. And these events are recorded by the Holy Spirit, not for the sake of those who perished but for the sake of succeeding generations, likewise for the sake of the papists, the pests of the last times, as Peter maintains.

But it nearly always happens that those who should be frightened

---

[63] The Roman mile is usually listed as equivalent to 1,482 meters; the Italian *miglio* is the same, or nearly the same, 0.925 miles according to the British and American measurement.

are most complacent and, on the other hand, that those who are in need of comfort feel anguish and despair. Thus the pope and the cardinals do not bother about this horrible example. Nor do they think that it concerns them, for they do not believe that there is a God. His wrath does not frighten them until they feel it. Therefore we must shun them, lest we become involved in the same punishments.

Christ, too, mentions this account more than once. He bids us remember Lot's wife (Luke 17:32) and declares (Matt. 10:15) that the people of Sodom will have a more tolerable judgment than the cities which heard the Gospel to no avail. But if those who disregard the Word are to be punished more severely than Sodom, what should we conclude about those who persecute the Word? Therefore Christ's words should be pondered well. If He does not want His Word to be despised, it is far less His desire that it be trampled underfoot and that men be killed on its account. Yet this is what the pope and his followers are doing, with the result that he fills the entire world with murder.

Accordingly, we, like Lot and Abraham, see evils so great that it is impossible to enlarge on them enough. These evils gravely torment the hearts of the godly, just as Peter states about Lot, too, that his eyes and ears were tormented every day. But we shall wait patiently until the Lord destroys these Sodomites of ours, and we shall put forth every effort to avoid being found doing the wicked deeds of the church of the pope.

Even though we, too, are troubled by our faults and, not to mention anything that is more grievous, are lazy and sleepy with regard to the Word, still nothing could happen to us that would be bitterer than the suppression and the loss of the Word. The world considers departing from the Word a light sin and thinks that being without it is a small loss. But among ourselves the awful verdict of Peter and Christ has weight; they say that the people of Sodom are saintly and righteous in comparison with the Roman Church, which not only despises but even persecutes the Gospel and kills the believers. Therefore Peter is right when he says (2 Peter 2:6) that God made this an example for those who will be ungodly in the future. And Christ says that the judgment of the people of Sodom will be more tolerable than that of such despisers.

Therefore let us comfort ourselves, for this account points out both truths: that the enemies of the church are to be punished and that the righteous are to be eternally saved, provided that we are like Lot and Abraham, that is, provided that we hold fast to the Word and to faith. The Lord knows, says Peter (2 Peter 2:9), both how to rescue the righteous and how to reserve the ungodly for destruction. Yet the ungodly do not believe this, and when they hear such examples applied to themselves, they laugh very pleasantly in a situation that is not at all funny — a situation that cannot be wept over enough and cannot be adequately lamented or expressed in words. Consider what a terrible disaster it was when in a single storm five cities, together with the men, the women, the children, the servants, the maids, the beasts of burden, and the cattle, were swallowed up at the same time, so that not even a straw remained from that entire region. What clearer example can one point out to show that God is sternly angry with the ungodly? Yet Christ and Peter say that this is a small punishment if you compare it with the punishment that awaits our papists, who are not only impenitent but are also stubborn and retain and defend manifest errors.

Moses uses the word "rain" to indicate that the storm was brought on through the instrumentality of the angels. Moreover, reason knows the things that commonly accompany storms: violent rains, whirlwinds, thunderclaps, lightning flashes, thunderbolts, and earthquakes. He also mentions brimstone, because the fire produced by storms is always sulphurous, and objects struck by lightning also have the odor of sulphur. Hence fire which fell down with a loud crash and thunder consumed the cities. But remember that this is the work of the angels and that such things do not happen accidentally, as the heathen suppose.

Furthermore, from the beginning of the world there have always been various examples of the wrath of God which have not been recorded, but those that have been recorded are very memorable; they teach us to shun sins, since God punishes sinners in such a horrible manner. During this year a goodly part of the earth in the territory of Naples near Puteoli vanished because of an earthquake and an inundation — not by some chance, as the papists think, but because of the sins of the people, of which there is no end.[64]

Christ very kindly and compassionately says (Matt. 12:32) that

[64] Earthquakes and floods struck Naples and Puteoli (whose modern Italian name is Pozzuoli) in 1538; see our Introduction, p. x.

if anyone sins against the Son, it will be forgiven him, but that to sin against the Holy Spirit — as the papists habitually do, who sin incorrigibly, knowingly, and from downright malice, even though, because of their natural endowment and without grace, they could refrain from such sins — that is assuredly an unforgivable sin. Who compels them to kill our people? Who compels them to make such bitter attacks on the acknowledged truth? Are they not compelled by their own will, which Satan also urges on?

David also sins, and very seriously, when he commits adultery and is the cause of an unjust slaying. But this was a sin of weakness, and it was forgiven when he acknowledged it and asked in faith that it be forgiven. But to persecute the Gospel and to persist in manifest idolatry contrary to so many warnings of the Holy Spirit, as though in contempt of the majesty of God (for I can properly call it contempt) — these are sins against the First Table, and certain destruction results from them.

Hence I have no doubt that in that light of the Gospel God will remove His elect from the people of Sodom and will gather the wheat into His barn. Thereafter — if the blaspheming papists continue to rage — the end will follow; that is, either the Last Day will come, or an extraordinary overthrow of the entire papacy will follow. For Peter is not lying when he calls Sodom (2 Peter 2:6) "an example to the ungodly," and the very nature of their sins is such that God cannot remain silent about them forever. Let us, therefore, thank God, who through His Son has delivered us from the coming wrath and guards us through His angels, lest we perish together with the Sodomites of our time.

But here we must not overlook Moses' expression "The Lord rained from the Lord." The Jews, above all, are offended by it and distort it in various ways. But the text states clearly that the Lord rains and that He rains from the Lord, for in this passage the name of God which is called the Tetragrammaton is used both times; and in the Hebrew there is added as a distinct syllable, and significantly, what is termed the accusative particle.[65] Therefore since Moses mentions the Lord twice by name, he is directing attention to two Persons, as they are called, of the Godhead and one Lord. St. Hilary learnedly

---

[65] Luther is referring to the Tetragrammaton or, as he usually called it in his writings against the Jews, the *Shem Hamphoras,* usually transliterated into English as *Yahweh.*

and correctly stresses this passage as proof that God the Father, who begets; God the Son, who is begotten; and God the Holy Spirit, who proceeds from the Father and the Son, are one God.[66]

Since the Jews are audacious, yes, even rash, they explain the particle as a pronoun, so that the sense is: "The Lord rained from Himself, the Lord." But who ordered them to have the audacity to do this in the case of God's Book? For if one were at liberty to trifle in this way with Holy Scripture, no article of faith would remain intact. Hence it is characteristic of the unbelieving Jews and of the godless papists to be teachers of the Holy Spirit and to teach Him what or how to write. But let us be and remain pupils, and let us not change the Word of God; we ourselves should be changed through the Word.

The Jews invent this misleading interpretation with their usual presumptuousness in order that they may not be forced to admit a duality of Persons in the Godhead. But we know from the Gospel that Christ keeps this mode of speaking everywhere; for He relates everything, both His sayings and His deeds, to the Father. He says (John 7:16): "My teaching is not Mine, but the Father's"; (John 14:9): "Philip, he who sees Me sees My Father"; (John 14:10): "The Father abides in Me, and I in the Father"; and (John 5:19): "Whatever the Father does, the Son does the same." What else is this than what Moses says: Christ teaches, Christ works, but from the Father or out of the Father. And John especially took delight in this form of speaking, to show that everything done and said by Christ is done and said as though by the true God, namely, by God the Father, who was not begotten but who begot the Son.

Let us, therefore, by no means be influenced by the scoffing of the Jews, who have before them this basic truth, though incorrectly understood, that there is only one God. After this they corrupt Scripture, which speaks of several Persons. But give them the answer: Of course, God is one; but through the Word the Holy Spirit has revealed about God that in the one divine Essence there are three Persons. This we adhere to and teach, and we rely not only on the authority of Scripture but also on the testimony of the New Testament.[67] For the Gospel speaks in a very special way and says that

---

[66] Hilary, *De Trinitate*, Book IV, ch. 29.

[67] A reflection of Luther's tendency (which he does not consistently observe) to identify the Old Testament as *Schrift* in the strict sense and the New Testament as *Predigt*.

Christ does everything and says everything, but from the Father; likewise (Matt. 28:18): "All authority in heaven and on earth has been given to Me"; that is, I am the true God, and between Me and the Father there is no difference except that I was begotten of the Father; but the Father is not begotten. Therefore Hilary and Augustine were correct in their statements when they made use of this passage to defend the article of our faith concerning the divinity of Christ.[68]

26. *But Lot's wife behind him looked back, and she became a pillar of salt.*

Lot's wife, who goes out with her husband, was undoubtedly a believing and saintly woman; otherwise she would neither have followed her husband in so great a disaster, nor would she have been seized by the angels and led out. Therefore let us reject the Jewish legends; for they make the nonsensical statement that she was inhospitable and refused the angels salt to season their food, and that for this reason she was turned into a pillar of salt.[69] The books of the Jews are full of such absurdities. Why do they not rather direct their attention to the account itself and carefully combine the circumstances, which prove clearly that this woman was not inhospitable but was godly and saintly, in whom faith was clearly discernible, since she follows her husband without hesitation and yet has this human experience that she looks back and perishes?

From the text it is clear that Lot's wife had entered the city of Zoar with her husband. Therefore — since women are rather weak by nature — she either forgot the command of the angels, or she thought there was no longer any danger after she had come into the city from the open country. But disobedience has its punishment, and she is changed into a pillar of salt.

No reason can be given why God acted in this manner. Perhaps the Dead and Salt Sea got its name from this pillar. But this pillar did not remain standing long; it was shattered together with the city and destroyed by a thunderbolt. But it may be that Moses calls it a pillar of salt, not because it was actually salt, but because it was similar to salt; for salt is white. Augustine, Chrysostom, Ambrose,

---

[68] On Hilary see p. 297, note 66; the reference to Augustine is to his *De Trinitate*, II, ch. 12.

[69] This is derived from Lyra *ad* Gen. 19:26.

and Gregory all pass over this passage in silence. Lyra alone, who follows the lead of the rabbis, often joins them in indulging in foolish rabbinical ideas.[70] Perhaps this happened through the extraordinary providence of God, in order that we may keep reading the sacred books and not merely be occupied with reading the commentaries of human beings, who often sin through their excessive inquisitiveness.

Therefore, without taking into account other things which contribute little to the subject matter, let us be satisfied with the fact that Lot's wife is held up to us as an example by Christ's teaching, for He refers to her when He says (Luke 9:62): "No one who puts his hand to the plow and looks back is fit for the kingdom of God." And in His earnest address concerning the Last Day He says (Luke 17:32): "Remember Lot's wife." From this we readily understand what it means to look back, namely, to depart from God's command and to be occupied with other matters — matters outside one's calling — like the man who has been commanded to follow Christ and wants to bury his dead first (Matt. 8:21).

Hence this is a sign or lesson and a warning not to allow ourselves to be hampered in our calling, as Peter in John 21:20 looked back at John but was rebuked by the Lord. For everyone should stick to his own calling and not concern himself with what others are doing. At the present time the papists beset us a great deal with the example of a former age during which everything lay in darkness. "Your doctrine," they say, "is new and unknown to our ancestors; therefore if it is true, all our ancestors have been condemned." They, too, are looking back and thus disregard the word they have before them. For what concern is it to us what kind of judgment God pronounced on those who departed this life in times past? The Word of God is being preached to us today; we must hear and receive it without any argument. We must not become questioners who ask God why He has brought the sound doctrine to light at this time and not in former times.

Thus this account teaches us to remain steadfast, for he who wants to be a Christian must not change his purpose: he must not look for another way or another Gospel. In this one and only way there is salvation; if you enter upon another, you have perished and are like Lot's wife. But so far as Lot's wife is concerned, this example

[70] Cf. Lyra *ad* Gen. 19:26 on the Jewish and Christian exegesis of this verse.

is instruction for us rather than a condemnation of the woman, who, I fully believe, was saintly and was saved; for one should have no other presupposition concerning God's mercy, especially since she has a splendid testimony of the life she has previously led, inasmuch as the angels themselves bring her out and she follows her husband.

But you will say: "Why does she perish in this manner?" My answer is: She was overcome by human weakness and, contrary to the angels' command, looked back toward those awful crashes. For this disobedience she suffers a temporal punishment. Nevertheless, her soul is saved, as Paul says (1 Cor. 5:5) about the incestuous man. Therefore one must hold fast to this teaching — that the saintly woman is compelled to suffer this punishment — in order that it may reach all succeeding generations. Christ says (Luke 17:32): "Remember Lot's wife."

But one must by all means entertain the hope that Lot's wife was not condemned for this reason. For there are many such examples in Holy Writ; they show that God afflicts His saints with temporal punishments in order that they may not perish with the world. And Paul says (1 Cor. 11:32): "When we are judged by the Lord, we are chastened, so that we may not be condemned along with this world." Accordingly, Lot's wife was chastened; but she was not condemned. In like manner, Aaron's sons, who were offering strange fire, were castigated as a sign for others and were not condemned (Lev. 10:1 ff.). I have the same conviction about the prophet who was killed by the lion (1 Kings 13:24). In that instance the body suffered because of disobedience; but nothing befell the soul, evidently in order that we may be admonished to fear God and may strictly keep the commands of God. Thus this pillar is truly a spice and the salt of wisdom; it admonishes us not to look back but to persevere, and, as Paul puts it (Phil. 3:13), to "strain forward to what lies ahead."

And we surely need the command because of the powerful enemy we have. Day and night he lies in wait for us and pursues us. It is for this reason that the evangelist John warns us so insistently to abide in the doctrine which we received in the beginning;[71] and Jude (3) directs us to contend earnestly for the faith once delivered to the saints. Looking for new dogmas and departing from the way

---

[71] Luther seems to be referring not to the Gospel of John but to 1 John 1:24 and related passages in the First Epistle.

which the Word points out is a most serious trial and plague for the church. Therefore Paul warns the Galatians (1:6) to beware of such teachers as put stumbling blocks in the way and lead off into byroads.

This evil has its origin in a loathing of the Word, and Satan originates this loathing with outstanding skill. Thus in our time Münzer departed from the Word and kept stirring up rebellions. When these had been put down, Carlstadt and the Sacramentarians disturbed the church. When they, too, were already giving way, the Anabaptists arose.[72] Thus the church is never without a trial; for the world does not continue on the proper and steady course of its calling but looks back like Lot's wife, who was punished temporally on this account as an example for those who would be ungodly in the future — an example to show that they would bring eternal punishment upon themselves if they did not adhere to the Word.

Perhaps Lot's wife was terrified by the awful crash of the thunderbolts and the collapsing cities and looked back for that reason. To be drawn away from the Word by new and strange ideas is, therefore, no joke or slight trial. When Arius spread his poison in the world, it was received with loud applause because it presented something new, something that had previously not been heard in the world.[73] Such were the beginnings of nearly all heresies; the world received them with open arms and admired them as though the earlier teachers had not been sound.

By her example Lot's wife warns us to beware of this poison of Satan in order that we may remain steadfast in the faith once delivered (Jude 3). But the world does not submit to this doctrine. Some gratify their own vanity with new doctrines; others look for glory, as Paul says (cf. 1 Tim. 6:5, 20). Thus nearly all are diverted from the true course.

From our own sentiments we shall readily gauge how hard it was for the saintly man Lot on such an occasion and because of such a sin to lose his very dear wife, with whom he lived for so many years and who had followed him so dutifully during so prolonged an exile.

[72] See, for example, p. 31, note 25.

[73] See *Luther's Works,* 22, p. 18, and the note there on the sources of Luther's knowledge about Arianism.

Therefore when Lot did not seem safe even in Zoar — for the mishap of his very dear wife justly frightened him — he took refuge on a hill near by, and there, with his daughters, he hid in a cave, lest they, too, lose their lives in a similar disaster.

27. *And Abraham went early in the morning to the place where he had stood before the Lord;*

28. *and he looked down toward Sodom and Gomorrah and toward all the land of the valley, and beheld, and lo, the smoke of the land went up like the smoke of a furnace.*

Here the saintly patriarch Abraham, the father of the promise, is presented as an observer of the awful punishment by which the five cities perished. This is evidently done for the purpose of giving special emphasis to the sternness of God's wrath in order to frighten the ungodly; for the very saintly man had interceded with God in behalf of those places. He had asked God not to destroy them. He is compelled, however, not only to weep over and patiently put up with the sins of others but even to behold with his own eyes the destruction of so many thousands of human beings. Moses wanted to indicate the nature and the magnitude of this trial; for Abraham undoubtedly had the thought which Ps. 89:47 expresses: "For what vanity Thou hast created the sons of men!" "I am not to believe, am I, that I alone of the children of God am being kept unharmed when God at one time is consuming so great a multitude of human beings by fire from heaven?"

This reflection and debate about the incomprehensible judgments of God causes hearts to murmur against God and gives occasion for terrible trials and doubts. Reflect! If you were in a city besieged by enemies and knew from God's Word or from a sure revelation that all the citizens were to be killed but you alone would be saved, and if you saw the enemy raging without any distinction — in such danger how long would you keep that confidence of yours concerning your safety? Abraham, too, was in such a situation. But he held firmly to his faith by thrusting aside those obstacles which were trying to shake his faith.

His grief was increased by the recollection that by a divine miracle this whole region was delivered from the power of the enemy six or seven years earlier, more or less. Thus it not only grieved him that the people who had been saved through him were perishing so wretchedly, but he also thought of the entire human race as he reasoned with himself: "If these people, for whom a miracle was performed and who were delivered by my hand, degenerated in so short a time and were overthrown, what hope is one to have about the entire human race?"

Therefore when — in the next chapter — Abraham proceeds to Gerar (Gen. 20:1), he is extraordinarily fearful; for he doubts that in this place there are people who fear God, and to the king, who remonstrates with him, he replies: "I thought that perhaps there is no fear of God in this place and that they will kill me because of my wife" (Gen. 20:11). What, I ask, was the source of these thoughts? Was it not a heart which had this thought: "If there was no fear of God in that Paradise, what will there be in the country of Palestine?"

This was Abraham's first trial. Moses describes it in detail and in words that carnal men do not understand. He says: As soon as dawn drew near, Abraham went out with the utmost concern, not only for the five cities in general but also for his nephew Lot, his wife, and his daughters, who, as he knew, were living in Sodom; but he did not know whether they had perished with the people of Sodom. For this reason he trembles and is full of fear. He is constrained to weep because of the sins of others and to dread every misfortune.

We must not suppose that Abraham was a block of wood and devoid of all human feelings. He was as godly and compassionate as anyone else. Consequently, he was concerned about the safety of the five cities and especially about the members of his family. Therefore he could not stay in bed. He gets up before daylight and has some hope that perhaps God will act more mildly. Full of hope, worries, and fears, he accordingly turns his eyes at once toward the well-known region to see whether it is still unharmed. Familiar are the sentiments we feel toward absent friends, the way Terence's Mitio is anxious about his son, who is tarrying too long.[74] In like manner, I am anxious about my dear Philip while he is at Frankfurt and now have a variety of thoughts about him.[75] Hearts affected in this

---

[74] The ultimate source of this reference is Aristotle, *Poetics*, ch. 9.

[75] This is an important key to the chronology of these *Lectures on Genesis;* cf. our Introduction, p. x. Philip Melanchthon had left Wittenberg for Frankfurt on January 31, 1539, and returned from there on or shortly after April 22 of that year. Thus these words would seem to fall into that period early in 1539.

manner feel nothing but troubles and worries. They think: "Ah, what are my friend, my nephew, my children, my fellow citizens, and others now doing?" Such was the state of Abraham's heart at that time; he was full of sighs and groans. Even though these facts are recorded by Moses in few words, they should not be looked at with carnal eyes; you must make the mood, yes, even the effect of the events your own, put yourself, as it were, into the situation before us, and examine your heart as to what you would have thought or done had you been in such a position.

But what happens while the saintly man has these anxious thoughts? "Behold," says Moses, "he saw smoke going up like the smoke of a furnace." Then indeed his amazement and grief increased, for so far there had remained a slight hope that God would act with greater leniency. But Abraham experiences the opposite. He sees קִיטֹר going up, that is, a transparent smoke without a flame. At night a dense smoke appears as if it were all fire; but that smoke was transparent, as smoke usually is when the fire is already almost out or is burning less intensely. When we see from a distance that a dense smoke is rising, we immediately draw the conclusion that there is a fire at that place; but there is still some hope that the fire can be extinguished. But when we see that transparent smoke, we assume that there is no longer a conflagration; then we conclude that everything has been destroyed by the conflagration. Thus when Abraham saw that thin smoke, he realized that the entire region had been consumed by fire.

What sighs and what groans followed after this sad sight! "Where is my dear Lot now? What is his fate? Is he alive? Are his wife and daughters alive?" Accordingly, Abraham burst into tears. Terrified, he bewailed the great disaster.

However, these facts are recorded for the sake of the ungodly in order to enlarge on God's wrath against sin, if by any means some may repent and cease sinning. The Jews make sport of these very serious matters, but the papists generally regard them with carnal eyes. They see that Abraham, Lot, and the other saints have their own wives and are occupied with the management of their homes. These things they consider worldly and unworthy of saints. They are offended by this outward appearance. But the deaths and the hell with which God has vexed His saints every day the papists neither see nor understand; yet Holy Scripture presents these things clearly enough — if they were not blinded by lusts and loveless,[76] as Peter (2 Peter 3:3) prophesies concerning them. Yes, they even laugh at these ideas. But the people of Sodom laughed, too. Nevertheless, there came such a horrible disaster upon them. We shall expect the same thing from our opponents, although, when they are punished, we shall be moved by compassion and shall mourn their destruction. Nor do I doubt that those who live after us will often wish for death; for such great disasters bring about a stupor, and then there is no room for weeping, as we are accustomed to do in less serious dangers.

29. *So it was that when God destroyed the cities of the valley, God remembered Abraham and sent Lot out of the midst of the overthrow, when He overthrew the cities in which Lot dwelt.*

What Moses has here added about Abraham is intended as a praise of prayer, for he clearly declares that God saved Lot not so much because of his own righteousness as because of the prayer of believing Abraham. (For Lot had already begun to be in danger because of his disobedience and delay. Therefore the angels chide him and say: "Lest you perish in like manner"; but his wife sinned more dangerously and for this reason was punished more severely.) It is as though Moses were saying: "God loved Abraham so much that He saved Lot because of him, for He did not want the heart of saintly Abraham to be saddened endlessly but left him this comfort, lest he have sorrow upon sorrow. Thus in all the accounts of the saints you see trouble alternating with deliverance, suffering with comfort, and tears with joy. Therefore they are the true Atlases who bear heaven on their shoulders, that is, sustain the burden of divine wrath and in such great disasters still keep their trust in mercy, even though they see the opposite. In the end they experience how great the power of believing prayer is.

Now follows the text about Lot and his daughters. It perplexes both the Jews and our own people, and causes them to ask many questions. Our fathers generally passed it over, either because they were hindered by other endeavors or because God so directed it, lest the church be burdened with a multitude of books. For this reason I myself hate my books and often wish that they would perish, because I fear that they may detain the readers and lead them away

[76] Here the Weimar edition and the Erlangen edition have ἄσοργοι instead of ἄστοργοι, which means "loveless."

from reading Scripture itself, which alone is the fount of all wisdom. Besides, I am frightened by the example of the former age.[77] After those who had devoted themselves to sacred studies had come upon commentaries of human beings, they not only spent most of their time reading the ancient theologians, but eventually they also busied themselves with Aristotle, Averroes, and others, who later on gave rise to the Thomases, the Scotuses, and similar monstrosities.

For this reason books should be limited in number, and among these books only those which lead the reader into a correct understanding of the Scripture should be given approval. And in the books of the fathers themselves we should value nothing that is not in agreement with Scripture; it alone should remain the judge and teacher of all books. To be sure, it is profitable to hear the confessors, whether they are dead and teach in their writings or are living and teach by word of mouth. Nevertheless, there should be a limit. And one should always observe this rule: that we read those who expound Scripture. Since we have no opinion of the fathers on this passage, we shall expound it as best we can.

30. *Now Lot went up out of Zoar and dwelt in the hills with his two daughters, for he was afraid to dwell in Zoar; so he dwelt in a cave with his two daughters.*

It was not without reason that Lot was afraid to remain in Zoar, for the four cities had already perished. They had been consumed by fire from heaven. Moreover, in the very city of safety Lot loses more than he had lost in the city of destruction. In Sodom he had lost his home, his household, his cattle, and his domestics; but here he loses half of his life, namely, his wife, a saintly woman endowed with most eminent virtues. Therefore he thought: "If my wife was not saved in the city of safety, perhaps the same danger will come upon me and my daughters tomorrow. Come, then, my daughters; let us go away to a safer place, where we can be safe from the

---

[77] Luther had repeatedly expressed himself this way about his books, but the problem had become acute during the 1530's. In 1533 there appeared a catalog of his existing works, to which he wrote a rather diffident foreword (W, XXXVIII, 133—134). Then, on June 13, 1536, Wolfgang Capito of Strassburg had asked Luther for permission to reprint his *Postil* and other works. To this Luther replied on July 9, 1537: "As for the disposition of my books in volumes, I am rather cool and disinterested *[frigidior et segnior]*; for I am aroused by a Saturnine hunger and would rather see them all devoured. I do not acknowledge any as my legitimate book except the book *On the Bondage of the Will* [1525] and the *Catechism* [1529]." W, *Briefe*, VIII, p. 99.

temptation because of which my wife perished." Accordingly, he leaves Zoar, and it, too, perishes immediately by fire from heaven and is consumed like the others; for the text states clearly that the entire region is to be destroyed. Consequently, Zoar, which was the fifth among these cities, perished too.

This, then, was the end of these cities. It was indeed a terrible disaster; and to frighten those who deride and persecute the Word, it should be impressed on them often. For there are enough, and more than enough, other sins in which we are all born and live; but the majority add this devilish malice, that they deride, blaspheme, and persecute the Word. To deride the Word of God is, therefore, the antecedent whose most certain consequence is to perish by brimstone and flaming fire, so that the godly are hardly able to see and bear this awful judgment.

Thus Lot, too, frightened by the example of his own wife, takes to flight; for no misfortune could affect him more closely unless it affected his own body. But of the evils there is not yet enough. Where he concludes that there will be certain safety, he encounters a greater danger. This is in accord with the common saying: "No misfortune comes singly." He hides in a cave, with the intention of avoiding the sight not only of the region that had already perished in flames but also of the human beings, the cattle, and the earth itself, lest there be some occasion for sinning. What, then, shall we suppose was his frame of mind? Undoubtedly he was in the utmost fear and anguish. But behold, a new evil overtakes him, as now follows.

31. *And the first-born said to the younger: Our father is old, and there is not a man on earth to come into us after the manner of all the earth.*

32. *Come, let us make our father drink wine, and we will lie with him, that we may preserve offspring through our father.*

33. *So they made their father drink wine that night; and the first-born went in and lay with her father; he did not know when she lay down or when she arose.*

This plan of the girls was certainly foolish. Therefore when carnal people, who look at Holy Scripture superficially, read things like this, they think of their own desires and suppose that these girls were crazed by lust. But they do not see the dreadful severity of God's wrath and the grief and near-desperation of these human beings. Nor are the Jews less rash; they argue that what Moses writes in this passage is impossible, that Lot could not have been unaware of his intercourse with his daughters.[78]

Above all, then, Moses must be defended against the suspicion of lying. Hence we declare that it is certain and beyond doubt that Lot and his daughters were in extreme fear and distress, not only because of the sad spectacle — that they saw such a great multitude of human beings suddenly perish — but also because of the misfortune in their family — that Lot had lost his very dear wife and that his daughters had lost their very lovely mother. If anybody is not crushed by this misfortune, he has a heart that is harder than adamant.[79]

Now it is also true that human beings who are in the height of excitement become mentally deranged and both say and do things which they later forget. For the mind, as though engulfed by the intensity of the excitement, is not conscious of itself. Thus Lot was undoubtedly aware of having had intercourse with his daughters, since coition is a shaking of the entire body and an excitation of soul and body. But why does Moses state that Lot was not aware of it?

My answer is: Moses does so in order to point out that Lot had been absorbed in the height of excitement and for this reason does not remember afterwards what he did. We observe the same thing in less serious situations, in the case of melancholy people and of lovers whose emotions are rather strong; they say and do many things which they later on no longer remember. For people in love are really out of their mind and invent dreams, as the poet says.[80] Hence it is nothing new for someone in unusual stupefaction to perform an act of which he later on has no recollection. Hence the Jews are poor dialecticians; for Scripture does not state that Lot was not aware of the intercourse but states that he got up and did not know that he had had intercourse. Moses is describing the intensity of the excitement and not, as those swine suppose, the allurements of lust.

Moreover, it tends to excuse the saintly man that he not only was in the height of excitement but had also been made drunk by

[78] Cf. Lyra *ad* Gen. 19:33.

[79] Ovid, *Epistulae ex Ponto*, IV, 12, 31.

[80] Vergil, *Eclogues*, VIII, 108.

his daughters. Thus two troubles come together: extreme excitement and drunkenness, something which easily engrosses those who are perturbed. Why, then, is it strange that Lot did not know in the morning what he did at night? A drunken man says something and is well aware of saying it, yet after sleeping he does not remember what he said.

These are my thoughts about this passage, for I cannot bear what those dogs maintain: that Moses is recording things that are impossible. These occurrences are common even in less serious perplexities, as when melancholy, love, or some other emotion grips the minds; then people do not always remember what they did. Therefore it is not an impossible but a daily and common occurrence for a human being to fall into love, hate, sorrow, or joy to such an extent that because of anger or delight he does not know what he is saying or doing, even though he is aware of saying and doing something.

I do not say that one can completely excuse Lot for this reason. Besides, the matter belongs into a different discussion. I am merely stating that what the text says in this passage about Lot is not impossible. He is intoxicated in a twofold way: his body with wine and his heart with cares. Therefore it is not strange that when he is sober, he does not know what he did when he was drunk. Moreover, this, too, helps us to learn to pay more careful attention to the sacred accounts and not to pounce upon Holy Scripture like swine spurred on either by hatred or by lust.

Lyra's opinion is incorrect when he implicates the saintly father Lot in such a great sin.[81] He sat in his monastery and did not see Sodom in flames, a spectacle which did not give any occasion for lust but engulfed the mind in the most violent disturbance. Since Lyra is not aware of this, he thinks that the drunken Lot may have danced in the cave and that these things took place after this. But his opinion is wrong, and he does not give due consideration to the account by paying attention to all the circumstances. If a boy inadvertently sets fire to a house, he is not for this reason regarded as an incendiary. Therefore the laws spare him. Similarly, when a brawl occurs and angry people engage in a fight, some things are excused in a civil manner because the sin has been committed inadvertently, not on purpose. Thus Lot was in such straits that

---

[81] See p. 308, note 78.

he did not know what he was doing. The godly have very tender hearts and, as Scripture says of them (cf. Is. 41:14), are like the most delicate little wood worms; but the obdurate and the proud readily despise everything. One should not judge in accordance with inexperienced hearts. No, judgment should be given in accordance with hearts that are terrified and are afraid of the wrath of God, especially at the time of a disaster as great as the one Lot experienced.

Therefore Moses is not recording impossible things; he is recording things that are natural and in harmony with experience. In support of this there is also the circumstance that he records that Lot went up into the hills and hid in a cave. For if his mind had not been perturbed, he would rather have gone to Abraham than to the hills; but because he was perturbed, he is incapable of forming any plan about doing anything.

One should have the same opinion about Lot's daughters. The weakness of the female sex is well known; but the peril in which they had been and the unexpected mishap of their mother, which they had witnessed, had seriously perturbed their minds. Thus they devise this plan, not because they are stirred up by lust but because of their extraordinary compassion for the entire human race. Consider their words more carefully. They say: "There is no longer a man on earth" and: "Let us preserve offspring from our father." These are words of despair and not of lust, even though they rest on a specious foundation. Lot's daughters thought: "God does not want to destroy the human race; He wants to preserve it. But now there is nobody left besides our father who could preserve procreation and the race. Therefore we must sleep with our father." Thus it is nothing but genuine concern for preserving the human race that troubles the saintly girls. The assumption that there is not a man left on the earth is ample reason for their disturbance. Hence hearts in such a state of agitation urge cohabitation with their father; it is not lust that does so.

I am saying this, not to excuse them but to set forth the true reasons for this deed. When these are discerned, the offense, which necessarily follows if you do not see these reasons, is extenuated. The father is saintly, and the girls are saintly; but both sin, yet not because of malice and lust but because of their great disturbance. Therefore nobody will be able to defend his own lust by citing their example. If they had been undisturbed and in control of their mental faculties, they would have refrained from incest and — as

Abraham does later on — would have comforted themselves with the omnipotence of God, who would be able to make human beings even from stones or call the dead back into life. But since they were disturbed, they conclude in accordance with their present state of mind: "If no man is left besides our father, we shall have offspring from our father. But he is an old man and will be ashamed of the deed. Therefore it will be necessary to make him drunk, in order that he may forget the present misfortune and in order that his senile body may be inflamed by wine. He will never do this when he is sober."

It is not without reason that Moses devotes so many words to his description of the foul deed. That so large a multitude of ungodly people has perished — this is horrible in itself; but that Lot, who saw this punishment, and his daughters fall into so great a sin — this is more horrible. Moreover, these facts have been recorded to frighten all the ungodly, yes, even the saints, lest they become smug. On the contrary, they should recognize the weakness, of which there are such horrible examples, and devote themselves more diligently to prayer and be watchful. Yet it behooves us to excuse the father as well as the daughters and not to magnify their guilt; for they are not sinning, like the ungodly, because of lust, idleness, smugness, and malice; they are sinning as a result of great perplexity. But a fall resulting from perplexity should in no wise be compared to one that comes about intentionally, since Lot would not have been made drunk so easily if his heart had not first been perturbed. So he sinned, but he sinned venially; that is, God forgave this sin out of mercy. For Lot would never have committed it if he had been sober and in possession of his mental faculties.

You will ask: "But why does God permit His own to fall in this manner?" Although we are not at liberty to inquire too eagerly into God's doings, yet here the answer is easy. God wants us to be well aware of our feebleness, lest we lapse into smugness. Thus Lot and his saintly household had seen the sins of the people of Sodom and had rightfully abominated them, but what happens to them now? The people who are so saintly pollute themselves with abominable incest, something which hardly ever happened among the people of Sodom or at least did not happen commonly.

Hence the reason is clear. God wants us all to humble ourselves and to glory solely in His mercy, because, so far as we are concerned, no one is better or saintlier than the other, and no one sins so gravely. If God should withdraw His hand, you will pollute yourself with the same sin. Therefore this awful fall teaches two lessons: (1) that you should humble yourself before God and (2) that you should continually pray to God for the guidance of the Holy Spirit. The nonsense of the Jews about the wine that was dispensed and about the philter prepared by his daughters must be utterly rejected. It was natural wine, such as that region produced; and it undoubtedly also had an excellent and smooth flavor. For previously Moses himself praised the fertility of that region highly when he called it a Paradise of God. Therefore Lot became drunk, not because he drank wine so excessively, but because his perturbed mind could not tolerate such excellent wine.

Moses does not mention how long Lot stayed in those hills; but if one considers the circumstances, it is likely that Abraham sought him and brought him to his own home and that he lived there with his daughters. For how could Abraham abandon his nephew who had been barely snatched from such a great catastrophe? How could he not have shown the kindliest affection for him who had now been deprived of all the property he had formerly had in such abundance, was now bereft of his wife, and finally was also defiled with incest, over which Abraham, as was proper, undoubtedly grieved deeply? For Abraham was a very kindhearted man.

The circumstances support these ideas, but the rabbis — or, to apply a more truthful name to them, the asses of the Jews — do not give consideration to such circumstances; they judge Scripture solely on the basis of their own filthy sentiments. Let those who are of that sort read Ovid, Martial, and their like. This passage deals with very great trials of very saintly people and with very violent conflicts of faith. Consider Abraham himself. Just as one wave sets another wave in motion, so trial and disaster, one after the other, befall him. His grief was very great because he was unable to save the five cities by his prayer. Furthermore, the necessary concern for his nephew Lot worried him; and after he knows that Lot is alive, he also learns about the incest. All these are matters of great importance.

But by what thoughts shall we suppose that Lot himself was tortured after he had learned that his daughters had been impregnated by him? If he had not heard numerous comforting discourses from Abraham, he would undoubtedly have died from grief and sorrow. Examples show what the result of extraordinary grief is, namely, that many suddenly die from this most violent poison. These ideas are more in accord with the truth than what Lyra propounds on the basis of the opinion of the Jews: that Lot sat in a tent under a fig tree and that both Lot and his daughters lived at ease in Abraham's home. On the contrary, it is more likely that they died.

What Lyra alleges about the name is similarly inept. He calls the older daughter the more shameless and charges that by this name she had given her son a mark to show that he was born as the result of incest.[82] For מוֹאָב means out of or from the father. The younger he calls more modest, since she gave her son the common and not disreputable name בֶּן־עַמִּי, that is, "son of my people."

But whatever may in the end be the reason for the names, history shows that these two nations were richly blessed above the others, except that it was forbidden for them to be admitted to the government. But how much more glorious it is that Ruth, the ancestress of Christ, was a Moabite! God had cast the rebellious Korah aside, but with what great gifts his descendants were endowed is shown by the very delightful psalms which are found among those of David. Thus this serves to comfort descendants; they should not despair of a blessing, even though their ancestors brought upon themselves God's curse and wrath because of their sins. "Why, then," you will say, "did the first-born daughter call her son Moab?" My answer is: It was by no means her intention to disgrace her son; she did so in order to remove the offense and to indicate that the cohabitation with her father occurred not from lust or desire but because of her perplexity. Hence she is excusing her disgrace and pointing out that she would have refrained altogether from this incest if her thinking had been rational. But since she was troubled by a concern which was not evil, it was not a disgrace for her to think that the preservation of the human race could not be maintained in any other manner.

34. *And on the next day the first-born said to the younger: Behold, I lay last night with my father; let us make him drink wine tonight also; then you go in and lie with him, that we may preserve offspring through our father.*

35. *So they made their father drink wine that night also; and the younger arose and lay with him; and he did not know when she lay down or when she arose.*

36. *Thus both the daughters of Lot were with child by their father.*

[82] Lyra *ad* Gen. 19:33.

37. *The first-born bore a son, and called his name Moab; he is the father of the Moabites to this day.*

38. *The younger also bore a son, and called his name Ben-ammi; he is the father of the Ammonites to this day.*

The younger gives her son this name also with a definite intention; for just as the older confesses her sin in her son's name and yet puts an end to the offense, since she has sinned because of the perplexity of her heart, not because of lust, so the younger comforts herself with this name Ben-ammi, since, even though he was born as the result of incest, God would not altogether cast him aside as part of His people. Moreover, it seems likely to me that these names were given to the sons as a result of the comforting addresses with which Abraham encouraged the women; for we shall not doubt that they had need of unceasing comfort and that Abraham, as the chief bishop, diligently did his duty in this situation. "My daughters," he said, "you have indeed committed a grievous sin; but do not despair on this account. God sees your hearts; He sees that you did not sin because of lust and lasciviousness but because in such great sorrow and fear your mind became insane, so to speak, and lost all control." This is the one part of the comfort which the mother expressed in the name Moab. Then he added this one: "It is not that you should fear that God will pass on your sin to your sons. He will bless your sons as a part of His people; He will not cast them aside."

This is the exposition of this chapter and indeed not a detailed one — for what can be done by me in detail in so great a mass of things to do? — but one that is simple and true. And you should remember that this account must often be impressed in sermons because of ungodly and smug people, of whom there is always the greatest abundance. Let us not become like the antinomians, who completely thrust the Law out of the church and foster smugness in their hearers. Their destruction is deserved. Moreover, Moses buries the patriarch Lot in this passage; that is, henceforth he will make no mention of him, and it is likely that Lot did not long survive after he had been tortured so much by grief and sorrow.

CHAPTER TWENTY

1. *From there Abraham journeyed toward the territory of the Negeb, and dwelt between Kadesh and Shur; and he sojourned in Gerar.*

I HAVE often stated that when Moses describes the life of Abraham, the saintliest patriarch of all, he does so very much in a manner which befits an ordinary citizen. He says nothing about miracles or about prodigious works and endeavors like those of which monks and hermits boast. He makes Abraham a very common human being who occupied himself with the affairs of the home; for he had a wife, he had children, he had numerous domestics, and with them he wandered hither and thither as necessity and convenience dictated. Hence there is here no semblance of extraordinary saintliness. Therefore the papists and especially the monks neither concern themselves much with these accounts nor read them attentively. But if in the case of this patriarch they were to see a novel form of clothing, strange customs, and a way of life different from that of all other human beings, then indeed they would extol him as a saintly man.

It is impossible to rid the world of this notion. It admires nothing except what is unusual. Therefore when it hears that Abraham wanders about so often and seeks new abodes, it says: "What is so unusual or praiseworthy about this? Abraham has this in common with many, and especially with beggars and other very ordinary people. Things worthy of praise have to be unusual to arouse admiration."

Thus it happens that these sacred accounts are disregarded, and some magician in the market place gets more admiration and a larger gathering when he spews fire than this saintly man, who walks in faith and in the Word and waits with the utmost patience and hope for the promise which God had made to him. This the papists do not see; they regard only the bare work, and in the work they do not consider the heart itself and the sentiment. They say: "Abraham wanders about and takes with him a wife and domestics. Therefore he is a plain layman. But if he had gone into the desert, if he had become a monk, this would have been admirable and worthy of being recorded." In short, the world wants to be amused with tricks but disregards and hates the truth.

Let us, therefore, be mindful of the Word, namely, that two chapters earlier [1] God Himself commands Abraham to go out and to traverse the land. Even though these words are clearer than this sun which we see, those moles do not see it; they admire only their cowls, vigils, and fasts. But what shall we suppose that the saintly man with so large a number of domestics suffered when he was wandering about among the heathen and was continually changing his abode? For he had to be suspended between heaven and earth, since he did not own a single foot of space.[2] This was surely a strange religion and more difficult than that of the monks. For how trifling a thing it is to put on a cowl and meanwhile be untroubled about food and peace, and even to enjoy glory and honor in very beautifully constructed monasteries! Therefore these accounts should not be passed over lightly; they were written by the Holy Spirit and were left for the churches in order that they might be read for the purpose of establishing faith.

Above, in chapter twelve,[3] Moses writes that Abraham came from Bethel toward Hebron to the valley Mamre, where the three brothers, the hosts of Abraham, were. He lived in that place about twenty years, more or less, and there Ishmael was born to him. There, too, he saw the destruction of Sodom; and after he had there received the promise about the son who would be born to him, he went from there to Gerar. Perhaps those three hosts of Abraham died and less godly heirs succeeded them, as is wont to happen, or he avoided a place so close to Sodom. But how much it cost to transfer his residence elsewhere Scripture does not indicate; it leaves this to the reflections of those of us who are maintaining a household.

Furthermore, during those twenty years Abraham undoubtedly converted many at Mamre. Meanwhile, however, the five neighboring cities situated in a very fertile region perished. For this is the

---

[1] By his reference to *supra capite secundo* Luther appears to mean "two chapters earlier," not the second chapter of Genesis; but what he has in mind would suit Gen. 12:1 ff. better.

[2] On the patristic backgrounds of this idea cf. *Luther's Works*, 13, p. 346, note 93.

[3] Although the original has "chapter twelve," the reference is obviously to Gen. 13:18.

way it usually happens: at first the world receives the Word with joy, but it soon loathes it again and in the end, as we see today, even abhors and hates it, since, of course, definite perils must be expected because of the Word, as Christ states in the parable of the rocky soil (Luke 8:6). It is natural, of course, for all human beings to desire eternal life; but they want it coupled with the advantages of this life. Yet Christ's statement is well known (Matt. 16:24): "Let him who wants to follow Me take up his cross"; that is, those who want to be heirs of eternal life must bear and suffer many afflictions.

And here Abraham both teaches and comforts us in an outstanding manner by his example. He is the heir of the entire land of Canaan, for God has promised it to him. Yet he does not own one footbreadth of the entire land, wanders about with his people — now here, now elsewhere — and has no definite abode; and in accordance with his own example his sons and grandsons are exiled too and have no definite abodes. But what is the purpose of this? Undoubtedly in order that we may learn that the saintly patriarch expected another kingdom and another possession than the one which was earthly and of this life. Therefore he remained a stranger in his own land — the land that God had promised him — doubtless in order to leave behind for the Pharisees the true understanding of Holy Scripture concerning the kingdom of God and concerning the main subject of the promise: that the land of Canaan is not the main subject of the promise. Otherwise Abraham, who, with his descendants, lived as a stranger in the very Land of Promise, would not have attained the promise. Therefore we, too, must live in this life as strangers until we reach the true fatherland and a better life, which is eternal. But a later age, as the history of the Pharisees shows, forgot the eternal promises, clung solely to the possession of the land of Canaan, and considered the kingdom of Christ a physical kingdom.

But the prophets and other saints pondered those wanderings of Abraham more diligently and warned that one must look for another country and fatherland than this physical and transient one; otherwise his physical land would have been given to Abraham himself, to whom it was promised. But not even a footbreadth became his during his entire lifetime. He even bought a burial place for Sarah with his own money (Gen. 23:16). This the prophets saw, but our papistic moles do not see it. They say: "Abraham had a wife. Hence he was a plain layman. Hence there is nothing spiritual in the account of him. Everything is ordinary."

But the Letter to the Hebrews (11:8-10) is of a different opinion, for it relates these ordinary things to the Spirit Himself and declares that those ordinary deeds were done in faith. In faith he took a wife, and in faith he wandered about; that is, everywhere he sustained himself with the divine promises or the Word and looked for a resting place or abode other than an earthly one. Of this present one he made use as of food and drink.

Hence let us, too, learn to use this life as an inn or a lodging place for the night. If you understand Abraham's wandering in this manner, you will not say that it was something ordinary; for it is a work of faith, and of a very fervent and strong faith at that. But the ungodly do not see this, as is written (Is. 26:10): Let the ungodly be done away with "that he may not see the glory of God." Works that result from the Word and are done in faith are perfect in the eyes of God, no matter what the world thinks about them — even if you should be merely a shepherd or an infant's nurse. But, as I have said, those moles see only those things that are showy. If you exhibit a monkey, an ugly and useless beast, in a public place, you will immediately find some who run up and admire it as a most beautiful beast. Thus the world admires strange and unusual works, but they have no understanding of faith. Besides, the works of God are always concealed under some lowly form. They do not shine in the world, but they do shine in the eyes of the heavenly Father. But let us now turn to the text.

From Hebron, Abraham proceeded toward the south and dwelt between Kadesh and Shur. Kadesh is on the border of the tribe of Judah toward the east, but Shur is in the tribe of Judah toward the west, near the mountainous regions that border on Egypt. Between these is situated גְּרָר, which means a "sojourn," for גֵּר is a "sojourner." Thus sojourner harmonizes with the name of a place. The guest is a sojourner, and the place has the name "sojourn," just as we use the term "hostelry." The purpose is to have you realize that even in that place Abraham was not a citizen but was a guest. Moreover, גְּרָר is a city of Palestine and almost the farthest toward the south. Furthermore, Palestine is not yet mentioned with any distinction. Perhaps it was not yet a kingdom, and the individual cities were ruled by individual kings.

2. And Abraham said of Sarah his wife: She is my sister. And Abimelech, king of Gerar, sent and took Sarah.

Here a new danger overtakes the patriarch Abraham; but before we expound the account, you should be reminded of the historical facts, which serve in an excellent way to bring about a correct understanding of Scripture. At that time Shem, Shelah, Serug, and Terah were living. Shem had seen the original world before the Flood. But we should not think that the saintly men lived in idleness; they publicly maintained the worship of God and gave instruction to the people of their households concerning the will of God, His promises, His Law, etc. Undoubtedly the neighboring households saw and heard this, and because of this opportunity Gentiles also arrived at the knowledge of the true God and were saved, even though they had not been circumcised. Thus at that time there were many well-established churches in the world. Yet there happened what we, alas, experience today too: at that very time there existed the greatest licentiousness and very wicked men, as the example of the people of Sodom proves. Nevertheless, in the neighborhood they had Abraham as a most excellent teacher, through whose kindness they had been delivered from the wrongs and the yoke of foreign kings.

The same situation prevails in our time. Germany has never had more talented and more learned men. But if you appraise the situation properly, there have never been more villainous men — men who by their eloquence, their knowledge of languages, and other gifts were able to give outstanding support to the church. These men hire out their service to tyrants and to the pope; they are the bitterest enemies of the church.[4] But you see that the same thing happened at the time of so many holy fathers. Let us, therefore, bear the ingratitude, the hatred, and the blasphemy of the world, just as those saintly men did. The seed does not find fertile soil everywhere, the rocks are sterile, the thorns and thistles choke the grain, and Satan lies in wait for the smug. Therefore let it be enough for us that some hear and receive the Word with fruit in spite of all this. But now let us look at the account.

Because Abraham fears for his life, he invents a lie in that new lodging place and calls Sarah his sister. Why does this happen? Evidently because God wants to teach us that even the saintliest

---

[4] It is not altogether clear whether Luther is referring to Erasmus with these harsh words.

fathers had human feelings and emotions, in order that we may not, as we are nevertheless commonly wont to do, think that they were stones or rocks — whom fears, suspicions, scruples, anger, and joys did not affect at all — and that they were like angels. But this is not the case; for no fear befalls an angel. Here, however, Abraham is full of apprehension and fears for his life. Hence Moses describes him as a human being, and he does this for our comfort.

Since Abraham has no definite word from heaven that his wife will be protected, he does what reason suggests and hopes that by such a lie he and his wife can be protected. The Holy Spirit does not always impel godly people; He lets them do some things in accordance with their own will and wish. When Elijah killed the prophets of Baal, he was impelled by the Spirit of God (1 Kings 18:40); yet later on, when Jezebel's wrath has been reported to him, he fears for himself, withdraws into the desert, and in this way looks out for his life (1 Kings 19:1-4). This he does of his own free will, for he is not commanded by God to withdraw. His reason kept telling him that he would be safe if he hid in the desert. Thus he who was most resolute when he killed the prophets was trembling here in his danger and thought that he would not be safe anywhere in Israel. These facts were recorded to comfort us, who have no other thought about the saints than that they were blocks and logs without feeling.

Therefore Paul and Barnabas correctly say of themselves (Acts 14:15): "We are mortal men like you." They are not afraid [5] to say this to idolaters, because the saints are not always impelled by the prompting of the Holy Spirit. They have their desires and afflictions just as everybody else does. Therefore they, too, engage in ordinary pursuits: they sow, plow, build, etc. Reason and diligence are adequate for doing these things; and although the ungodly, too, do similar things, nevertheless, in the case of the godly, these things are pleasing to God because of the faith in which the godly live. Therefore they do nothing out of the ordinary except by special impulse of the Holy Spirit and when commanded by a definite word; otherwise they continue in and live with normal sentiments and endeavors. They do not engage in extraordinary works, as the pope's saints do, who regard a change of garment, a change of place, living alone, and separation from the remaining mass as saintliness, and who

---

[5] We have accepted the suggested emendation by the Weimar editors and have read *verentur* instead of *veretur*.

meanwhile pay no attention to the fear of God and the love of God, as they strain out a gnat and swallow a camel (Matt. 23:24).[6]

Abraham was not of that sort. Although he was saintlier than all the monks who ever were, are, or will be, he was nevertheless apprehensive. He fears for his life when he comes to the unknown people of Gerar. Since the wickedness of the Sodomites was so great, he suspects that there is no fear of God in this place either. Similarly, Shem and his forefathers were heads of households; they had the Word, and they instructed the church. Let us, too, abide by what God has ordained. If God wants to do something extraordinary through you, he will call you and will point out opportunities. Avail yourself of them. If this does not happen, let everyone nevertheless rejoice that he is in a divine calling when he assumes and performs these ordinary duties of this life.

The papists flaunt their canons and the decrees of the fathers, even though these canons and decrees have no divine authority. Yet the papists adore them. Meanwhile they pay no attention to love, hope, and faith. Indeed, because they persecute the Word, they are the enemies of faith. Shun them, and follow in the footsteps of the saintly men, who did not shrink from being associated with ordinary people and had no regard for their own ease but submitted to the common hardships of this life and had wives and families whom they supported by their diligence and labor, just as all sensible heads of households are commonly wont to do, even among the heathen.

"But are these ordinary works?" you will ask. Nevertheless, they are commended by Holy Scripture, which bears witness that man was created for the duties of the household and of the state. Hence these ordinary works are God's order. What more glorious commendation are you asking for, or what clearer testimony? Hence when a maid milks the cows or a hired man hoes the field — provided that they are believers, namely, that they conclude that this kind of life is pleasing to God and was instituted by God — they serve God more than all the monks and nuns, who cannot be sure about their kind of life. Therefore set these accounts against the traditions and canons of men; for here there is the testimony of the Holy Spirit, who says of His saints that they lived in the faith, the Word, and the confession but were like the rest of men in all other respects. Thus Paul says

[6] Luther adds the German: *Es sind mucken saiger und cameel schlucker.*

to the heathen (cf. Acts 14:15): "We are men just like you"; that is, we are similarly affected. We grieve when there is trouble, and we rejoice if our affairs prosper in accordance with our way of thinking.

I impress these facts frequently and gladly, and I know that this is not done without fruit. Evidently this false notion is so deeply fixed in the hearts of all men that we admire only what is rare, strange, and unnatural. Let us rather remain pupils of the Holy Spirit and of Scripture, and let us imitate the lives and the deeds of those whom Scripture praises and presents as examples. Let us not bother about the fact that in accordance with a special call Abraham was a warrior and killed four kings. He did this by a special command. When God wants you to do something of that sort, he will give you a command to that effect, not indeed from heaven through angels but through the constituted authority. If this does not happen, refrain from extraordinary deeds, and keep in mind Abraham in his calling as head of the household. Even if, as the papists maintain, you do works of the laity, these are nevertheless truly spiritual, because of faith and the Word. A monk cannot take such pride in his cowl and in his monastery, no matter if he has the canons of the fathers or the decrees of the pope in his favor. If the canons, together with their councils and decrees, have in them anything that is good, they are in agreement with Holy Scripture; but if they are not in agreement, we do not bother about them at all, but properly even shun and reject them as suspect. Moreover, in harmony with the testimony of Scripture, we praise civil works; for God wanted us to bear the common hardships and misfortunes of human nature, and He tells us not to despair in them but to be confident that He will be with us. Indeed, He has provided us with natural reason, by means of which we are to exercise control over those civil works, lest we tempt God, who makes the earth subject to us. But let us now turn to the historical account.

The text states that King Abimelech seized Sarah. Here the question arises how it is likely that Sarah was seized because of her beauty — and at that not by some ordinary man but by the king himself — although by this time she was an old woman full of years, since she evidently was seventy-five years old. As a rule, physical beauty is not praised at that age. Therefore that generation must have been more vigorous and of a far stronger constitution than is the case today. Now the women who have reached approximately their fortieth year are no longer fit for childbirth. Septuagenarian Sarah is not only praised because of her beauty, but she still hopes to bear a child. Consequently at that time people were more moderate and, in my opinion, were also aided by a mild climate. Today we not only injure and weaken our bodies by gluttony, but we also contaminate the climate by our sins; that is, we provoke God, with the result that the inclemency of the weather is greater than it was in those times.

Then, too, God wanted His great blessing to be apparent among His own people, namely, that the youth of those who fear Him is renewed like the eagle's (Ps. 103:5; Is. 40:31), and their godliness blossoms forth in their bodies, as Scripture bears witness concerning Moses, Joshua, Caleb, and others that they retained their youthful powers even at a rather advanced age. Of course, it is also universally true that a moderate way of life greatly assists nature. On the other hand, even the strongest bodies are ruined by intemperance; and when they accumulate diseases, they hasten their death.

3. *But God came to Abimelech in a dream by night and said to him: Behold, you are a dead man because of the woman you have taken; for she is a man's wife.*

By this procedure, which he supposed would be a means of safety, Abraham exposes his wife to danger. And he did not sin by resorting to such a plan; for where there is no higher word to guide us, we are right in following our reason. But I am speaking about civil matters; for so far as spiritual matters are concerned, God has made everything abundantly clear in His Word. But outward and physical matters He has put under the control of reason, and, to state it simply, they have no need of the exhortations of the Holy Spirit. What they need is diligence, persistent effort, and care; otherwise we are tempting God.

So far as the account is concerned, King Abimelech is described as a godly king. Therefore he was undoubtedly one of the number of those who heard the patriarchs Shem, Shelah, and others. For it is significant that Moses states clearly that God considered him worthy of being spoken to. It was not an angel who came to him, the text says; it was God. Hence special note must be taken of this. You will say: "Why, then, did Abraham fear such a godly man?" I think that this happened because of the horrible example of the five cities. For there he encountered such great human wickedness that according to God's own testimony not five righteous men were found in that entire region. "If, then," so he thought, "in this blessed land, which had the most distinguished patriarch Shem as a teacher in the neighborhood, there was so much ungodliness and crime, I shall find ungodly Sodomites, murderers and adulterers wherever I go." I suppose that this fear arose as a result of such a thought; for our own misfortunes, as the Greeks elegantly express it, teach us that one learns by experience.[7]

Nor could a sensible person regard this reasoning with contempt. For if you saw lightning strike one or the other city where you had hoped to find well-established churches, what hope would you have concerning the others, which are notorious for adultery, usury, gluttony, luxury, deceits, frauds, etc., as nearly all the commercial centers throughout Germany are today? Thus by their sins the people of Sodom so troubled Abraham's saintly heart that he gave up hope concerning all other men. Experience led him[8] to that way of thinking, and indeed without sin.

Therefore Abraham fears for his life, and not without reason, if we carefully consider the circumstances. The promise had been given to him that Sarah would give birth in this year, and the promise was clearer and surer because the name Isaac had been assigned to his son. After this joyful announcement there ensues the very grievous overthrow of the five cities, about which Abraham was so greatly concerned that he interceded for them with God. But he met with refusal on the ground that the wickedness of those people was so great that not five righteous men were found among them. Thereafter misfortune befell the family. For Lot was Sarah's brother; and first his wife is taken from him, and then he commits incest because of the foolishness of his daughters. No wonder these many great evils, which occurred within one year, broke the heart of the saintly man so that he supposed that nothing was safe anywhere! Those who do not take note of these circumstances do not understand the account. For this reason they even read it with contempt. To me indeed it seems remarkable that in such great sorrow Abraham was able to beget a child.

---

[7] The play on the similarity of the Greek words παθήματα and μαθήματα is at least as old as Herodotus, *History*, Book I, ch. 207.

[8] We have followed the Weimar editors in reading *eum* for the *eam* in the original.

But these facts serve to teach us how God is wont to train his saints. Because Abraham had a wife from whom he begot a son, the monks think that he led a sensual life; but they do not see the manifold and most grievous trials and dangers which befell him during this one year. For they are unacquainted with the spiritual conflicts by which God continually trains the faith of the saints.

In the papacy there is a book containing the legends or accounts of the saints.[9] I hate it intensely, solely for the reason that it tells of revolting forms of worship and silly miracles performed by idle people. These legends and accounts actually accomplish only one thing: they increase contempt of the government and of the household, yes, even almost of the church itself. Therefore such tales should be shunned and utterly rejected, for the chief thing of Christian doctrine is faith. About this the entire book does not mention a single word anywhere. It is occupied solely with praising monasticism and monkish works, which are altogether at variance with the customary ways of people.

Similarly, the papists today bestow exaggerated praise on the originators of monasticism and say that they were saintly men. But what concern is this of ours? We are not debating whether Augustine and others were saintly. But if there is to be a discussion about saintliness in general, is not Paul saintlier? Indeed, is not Christ saintlier? Why, then, do we not follow these? Why do we not embrace their canons or doctrine, since we are sure that if we hear and follow Christ, we are pleasing God?

This saintliness should be enough for us. We should seek no other saintliness through extraordinary works outside our calling. The Carthusians eat no meat throughout their entire life. Why? A saintly man has so decreed. But is it sufficient to give this answer? How much more correctly the very wise man Augustine answered! Above others he had the illumination which caused him to say that he reads the writings of the earlier fathers in such a way that he does not believe them — no matter how great their influence may be because of their saintliness and learning — unless they are in agreement with the Scripture.[10] Both saintliness and learning are splendid and very high distinctions; but they are not sufficient for faith, which

---

[9] Luther is probably referring to the *Legenda aurea* of Jacobus de Voragine.

[10] A representative statement is in Augustine's *Epistle* LXXXII, ch. 1, *Patrologia, Series Latina*, XXXIII, 277.

must rely on the Word of God alone. This statement of Augustine sets forth a very fine judgment against all human traditions. If you adopt it, you will say: "No matter how great the influence of the pope may be because of his erudition, instruction, saintliness, wealth, and power, let him go where he wants with his sanctimony, instruction, and the rest of his gifts; we shall not listen to him unless he produces Holy Scripture."

We need this caution, for our gentlemen jurists are not yet ceasing to praise their silly and ungodly canons and to protect and defend the authority of the popes.

But I return to Abraham. You see him described as walking in faith, performing many good works, and enduring many misfortunes. Let us follow him and other patriarchs like him, for we have better examples than those which the pope sets before his people in his legends. And those very fathers whom the papists praise observed their traditions in genuine freedom and bade them be observed in the same way. But the pope does not do this; he fastens halters on consciences and makes the traditions binding. For the laws which he commands to be observed, he commands to be observed under penalty of damnation.

But the devil should speak in this manner, not a bishop. Therefore Paul is right when he calls the pope a son of sin and perdition (2 Thess. 2:3) who gives rise to nothing but sin and perdition. For this reason the pope should be driven out of the church, which Christ wanted to be free, as Paul says (2 Cor. 1:24): "We do not lord it over your faith." Paul did not want the church to be subject to the tyranny of teachers, for he recognizes only one teacher, Christ, whom he serves in true humility.

Though Abraham was plagued and tempted in so many different ways during this year, eventually he also found solace; for his wife is returned to him by the king, he is received into the friendship of the king, and generous hospitality is offered him. About the lie we have spoken above, when we dealt with a similar account; for when Abraham was in Egypt ten years before this, he experienced the same thing that happened to him here in Gerar.[11]

But in the schools they debate about three kinds of lies: the jocular, the obliging, and the injurious or infamous lie. Actually,

---

[11] See the earlier discussion, based partly on Augustine, in *Luther's Works*, 2, pp. 291 ff.

however, there is only one kind of lie, namely, that which harms one's neighbor in his soul, as the lie of Satan, in his body, or in his possessions and reputation. For the jocular lie — when we fabricate something — serves to instruct the youth, as when short fables are told to them and when they are frightened by fictitious characters, as on the stage.

Similarly, the so-called obliging lie is also invented for the advantage of one's neighbor. Thus in Luke (24:28) Christ pretended that He would go farther. Saul's daughter asserts that David is lying in bed (1 Sam. 19:11-17). This is the kind of lie we are now discussing. Sarah pretends to be a sister and not a wife. But because Abimelech believes that she is a sister and brings her to his house — even though he sins in ignorance — God nevertheless punishes him, though not to the point of damnation; He does so in mercy. Moreover, this is sure proof that Abimelech was a saintly man, since God speaks with him and earnestly admonishes him not to sin so imprudently.

All this serves to commend to us the patriarch Abraham, whose faith wrestled bravely in this peril. For it was no slight adversity or one to be esteemed lightly that his wife was taken from him, and by the king himself at that, and at the time when a seed had been promised to him. The Lord, you see, had designated the very time. "In this year," He said, "Sarah will bear your son Isaac." While Abraham is living in this hope, he loses his wife. He does not know when the Lord will restore her to him, yet he concludes in firm faith that God's promise will not be without effect. Hence his heart was troubled in various ways when he regarded the conduct and examples of the world, and he was compelled to have doubts about the outcome. For it is well known what tyrants are wont to do; they frown on any opposition to their desires. The very fact that Abraham's wife was taken from him when he arrived strengthened his conviction — at which he had already previously arrived — that among these people there was no fear of God.

But just as Abraham's heart indulged in these thoughts and was despondent and discouraged, so, on the other hand, as often as he thought of God and of His promise, he gained the sure hope that Sarah would be restored to him unharmed. In this way he overcame the thoughts of the flesh by faith; he adduced the Word against them and added a fervent prayer. And when God is called upon,

He is soon at hand and does not abandon His own in dangers. For it is impossible for one who believes in His promise to be forsaken. God would rather break asunder the heavens than disregard believers.

I have no doubt that David had this passage in mind when he thanked God in Ps. 107:6-7 for the help that was shown in the time of trouble. "Then they cried to the Lord," he says, "in their trouble, and He delivered them from their distress; He led them by a straight way till they reached a city to dwell in."

Learn, therefore, from this passage what a great thing faith is and how pleasing a sacrifice a believing heart is to God. When Abraham has been left in the lurch by his own counsel, he is saved by the promise. Hence if we, too, are living in dangers — as is utterly inevitable, provided that we want to be true Christians — let us trust in the Lord's help, which the promise makes certain for us in accordance with the declaration (Ps. 50:15): "Call upon Me in the day of trouble; I will deliver you."

Many difficulties are put in the way of those to whom the government of the state has been entrusted. Therefore most of them neglect their duty and are afraid of incurring displeasure. But all fear should be put aside, and what the Word commands should be done in faith. For if an officer of the state is unwilling to punish a murderer or an adulterer because that murderer or adulterer inspires fear by reason of his power and wealth, and is able to harm the state, such an officer acts contrary to his duty and the will of God. He should rather be mindful of the promise, which says (Rom. 13:1-2): "All power is from God, and he who resists the power resists God." In accordance with this promise, he should proceed with the punishment of the wicked. But if hatred or enmity results, he should commend himself and his welfare to the Lord in faith; then he will feel that he is being defended by God. He who does not have this faith will connive at public crimes and so violate God's command and therefore bear His punishments.

Moreover, the works of a faithful officer of the state are far superior to those of the hermit Antony and of the others, who indeed can also be saints but are among the minor ones. Like women, they are afraid and shun dangers. But the bishop who remains among his fellow citizens without fear awaits the sword of the tyrant, as Cyprian did.¹² Similarly, a faithful ruler, like Constantine and Theodosius, and faithful heads of households, each in his own station, are exposed to countless dangers; but because they are sure of their calling, they call upon God and so are delivered by faith.

These conflicts prepare the saints and thus keep them from being soft like the hermits, who endure nothing except what they bring upon themselves. The tyranny of rulers, who were scattering the churches everywhere, can excuse the hermits, Antony and others, who for this reason should be given a place among the saints, but as weak and fearful ones. But in one year Ambrose lives a saintlier life and does more good works than Hilarion in all his seventy years. Ambrose lived in the ordinary manner, and he lived unmarried, not because of some compulsion but voluntarily, just as marriage is a voluntary matter. In addition, he taught publicly. Privately he comforted some and reproved others whenever he had the opportunity to do so, and he was most zealous in the defense of the church. Even though these works are considered insignificant, they nevertheless excel all the works and worship of all the monks.

Therefore it is important to have a position of authority in the household, in the state, or in the church; for these are the orders that were instituted by God.¹³ Hence those who live in them, even though they will not be free from dangers, should nevertheless — because they have the command concerning prayer — hold fast to the certain hope of help.

If you want to know something about the life of Christians or about the legends of the saints, no matter what they are, I shall tell you in a few words. If you are a Christian, no matter in what order you are, God will trouble you in various ways through the devil, the world, and the flesh; and He will do so in this ordinary life, which is without any special outward show. Therefore faith and prayer should be conspicuous throughout the entire life of Christians. Everywhere in the account of Abraham you see an example of this. There is danger that his wife is being taken from him. But even though he cannot shut grief out of his heart, he does not utterly despair but calls upon God and believes that God will bring help. And as he believes, so it happens. "He rebuked great kings on their

---

¹² A reference to the martyrdom of Cyprian in Carthage, September 14, 258.

¹³ Cf. p. 217, note 45.

account," says Ps. 105:14. So Abimelech, too, is rebuked on account of Abraham.

"God came to him," says Moses. What he means is that God came with terror and not as He is in the habit of doing when He takes on the usual appearance of a human being, a dove, or a lamb. But He does this in order to show that He is concerned about Abraham. About the three kinds of prophecy we have spoken above, namely, prophecy per se, visions, and dreams.[14] So far as dreams are concerned, there is the well-known rule that such revelations must be scrutinized with respect to their relation to the Word and to faith. If they are not in harmony with the Word or destroy faith, they are of Satan.

In the Hebrew our translation into Latin — *iuncta marito*, "joined to a husband" — is בְּעֻלַת בַּעַל, that is, "married to a husband." Now the word בַּעַל is familiar, for it denotes a husband. Furthermore, by this name people designated definite idols and boasted that these idols were united with God as a bride is united with the bridegroom. Hence Hosea (2:17) states: "I will remove the names of the בְּעָלִים from her mouth"; that is, they will no longer have a multitude of gods or idols; they will have Me alone as their true God, whom they will accept in true faith, just as I shall accept them in true love.

In this manner the word is employed in this passage too. Sarah is married to a husband; that is: "You are doing wrong by loving a woman who has her own husband, by whom she is loved and whom she loves in turn; therefore keep away from her, and return her to her husband." This is such a forceful preaching of the Law that unless God had preserved the king, he would have died immediately from grief and fear. But he buoys himself up by faith and concludes that God is just. Thus he asserts his innocence.

4. *Now Abimelech had not approached her; so he said: Lord, wilt Thou slay an innocent people?*

5. *Did he not himself say to me: She is my sister? And she herself said: He is my brother. In the integrity of my heart and the innocence of my hands I have done this.*

God comforts Abraham in a twofold manner: first, by seeing to it that his wife is restored to him; secondly, by showing him that the citizens in Gerar were not as wicked as those in Sodom. There they

---

[14] See the earlier discussion in *Luther's Works*, 2, pp. 218—219.

did not keep away even from men; but here the king, after he has been warned by God that Sarah was a married woman, keeps away from her. And praise is properly bestowed on his moderation and chastity because he did not immediately yield to a mad impulse of lust, arrange a wedding, and attack his guests, as the people of Sodom did; but at his home he was honorable in his treatment of the woman he had taken. As soon as he learned that she was married, he released her. Hence he was one of the saintly kings who undoubtedly ruled his people in a godly manner, just as the little verse declares: "The entire country conforms to the king's example." [15] It was an extraordinary comfort for Abraham to find such a king even among the uncircumcised. For this thought or trial disturbed him greatly, that prompted by the example of the people of Sodom, he had been forced to conclude that the entire world was corrupt and without fear of God. By so clear an example this thought is driven out of him, with the result that where his fear is greatest, there he finds people who are most blameless and truly saintly.

Moreover, this passage also serves to praise marriage, which, as we know, was not only originated by God but, as we learn and see here, is protected by God, just as the Sixth Commandment not only forbids acts of adultery and lust but is also a barrier and safeguard for marriage, lest it be dishonored.

The prayer with which Abimelech excuses himself before God deserves our careful examination. He does not despair at once because of that awful preaching of the Law which he hears from the Lord: "You will surely die"; but first he asserts his innocence. Furthermore, he has firm hope in God's justice, that is, in His compassion. For God's justice is not, as they have taught in the schools, the severity, sternness, or violent anger with which God condemns; it is the justice through which He has mercy on the humble as He protects them against unjust violence and punishes the guilty.[16] For both are just: punishing the evildoers and protecting the innocent. He who knows that God is just in this way will readily withstand terrors and will find a place of rest. But what Abimelech states in

[15] Claudian, *Panegyric* on the consulship of Honorius, 299.

[16] A reflection of Luther's struggle to find the meaning of "the righteousness of God." See his "Preface" to the Latin edition of his writings (1545), *Luther's Works*, 34, pp. 336—337.

this passage is also required, namely, that he have a pure heart and innocent hands. This means that it is necessary to have a good conscience. But since those who yield to sin and to the flesh cannot have a good conscience, they must, if they are to be converted, first be frightened, and not slightly at that, but in such a way that they do not know where to turn, as we see in Peter and in David. Since they are conscious of their guilt, they do not excuse themselves; but when they acknowledge their sin, they are wretchedly perplexed and humbled. Yet they eventually lay hold of mercy and thus are reconciled through faith, which accepts the Mediator.

But why does Abimelech, when he alone is addressed, involve the entire nation in his answer? He does not say: "Wilt Thou kill me a just man?" but: "Wilt Thou kill a just nation?" A possible answer is that he had a large household establishment, that Sarah had been brought to him by others, and that in this way not only the king but also the people had sinned.

But it is more in accord with the truth to say that the saintly king involved the whole nation because he had a good knowledge of sacred matters. Accordingly, he concluded on the basis of examples and experience that an entire people is often punished because of an ungodly king, just as God also blesses an entire kingdom because of a saintly ruler. Thus He granted prosperity to all Syria on account of Naaman, but because of David's sin he smote the entire nation of Israel. These facts even the heathen learned from experience, just as there are the lines of Hesiod to the effect that often an entire city is punished because of the sin of one person.[17] And Horace speaks the truth when he says: "Whatever folly the kings commit, the Achaeans are punished."[18]

Furthermore, the fact that Abimelech mentions not only his own person but the entire people gave emphasis to his prayer for pardon. Then it is also true that there is no greater misfortune for kingdoms than the decease of pious and saintly rulers.

But it is not enough for the king to assert his own innocence; he also relates the circumstances and passes the guilt on to others. He says: "Without anyone compelling him, Abraham declared of his own free will that this woman was his sister; indeed, when she herself was asked, she corroborated the statement that she was his

[17] Hesiod, *Works and Days*, 238.
[18] Horace, *Epistles*, I, 2, 14.

sister and not his wife. Why did they lie? For if I had known how matters stood, I would never had made this attempt."

What shall we answer here? Abraham and Sarah are accused by the saintly king. Hence either the king is lying or Abraham and Sarah committed a sin. My answer is: The saints, however great, should not always be excused when they sin; for although Abraham is full of faith, nevertheless in this instance he fell through weakness and feared for himself. You will say: "But he had a reason, for he was distressed to such an extent by that wretched downfall of the people of Sodom that he was forced to fear when there was safety." Even if this cause of fear could not be regarded lightly or excluded, it nevertheless does not entirely excuse Abraham.

In the first place, this fear was a sin; and, as usually happens, this sin results in the other one. He lies, and he instructs his wife to lie. But in the saints these sins are venial. John states (1 John 1:8): "If we say that we have no sin, the truth is not in us"; and we have the article of the Creed: "I believe in the forgiveness of sins." Therefore we shall not excuse Abraham entirely but shall include him, too, in the sinful mass, yet in a one which, although it is not ungodly, nevertheless has in it the remnants of sin. This is also proved by the fact that God Himself does not excuse Abraham but accepts the king's excuse.

The saints daily commit many such sins; for they, too, are carried away by occasions. But these sins differ from the sins of the ungodly, which deny the faith and militate against the acknowledged truth. Abraham is not that kind of man. Yet he feels the law of his members (Rom. 7:23), which sometimes tears him away from the right way, namely, when he is not excited by fervent faith, when the days are evil and times of tribulation are at hand, just as we, too, daily experience in ourselves.

Therefore you must note that the saints should not always be excused from all sins; for the conclusion that they, too, had bodies or flesh and felt their passions, which original sin left even in such as were reborn in faith, serves to comfort us.

But here another question turns up. Why does God allow such sins to be committed by His own? Why does He permit His own to stumble in this way? The most appropriate answer to this question is given on the basis of the outcome. God permits it to happen this way in order that He may have the opportunity to achieve many good results. The saints do not fall in order to perish; they fall in order that God may bestow rich blessings on them by heaping greater benefits on them, as is written (Rom. 8:28): "We know that all things work together for good for the saints," and a gloss to this passage adds: "Even their very failings."

No one can have any doubt that God sends tribulation and misfortune to the end that they may benefit us; for Paul's statement is well known (2 Tim. 2:12): "If we suffer with Him, we shall also reign with Him." Yes, God even makes up for our misfortunes.

The sons of Israel sell their brother Joseph. He is led away to Egypt as a slave, and there a new misfortune is contrived for him by an adulterous woman; but in the end he is acquitted with honor and is right in telling his brothers (Gen. 50:20): "You meant evil against me, but God meant it for good."

But, as I have said above, not only the passive evils that are inflicted on us result in good, but also the active ones, that is, the evils which we ourselves do. "How can this be?" you say. Because when a godly person is aware of his fall, he becomes ashamed and is perturbed. Thus his fall leads first to humility and then also to fervent prayer. It is for this reason that Solomon says (Prov. 24:16): "A righteous man falls seven times in a day and rises again." For they do not persist in their sins; they groan and grieve. Moreover, the evil which remains in our flesh is like a spur which urges us on, with the result that we are angry with ourselves, condemn ourselves, and cry out with Paul (Rom. 7:24): "Wretched man that I am! Who will deliver me from the body of this sin?" Lord, take away and crucify our flesh! Thus faith grows by reason of our failings, the seeds of which remain in our flesh.

Therefore God leads His saints in a wonderful manner, as the psalm (4:3) states. "With the pure Thou dost show Thyself pure; and with the crooked Thou dost show Thyself perverse" (Ps. 18:26). But these statements should not be understood as though we maintained that a failing is something good. For a failing remains something intrinsically evil; but in the case of the saints it becomes the occasion for something good, according to the statement (Ps. 18:25): "With the blameless man Thou dost show Thyself blameless." Whatever the saints do is sanctified; that is, even if those fall who are saintly or justified or believe and fear God, their faith is nevertheless disciplined and increased. To this extent God is wonderful in His saints.

Thus Abraham, who has a fervent faith, is tried to such an extent that he fears for his life and by his lying causes his wife to be taken from him. This is a failing, but what benefit results from this fall? Clearly this: His faith and prayer are kindled anew, and his wife is returned to him. Furthermore, the godly king associates with Abraham so closely that because of this opportunity Abimelech becomes more enlightened, arrives at a more perfect knowledge of God, and is helped by Abraham's prayers. And King Abimelech experiences death and punishment, not indeed for his destruction, as it seems, but in order that God may have the opportunity to perfect him and to include him in the church of Abraham.

These are God's wonderful works in the saints, that is, in the believers. They are not ungodly, and they do not continue in their sins. Yet they often fall through weakness; but their fall results in something good for them, because they are saintly.

On the other hand, the psalm (18:26) states: "With the crooked Thou dost show Thyself perverse"; for their merits or good works (we may use this term) work together for them for evil because they misuse God's noblest gifts — their intellect, eloquence, erudition, physical strength, beauty, etc. — against God and gradually become hardened, are blinded in their ungodliness, and eventually become so proud that to themselves they appear to be gods above the rest. This perversion of their gifts is clearly observable.

It has happened to me, too, that I often stumbled and ventured upon many very foolish measures. Therefore God, who controls all things, did not grant success. Then I was abashed. I began to hate myself and to be angry with myself. Moreover, since I had been humbled, I was then all the more zealously on my guard, lest I be deceived by the plans of the flesh; and I clung more carefully to the Word. But I thanked God for having so wonderfully changed my plan and for having granted another outcome, one that was far better than I had intended. It happened this way when we were at Smalcald. We declined to take part in the pope's council; but it would have been far better not to have declined if only the council had been held under fair terms.[19]

Thus it happens in our entire life that we do, plan, and say many things in a faulty way. But God uses these faults to humble

[19] This expression of regret over the actions at Smalcald in 1537 may reflect the attitude of Luther's editors rather than his own.

His saints. He turns our faults to better account. Perhaps He would not have done this if we did not have these failings.

These are theological matters which we do not tell to the canonists and sophists, who studiously distort and jeer at such ideas of ours. We tell them to the saints. Even though they do not indulge the flesh, they are burdened with sin, not because of wickedness but through weakness. When they are faint, they should not despair; then they should consider God's plan. He exalts His saints, as the psalm (4:3) states; that is, He guides them with a wonderful plan, just as it is very wonderful that He lets His saints fall in order to humble them, to kindle their faith and prayer, and to keep smugness away. For the statement (Rom. 8:28) is true: "For the elect all things work together for good." And Ps. 18:25 says: "With the blameless man Thou dost show Thyself blameless."

Thus Abraham falls into a sin here, but it becomes an opportunity for converting the king and the kingdom. This is indeed a marvelous work of God, who leads and guides His saints in a wonderful manner to keep them in the saintliness of fear and in the confidence of faith. This faith would utterly collapse if that weakness did not remain in the saints, for the abundance of the gifts of grace would make them arrogant.

We see this in the ungodly, who turn their good things into evils and make them cause evils for themselves; for they glory in their gifts, do not give thanks to God, and do not relieve the want of the brethren but think that they are gods and lords of others. Thus, just as for the saints all things turn out for good, so for the ungodly all things turn out for evil.

Furthermore, you should note here, too, that God is no antinomian;[20] for He begins His opportunity with the Law, but later, after He has allowed Abimelech's innocence, He absolves and comforts him, and also blesses him in various ways. This is the divine and proper procedure. Abraham and Sarah get into dangers because of their sin, but these dangers cause something that is good; for in this way the king associates himself with the house and the church of Abraham.

6. *Then God said to him in the dream: Yes, I know that you have done this in the integrity of your heart, and it was I who kept you from sinning against Me; therefore I did not let you touch her.*

[20] See p. 222, note 48.

7. *Now then restore the man's wife; for he is a prophet, and he will pray for you, and you shall live. But if you do not restore her, know that you shall surely die, you and all that are yours.*

This is a very delightful address. In His own words God absolves Abimelech of all sin. "I know," He says, "that your heart is pure"; that is, "I know that you truly fear Me and that you are not going to do anything against My will out of wickedness. For this reason I have also kept you from sinning. Moreover, when I rebuked you rather severely in the beginning, I did so for the sake of the outcome, namely, that Abraham might receive comfort and you might come to a fuller knowledge of God by associating with the house of Abraham. Thus My hand has been with you to keep you from sinning against Me."

These are words of extraordinary grace, as though God were saying: "I am your Protector and Keeper. Not only shall you suffer no harm to your body and your property; but, more than this, you shall suffer no harm to your soul. At first it seemed to you that I was angry with you. In reality, however, I am angry with you in this way in order that I may not be compelled to be angry. Thus I Myself am holding My anger in check in order that you may be without sin, that Abraham may have comfort, and that your whole kingdom may be converted." What more pleasing image of God can one imagine?

Therefore the Jews are stupid asses when at this point they invent the fiction that the godly king was so stricken in his body that he could not touch Sarah.[21] In this passage, however, you hear something different, namely, that God is not afflicting the body but is keeping the heart of the king chaste. For the body can be afflicted, and in spite of this the heart meanwhile burns with lust. Therefore one should take note of this passage, which points out that God is the Protector of His saints and keeps them from sinning.

It is an extraordinary sign of mercy and grace that God speaks at such length with Abimelech in his dreams, just as, on the other hand, it is a sure sign of anger when He keeps silence. Yes, even if God speaks and rebukes in anger, His grace is nevertheless there; for it is impossible for men not to be improved and not to become more pious because of the Word. For God is not an idle talker.

---

[21] Lyra *ad* Gen. 20:6.

Whatever He says is important and profitable. Abimelech knew Abraham as an exile and stranger; but from God's address he learns that he is a prophet of God, that is, a distinguished servant of God, than whom the world has nothing more sublime, since he was commanded by God to teach the world about God and through the preaching of the Word to gather a church for God in the world.

At that time Shem, Shelah, and other patriarchs were still living, but it was Abraham alone whose house God had chosen to be the church and to whom He had given the promise that through his Seed all the families of the earth would be blessed. Hence it is God's voice which declares that he is the high priest in whose house would surely be found the Word of God, forgiveness of sins, and eternal life.

Accordingly, we can imagine how great Abraham's standing with this king was from now on, for Abimelech hears God Himself call Abraham a prophet. Therefore the king received him most courteously and heard from him heavenly wisdom about the Son of God, who would be born from Abraham's house and would redeem the human race, and thus, after removing the curse, would bring everlasting blessing.

Thus Abraham is appointed bishop and teacher by God's voice; but the king, together with his citizens, is a pupil and hearer. Moreover, God blesses that place by letting Isaac be begotten and born there; and the Holy Spirit — but not circumcision — is given to the Gentiles, although those Gentiles, who had been taught by the Word, knew and believed that there is no other God than the One who would be born from Abraham's circumcised people.

These, of course, are the great benefits that result from the true doctrine: God's glory, fulfillment of the Decalog, and redemption from death and hell. Therefore the godly understand why Moses recorded these facts, namely, to confirm the promise of faith that the Gentiles also belong to the church of Abraham, even though they have not been circumcised. Accordingly, these changes continue in the world: the unrepentant people of Sodom fall to their destruction, but Gerar is converted. Thus today some become obdurate and utterly blind. On the other hand, some believe the Word and are enlightened by it.

Because God says that Abraham will pray for the king, you see how beautifully Scripture is everywhere in agreement; for everywhere it places the Spirit of grace and of supplication side by side. Thus Abraham is a prophet in order that he may teach the knowledge of God in the world. At the same time he is a priest in order that he may pray not only for himself but for his church, yes, even for the Gentiles who associate themselves with it. For God says: "He will pray for you." With this statement He calls the king and his people to the church of Abraham, and the Gentile, like a wild olive tree, partakes of the rich sap of the olive tree and is grafted on it (Rom. 11:17). Abraham, however, is thus praised by God as a very great teacher and as one who prays or petitions with very great power.

But you will ask: "Why does not God do such things without Abraham? What need is there for such a long address?" My answer is: "God honors the man who honors Him; and because Abraham confesses God, God, in turn, confesses him, honors him with a most noble testimony, and places under him the king and the entire kingdom, in order that they may become his pupils."

Concerning prayer we have stated rather often that even though God is ready to give us everything we need, He has made it necessary for us to pray, in accordance with the statement (John 16:24): "Ask, and you will receive." But we should pray not only for our own sakes but also to offer to God the worship that is due Him. For he who prays confesses that God is gracious, merciful, and forgiving. Therefore just as the Word must always be taught and emphasized in the church, so prayer must always be practiced, in order that grace may abound, that the incipient gifts may grow in us, and that the glory of God may be increased everywhere.

But why does God repeat the threat at the end? Evidently because the obdurate continually relapse into sin. Thus even though Pharaoh has been admonished so many times, he by no means relaxes his tyranny. And Saul often defends David and accuses himself, yet he reverts to his natural disposition and attempts to destroy David. Similarly, the rocky soil receives the seed, but it produces no fruit. "Do not be such a one," says God to Abimelech, "or you will surely die." Even though many beware of outward offenses, they nevertheless eventually become smug. It is the wicked doctrine of the sophists that a single spark of love is sufficient for eternal life.[22] They do not know that the Word must be emphasized by hearing

---

[22] Luther is referring to the scholastic notion of an "act of charity" as an expression of love toward God; such an act has the power to blot out mortal sin.

it daily and that prayer must constantly be urged if we want to remain in grace. Consequently, this repeated threat serves to encourage the king to abide in the grace which has been bestowed on him, for it threatens him with death if he sins. But those who are smug destroy themselves.

8. *So Abimelech rose early in the morning and called all his servants, and told them all these things; and the men were very much afraid.*

These words should be carefully noted, for they present a very fine example of repentance. Abimelech does not put off from day to day making amends for his deed, as we procrastinators are in the habit of doing. When we are moved by some pious emotion, we promise to make amends at a future time. In his dreams Abimelech hears the sermon about bewaring of sin. Therefore as soon as day breaks, he at once assembles his entire court and explains what has occurred. Next he calls Abraham also and returns his wife to him. Thus he who was a king now becomes a bishop of his kingdom and spreads the fear and knowledge of God among his own people also, in order that they, too, may fear God and have respect for the Word.

It is a most excellent gift of God when a king becomes a teacher, that is, when a godly officer of the state makes religion the object of his earnest concern. Abimelech knew God even before Abraham's arrival and had ruled his people in a godly fashion, but that knowledge of God was of a more general nature. Now, when he happens to hear Abraham, he learns to look at God more closely, as it were, since he knows that Abraham will be the father of the Blessed Seed. This knowledge of God Abimelech spreads among his subjects.

Today many say that they would embrace the Gospel if the kings themselves were to preach it, but that sensible people are repelled because most preachers are so wretched, poor, despised, and downright plebeian. But those who say this are lying, for the ungodly always disregard and despise the Word, whether angels teach it from heaven or kings teach it in the world.

For what do they miss in us? Did not our most illustrious prince of sacred memory, John, Elector of Saxony, teach the Gospel of Jesus Christ in the year 1530 through his frank confession at the Diet of Augsburg in the presence of Emperor Charles and all the imperial estates, and not he alone but with him and after him many others? [23]

Therefore this subterfuge is empty and deceptive. For if God were to send angels from heaven, as He sent them to Sodom, the ungodly would still not believe. Away with the devilish rhetoric of those who bring up the lowliness of the teachers as an excuse and look for distinguished, brilliant, and powerful preachers, as the Jews say John 7:48-49: "Does anyone of the rulers and the Pharisees believe on Him? Verily, this people, which does not know the Law, is accursed."

But these devilish subterfuges with which the ungodly adorn their obstinacy will collapse, and God will punish such outstanding contempt of the Word. Of what benefit was it that the angels came to Sodom and that Lot was a person who led a blameless life and with whom his fellow citizens could find no fault?

But there are some who uphold their contempt of the Gospel under another pretext. They say: "What good has resulted from it?" With this battering-ram, so to speak, they are trying to knock down our entire doctrine. But the hearts of the godly must be fortified against these offensive statements. Why do they not listen to Paul, who says (1 Cor. 1:26) that not many noble, not many wise men, have been called? But when he says "not many," the fact remains that there are nevertheless some. Thus at Abraham's time not many kings embraced the true doctrine. Yet Abimelech embraces it and becomes a teacher of his church.

Thus at the Diet of Augsburg there were many princes who detested our doctrine; yet there was also John, Elector of Saxony, of sacred memory, who confessed Christ with great courage before the entire world.

But if you ask what good has resulted from our doctrine, tell me what good resulted from Lot's preaching in Sodom. Surely this, that they were consumed by fire from heaven after they had heard the Word without fruit and in vain. Such a punishment will also overtake our despisers in due time, and we see that they are becoming blinder and more irrational from day to day. This is the beginning of their downfall. But you should take note of these facts in order to overcome the dialectic with which Satan blinds the eyes and hearts of many.

[23] John the Constant, who was Elector of Saxony from 1525 to 1532.

The attitude of the whole world is expressed in the familiar German proverb: "If you were to carry someone on your back as far as Rome and were to set him down roughly, all thanks would be lost." Our doctrine frees all nations from the torture and tyranny of Satan, from sin, from eternal death, from the countless monstrosities of the pope, and from the notoriously heavy burden of conscience. But the thankless world is not aware of these countless kindnesses of God. If any slight trouble occurs, if some either seize the property of the church or talk or live with a little less self-restraint, they exaggerate this fact endlessly. Such men are not pupils of the doctrine but are merely looking for the bad things they observe in those who profess the Gospel and for what seem to be faults. Upon these things they seize in order to revile our doctrine with a view to suppressing it.

But why is not Abraham's ministry also blamed for the destruction of Sodom that followed upon it? If the people of Sodom had survived, they would undoubtedly have placed all the blame on him, because he had been too close a neighbor to them; for they had long since forgotten that they had been delivered through his kindness. Such is the way of the world.

But by "world" I mean not only people of the lowest station but also the best, who stand out because of their wisdom and ability. They are the main ones. Because of a slight adversity they forget all the very great blessings bestowed on them, pass judgment on the doctrine of the Gospel, and begin to hate it.

Alas, we too, who have the Word and boast of it, easily forget the other blessings of God when we have been distressed by insignificant troubles. God has given me a healthy body until my fiftieth year;[24] He has given me a wife and children, and, above all, a fairly extensive knowledge of His Word. Now, when either dysentery or a stone plagues me at times, this one evil drives away the remembrance of all the other good things.

Thus God gives to the world the sun, rain, and other advantages; but if a plague or a famine occurs once within ten or twelve years, an outcry and complaint arises, and immediately the blessing of the former years vanishes. But it is a heavy cross to live amid such great wickedness of people who esteem the blessings of God lightly.

---

[24] Although Luther was afflicted with various diseases and discomforts, it was not until 1537 — about two years before he spoke these words — that he suffered an attack of stones so serious as to be almost fatal.

We should do the opposite and bear patiently the rather light and few troubles in comparison with the vast sea of blessings with which God daily overwhelms us. For when all our troubles have been brought together in one heap, what are they in comparison with this one gift, that God has revealed His Word to us? Accordingly, those who disregard the boundless blessings of the doctrine because of some inconveniences — do they not work great harm?

How much more correct Paul is when he says (2 Cor. 4:17-18) that our afflictions are temporary and light, but that the glory with which God will make up for them will have measureless significance for those who look at what is invisible, not at what is visible!

But Paul is preaching this in vain, for the world does not believe. It is wholly occupied with what is visible; it pays no attention to what is invisible and regards it as worthless. The merciful Father has given His Son, who died for our sins. He, in turn, demands of us that we confess His name before the world and also lose our life for His name's sake; and He promises that eternal rest and boundless glory will follow upon this small cross. What can be more delightful than this promise, which promises so sure a deliverance from eternal death? Besides, it is the nature of our life that eventually we must die. Why, then, do we not rather die for the sake of Christ's name?

But our nature does not permit a proper comparison between the greatness of our blessings and the smallness of our troubles. In accordance with its way, the flesh always obscures the greatness of the blessings, which are infinite, with the troubles, which are finite to the highest degree.

Therefore let the list of God's blessings, physical as well as spiritual, be constantly in view, and we shall see that where there is a drop of evil, there is an ocean of God's benefits on which we should expatiate with divine rhetoric, as Paul does in an excellent manner; for with a single word he exhausts all the perils and inconveniences about which the world can complain.

The lot of those to whom God has entrusted the ministry of the Word is uncertain: They are driven out of their homes, are slain, and are burned. You will say: "Are these not evils?" Paul's answer is: "They certainly are, but they are light and momentary. Moreover, they result in an eternal and boundless advantage" (cf. 2 Cor. 4:17).

Paul sees and believes this. The world, however, neither sees nor believes it but is entirely occupied with the present things.

Therefore, as the German proverb states: "If you carry it on your shoulders as far as Rome and set it down rather roughly, all thanks is lost." [25] The world wants to feel no cross, no slight inconvenience, and no straw of evil, although it itself is full of beams and is vexatious and burdensome, especially for the church.

Therefore let us who are Christians overcome and make light of those monstrous fictions of the devil, and, on the other hand, let us place great stress on the benefits of God. For all our afflictions are really very small, and it is a minute little cross which we are bearing if we compare it with the benefits which have accrued to us from the creation, redemption, and sanctification and which will be more manifest in the life to come (Rom. 8:18).

But let us return to the account. The disaster of the people of Sodom which the patriarch Abraham was compelled to witness was great. Therefore God comforts him with another example, which is not sad but is most gladsome and delightful, namely, that the heathen king Abimelech becomes a bishop and teaches the Word of God at his court. The text says: "He called all his servants." And this preaching was not in vain. For Moses adds: "And they were very much afraid."

Accordingly, this is a very fine contrast. Abraham had delivered the people of Sodom and the neighboring cities, and he had not only bestowed this physical benefit on them but had also given instruction about the true knowledge and worship of God. Lot, too, who lived in Sodom itself, was not silent; he endeavored to spread the knowledge of God, and he freely confessed his faith. But the ungodly citizens ignored both these teachers and not only did not fear God but even held Him in contempt.

But here you observe the opposite among the people of Gerar. When they hear the Word from their king, they humble themselves and are converted to God. They had no knowledge of the king's dream, nor had they seen it; but they believe him when he tells about it and they receive it as the Word of God and are afraid, yet in such a fashion that they preserve their hope in the grace of God; and they give rich gifts to Abraham.

Moses relates these facts in a few words. He does not enlarge on them, as the historians of the heathen do, but leaves this to the reader. Yet all these events serve to comfort Abraham, who had been

---

[25] Here Luther quotes the proverb in Latin; on page 342 he quotes it in German.

[W, XLIII, 122, 123]

filled with terror by the example of the people of Sodom and supposed that there was no longer any fear of God in the world. But through this occurrence God showed him that although most people in the world are wicked, He nevertheless has His little church, even though it is small and hidden.

In the Books of the Kings (1 Kings 19:18) God comforts Elijah in the same way; for when Elijah complained that he was the only one left who adhered to the true worship, God answers him that there are still 7,000 remaining, all of whom are uncorrupted and worship the true God.

Since the ingratitude and the wickedness of the burghers, the peasants, and the classes of every kind are so great, we, too, are often driven to conclude that the entire world is possessed by Satan. Moreover, the very sad spectacle troubles the hearts of the godly. But one must hold fast to the hope which is here set before Abraham: that nevertheless there are some pious and saintly people still living. For God is not without a people. He is a God of mercy and of judgment. Therefore He preserves and guides those who are not impenitent but humble themselves and seek forgiveness. Thus Ps. 12:1 states: "The faithful have vanished from among the sons of men"; that is, the world casts aside and hates the truth and the Word. Yet at the end the Lord says (Ps. 12:5): "I will arise because of the poor." Therefore there always remain some who keep and receive the Word.

Thus when Christ had departed from Jerusalem because the Jews were about to stone Him, He again came to Jerusalem, and He said in continuation that there are twelve hours in the day (John 11:9); that is, that in time hearts are changed and that some change their wickedness for the better. Accordingly, things change. At one place a very sad spectacle engages Abraham's attention, at another he receives comfort. Here in his exile he meets godly people who receive him kindly and respect him as a prophet of God.

In addition, Abraham has the greater comfort that Sarah conceives and makes the hope of an heir certain. Thus God shows abundantly that He tenderly loves His saints, that is, those who believe His promises. To be sure, He permits them to be vexed in various ways. Nevertheless, He faithfully keeps His promises. Therefore let no one despair even in the greatest afflictions, but let us all maintain with the utmost steadfastness that heaven would sooner fall down than that God would forget His promise.

One should have the same thought about Lot and his daughters. Although Moses relates nothing about them, they undoubtedly took refuge with Abraham as the father of the promise. They expected to hear from him comfort against the many great troubles into which they so suddenly fell. Accordingly, in addition to the fact that association with the people of Gerar, who feared God, mitigated their grief — while the people of Sodom, as Peter says (2 Peter 2:8), had vexed both the eyes and the ears of the saintly persons — Abraham himself, as the supreme bishop, absolved them from incest. For even though he could neither excuse nor approve their deed, he nevertheless presented God to them as forgiving and as feeling pity for our weakness. He said: "The deed cannot be undone. Therefore God now demands nothing of you except that you acknowledge your sin and hope for His mercy for the sake of the promised Seed."

Toward the sons who were born from Lot's daughters Abraham undoubtedly displayed affection, just as grandfathers are wont to do toward grandsons; and he promised them kingdoms. Therefore for them, too, the misfortune by which they were humbled resulted in a comfort. For Abraham could never have had any rest if he had not known that Lot and his daughters had been reconciled with God. Therefore we who believe the promise have a God who indeed tries us but does so with a slight and momentary affliction, as Paul calls it (2 Cor. 4:17). For we do not act like those irreligious people who say: "What good results from the Gospel? For we know that Abraham believes in God, but what good did it do him? He is compelled to leave his native country, to go into exile, and there to endure countless misfortunes among the heathen." These things the world considers to be evils, and we do not deny that they are evils; but we maintain that they are light and momentary evils if, in contrast, you look to the importance and the eternal duration of the good things.

But only the believers do this, only those who look to what is invisible, not to what is visible; that is, who cling to the Word in simple faith. Yet, as we have stated above, even in temporal affairs the good things outweigh the evil. But how much truer this is in the church! Here the voice of Christ is heard (Matt. 11:29-30): "My burden is light," namely, for those who believe My Word; "and My yoke is easy," namely, if we look to Christ, who has promised that He will refresh us, just as He adds: "You will find rest for your souls."

The verb "you will find" indicates that for a time the godly will be without rest. But that time of no rest is brief. Moreover, the rest of their souls which the believers will find will be important and eternal.

Far from either believing or understanding this, the ungodly do not even have a proper knowledge of the good things they now have and enjoy every day. For if they lead a most pleasant life for a whole half century and nothing but a slight fever lasting a few days attacks them, they forget all previous benefits and all but act like madmen because of their impatience. This is a horrible blinding that comes from Satan, who obscures these benefits. I myself hate Pliny very much because he accuses nature as though she were always a stepmother and not rather one who nourishes. He makes a great hullabaloo about poisonous animals, snakes, crocodiles, etc.[26] But the infinite excellence of so many cows, bulls, sheep, birds, fish, and human beings he does not see. Indeed, he does not see even the sun and the moon. Holy Scripture does not speak about the creatures in such a manner. Indeed, the rhetoric of the Holy Spirit attaches more importance to the things that are good than it does to the things that are evil. Satan is in the habit of doing the opposite, even though the circumstances themselves clearly indicate that where there is one hideous snake or dragon, there are a thousand cows, and where there is one wolf, there are a hundred sheep.

9. *Then Abimelech called Abraham and said to him: What have you done to us? And how have I sinned against you, that you have brought on me and my kingdom a great sin? You have done to me things that ought not to be done.*

Frightened by God's address, King Abimelech humbles himself after his sin has been disclosed to him. After he has humbled himself, he hears the pardon for his sins and accepts the comfort. Now he adds his confession. Finally there follow all kinds of good works. Through them he shows his love toward the exiles. Furthermore, these words of his confession are not to be understood as though the king alone were speaking them; but they are the public utterance of the entire kingdom, that is, of the king and of his subjects.

This is a clear example that even before the birth of Christ, yes, even before the Law was given, many who were not circumcised were

---

[26] Luther is thinking of passages like Pliny, *Natural History*, VIII, 25.

joined to the church of the circumcised and were saved. "For the ways of the Lord are unsearchable" (Rom. 11:33), and the dream of the Jews that God cast away all the Gentiles and wanted to be known and worshiped solely by those who are circumcised is a rash fabrication.

Our translator into Latin assumes that these words of the king are a protest, but he is speaking as one who has no experience with spiritual matters and with trials.[27] For the king is not remonstrating with Abraham, but out of a contrite and troubled heart he is complaining in utmost humility about the cause of such a great misfortune. He is one of those who say with Job (23:15): "I took fright at all my deeds," and with David (Ps. 19:12): "Who discerns his faults? Cleanse me of my hidden faults." Likewise, James (3:2) states: "We all make many mistakes." For to hear the Word of God is not play or sport. When it strikes the heart, it is like a thunderbolt which overthrows even the most strongly fortified places by its force, as the account of Paul shows when he was dashed to the ground on the journey to Damascus (Acts 9:4). There he heard no high-sounding words; but he felt that his spirit was being crushed, as the Lord says in the Book of Jeremiah (23:29): "My words are not feeble, but a fire and a hammer which shatters rocks." Paul hated the Gospel with such an obstinate heart that he was like an immovable rock. Yet he is shattered by the hammer of the Word. For "God kills and brings to life; He brings down to Sheol and raises up" (1 Sam. 2:6).

Accordingly, God does not speak with us as one human being speaks with another. "His words are like a two-edged sword by which hearts are pierced" (Heb. 4:12). Therefore our hearts are not proud but are humbled to the utmost; they do not boast of works or merits, but with Job they take fright of all their works. Nor do they find anything to set against God's wrath, but they see and feel that even their righteous works are unclean and polluted before God. Thus Augustine's famous statement is often repeated: "Woe to the life of men, be it ever so praiseworthy, if mercy has been withdrawn!"[28]

From such a sentiment the king, too, is speaking here. He does not remonstrate with Abraham as one who is righteous and does not

---

[27] The colon between *loquitur* and *ut inexpertus* in the original seems to be misplaced.

[28] Perhaps a reference to Augustine, *De correptione et gratia*, ch. 13, par. 41, *Patrologia, Series Latina*, XLIV, 941—942.

deserve this injustice. He has a contrite spirit; and, because he hears from God that he has sinned unknowingly, he is looking about for the reason. Then, because he hears from God Himself that Abraham is a prophet of God, he deplores his misfortune: "Come, saintly prophet, tell me what my sin is. What have I done or perpetrated that I fell into that mistake and thought about marrying your Sarah?" For contrite hearts are in the habit of acting this way; they cannot rest until they hear what their sin is, in order that they may be able to find a remedy.

But Abraham had stated that Sarah was his sister, and this had been the occasion for the king's sinning; for if Abimelech had known that Sarah was Abraham's wife, he would never have resolved to marry her or take her away. Therefore he thinks: "Some other sin by which I deserved to fall into this sin must have preceded." Consequently, he does not remonstrate; but he trembles, is agitated, and seeks peace of conscience. He is not aware of anything, yet he feels that he has sinned somewhere, in accordance with the statement (James 3:2): "We all make many mistakes." For we commit many sins even without knowing it.

It is for this reason that Christ advises us to pray (Matt. 6:12): "Forgive us our trespasses" and also tells us to forgive others their trespasses. For the remnants of sin remain in us and require daily forgiveness.

The pope, together with his frogs and dogs, boldly barks against us that we reject good works or forbid them. But we tell and urge all people to do good works. Yet we reject the teaching that any good works, be they ever so numerous, must be set over against the judgment of God. This is what King Abimelech means here; for his frightened conscience thinks about nothing but his sin and refrains from all boasting and self-confidence, no matter how many good works it may have.

In this sense one must understand the statement of Gregory: "It is characteristic of pious hearts to acknowledge guilt even where there is no guilt."[29] The pope, as befitted the Antichrist, distorted this statement to establish his tyranny. He wanted to be feared in this manner. But this was wicked. For only before God should one acknowledge guilt which does not exist, not before men. I can truth-

---

[29] Luther may be thinking of Gregory's counsel in his *Liber regulae pastoralis*, Part III, chs. 29—30, *Patrologia, Series Latina*, LXXVII, 107—112.

fully say that I have not committed adultery and have not stolen, but I cannot say in general that I have committed no sin against the Sixth and Seventh Commandments.

For in these circumstances I must be afraid of God's judgment, even though I am not conscious of anything. Sin has not yet been done away with, nor has it been completely buried; and to have restrained one's hands is not enough for God. He condemns even the lust of the heart. Therefore we are right in acknowledging before Him guilt where there is no guilt, that is, where we are not conscious of anything. We are right in saying with David (Ps. 19:12): "Who can discern his errors? Cleanse me of my hidden faults." For God holds even our original sin against us, but the pope holds nothing of that sort against us. He is neither God nor the judge of original sin. Therefore if he accuses us unjustly, he must be resisted, and there should be no room for the tyrannical statement which has its origin in the mouth of Satan: "Our pronouncements, even though unjust, must be feared." Indeed, you must say that these pronouncements must be resisted and that here neither the authority of Saint Gregory nor that of any other human being should have any weight. For the pope is not God, to hold any guilt against us. God, however, always regards us as responsible and answerable to Him.

Accordingly, you have here an example of an extraordinary confessor who is afraid of sin where there was none, that is, where he was conscious of none. To be sure, he heard the absolution from God; but once his heart has been frightened, he is unable to find enough rest but is troubled by his worries. Even though this happens with great torment of hearts, it is nevertheless pleasing to God, in accordance with the statement: "My Spirit will dwell with a contrite heart." [30] Proof that this is the sense of this confession is the fact that the king entreats Abraham a second time and says: "What did you see, that you did this deed?" The emphasis is on the verb "see," for to see is peculiar to prophets to whom God reveals His will through visions. It is as though the king were saying: "I know that you are a prophet. Come now, tell me whether you have had any revelation concerning this plan of yours and whether you said by a definite command of God that your wife is your sister. Surely some guilt is at the bottom of this. I am not conscious of it. Nor is my people conscious of it. If we have done any wrong, please say so, and we shall repent."

[30] Apparently a reference to the Latin of Is. 57:15.

11. *Abraham said: I did it because I thought: There is no fear of God at all in this place, and they will kill me because of my wife.*

12. *Besides, she is indeed my sister, the daughter of my father, but not the daughter of my mother; and she became my wife.*

13. *And when God caused me to wander from my father's house, I said to her: This is the kindness you must do me: at every place to which we come, say of me: He is my brother.*

Abraham does two things. He excuses himself, and he frees the king's conscience. It is as though he were saying: "God has given me no command, nor have I seen any prophetic vision. Therefore you should have no fear whatever. The one true reason for this deceit was this: after I had left my homeland, I migrated also from Hebron, where for many years I was a neighbor of the people of Sodom, and by means of my sword the Lord delivered that entire region. Through my prayer and diligent intercession I, too, wanted to deliver them from the wrath of God; but because of their persistent wickedness I was unable to do so. When I became aware of this wickedness, I thought — I admit it — that there were nowhere any human beings who had any fear of God. Accordingly, since I feared for my life, I thought that I could save myself by this means. Full of troubles and misfortunes, I therefore adopted this plan. I beg you to forgive me."

These accounts deserve to be read, for they tell of the ceaseless mortification of the saints. Therefore they are very useful for the proper regulation of one's life. How much easier it would have been for Abraham to present his neck to the executioner for inflicting the deathblow in one hour than to be killed daily in this manner! Moreover, by these examples the godly heart is trained for faith, hope, and all Christian virtues. Therefore they should be read frequently; for whenever a new misfortune befalls, God has new sermons or addresses by means of which He mitigates these misfortunes.

You see nothing of this sort in the common legends or accounts of the saints, which, when they get to their main point, extol celibacy. But it would have been far easier for Abraham to do without a wife than to be vexed by so many inconveniences. But since he has the sure promise of descendants, he bears the cross which the Lord places on him. He is not at all disturbed by the fact that this kind of life is entirely without any outward appearance of sanctity.

First Abraham had excused himself before the king by stating that whatever he did, he did as a result of his fear and perplexity after those extraordinary misfortunes; for he thought that in Gerar, too, the same sins and the same ungodliness he had encountered in Sodom and Egypt were prevalent. Now he adds another excuse. It has to do with Sarah herself. But this entire lengthy explanation serves to comfort the king, for it is very difficult to buoy up a heart that is really frightened. Abraham sees this, and therefore he resorts to a rather lengthy speech. He says: "My wife had some reason for stating that she is my sister; for she actually is my sister, but not in the sense in which you understood it. I used the word figuratively — not indeed because I hated you, but out of fear — for the term 'sister' is something used in its strict sense and sometimes in its broad meaning. I called her sister in the wide sense, but you understood it in the strict sense."

Furthermore, the question arises here how Abraham can say that Sarah is the daughter of his father Terah; for Moses states clearly that Terah had three sons — Nahor, Haran, and Abraham — and that Lot was Haran's natural son, but that Lot was Sarah's brother. But of Sarah he does not state that she was Haran's natural daughter, unless perchance you imagine that she had two names and that above, in the twelfth chapter, she is called Iscah.[31] But since this is a little too farfetched, it remains for us to conclude that Sarah was the stepdaughter of Haran. Because he died before his father Terah, she was brought to Terah's home and was reared there. From then on she was called Terah's daughter. Consequently she was neither the natural nor the legitimate daughter of Haran; she was adopted when he married the widow. If we accept this idea, the debate whether Abraham could marry his brother's daughter is already cut short; for the Law does not prohibit marrying a brother's stepdaughter.

Where our translation has: "When God caused me to wander from my father's house," the Hebrew is: "After אֱלֹהִים, gods, had caused me to wander." One must consider the passage carefully and note it well. It is otherwise common usage to employ the plural noun אֱלֹהִים for the name of God; but in this passage there is added to the plural noun אֱלֹהִים a verb that is also in the plural "They caused to wander." The Jews cavil at this passage with their familiar mis-

---

[31] Although the original has "twelfth chapter," the actual location of the passage is in the eleventh chapter; cf. also *Luther's Works*, 2, pp. 238 ff.

representation, as though Moses were speaking in this way to show respect.[32] But let us conclude that Moses' intention is the same as it was in the first chapter (Gen. 1:26), where God says: "Let Us make man," namely, to show clearly that in the absolutely uncompounded Divinity there is a plurality of Persons: the Father, the Son, and the Holy Spirit. And we are not inventing this; we derive this wisdom from the Word of God, which is plain and clear and should not be perverted by us as the Jews pervert it, especially since Holy Scripture is in such beautiful agreement and the New Testament so clearly proves the same thing.

Furthermore, Abraham undoubtedly wanted to employ this mode of expression before the king with the definite purpose of instructing him about the mystery [33] of the Trinity, namely, that God is Three and One and that the promised Seed of the woman is the eternal Son of God. And the saintly prophets learned from Moses, who read Holy Scripture far more diligently than either we or the Jews do today. The Jews read the sacred writings in such a manner that they are blinded more and more.

"To wander" is a familiar verb. Abraham wants to point out that he left his native land without knowing where he was going, that he was merely obeying the Word of the Lord, but that later on the Lord had shown him this place of the land of Canaan. Furthermore, he wants to point out that he is dwelling here in such a manner that he has nothing of his own but is compelled to wander now here and now there. In short, he points out that he is wandering in this manner in a strange region by divine command, lest Abimelech suspect that he has been expelled and is roaming about because of his own fault. Abraham says: "It is God's plan and will which compels me to do so; otherwise I would have remained among my own people."

Here one should also note that Abraham says that he spoke most respectfully to his wife. He did not give an order and did not say: "You must obey me; I compel you; I demand from you." No, he said: "I beg you," and he does not consider her action obedience; he considers it a favor, as though by a superior person, in accordance with Peter's precept (1 Peter 3:7): "Bestow honor on the female sex." But why did Moses record this? Doubtless in order to present

[32] See Lyra *ad* Gen. 20:13.

[33] The original has *ministerio;* we have followed the Erlangen edition and translated *mysterio.*

an example of a very fine marriage, something which is indeed a rarity on earth but is most pleasing both to God and to men.

Therefore by means of this very example Peter exhorts spouses to learn to love each other and to treat each other with respect and not as people are now in the habit of doing. Husbands generally are lions in their homes and are harsh toward wives and domestics. Similarly, the wives generally domineer everywhere and regard their husbands as servants. But it is foolish for a husband to want to display his manly courage and heroic valor by ruling his wife. On the other hand, it is also unbearable if wives want to dominate. Such marriages — where both are capricious — are common, as the proverb has it: "Three things are rare, but they are pleasing to God: harmony among brothers, love among neighbors, and accord between spouses." The reason is that people generally enter into this kind of life without prayer and, like swine, regard only what is carnal. Therefore the wife does not see what is truly good in her husband. On the other hand, the husband sees in his wife only what displeases him. Since there is no mutual tolerance between them, quarrels and countless outbursts of anger arise.

Therefore this example deserves frequent attention from married people, in order that they may learn how to live together amicably. For one who is unwilling to overlook anything but wants to go to extremes in all his demands will lead a most wretched life. Besides, he will be irksome to others; for, if I may say so, this life is truly scurvy, ulcerous, and full of troubles. Therefore one who lives in it will not find favorable conditions everywhere. "Where there is fire," they say, "there is bound to be smoke." Thus troubles are everywhere added to favorable conditions, but pious hearts will bear the troubles with patience and thank God for the favorable conditions.

The fact that Abraham gives Sarah the all-inclusive instruction: "In every place to which we come say that I am your brother" is evidence of his great weakness and inordinate fear; for it indicates that he is afraid not only of the people of Gerar but also of all other men. For this reason he did not have the courage anywhere to admit that Sarah was his wife.

But why does Moses record this conduct, hardly creditable, about such a great man? He does this for our sakes, for the virtues of the saints should be praised in such a manner that we nevertheless conclude that they were human beings and that they both had and endured something human. Thus James 5:17 states that "Elijah was a man of like nature with ourselves." Paul tells the heathen concerning himself and Barnabas (Acts 14:15): "We are mortal men like you." And Peter tells Cornelius (Acts 10:26): "I am a man like you."

Moreover, even though the faith of Abraham is given high praise by the prophets and apostles, the account nevertheless shows that he often returned to his habitual weakness. For God really leads His saints in a marvelous manner. Sometimes they simply go along like other men, and their faith seems to be buried, so to speak; again, at another time, they are full of the Spirit and perform marvelous deeds, as I pointed out above concerning Elijah, who slew the false prophets with great courage, then trembled when he was informed of Jezebel's fury, and withdrew into the desert.[34]

The Holy Spirit has recorded these facts for our comfort, in order that we may be certain that the saintly men were not unfeeling stocks or stones, such as the pope invents. Jerome writes about Hilarion that for forty years he used no bread and until his seventieth year drank nothing but water.[35] Because this is unnatural, men admire him.

But you hear nothing of this sort about Abraham. He eats, drinks, and works like other men. But if you consider his faith, hope, love, humility, and true mortification, he far surpasses all Hilarions and Antonys. These men, too, had their torments (if I may call them such) and crosses, but they were voluntary and self-elected or freely imposed.

But by the Lord's command Abraham is compelled to travel about as a wanderer from nation to nation, not to have a fixed abode anywhere, and to see terrible disasters which he himself did not choose but got into by the Lord's command and bore patiently. The papistic saints, on the other hand, are most impatient even in trivial situations. How impatient Jerome himself is, since a single little word provokes him to write invective! Therefore let us direct our attention to the saints whose examples the Holy Spirit sets before us — the saints who are full of faith, love, and humility. Yet outcroppings of human weaknesses occur, in order that weaker people may have comfort. Indeed, in our flesh God's Son Himself was weak, tired, afraid, fled from dangers, etc.

[34] See p. 320.

[35] According to Jerome, *Vita S. Hilarionis eremitae,* ch. 11, *Patrologia, Series Latina,* XXIII, 33—34, Hilarion did not eat bread for sixteen (not forty, as Luther has it) years.

14. *Then Abimelech took sheep and oxen, and male and female slaves, and gave them to Abraham, and restored Sarah, his wife, to him.*

15. *And Abimelech said: Behold, my land is before you; dwell where it pleases you.*

After Moses has related that the king was thoroughly frightened by the Word, he next — in order that nothing that could be desired in a godly king may be lacking — tells us about the love which the king had after being absolved from sin and after confessing his sin before Abraham and his entire court. He did not expel the foreigner Abraham, as we heard above about Pharaoh (Gen. 12:20); but he bestows royal gifts on him, giving him oxen and sheep, male and female slaves, and permitting him to dwell in whatever place he wishes. It is as though the king were saying: "You are a prophet; you have the Word and teach it. Therefore in keeping with the duty of a king it is incumbent on me to help, honor, defend, and support you."

Such is the respect Abimelech feels for the ministry of the Word or the priesthood. Therefore all kings and princes should direct their attention to this example. Usually, however, they prefer to be like Pharaoh rather than like Abimelech. This example also serves to comfort the churches, for God does not forsake His own forever. We have heard of the trouble and the misfortunes which godly Abraham endured. If he had not sustained himself with God's promise, it would not have been surprising if he had died from sorrow; and it is likely that in that year pious Lot died from grief. But at the opportune time God comes truly as a helper in tribulation and opens the kingdom of the people of Gerar to Abraham that he may live in it untroubled and safe, and also that Sarah may have a quiet place in which to bear her son.

In this way God comforts His afflicted church. For He does not subject it to tyrants forever, but sometimes He gives godly kings and princes who support the churches and confer benefits on them. In our times the most illustrious electors of Saxony were men of that kind. They believed that the care of the churches was their main concern. Hence they established schools and provided capable ministers for the churches that had been miserably neglected, while others persecuted the Word and troubled the churches with their tyranny.[36]

---

[36] The electors of Saxony were Frederick the Wise (1487—1525), John the Constant (1525—32), and John Frederick the Magnanimous (1532—47).

But Abimelech realizes what a great gift it is to have in his kingdom the Word of God, the worship of God, the church of God, and a prophet of God. Therefore he is so generous toward this guest and shows him the highest honor. He offers him not only a place to dwell but also the use of the things he may need for his convenience.

Therefore this king belongs in the catalog of the saintly rulers whose duty it is to support the prophets and defend the church of God, not to build monasteries. But even though men who do this are rare, nevertheless this example of Abimelech should be praised in the church and shine.

Even among our own people there are today many who seize the income of the churches and defraud the godly clergy of their salary. The papists, who are wholly possessed of Satan, even add persecution and the sword. Consequently, they will have their rewards, but these rewards will be far different from those which Abimelech received because of his godliness. Abraham prays for him, and he is healed. But the tyrants have the prayers of the church against them and will be delivered to everlasting death.

Thus in Abraham this account presents, in the first place, an example for preachers. From it they are to learn how God is wont to train His saints in the greatest virtues — in faith, hope, and love — in order that they may be able to forgo and to suffer, and may learn to hope for deliverance. These are the real duties of those who are prophets or teachers. In Sarah this account presents an example for mistresses of households; in Abimelech it presents an example for rulers. Moreover, the city of Gerar merits praise because the son of the promise was conceived and born there; and I am amazed that this place is not mentioned anywhere else in Scripture.

16. *But to Sarah he said: Behold, I have given your brother a thousand pieces of silver. Behold, it is a covering of the eyes for you in relation to all who are with you and all others. In this manner she was rebuked.*

This passage is somewhat difficult because of the grammar, and for this reason the translators differ to an extraordinary degree. Nevertheless, the meaning can easily be gathered from the circumstances. Moses states clearly that what the king gave he gave to Abraham, not to Sarah. For this is what the king says: "I have given your brother" — namely, to him whom you call brother — "but to you

I have given nothing." Furthermore, he adds the reason why he is giving Sarah nothing: "This," he says, "will be a covering of the eyes for you."

It is not surprising that there are some passages of Holy Scripture which cannot be adequately understood. Who today understands the writings of the scholastics after the Parisian style of language has come to an end? [37] For when the subject matter and familiarity with the subject matter vanish, then the words cannot be understood either. One who has not studied law does not understand legal terms at all. Similarly, medicine has its own special terms. Likewise astronomy, which nobody understands unless he first masters the subject matter.

Moreover, it is certain that after the Jews had denied Christ, they lost the subject matter. For this reason they are incapable of teaching anything sound and torture themselves in vain with matters of grammar. They often assign ten different meanings to a single word; for "they have lost the light of the words," [38] namely, the subject matter. Thus in this passage the difficulty lies in the words when Abimelech says: "It will be a covering of the eyes for you." For you do not know whether the covering is to be understood in a passive or an active sense. But the last clause is fraught with greater difficulties, especially if one consults the translators.

Burgensis finds fault with Lyra. Santes, too, is at variance with the others. Jerome adds the word "remember," in order to complete the meaning; and his translation into Latin is undoubtedly *reprehensam*. But unlearned people have corrupted the passage and have it *deprehensam*.[39] For *reprehendere* is a well-known word. It means "to rebuke," "to censure," "to punish," "to set right," as in Ps. 6:1: "Lord, rebuke me not in Thine anger" and in Is. 1:18: "Reason with Me."

But let us disregard the grammatical discussion and consider the sense, which I think is very simply this: "To you," the king says to Sarah, "I am giving not even a penny, in order that you may have a covering of the eyes, that is, a sure proof of your chastity, that I have not touched you. For if I gave a gift to you especially, I would

---

[37] Luther seems to be referring to the humanistic restoration of Ciceronian Latin in place of the Latin of the medieval theologians.

[38] See *Luther's Works*, 2, pp. 14—15.

[39] Cf. *Luther's Works*, 1, Introduction, p. xi.

be suggesting to others the suspicion that your decency has been violated." Hence I understand the covering of the eyes in a passive sense. I take it as an unusual expression. Just as we say in Latin *obstruere os*, "to stop someone's mouth," so they say that they will cover the eyes; that is: "They will not have the courage to accuse you but will rather bear witness that you have kept your decency unimpaired."

The clause at the end should support this idea: "And she was rebuked or censured"; that is, not only was no gift bestowed on her by the king, but she was even rebuked, not out of hatred but out of genuine love. For in this way the king had regard for Sarah's reputation and decency. This I consider to be the true sense of this passage. I am unable to say anything about the value of the thousand pieces of silver; but since the king gives them as a gift, I suppose that this was no small sum of money.

17. *Then Abraham prayed to God; and God healed Abimelech, and also healed his wife and female slaves so that they bore children.*

18. *For the Lord had closed all the wombs of the house of Abimelech because of Sarah, Abraham's wife.*

This little sentence proves, in the first place, that Abraham was a prophet of God. In the second place, it bestows the high praise on the church of Abraham that it is truly the church of God out of which the Savior of the human race is to be born. For Abraham was the father of the promise, and wherever he wandered, he carried with him the promise concerning Christ, who would be born from his seed; he did not carry gods with him, as Aeneas did.[40]

Therefore, just as in the Book of Acts Peter teaches Cornelius that there is salvation solely through God's Son, who became the sacrifice for us on the cross, so Abraham instructs godly King Abimelech about the Promised Seed and the plurality of Persons in the Godhead. This was a prophetic work, to which is joined that other work of intercession or prayer, which is immediately heard. For it is impossible for the prayer of a righteous man to be of no effect, since the promises cannot lie (John 16:23): "If you ask anything of the Father, He will give it to you in My name." Likewise (Luke 11:10): "Everyone who asks will receive."

[40] Probably an allusion to Vergil, *Aeneid*, III, 12.

When the text states that the female slaves were healed, it refers to the female slaves who were the king's subjects, just as we read in the Book of Kings: "Are you the servant of Saul?" That is: "Are you his subject?" I have said that the disgusting fiction that Abimelech was stricken in his genitals should be utterly rejected. In the first place, he was stricken enough in bed by God's voice. For such dreams do not depart without greatly impairing all powers, as the example of Daniel proves. He lay seriously ill for several days after his conversation with the angel.

In the second place, the king was troubled by a sad sight. He saw that his wife was exposed to danger in childbirth, and he heard that the same thing happened to the wives of his subjects more frequently than was usually the case. Therefore I do not believe that the king was stricken in his private parts, but that he became ill as a result of the castigation he heard in his dream: "You will surely die"; then, too, as a result of the danger to his wife, whom he sees bearing the punishment for his sin and unable to give birth. For the Lord had closed or constricted all wombs so that they could not bear children.

In its proper sense the Hebrew word רֶחֶם designates the place where the fetus lies in the mother's uterus. By synechoche it is sometimes used for the entire woman. It is also employed in the sense of mercy and compassion, which is especially attributed to this sex, since by nature it was made or created to love, nourish, pity, etc. The female sex has this disposition toward compassion to a greater extent than men. Because of this disposition women are called רֶחֶם. Indeed, God, too, calls Himself רֶחֶם, because He is the compassionate One who will not cast us aside when we are in misfortune but has mercy on us and cherishes us.[41]

Therefore the punishment of the women of Gerar was not only the labor of childbirth; it was their despair of bringing forth children. Women know how great a calamity this is. Hence all were amazed because so many women were in labor and yet could not give birth. But they were suddenly healed through Abraham's prayer, and in their peril they learned of the king's sin and believed that Abraham was a true prophet of God and that the true church of God was in his house. They were converted to the God of Abraham, whom, to-

---

[41] The words for "womb" and for "mercy" have the same root in Hebrew.

gether with Sarah, the Lord wanted to comfort by making it possible for her to conceive.

Where our translation has "because of Sarah, Abraham's wife," the Hebrew has "because of דָּבָר," "the word or affair of Sarah," just as there is a book with the title *The Words of the Days*, that is, the events of the times.[42] In short, in this account Moses presents an example of prayer and the answer to prayer. He shows how tenderly God loves His believers, how solicitously He takes care of them, and how generously He aids them, in order that we, too, may learn to believe and to look for His help at the appropriate time.

This passage is a fine proof and example for the papists. They say: "Abraham accepts gifts from the king and prays for him. We are doing the same thing in our monasteries. Therefore we are right when we accept the gifts that are offered, likewise the honors and the prestige. Why should we refuse these when we see that Abraham does not refuse them? For he readily lets himself be glorified and enriched. Why, then, should we pray gratis, as you Lutherans teach?"

My answer to this argument is simply this: "Do the same thing Abraham did, and we shall give you everything." It is easy to imitate Abraham by receiving from others, yes, even by running to and fro and extorting money under the pretext of prayer; but to imitate his prayer is surely not easy, and a man of prayer, such as Abraham is, deserves not only to be fed but also to be honored, just as Paul says (1 Tim. 5:17) about ministers of the Word that they are worthy of double honor, and, as Christ says (Matt. 10:10): "The laborer deserves his reward."

The story is told about St. Ulrich that he fed a certain beggar in order that the beggar might pray for him every day. But one day it happened that the steward overlooked the beggar and did not give him his customary portion. For this reason the beggar, in turn, neglected his praying. Because Ulrich had met with some misfortune and had been exposed to danger on that day, he asks the beggar whether he had prayed for him on that day. The beggar says that he had not and adds as the reason that on that day the steward had not given him anything. Then Ulrich scolds the steward for having deprived him of the beggar's intercession by his niggardliness. "Well,"

---

[42] Apparently a reference to the Hebrew title of the Book of Deuteronomy; cf. *Luther's Works*, 9, p. 9.

says the steward, "how much do you suppose praying one Our Father is worth?" Ulrich sends him to Rome to inquire how high he should estimate the value of one Our Father. The pope's answer is: "A penny." When the steward laughed, the pope gives a second answer, namely, that he estimates its value to be that of a gold piece. His third answer is: "The whole world with all its wealth could not pay for one Our Father." [43]

Perhaps answers like these have been invented, but they are surely not related without fruit or in vain. Hence if the papists rightfully want to have possession of such rich benefices, they, too, should pray; but since prayer demands faith in Christ — while they are not only without faith but even hate and persecute the Word on which alone faith relies — there can certainly be no prayer among them. For them prayer is merely a work of the tongue; they bellow and shout in the churches without any understanding and have no correct knowledge either of their own misery or of God's mercy. But prayer without understanding is also without devotion, since there is no desire for something of which one has no knowledge.

Thus the prayer of the papists is a tedious work and a most irksome chore; it is worth not even a penny in the eyes of God. Indeed, it is an abomination, since the papists are without faith and do not give God His honor; for He wants to forgive gratis, and for Christ's sake He wants to give us the things we need.

This no monk believes. Yet they cover their wickedness with a false lid by saying that the church has given orders to shout in the churches in this manner and that by authority of the pope they are exempted from praying and are merely obligated to read psalms. Thus in the decrees there is the very widely known statement that attention to the words is the only thing required.[44]

Who would not detest those who pray or petition in this manner? Therefore their churches are truly schools of the devil and should be stripped tenfold of their prebends: first, because they do not pray, for they are without faith and do not understand what they are praying; secondly, they make prayer a work of the tongue and worship of God a threshing of words, while in reality they blaspheme Christ in all their prayers. But sins of commission — for we may call them

[43] St. Ulrich, Bishop of Augsburg, who died in 973.

[44] The principle is quoted as *Nullam attentionem esse necessariam nisi verborum*.

such for the purpose of teaching [45] — are far more horrible than sins of omission.

Therefore since the monks and the canons rate their prayers so highly that they even sell them, nothing can be mentioned that is more wicked than they are. But those who, like Abraham, have the Word are true men of prayer and have no doubt that they are children of grace, because they have been called, have been taught by the Holy Spirit through the Gospel, and are filled with the knowledge of Christ, through whom they have been made heirs of God. This glory, which comes from heaven, not from us, must be there when we want to pray. For unless we believe that we please God, how can we think of a prayer that it is pleasing to God? But he who has doubts about this matter — as all papists must have doubts about it — will pray in vain.

On the other hand, those who believe that they are in the state of grace because of the Son of God pray without ceasing even when they are doing something else. For there is in them the unutterable groaning (Rom. 8:26), which neither keeps quiet nor rests but day and night fills the entire world, yes, even heaven itself with its cries. Of this groaning the papists are not aware. Therefore they accuse us publicly of not praying at all; but they boast that they pray day and night, although they do not know what true prayer is, much less what true prayer achieves and how effective it is. Yet they prate much about the merit of prayer.

So far as the words are concerned, they pray the Lord's Prayer with us; but they neither realize nor understand what they are praying. They do not know what the name of God is; they do not know how it is hallowed; they do not know what the kingdom of God is. And how could they really pray for the hallowing of His name and for the coming of His kingdom when they blaspheme the name of God, that is, blaspheme sound doctrine and persecute the church?

But we who hold fast to the Word are cognizant of the perils Satan devises for the church, and we are aware of the power of the kingdom he has in this world. Therefore we cry with genuine fervor: "Hallowed be Thy name," that is: "Give us saintly and godly teachers in the church to make known Thy name to the world that Thou art compassionate and that Thou dost pardon sins because of Thy Son, who was crucified for us, and that Thou dost want to bestow eternal

---

[45] The Latin term for "sins of commission" is *peccata affirmativa*.

life, in order that all men may put their trust in Thy compassion, call upon Thee, praise Thee, and give thanks to Thee." For this is hallowing God's name. "Thy kingdom come," that is: "Give Thy Holy Spirit to rule and preserve us, lest we fall back into the kingdom of Satan, who tries to do away with the Word, faith, and all worship of God."

When we pray in this manner, we ourselves, too, are prophets or sons and pupils of the prophets. Nor is it necessary that future events be revealed to us. For the office of a prophet it is enough that we understand Scripture and are able to teach others and also to help one another with prayers. For he who is not a prophet is unable to teach, pray, and do any good work.

Therefore the name "prophet" belongs equally to all Christians, and he who denies this also denies that he has been baptized and has been instructed through the Word. There is at least this difference, that some have the Spirit of God more abundantly, others less abundantly. Even though He is not in me in such abundance as He was in Elijah, nevertheless, according to His measure, He is in me also. Therefore I both teach the Word and pray for the church. Though Abraham had a greater measure of the Spirit, he did not have a different Spirit. Nor did he have a different Lord and God.

Therefore the papists defend their greed and rapine in vain by citing this example of Abraham. For them good works consist in reciting psalms in the temple without feeling and understanding, wearing a hair shirt, and abstaining from meat but not from fish and wine. In their estimation these works deserve such great wealth and such rich prebends.

But the Holy Spirit and Scripture preach otherwise about good works, namely, that for a good work it is necessary to believe that one is in favor with God because of Christ. If this foundation stands, then everything is holy, whether you teach the Word or comfort the afflicted, whether you bear either your own weaknesses or the wrongs of others. For this reason Christ says (John 14:12): "Truly, truly, I say to you, he who believes in Me will do the works that I do; and greater works than these will he do."

But what kind of works did Christ do? Surely works that pleased His heavenly Father. He denounced the Pharisees, and He comforted the humble. These works were pleasing to God. But even when He slept in the ship, even when He made a journey, ate and drank, He pleased God. "The same thing" He says, "happens to those who believe in Me." "But," say the papists, "those are works of laymen and citizens. One should frown, shun association with people, and do nothing that resembles the actions of others." Thus, of course, they clearly prove that they know nothing about good works, about which they are nevertheless constantly screaming; and they make accusations against us, as though we did nothing that is good. Meanwhile they enjoy the riches of the world, by which they are dunged and fattened. But their destruction will come suddenly. Naturally, we are praying for them, but if they obstruct our prayers by their impenitence and it is necessary for this Sodom to go to ruin and perish, still our prayer for poor Lot and his household will produce results.

Index

By WALTER A. HANSEN

Aaron 5, 231
  sons of 284, 300
Abarim 287
Abbots 153
Abel 106, 250
Abimelech 115, 322, 323, 327, 330, 331, 332, 335, 336, 337, 338, 339, 340, 341, 344, 347, 349, 356, 357, 358, 359, 360
Abiram 15, 17, 280
Abraham ix, x, 5, 9-22, 24, 26, 28-30, 32-36, 38, 41, 43-49, 53-55, 57-66, 71, 74-79, 81 to 88, 90-105, 107, 109-116, 118, 119, 121, 123-129, 131 to 133, 135, 141-145, 147-150, 152-158, 161-168, 172, 174, 176-179, 181, 192 to 196, 198, 199, 201, 203, 205-207, 209, 210, 212, 216-222, 224-226, 228, 230, 231, 233, 236, 238, 239, 244-248, 260, 261, 266, 267, 277, 282, 284, 294, 295, 302-305, 311-333, 336-338, 341, 344 to 346, 348-356, 359, 361, 363, 364
  common father of Gentiles and Jews 106
  example for preachers 357
  friend of God 31
  gentle, kind, and generous toward exiles 180
  has a fervent faith 335
  ministry of 324
  not an ungenerous or niggardly host 197
  obedience of 169, 170, 171, 173, 175
  praised by God as a very great teacher 339
  prayer(s) of 232, 234, 235, 335, 360
  truly remarkable man in his faith 120
  victory of 3, 4, 6, 7
Abram 3, 10, 12, 38, 42, 45, 46, 61, 74, 88, 112
Absolution 272, 275, 350
Achaeans 332
Acts 84, 90, 130, 359
Adam 16, 17, 40, 42, 47, 56, 97, 103, 133, 138, 139, 141, 171, 173, 175, 179, 184, 206, 270, 272, 274
  old 5
Adolescence 279
Adoration 118
Adulterer(s) 46, 222, 223, 224, 254, 279, 324, 328
Adultery 5, 227, 233, 254, 258, 259, 296, 324, 331, 350
Adults 103, 110, 112, 171, 233
Aeneas 359

Aeneid, by Vergil 369 fn.
Aeschylus 49 fn.
Affliction(s) 9, 18, 22, 32, 35, 36, 38, 63, 64, 68, 69, 70, 71, 73, 101, 249, 264, 317, 320, 343, 344, 345, 346
Africa 63
Agatha, St. 125 fn.
Agnes, St. 125 fn.
Agricola, Johann 243 fn.
Ahaz 30, 216
Ai 164, 180
ἀκρισία 263
Alexandria 217
Allegory 28, 55, 72, 141, 192, 237 fn., 293
Alms 168, 215
Altar(s) 32, 143, 280, 281
Amalekites 172, 283
Amazons 189 fn.
Ambition 5, 6, 13, 15, 65
Ambrose 165, 194, 298, 329
Ammonites 228
Amorites 40
Amos 10, 274
Amram 34
Amyris 281
Anabaptists 5, 13, 15, 191, 301
  hold that Baptism must be repeated 103
Analogia 11 fn.
Anarchy 130
Andria, by Terence 47 fn.
Angel(s) 18, 29, 58, 61,

64, 66, 69, 71, 74, 75, 80, 99, 108, 164, 165, 167, 178, 181, 187, 188, 194, 199, 200, 207, 208, 212, 215, 218, 219, 220, 228, 232, 243, 244, 246, 247, 248, 249, 252, 258, 263, 264, 266, 267, 268, 269, 270, 271, 272, 273, 274, 277, 280, 284, 285, 286, 295, 296, 298, 300, 305, 320, 322, 323, 340, 341, 360
  ministry of 60, 62
  of Satan 5
  worship of 275
Anger 58, 59, 239, 309, 320, 331, 337, 354
Animal(s) 32, 66, 293
  clean 250
  poisonous 347
  unclean 250
Antichrist 121, 122, 123, 221, 349
Antinomian(s) 223, 239, 240, 243, 269, 314, 336
  assert that threats of Law have no place in the church 281
Antiochus 121
Antony, St. 131, 196, 216, 217, 275 fn., 328, 329, 355
Anxiety 42, 234, 237, 282, 286
ἀορασία 263 fn.
ἀορισία 263
ἀοριστία 263 fn.
Aphrodite 201 fn.
Apostate 275
Apostle(s) 5, 6, 16, 56, 63, 77, 84, 114, 125, 147, 152, 164, 185, 203, 258, 355
Apparition(s) 10, 166, 168
Apples 149
April 123
Arabia

Deserta 162
Felix 162
Petraea 162
Arabs 66
Arianism 301 fn.
Aristocrats 253
Aristotle 50, 85, 122 fn., 226 fn., 303 fn., 306
Arithmetic 130
Arius 301
Ark 13, 19
Arphaxad 233
Arrogance 5, 14, 131
Ars amandi, by Ovid 47 fn., 248 fn.
Ars poetica, by Horace 68 fn.
Asmodeus 58
Asphalt 222
Ass(es) 86, 149, 312, 337
  wild 66
Assyrians 270
ἄστοργοι 305 fn.
Astronomers 289
Astronomy 358
Athenaeus 281 fn.
Athens 51 fn.
Augustine, St. 10, 11, 81 fn., 107, 130, 159, 160, 165, 187, 191 fn., 192, 194, 199, 257, 258, 260, 288, 298, 325, 326, 348
Atlases 305
Augsburg 362 fn.
Austria 77
Authority 13, 69, 81, 118, 255, 257, 259, 298, 322, 329
  divine 272, 273, 321
  of Christ 114
  of church 213
  of Moses 93
  of parents 240
  of pope(s) 326, 362
  of Scripture 27, 57, 297
  of St. Gregory 350
  threefold 279
Autodidact 5 fn.
Avarice 233
Averroes 306
Axiom(s) 213, 214

Baal 144
  prophets of 320
Babel 170, 230
Babylon 60, 274, 280, 285
  king of 10
Babylonians 278
Baker 197
Balaam 280
Banquet(s) 195, 197, 198, 251, 253
Baptism 29, 37, 82, 90, 92, 95, 101, 103, 104, 106, 107, 108, 109, 110, 111, 124, 146, 147, 155, 165, 167, 168, 220, 272, 273, 274, 275, 288;
  see also Sacrament(s) of Christ 87, 193
Barnabas 320, 355
Bashan 197
Bathsheba 45
Battering-ram(s) 9, 213, 341
Beastliness 256
Beersheba 180
Bees 183
Beggar(s) 183, 188, 209, 315, 361
Believer(s) 29, 52, 87, 90, 131, 152, 153, 185, 188, 198, 269, 294, 321, 328, 335, 346, 347, 361
Bellum Catilinarium, by Sallust 284 fn.
Belly 14, 149, 200
  brutes of 197
Ben-ammi 314
Benedict, St. 165, 200 fn.
Benjamites 279
Bernard 165, 225, 291
Bethel 164, 180, 316
Bethlehem 216 fn.
Bible 37, 207 fn., 275; *see also* Holy Scripture(s), Holy Writ, Sacred Scripture, Scripture(s), Word of God
  German translation of 66

INDEX

Birds 32, 33, 34, 179, 347
Bis dat qui cito dat 284 fn.
Bishop(s) 5, 98, 153, 179, 222, 240, 242, 245, 280, 314, 326, 328, 338, 340, 344, 346
  of Augsburg 362 fn.
Bitumen 243
Blamelessness 78
Blasphemy 162, 173, 240, 278, 319
Blessing(s) 9, 13, 14, 15, 25, 45, 48, 54, 56, 57, 64, 65, 68, 73, 74, 99, 104, 107, 111, 120, 134, 135, 143, 145, 146, 147, 148, 149, 150, 152, 154, 157, 158, 162, 163, 208, 212, 220, 221, 274, 313, 323, 334, 338, 342
  physical 12, 28
  sea of 343
Blindness 23, 97, 102, 133, 264, 265, 266
  miraculous 263
  natural 263
Bloodshed 13
Boils 270
Book(s) 37, 38, 69, 305, 306
  of heathen 245
  of Moses 237
  sacred 299
Book of Acts 359
Book of Deuteronomy 361 fn.
Book of Genesis 210, 227
Book of Jeremiah 269, 348
Book(s) of Kings 284, 345, 360
Book of Wisdom 8
Brandenburg 66 fn.
Bread 50, 51, 59, 149, 159, 160, 181, 184, 185, 186, 190, 198, 220, 225, 243, 244, 246, 267, 290, 298, 355
  baked in ashes 197
  unleavened 250, 251
Breast(s) 83
Breitenbach, Georg 66
Bride 8, 277, 283, 330
Bridegroom 8, 330
Briefe, by Luther 306 fn.
Brigands 113, 150, 234
Brimstone 190, 224, 295, 307
Bulls 347
Burgensis 358
Burghers 182, 227, 249, 345
Burgomaster 49
Butter 198, 211

Cadaver 150
Cain 13, 16, 56, 96, 106, 111, 250, 272
Cakes 196, 197, 198
  unleavened 250
Caleb 323
Calf 196, 197, 198, 280
Calling 30, 62 fn., 65, 118, 128, 130, 131, 172, 204, 209, 267, 274, 290, 299, 301, 321, 322, 325, 329
Camel 321
Canaan 9, 10, 27, 28, 31, 32, 33, 34, 36, 38, 39, 41, 52, 66, 83, 100, 112, 113, 114, 116, 119, 120, 149, 151, 156, 180, 188, 190, 209, 222, 251, 317, 353
Canaanites 40
Candles 273
Canons 121, 197, 242, 254, 322, 326, 363
Capito, Wolfgang 206 fn.
Captatio benevolentiae 288 fn.
Captivity 37, 150, 226
  Babylonian 36
Cardinals 153, 240, 242, 254, 268, 294
Cares 3, 159
Carousing 182

Carrensis, Hugo 26
Carthage 329 fn.
Carthusians 325
Catachresis 192 fn.
Catechism, by Luther 306 fn.
Cathedrals 245 fn.
Cato 11, 67
Catonis disticha 11 fn.
Celibacy 44, 47, 97, 182, 202, 204, 210, 211, 351
Celibates 44, 208
Censorinus 213
Ceremony 29, 91, 101, 144, 250, 281
Chaff 150
Chaldea 181
Charity 189, 339 fn.
Chastisement(s) 60, 70
Chastity 208, 211, 216, 224, 254, 331, 358
Cheese 211
Childbirth 134, 136, 323, 360
Children 9, 12, 15, 34, 43, 45, 46, 47, 48, 59, 68, 93, 94, 96, 97, 100, 102, 104, 112, 122, 133, 134, 138, 144, 145, 149, 159, 162, 171, 177, 179, 181, 201, 203, 204, 205, 214, 222, 225, 231, 232, 238, 239, 240, 253, 257, 261, 264, 266, 269, 279, 283, 295, 302, 304, 315, 342, 360
  of flesh 19
  of grace 363
  of promise 19
  of spirit 19
  of wrath 136
Christ; *see also* Mediator, Messiah, Redeemer, Savior, Son of God
  day of 219
  divinity of 298
  has rendered satisfaction for your sins 214
  Head of church 213

humanity of 219
et passim
Christian(s) 38, 51, 59 fn., 78, 92, 110, 132, 133, 155, 160, 165, 168, 180, 189, 223, 240, 265, 299, 328, 329, 344, 364
Christus enim est fac totum 90 fn.
Chrysostom 298
Church(es) 3, 8, 14, 16, 17, 19, 20, 27, 31, 48, 50, 54, 58, 61, 66, 70, 72, 77, 81, 98, 101, 107, 109, 111, 112, 113, 114, 120, 122, 123, 124, 125, 127, 134, 135, 136, 140, 143, 145, 147, 151, 152, 155, 158, 160, 161, 164, 168, 170, 174, 179, 180, 181, 182, 187, 188, 189, 190, 191, 192, 196, 197, 202, 204, 213, 217, 218, 223, 224, 225, 227, 233, 234, 238, 242, 243, 249, 250, 260, 263, 269, 274, 278, 279, 281, 285, 287, 291, 305, 314, 316, 319, 321, 324, 325, 326, 329, 335, 336, 338, 339, 341, 342, 344, 345, 346, 348, 356, 359, 360, 362, 363, 364
  always has a common treasury 178
  catholic 106
  early 84
  enemies of 295
  false 55, 56
  fathers ix
  government of 53, 55
  Latin 26
  monastic 245 fn.
  never without a trial 301
  of Gentiles 37, 153
  of Isaac 162

of saints 222
pope's 280, 286, 294
Roman 294
true 13, 15, 35, 38, 56, 227, 228
Cicero 67, 262 fn.
Circumcision 22, 76, 77, 79, 80, 81, 82, 83, 84, 85, 86, 87, 88, 89, 90, 91, 92, 93, 94, 96, 97, 98, 99, 101, 103, 104, 105, 106, 108, 109, 110, 111, 112, 113, 115, 116, 120, 123, 124, 125, 127, 128, 129, 131, 132, 133, 134, 135, 136, 137, 140, 142, 143, 144, 145, 151, 162, 170, 171, 174, 175, 176, 208, 250, 338
  limited and confined within definite bounds 126
  not instituted as something permanent 100
  of no avail for righteousness 78
  spiritual, true, and perfect 141
City of God, by Saint Augustine 81 fn.
Classics ix
Claudian 331 fn.
Clement VII, pope 144
Clergy x, 357
Cleric 128
Cloisters 284
Clothing 50, 52, 315
Clouds 139
Cochlaeus, Johannes 193 fn.
Cohabitation 310, 313
Coition 308
Comfort(s) 3, 10, 33, 38, 52, 58, 62, 63, 65, 73, 124, 135, 184, 241, 243, 271, 291, 305, 314, 320, 331, 337, 345, 346, 347, 355
  hidden 15

Comfortat pauperes ecclesiae, et damnat rebelles 242 fn.
Comforter 205
Commentariorum in Epistolam ad Ephesios libri tres, by Jerome 83 fn.
Communion 155, 281; see also Eucharist, Holy Supper, Last Supper, Lord's Supper, Sacrament(s)
Compassion 71, 134, 189, 240, 249, 285, 286, 305, 310, 331, 360, 364
Compostela 109
Conceit 186
Conception 206
Confession 57, 118, 182, 183, 187, 189, 199, 241, 273, 321, 340, 347
Confessions, by St. Augustine 160 fn.
Confitemini 155
Conscience(s) 25, 125, 214, 222, 223, 224, 326, 351
  frightened 349
  good 128, 332
  heavy burden of 342
  peace of 349
  terrors of 8 fn.
  unquestioning 196
Consolation 54
Constantine 328
Continence 208, 210
Contradiction in terms 119
Contrition 242
Convents 275
Corinthians 283
Cornelius 81, 355, 359
Council 213 fn., 335
Counselors 253
Courtesy 186, 252
Covenant(s) 41, 83, 85, 90, 91, 92, 99, 102, 104, 111, 115, 116, 123, 126, 127, 128, 138, 161, 184

of circumcision 76, 78,
  81, 86, 103, 105,
  162, 163
 of Isaac 163
Cowl(s) 51, 118, 316,
  322
Cows 177, 321, 347
Creed 109, 333
Criminals 113, 250
Crocodiles 347
Cruelty 34, 178, 181,
  182, 235, 252
Curiosity 11, 139, 200,
  201
Curse(s) 29, 99, 146,
  313, 338
Cyprian 191, 329
Cyril 194
Cyrus 81, 89

Damascus 12, 16 fn.,
  181, 348
Damnation 70, 173, 326,
  327
Danger(s) 3, 5, 6, 30,
  31, 46, 53, 63, 76,
  78, 108, 117, 120,
  137, 138, 140, 173,
  214, 256, 259, 260,
  261, 264, 267, 284,
  285, 288, 289, 292,
  298, 302, 305, 306,
  307, 320, 323, 325,
  328, 329, 336, 355,
  360, 361
 of vainglory 4
Daniel 90, 121, 274, 360
Darius 89
Dathan 15, 17, 280
David 4, 5, 13, 27, 30,
  31 fn., 36, 37, 44,
  45, 79, 117 fn., 141,
  145, 152, 165, 235,
  248, 260, 283, 290,
  296, 313, 327, 328,
  332, 339, 348, 350
Day of Judgment 40;
  see also Day of the
  Lord, Last Day
Day of the Lord 35;
  see also Day of
  Judgment, Last Day

De catechizandis rudibus,
  by St. Augustine
  107 fn.
De consideratione, by
  Bernard of Clairvaux
  225 fn.
De correptione et gratia,
  by St. Augustine
  348 fn.
De divinis nominibus, by
  Pseudo-Dionysius
  274 fn.
De doctrina Christiana,
  by St. Augustine
  192 fn.
De officiis, by Cicero
  262 fn.
*De situ et nominibus lo-
  corum Hebraicorum,*
  by Jerome 199 fn.
De Trinitate
  by Hilary 61 fn.,
  297 fn.
  by St. Augustine
  191 fn., 192 fn.,
  298 fn.
Dead Sea 298
Death 4, 8, 11, 28, 33,
  38, 40, 62, 63, 79,
  105, 119, 120, 125,
  134, 136, 138, 140,
  173, 175, 207, 211,
  215, 216, 223, 258,
  264, 277, 305, 323,
  335, 338, 340
 Christ's 141, 214
 civil 143
 eternal 21, 39, 225,
  342, 343
 everlasting 357
 of Son of God 124
 spiritual 143
 victory over 160
Debauchery 258, 259
Decalog 121, 217, 338
Decius 125 fn.
Decretals 155
Despair 4, 63, 72, 276,
  294, 310
Devil 8, 25, 77, 180, 229,
  252, 264, 265, 279,
  326, 329; *see also*
  Satan

delusions of 275
 kingdom of 49
 monstrous fictions of
  344
 schools of 362
Dialectic(s) 9, 84, 191,
  194, 341
Dialectician(s) 101, 119,
  195, 213, 308
Dialogorum libri quatuor,
  by Gregory 168 fn.
Diet of Augsburg 340,
  341
Dietrich, Veit ix
Diocletian 125 fn.
Dionysius 166, 274
Disciples 61, 92, 104,
  172
Discipline 48, 59, 98,
  203, 229, 231, 245,
  252, 253, 254, 256,
  279
Disease(s) 6, 48, 65,
  139, 202, 248, 271,
  323, 342 fn.
Disobedience 47, 48, 62,
  135, 172, 175, 284,
  285, 286, 298, 300,
  305
Dispensation 126, 144
Divine Majesty 21, 109,
  138, 148, 166, 171,
  230, 270, 272, 279
Divorce 258
 Jewish 259
Doctors 29, 153
Doctrine 22, 23, 77, 91,
  94, 95, 110, 117,
  138, 161, 183, 185,
  186, 193, 200, 221,
  222, 224, 226, 243,
  286, 300, 301, 339,
  343
 Christian 325
 of antinomians 223
 of creation 288 fn.
 of Gospel 342
 of justification 107
 of Law 132, 133
 of papists 172
 of pope 124
 of resurrection of the
  dead 10

of Trinity 192, 219, 245
of wrath 242
Pharaonic and pharisaical 227
profitable 15, 143, 252
scholastic 25
sound 14, 25, 241, 299, 363
true 57, 265, 338, 341
Dogs 78, 309, 349
Domina mea 146
Dominic, St. 196
Dove 193, 194, 330
Dragon(s) 37, 271, 347
Dream(s) 10, 11, 12, 18, 113, 167, 177, 275, 308, 330, 337, 340, 344, 348, 360
Drones 183
Drunkenness 9, 233, 248, 309
Duke
of Brandenburg 66 fn.
of Saxony 66 fn.
Dung 277
Dupin, Louis E. 276 fn.

Eagle 323
Ears 136, 155, 190, 255, 294, 346
of grain 177 fn.
Earth 39, 40, 63, 80, 89, 124, 139, 150, 168, 188, 196, 205, 206, 220, 229, 235, 243, 244, 271, 292, 293, 298, 307, 310, 316, 322, 338
seven ages of 141 fn.
Earthquakes x, 221, 295
Eber 233
Eclogues, by Vergil 308 fn.
Edomites 152
Effeminacy 254
Egypt 31, 34, 35, 61, 74, 81, 88, 96, 113, 154, 180, 181, 188, 235, 261, 318, 326, 334, 352
four-hundred-year affliction in 32

Egyptian(s) 32, 49, 81, 89, 259
εἰκαῖα 213 fn.
Elbe 282
Election 169
Eliezer 12, 16, 54, 55
Elijah 269, 271, 320, 345, 354, 355, 364
Elisha 89, 263, 269
Elizabeth 29, 134
Eloquence 67, 154, 186, 319, 335
Embryos 206
Emperor Charles 340
English 296 fn.
Enoch 39, 79
Epicureans 118, 242, 268
Epicurus 243
ἐπιείκεια 262 fn.
Epiphanies 168
Epistle to the Hebrews 35, 79
Epistles, by Horace 128 fn., 332 fn.
Epistolae
by Pseudo-Dionysius 166 fn.
by Seneca 254 fn.
Epistulae ex Ponto, by Ovid 308 fn.
Erasmus 67, 319 fn.
Erfurt 49, 50 fn.
Erlangen edition 215 fn., 227 fn., 240 fn., 305 fn., 353 fn.
Error(s) 38, 97, 108, 117, 145, 146, 160, 168, 195, 217, 237, 240, 273, 275, 280, 295, 350
Turkish and Jewish 25
Es war mit jnen auff die neige kommen 207 fn.
Esau 13, 16, 56, 96, 103, 145, 148, 152
Eternity 39, 149
Etymology 100
Eucharist 37, 109, 110, 111, 122, 124, 146, 213, 375; *see also* Communion, Holy Supper, Last Sup-

per, Lord's Supper, Sacrament(s)
Eunuch 81
Evangelicals 227
Evangelist(s) 205, 300
Eve 56, 97, 133, 134, 139, 184, 206, 270, 282, 287
Evildoers 40, 235, 331
Evodius 11 fn.
Excommunication 57, 242
Exegesis
Christian 299 fn.
Jewish 299 fn.
Exodus 35
Externalist 276
Externals 272, 273, 275, 276
Eyes 130, 136, 150, 173, 185, 186, 193, 194, 196, 215, 226, 263, 278, 294, 302, 303, 341, 346, 358, 359
carnal 304
pigs' 210
Ezekiel 223, 247, 248, 280, 292

Fabian, St. 125
Factions 16
Faith 21, 22, 23, 24, 25, 29, 30, 31, 33, 36, 37, 44, 45, 67, 70, 72, 75, 78, 79, 80, 83, 85, 87, 89, 94, 95, 96, 102, 103, 104, 105, 107, 110, 111, 112, 113, 114, 118, 120, 124, 128, 133, 135, 137, 140, 141, 143, 146, 147, 148, 149, 151, 152, 153, 154, 156, 162, 163, 166, 170, 171, 174, 175, 176, 185, 186, 188, 190, 191, 192, 194, 195, 199, 200, 204, 206, 208, 210, 211, 212, 215, 216, 217, 218, 224, 230, 231, 235, 260, 264, 265, 270, 271,

INDEX

289, 291, 295, 297, 300, 301, 302, 312, 315, 316, 318, 320, 321, 322, 325, 326, 328, 329, 330, 332, 333, 334, 336, 338, 344, 346, 351, 357, 362, 364
  Abraham's 3, 20, 28, 106, 125, 173, 196, 198, 327, 335, 355
  alone justifies 19, 26
  analogy of 168
  inactive 169
  righteousness of 177
  unity of 108
Faithfulness 4
Fanatics 110, 211
Fasts 168, 316
Fatness 197
Fear(s) 7, 8, 10, 13, 14, 21, 25, 216, 242, 264, 307, 314, 320, 324, 328, 330, 336, 351, 352
  of God 48, 128, 218, 221, 222, 224, 225, 227, 230, 233, 237, 241, 248, 252, 255, 303, 321, 327, 331, 340, 345
Female(s) 48, 111, 129, 132, 202, 215, 255, 270, 272, 274
Fetus 64, 205, 206, 360
Fides [charitate] formata 21 fn.
Fire 190, 221, 222, 223, 225, 229, 243, 264, 270, 271, 273, 274, 278, 285, 293, 295, 300, 302, 304, 306, 307, 309, 315, 341, 348, 354
  eternal 268
First Commandment 80, 116, 237
First Table 4, 5, 6, 98, 101, 159, 240, 296
Fish 347, 364
Flattery 230
Flax 223, 224
Flesh 6, 8, 9, 13, 15, 32,
34, 48, 51, 64, 77, 82, 88, 93, 94, 95, 96, 97, 101, 102, 105, 107, 112, 124, 132, 135, 136, 137, 141, 142, 152, 155, 158, 177, 178, 192, 199, 202, 205, 211, 225, 230, 252, 253, 261, 265, 268, 272, 276, 279, 327, 329, 332, 333, 334, 335, 336, 343, 355
children of 19
filthy deeds of 42
imprudent and complacent 40
lusts of 22
mortification of 174
pride of 63
Flippancy 179
Flood(s) x, 19, 140, 229, 233, 234, 236, 239, 241, 268, 293, 295, 319
Food(s) 48, 50, 52, 146, 181, 200, 217, 222, 228, 247, 248, 274, 298, 316, 318
Fool 67, 229
Foot washing 189
Foreskin 79, 82, 88, 102, 132, 135, 137
  of the heart 141
Forgiveness of sins 7, 12, 39, 109, 158, 214, 224, 228, 265, 333, 338; *see also* Remission of sins
Fornication 47, 254, 259
Fortune 52, 226, 229, 248
France 41 fn.
Francis, St. 109, 196
Frankfurt x, 303
Frau 146
Frederick the Wise 356 fn.
Freedom 32
Frogs 349

Gabriel 80, 232
Gadding 201
Galatians 23, 29, 35, 84, 187, 301
Gallows 50, 123
Gambling 182
Garrulousness 201
Gellius 213, 214 fn.
Genealogy 42
Genesis 233, 316 fn.
Genitals 360
γενόμενος ἐν ἑαυτῷ 18
Gentiles 28, 89, 90, 91, 92, 93, 94, 95, 96, 97, 98, 99, 104, 105, 106, 107, 110, 111, 112, 113, 114, 115, 116, 118, 121, 127, 128, 129, 131, 132, 142, 143, 144, 145, 147, 151, 152, 162, 177, 189, 209, 261 fn., 319, 338, 339, 348
  church of 37, 153
Gerar 303, 316, 321, 326, 330, 338, 344, 346, 352, 354, 356, 357, 360
German 206, 248 fn.
Germans 147, 248, 251, 283
Germany 60, 153, 249, 252, 254, 278, 319, 324
Gerson, John 276, 277
Gideon 30
Girl(s) 103, 147, 160, 183 fn., 257, 266, 278, 307, 310
Gloria in Excelsis 155
Gluttony 248, 323, 324
Gnat 321
God
  Deliverer and Liberator from death 33
  faces of 166, 167
  fear of 48, 128, 218, 221, 222, 224, 225, 227, 230, 233, 237, 241, 248, 252, 255, 303, 321, 327, 331, 340, 345
  goodness of 4, 241

in His essence is incomprehensible 138
is by nature merciful 103
is long-suffering and patient 40
is immortal and eternal 110
is no respecter of persons 64
is provoked to wrath if we neglect prayer 292
is *sui generis* 118 fn.
kindness of 12
kingdom of 49, 95, 104, 105, 130, 153, 170, 184, 224, 254, 299, 317, 363, 364
knowledge of 48, 51, 72, 75, 81, 95, 107, 114, 117, 125, 153, 162, 233, 269, 289, 319, 335, 337, 338, 340, 344
patience of 40, 156
reconciliation with 12
sees innermost thoughts of heart 161
shows no partiality 129
uncovered 276
will of 14
wrath of 8, 44, 60, 72, 134, 214, 224, 233, 234, 236, 237, 238, 239, 241, 242, 243, 264, 269, 278, 281, 292, 294, 295, 302, 304, 308, 310, 313, 348, 351
et passim
Goddess 83
Godhead 276, 296, 297, 359
Godlessness 82
Godliness 98, 117, 128, 170, 182, 203, 258, 261, 269, 323, 357
chief points of 118
Godly 8, 11, 36, 40, 63, 71, 77, 118, 129, 135, 140, 159, 179, 185, 189, 197, 221, 228, 236, 241, 244, 245, 250, 269, 270, 271, 292, 294, 307, 320, 341, 345, 347
sometimes suppose that God is sleeping 229, 230
Gog 64
Gold 186, 190, 199, 211
Gomorrah x, 131
Gospel 9, 66, 76, 77, 85, 95, 97, 121, 124, 125, 129, 131, 133, 167, 168, 189, 221, 223, 224, 232, 237, 263, 265, 272, 273, 275, 281, 290, 294, 296, 297, 299, 340, 341, 346, 348, 363
doctrine of 342
of John 300 fn.
Gossip 209
Government 36, 113, 122, 130, 131, 143, 150, 226, 227, 233, 255, 256, 259, 271, 279, 280, 313, 325, 328
of church 53, 55
Grace 21, 22, 44, 68, 69, 77, 90, 95, 96, 97, 99, 102, 104, 107, 111, 112, 124, 125, 130, 131, 133, 134, 136, 142, 143, 146, 155, 156, 161, 165, 167, 169, 182, 206 fn., 222, 228, 237, 265, 296, 336, 337, 339, 340, 344, 363
is truly immovable and unchangeable 8
suspension of 7
Grain 150, 319
ears of 177 fn.
Grammar 70, 72, 73, 87, 357, 358
Grammarian 262
Gratitude 49, 51, 73, 157, 227
Greece 63
Greed 6, 182, 223, 231, 364
Greek Anthology 48 fn.
Greeks 48, 281, 324
Gregory 114, 168, 299, 349, 350
I 188 fn.
VII 188 fn.
Grief 12, 14, 68, 134, 228, 242, 252, 302, 304, 312, 314, 329, 330, 346, 356
Grikel 243 fn.
Gut macht Mut 248 fn.

Hagar 42, 44, 45, 46, 52, 53, 54, 55, 56, 57, 58, 59, 60, 61, 62, 63, 64, 65, 68, 69, 70, 71, 72, 73, 74, 75, 76, 99, 145, 192, 208
Ham 56, 97
Hamites 97
Hannah 134
Haran 352
Harlot 108
Hatred 6, 50, 57, 115, 129, 152, 158, 179, 189, 203, 281, 309, 319, 328, 359
Hausteufel 58 fn.
Haughtiness 54, 56, 59
of Saracens 65
Health 129, 248
Heathen 32, 33, 35, 41, 43, 60, 64, 76, 82, 83, 84, 85, 88, 89, 96, 100, 110, 113, 116, 123, 128, 135, 145, 160, 175, 201, 203, 221, 245, 259, 283, 293, 316, 321, 322, 332, 344, 346, 355
know that there is a supreme deity 117
Heaven 17, 18, 50, 51, 121, 138, 139, 143, 147, 165, 186, 187, 190, 193, 196, 199, 202, 217, 224, 228,

INDEX

230, 239, 242, 243, 255, 268, 270, 271, 273, 274, 275, 276, 278, 291, 293, 298, 302, 305, 306, 307, 316, 320, 322, 328, 340, 341, 345
  birds of 32, 33
Hebrew 100, 164, 197, 266, 296, 330, 352, 360 fn., 361
Hebron 180, 316, 318, 351
Hell 9, 19, 28, 40, 89, 132, 139, 143, 230, 304, 338
Henning, Dr. 215
Hercules 189
Heresy 56, 97, 271, 280, 301
Heretic(s) 8, 14, 147, 272, 273
Hermit(s) 66, 113, 131, 139, 202, 217, 315, 328, 329
Herod 88, 167
Herodotus 281 fn., 324 fn.
Heroes 39
Hesiod 332
Hezekiah 156, 270, 278
Hie wonet Gott 248 fn.
Hilarion 329, 355
Hilary, St. 61, 191, 194, 296, 297 fn., 298
Hiram 112
History, by Herodotus 281 fn., 324 fn.
Holstein 249 fn.
Holy Land 74
Holy Scripture(s) 6, 8, 11, 12, 18, 25, 27, 29, 35, 37, 51, 68, 84, 87, 141, 164, 194, 297, 304, 307, 309, 317, 321, 322, 326, 347, 353, 358; *see also* Bible, Holy Writ, Sacred Scripture, Scripture(s), Word of God
  is in excellent agreement with itself 247

Holy Spirit 4, 8, 9, 11, 12, 20, 21, 24, 30, 35, 36, 38, 52, 53, 56, 58, 69, 97, 102, 113, 115, 124, 138, 161, 165, 167, 194, 195, 200, 206, 208, 211, 212, 217, 219, 224, 237, 241, 242, 243, 244, 247, 248, 265, 275, 281, 288, 293, 296, 297, 312, 316, 320, 321, 322, 323, 338, 353, 355, 363, 364
  rhetoric of 347
  et passim
Holy Supper 166; *see also* Communion, Eucharist, Last Supper, Lord's Supper, Sacrament(s)
Holy Writ 300; *see also* Bible, Holy Scripture(s), Sacred Scripture, Scripture(s), Word of God
Honey 140, 183
Honorate Deum in vobis invicem 187 fn.
Honorius 331 fn.
Hood 146
Hope 19, 24, 33, 37, 40, 44, 58, 63, 99, 123, 124, 129, 134, 149, 154, 167, 179, 210, 212, 255, 260, 292, 300, 303, 304, 315, 321, 324, 329, 331, 344, 345, 351, 355, 357
  of conceiving and bearing a child 211
  of fruitfulness 211
  of mercy 237
  of offspring 208
Horace 68, 69, 128 fn., 332
Horns 62
Horse(s) 149, 218
Hosea 70, 330
Hospitality 177, 178,

179, 180, 181, 182, 184, 185, 187, 188, 189, 196, 197, 198, 199, 202, 244, 245, 246, 249, 258, 326
  in Luther's home 183 fn.
Hospitals 181
Houses of ill fame 258, 259
Hugo de Sancto Caro, cardinal 26 fn.
Hull 149, 150, 151
Hunger 179, 180, 184, 232
  Saturnine 306 fn.
Husband(s) 42, 44, 46, 47, 49, 53, 54, 55, 56, 57, 58, 133, 134, 201, 203, 204, 205, 207, 208, 209, 210, 211, 212, 216, 217, 288, 298, 300, 330, 354
Hut 184, 199
Hyperbole 259
Hypocrisy 189
Hypocrite(s) 89, 182, 203, 246, 269, 275

Idol(s) 216, 330
Idolater(s) 222, 272, 320
Idolatry 13, 60, 164, 221, 296
Iekel 243 fn.
Immortality 11, 28, 110, 123, 149, 268
Impatience 9, 25, 217, 347
Impenitence 230, 365
Incarnation 136
Incest 254, 310, 311, 312, 313, 314, 324, 346
Indecency 171
Indifference 23
Infant(s) 103, 104, 105, 110, 133, 138, 140, 143, 161, 174, 206, 274, 318,
  soul of 137
Ingratitude 49, 51, 52, 146, 196, 218, 227, 234, 288, 319, 345

Inhospitality 178, 182
Inhumanity 178
Initium Evangelii 6 fn.
Innkeepers 198, 204
Inquisitiveness 201, 282, 299
Insemination 208
Institutio oratoria, by Quintilian 73 fn.
Intercession(s) 239, 351, 359, 361
Intoxication 268
Inundation 295
Irascibility 51
Iron 191
Isaac 16, 17, 34, 63, 65, 74, 80, 92, 94, 95, 96, 112, 118, 147, 148, 152, 154, 156, 161, 176, 177, 192, 205, 206, 324, 327, 338
  church of 162
  covenant of 163
Isaiah 37, 59, 69, 70, 71, 82, 107, 121, 123, 155, 156, 164, 169, 193, 222, 249, 255, 283
Iscah 352
Ishmael 13, 56, 63, 64, 65, 66, 69, 70, 75, 76, 78, 80, 89, 93, 94, 95, 98, 99, 111, 112, 114, 145, 147, 153, 154, 157, 158, 161, 162, 163, 175, 176, 192, 316
  circumcised in his fifteenth year 126
Ishmaelite(s) 69, 161, 163
Israel 28, 32, 36, 82, 89, 133, 146, 292, 320, 332, 334
Italy 63, 252, 254
Iuncta marito 330

Jabesh Gilead 228
Jacob 16, 17, 65, 92, 103, 118, 145, 146, 148, 154, 235

Jacobus de Voragine 325 fn.
James, St. 109, 159, 292, 348
Japheth 97
Jealousy 51
Jeremiah 36, 41, 70, 82, 237, 269, 348
Jerome 66, 83 fn., 199, 216, 257, 355, 358
Jerusalem 77, 84, 89, 91, 94, 164, 169, 233, 234, 345
Jewel 29
Jews 12, 21, 34, 36, 37, 38, 42, 46, 47, 48, 59, 64, 66, 67, 68, 71, 76, 77, 78, 79, 80, 82, 83, 84, 85, 86, 87, 88, 89, 90, 91, 92, 93, 94, 95, 96, 97, 98, 99, 100, 102, 104, 106, 107, 108, 109, 110, 111, 112, 113, 115, 116, 121, 122, 125, 129, 131, 133, 135, 136, 142, 143, 144, 145, 148, 150, 151, 152, 162, 163, 164, 177, 190, 191, 192, 193, 194, 208, 232, 248, 250, 251, 258, 261 fn., 263, 274, 296, 297, 298, 304, 305, 312, 313, 337, 341, 345, 348, 352, 353, 358
  are poor dialecticians 308
  killed Christ out of pure malice 228
  maintain that circumcision is to continue forever 127
  rabid pride of 81
  scoffing of 219
  sexual relations of 210
  were an exceedingly thrifty people 197
Jezebel 320, 355
Job 44, 81, 89, 106, 264, 270, 348

John 96, 107, 127, 129, 134, 159, 229, 297, 299, 333
  Elector of Saxony 340, 341 fn., 356 fn.
  Frederick the Magnanimous 182 fn., 356 fn.
  the Baptist 150, 202, 284
Jonah, 81, 89, 232
Joseph 81, 88, 96, 115, 154, 177, 182, 235, 280, 334
Joshua 280, 289, 323
Judah 74, 145, 251, 318
Judaizers 77
Judas 16, 17, 62
Jude 278, 300
Judea 61, 278
Judgment(s) 15, 25, 30, 42, 57, 62, 107, 114, 213, 220, 224, 225, 229, 230, 240, 260, 261, 263, 268, 275, 292, 294, 307, 310, 326, 342, 345
  of God 138, 139, 140, 173, 233, 236, 237, 241, 243, 269, 276, 299, 302, 349, 350
Julius II, pope 41 fn.
Jurists 42, 260, 262, 326
Just 234, 235
Justice 224, 230, 242, 331
Justification 39, 67, 107, 175
Juvenal 48 fn.

Kadesh 74, 318
καθάρματα 180
Kernel(s) 147, 150, 151
Keturah 112, 162
Kindness(es) 12, 49, 50, 51, 52, 59, 60, 68, 69, 70, 73, 83, 99, 117, 126, 137, 154, 165, 178, 183, 184, 185, 186, 187, 189, 197, 199, 218, 225, 226, 235, 247, 288, 319, 342
King(s) 43, 52, 64, 65,

INDEX

89, 113, 117, 123, 128, 147, 148, 149, 150, 151, 152, 157, 159, 161, 174, 184, 188, 199, 226, 233, 245, 253, 261, 270, 303, 318, 319, 322, 323, 326, 327, 329, 330, 331, 332, 333, 335, 336, 337, 338, 339, 340, 344, 347, 348, 349, 350, 351, 352, 353, 356, 357, 358, 359, 360, 361
of Ammonites 228
of Babylon 10
of Bashan 197
Kingdom(s) 14, 79, 91, 100, 107, 113, 114, 115, 126, 127, 150, 151, 152, 160, 250, 283, 318, 332, 336, 337, 339, 340, 346, 347, 357
Christ's 77, 163, 172, 317
eternal 29
Mosaic 251
of devil 49
of forgiveness of sins and grace 228
of God 49, 95, 104, 105, 130, 153, 170, 184, 224, 254, 299, 317, 363, 364
of God's Son 7
of Satan 364
Turkish 229
Kitchen 204
Knowledge 49, 68, 69, 71, 73, 88, 109, 140, 149, 188, 203, 221, 265, 273, 286, 342, 347, 362, 363
of God 48, 51, 72, 75, 81, 95, 107, 114, 117, 125, 153, 162, 269, 289, 319, 335, 337, 338, 340, 344
of languages 319
of sacred matters 332
of Trinity 195
two kinds of 67

Kohath 34
Korah 15, 17, 280, 313
Koran 63
  Mohammedan monstrosity 77

Laban 235
Laity 213, 322
Lake
  of asphalt 222
  of bitumen 243
Lamb 250, 251, 330
Land of Promise 317
Language, Parisian style of 358
Last Day 38, 159, 178, 182, 187, 190, 196, 296, 299; *see also* Day of Judgment, Day of the Lord
Last Supper 205; *see also* Communion, Eucharist, Holy Supper, Lord's Supper, Sacrament(s)
Latin
  Ciceronian 358 fn.
  of medieval theologians 358 fn.
Latins 48
Lattices 8
Laughter
  Abraham's 154
  Sarah's 212, 216
Law(s) 23, 24, 25, 26, 32, 46, 47, 48, 62, 65, 66, 69, 75, 76, 77, 78, 83, 84, 85, 89, 90, 91, 92, 94, 103, 106, 112, 113, 121, 125, 126, 127, 128, 131, 135, 137, 143, 144, 145, 150, 151, 156, 163, 164, 215, 221, 222, 223, 224, 225, 237, 241, 250, 251, 256, 259, 260, 261, 262, 265, 269, 281, 309, 314, 319, 326, 330, 331, 333, 336, 341, 347, 352
ceremonial 100

doctrine of 132, 133
moral 100
righteousness of 59, 96
seemingly foolish 136
works of 20, 22, 29
Lawrence, St. 125
Layman, 128, 315, 318, 365
Lazarus 16, 65
League of Cambrai 41 fn.
Lectures on Deuteronomy, by Luther 237 fn.
Lectures on Genesis, by Luther 47 fn., 249 fn.
  chronology of ix, 3 fn., 303 fn.
Legalists 262
Legenda aurea, by Jacobus de Voragine 325 fn.
Leipzig 66 fn., 249 fn.
Leo, pope 268
Lepers 50, 183
Letter to the Hebrews 19, 157, 178, 206, 220, 318
Levi 34, 35, 251
Levites 164, 280
Liber regulae pastoralis, by Gregory 349 fn.
Licentiousness 259, 319
Lie(s) 63, 193, 258, 319, 320, 327
  of monks 196
  three kinds of 326
Life 40, 45, 49, 50, 52, 55, 63, 64, 65, 68, 81, 83, 119, 121, 138, 139, 140, 160, 204, 205, 206, 207, 209, 211, 215, 216, 221, 228, 248, 258, 280, 283, 285, 300, 306, 311, 315, 318, 319, 320, 321, 323, 324, 329, 335, 343, 344, 347, 351, 354
active 275
blameless 98, 341
burdensome 218
civil 189, 202

contemplative 275, 276
corrupt 284
domestic 51, 62
earthly 125
eternal 25, 27, 28, 39, 41, 86, 92, 99, 110, 111, 118, 120, 124, 141, 142, 148, 149, 153, 155, 156, 158, 167, 214, 317, 338, 339, 363
everlasting 73, 123
future 141, 168
in the church 217
in the home 217
in the state 217
monkish way of 284
of godliness 128
of inactivity 129
of married people 54, 214
physical 86
sensual 325
troubled and wretched 39
various ranks in 142
various stations in 143
Linguists 81
Lion(s) 30, 37, 271, 284, 300, 354
Locusts 10
Logic 26, 85 fn., 137, 205
Logicians, medieval 118 fn.
λογίζεσθαι 22
Lombard, Peter 133 fn., 137 fn., 139, 193 fn.
Lord's Prayer 121, 288, 363; see also Our Father
Lord's Supper 29, 108, 165, 166, 213, 220, 272, 273; see also Communion, Eucharist, Holy Supper, Last Supper, Sacrament(s)
Lot 52, 61, 131, 179, 188, 226, 230, 232, 234, 236, 240, 241, 242, 243, 244, 245, 246, 247, 249, 252, 253, 254, 263, 265, 271, 272, 277, 280, 282, 283, 284, 285, 287, 291, 292, 295, 309, 314, 324, 341, 344, 352, 356, 365
daughters of 256, 257, 258, 259, 260, 261, 264, 266, 267, 268, 269, 278, 302, 303, 304, 306, 307, 308, 309, 310, 311, 312, 313, 324, 346
prayer of 289, 290, 312
wife of 240, 264, 267, 286, 294, 298, 299, 300, 301, 302, 304, 305, 306, 307, 308, 324
Louis XII of France 41 fn.
Louse 52, 53
Love 23, 24, 25, 31, 52, 58, 71, 94, 99, 170, 184, 185, 200, 231, 233, 235, 240, 277, 308, 309, 330, 339 fn., 355, 356, 357, 359
of God 321
of one's neighbor 84
services of 196
works of 189
Lucifer 139
Luke 18, 212, 270, 327
Lüneberg 249 fn.
Lupus est in fabula 67 fn.
Lust(s) 22, 42, 43, 47, 48, 57, 135, 141, 210, 223, 226, 239, 259, 305, 307, 308, 309, 310, 311, 313, 314, 331, 337, 350
Luther ix, x, 7 fn., 8 fn., 18 fn., 21 fn., 26 fn., 28 fn., 34 fn., 41 fn., 44 fn., 48 fn., 49 fn., 50 fn., 52 fn., 59 fn., 61 fn., 62 fn., 66 fn., 67 fn., 85 fn., 103 fn., 110 fn., 114 fn., 117 fn., 118 fn., 120 fn., 122 fn., 125 fn., 130 fn., 139 fn., 144 fn., 156 fn., 182 fn., 183 fn., 191 fn., 205 fn., 206 fn., 207 fn., 213 fn., 237 fn., 242 fn., 243 fn., 244 fn., 248 fn., 249 fn., 252 fn., 254 fn., 261 fn., 275 fn., 276 fn., 288 fn., 291 fn., 296 fn., 297 fn., 300 fn., 301 fn., 306 fn., 316 fn., 319 fn., 321 fn., 325 fn., 331 fn., 335 fn., 339 fn., 342 fn., 344 fn., 347 fn., 349 fn., 355 fn., 358 fn.
Luther and His Times, by E. G. Schwiebert 183 fn.
Luther the Expositor, by Jaroslav Pelikan 5 fn., 227 fn., 233 fn., 272 fn., 273 fn.
Lutheran(s) 361
quondam 193 fn.
Luther's Works ix, x, 7 fn., 8 fn., 18 fn., 19 fn., 27 fn., 28 fn., 34 fn., 39 fn., 42 fn., 47 fn., 51 fn., 62 fn., 67 fn., 71 fn., 77 fn., 96 fn., 106 fn., 108 fn., 116 fn., 117 fn., 118 fn., 120 fn., 123 fn., 125 fn., 130 fn., 182 fn., 184 fn., 192 fn., 193 fn., 215 fn., 216 fn., 217 fn., 222 fn., 230 fn., 233 fn., 237 fn., 248 fn., 254 fn., 261 fn., 262 fn., 265 fn., 267 fn., 268 fn., 272 fn., 274 fn.,

INDEX

275 fn., 277 fn., 286 fn., 288 fn., 301 fn., 316 fn., 326 fn., 330 fn., 331 fn., 352 fn., 358 fn., 361 fn.
Luxury 238, 324
Lyra ix, 16 fn., 23, 26, 27, 28, 34, 47 fn., 64 fn., 67, 71 fn., 72, 188 fn., 205 fn., 230 fn., 232 fn., 246 fn., 250, 251, 257, 258, 259, 263, 266, 268, 269 fn., 298 fn., 299, 308 fn., 309, 313, 337 fn., 353 fn., 358

Madonna 146
Magdalene 263
Magi 167
Magic 264
Magician 315
Magnificat 155
Magog 64
Male(s) 48, 101, 102, 104, 127, 129, 132, 133, 135, 136, 137, 144, 148, 202, 208, 215, 228, 255, 270, 272, 274
  three separate kinds of 142
  uncircumcised 103
Malice 51, 193, 228, 229, 230, 231, 236, 296, 307, 311
  of Satan 158
Mammon 100
Mamre 184, 234, 244, 316
Manhood 6
Manichaeans 160
Manna 274
Mark 124
Marriage(s) 12, 14, 16, 42, 43, 45, 47, 48, 53, 58, 202, 204, 214, 256, 259, 269, 277, 329, 331, 354; *see also* Matrimony
  of patriarchs 211

perils of 55
was divinely instituted 210
Martial 312
Martyr(s) 125 fn., 264
Mary 109, 115, 241, 276; *see also* Virgin Mary
Mass(es) 128, 168, 215, 217, 267
Master of the Sentences 133, 135, 137, 140, 193
Maternity 44
μαθήματα 324 fn.
Matrimony 43, 45, 121, 210; *see also* Marriage(s)
Matron(s) 201, 211
Maximilian I 41 fn.
Meat 202, 325, 364
Mediator 26, 332; *see also* Christ, Messiah, Redeemer, Savior, Son of God
Medicine 216, 223, 224, 232, 271, 358
Meinhold, Peter x
Melanchthon, Philip x, 19 fn., 103 fn., 262 fn., 263 fn., 303 fn.
Melchizedek 35, 234, 267
Menses 208
Merchant 251
Mercy 7, 8, 22, 23, 25, 33, 44, 49, 60, 65, 68, 69, 97, 115, 120, 128, 134, 140, 143, 145, 156, 157, 158, 166, 167, 168, 171, 172, 221, 224, 225, 235, 240, 242, 283, 287, 288, 292, 300, 305, 311, 327, 331, 332, 337, 345, 346, 348, 360
  hope of 237
  works of 180
Messiah 36, 37, 92; *see also* Christ, Mediator, Redeemer, Savior, Son of God

Metaphysics, by Aristotle 50 fn., 122 fn.
Metonymy 146
Micah 237
Michael 80, 232
Midian 162
Miglio 293 fn.
Mile
  Italian 293
  Roman 293 fn.
Milk 198
Millstone
  lower 237
  upper 237
Minister(s) 48, 181, 182, 187, 190, 218, 220, 232, 240, 241, 356, 361
Ministry 165, 232, 237, 241, 272, 277
  Abraham's 342
  of angels 60, 62
  of human beings 274
  of prophets 37
  of teaching 5
  of Word 111, 124, 155, 164, 167, 168, 233, 240, 288, 343, 356
Miracle(s) 31, 64, 68, 109, 117, 145, 206, 210, 226, 260, 262, 263, 270, 289, 302, 303, 315, 325
Misanthrope 51
Misanthropy 51 fn.
Misery 179
Misfortune(s) 25, 33, 120, 124, 135, 180, 185, 248, 252, 264, 265, 288, 303, 307, 308, 311, 322, 324, 326, 332, 334, 346, 348, 349, 351, 352, 356, 360, 361
Mitio 303
Moab 313, 314
Moabite 313
Moabitess 133
Moderation 241, 262, 331
Modesty 201, 202, 246, 247, 249, 253, 259

Moles 316, 318
  papistic 317
Monastery 7, 62, 130, 217, 252, 275, 276, 284, 309, 316, 322, 357, 361
Monasticism 325
Money 283, 317, 359, 361
Monica 159, 160
Monk(s) 51, 66 fn., 118, 128, 130, 139, 145, 153, 165, 166, 168, 180, 200, 203, 204, 218, 245, 275, 276, 289, 315, 316, 321, 322, 325, 329, 362, 363
  Augustinian 130 fn.
  Carthusian 252
  have had various discussions about obedience 170
  lies of 196
Monkey 318
Monogram 23
Moon(s) 86, 273, 347
  full 164
  most convenient indicator of time 163
Morals 201, 213, 227, 249, 252, 254
Moravia 77
Mortality 268
Moses 3, 5, 7, 10, 11, 12, 15, 18, 19, 23, 26, 27, 28, 32, 34, 35, 36, 41, 43, 46, 56, 58, 61, 62, 63, 74, 75, 76, 77, 78, 79, 80, 81, 82, 84, 86, 88, 90, 91, 92, 93, 94, 96, 97, 98, 100, 115, 134, 141, 143, 152, 156, 161, 163, 164, 165, 166, 168, 169, 173, 177, 180, 181, 185, 186, 191, 196, 197, 198, 200, 201, 203, 205, 209, 218, 219, 220, 225, 229, 231, 243, 244, 247, 248, 250, 251,
252, 253, 255, 257, 259, 261, 263, 267, 271, 272, 278, 280, 282, 286, 290, 292, 293, 295, 296, 297, 298, 302, 303, 304, 305, 308, 309, 310, 311, 312, 314, 315, 316, 320, 323, 330, 338, 344, 346, 352, 353, 354, 356, 357, 361
  books of 237
Motherhood 44, 49
Mule 149
Münzer, Thomas 5, 13, 15, 30, 31 fn., 165, 260, 301
Murder(s) 5, 227, 258, 294
Myconius, Friedrich x
Myrrh 283

Naaman the Syrian 81, 89, 235, 332
Nag, lazy 128
Nahash 228
Nahor 352
Naomi 133
Naples x, 295
Natural History, by Pliny 347 fn.
Nature 8, 47, 48, 52, 53, 56, 68, 85, 127, 152, 165, 199, 206, 221, 226, 227, 254, 255, 258, 262, 298, 323, 343, 347, 360
  divine 194
  human 276, 322
Nebuchadnezzar 10, 11, 89
Neighbor(s) 25, 84, 118, 122, 125, 198, 203, 204, 209, 226, 240, 277, 278, 327, 342, 354
New Testament 46, 69, 73, 92, 101, 103, 109, 110, 146, 147, 166, 169, 174, 194, 222, 297, 353

Nicomachean Ethics, by Aristotle 85 fn.
Ninevites 81, 89, 289
Niphal 253 fn.
Noah 39, 141, 233, 241, 250, 268
Nobility 260
Nobles 182, 227, 249
Noctes Atticae, by Gellius 214 fn.
Nolo episcopari 5 fn.
Non attendas, quis, sed quid dicatur 287 fn.
Number seven 141
Nuns 128, 204, 209, 275, 277, 321
  works of 201
Nut 147, 148, 150, 151

Oak of Mamre 184
Obedience 80, 100, 172, 174, 203, 204, 248, 273, 283, 284, 353
  of Abraham 169, 170, 171, 173, 175
Obstruere os 359
Ocean 39
  of God's benefits 343
Oecolampadius 5
Office 281
  episcopal and papal 5 fn.
  of ministry 232
  of prophet 364
οἰκουρός 201
Old Testament 31, 39 fn., 46, 73, 88, 103, 104, 147, 297 fn.
Omnipotence 137, 260, 311
On Commerce and Usury, by Luther 249 fn.
On the Bondage of the Will, by Luther 306 fn.
Oppositum in adiecto 119 fn.
Orator 73
Orestes 189
Orientals 251
Our Father 362; *see also* Lord's Prayer

INDEX

Ovid 47 fn., 248 fn., 308 fn., 312
Ox(en) 30, 86, 149, 356
  lazy 128

Palestine 176, 180, 303, 318
Pan 201 fn.
Panegyric on the consulship of Honorius, by Claudian 331 fn.
Papacy 37, 44, 51, 62, 107, 124, 166, 172, 179, 181, 196, 204, 210, 229, 243, 296, 325
Papist(s) 13, 26, 78, 84, 97, 98, 107, 109, 118, 153, 161, 181, 193, 201, 202, 203, 210, 211, 213, 217, 266, 267, 286, 293, 295, 296, 297, 299, 304, 315, 321, 322, 326, 357, 361, 363, 364, 365
  doctrine of 172
Paraclete 69
Paradise 42, 61, 171, 173, 179, 184, 282, 287, 293, 303, 312
Parent(s) 43, 45, 68, 99, 122, 131, 133, 144, 177, 198, 203, 205, 231, 233, 257, 258, 274, 279, 284
  authority of 240
Parthenion, Mt. 201 fn.
Passover 250, 251
Pastor(s) 174, 249
παθήματα 324 fn.
Patience 24, 51, 54, 55, 57, 68, 70, 120, 211, 212, 315, 354
  of God 40, 156
Patriarch(s) 14, 34, 49, 52, 53, 54, 57, 61, 81, 99, 109, 114, 115, 124, 131, 155, 157, 159, 164, 165, 167, 170, 175, 178, 179, 182, 185, 186, 190, 196, 197, 228,
230, 232, 233, 234, 245, 250, 302, 314, 315, 317, 319, 323, 324, 326, 327, 338, 344
  marriages of 211
Patrologia
  Series Graeca 166 fn., 274 fn.
  Series Latina 11 fn., 61 fn., 83 fn., 107 fn., 125 fn., 130 fn., 133 fn., 137 fn., 168 fn., 193 fn., 199 fn., 217 fn., 225 fn., 288 fn., 291 fn., 325 fn., 348 fn., 349 fn., 355 fn.
Paul, St. 4, 5, 6, 14, 17, 18, 19, 20, 21, 22, 26, 28, 29, 31, 35, 39, 40, 55, 59, 62, 64, 70, 76, 77, 80, 81, 83, 84, 85, 86, 90, 93, 96, 97, 98, 99, 102, 103, 105, 108, 117, 121, 124, 125, 130, 139, 147, 148, 149, 152, 155, 156, 158, 167, 176, 180, 181, 182, 187, 192, 197, 199, 200, 201, 213, 222, 224, 225, 239, 240, 254, 264, 269, 270, 271, 273, 275, 277, 283, 286, 288, 290, 291, 300, 301, 320, 321, 325, 326, 334, 341, 343, 346, 348, 355, 361
  ascribes righteousness to faith 23
  best and most learned interpreter of Moses 94
  excellent definer and expert dialectician 101
Peasants 30, 182, 227, 260, 345

Peccata affirmativa 363 fn.
Pedantry 5 fn.
Peloponnesus 281
Pentecost 250
Peril(s) 6, 129, 135, 146, 179, 180, 188, 190, 209, 210, 223, 225, 243, 244, 258, 277, 310, 317, 327, 343, 360, 363
  of marriage 55
περιψήματα 180
Persecution(s) 31, 179, 180, 185, 198, 244, 357
  physical 184
  spiritual 184
Persians 67
Peter, St. 18, 31, 40, 44, 58, 63, 112, 124, 127, 129, 169, 172, 180, 209, 231, 252, 260, 261, 270, 273, 291, 293, 294, 295, 296, 299, 305, 332, 346, 353, 354, 355, 359
Phaedrus 276 fn.
Phantoms 11
Pharaoh 10, 32, 88, 96, 106, 115, 177 fn., 231, 285, 339, 356
Pharisee(s) 9, 89, 90, 107, 269, 317, 341, 364
φιλάνθρωπον 68 fn.
Philemon 181
Philip 297
Philistines 188
Philologian(s) 67, 83, 267
Philologists 70
Philosophers 85, 226, 268, 270
Philosophy 193
Phocis 189 fn.
Physician(s) 10, 11, 206, 262, 271
Physics, by Aristotle 226 fn.
Piety 48, 62, 63, 124, 226

Pigs 210, 249
Pilgrimage(s) 202, 216
Pillar of salt 298
Pindar 189 fn.
Plague(s) 248, 264, 271, 301, 342
Plain of Mamre 184
Pliny 347 fn.
Poema 262
Poet(s) 49, 128, 308
Poetics, by Aristotle 303 fn.
Poison 210, 216, 301, 312
Polygamists 46
Polygamy 45, 46, 47
πολύμαστος 83
Pope(s) 13, 14, 17, 21, 35, 37, 40, 57, 63, 109, 128, 144, 153, 158, 166, 173, 174, 179, 182, 190, 202, 221, 222, 227, 229, 237, 240, 242, 245, 257, 268, 271, 286, 294, 319, 320, 322, 335, 349, 350, 355, 362
  authority of 326
  countless monstrosities of 342
  doctrine of 124
  removed cup from Eucharist 122
  traditions of 121
Postillae in vetus et novum testamentum, by Cardinal Hugo de Sancto Caro 26 fn.
Potiphar 162
Poverty 203
Pozzuoli 295 fn.
Prayer(s) 6, 9, 60, 75, 155, 160, 161, 165, 168, 174, 204, 236, 260, 270, 271, 287, 291, 292, 305, 311, 312, 327, 329, 331, 332, 334, 336, 339, 340, 351, 354, 357, 359, 361, 363, 364, 365

Abraham's 232, 234, 235, 335, 360
  demands faith in Christ 362
  for forgiveness 25
  Lot's 289, 290, 312
  parts of 288
Preacher(s) 78, 129, 234, 340, 341, 357
  should give consideration to vices and virtues, punishments and rewards 132
Prebends 362, 364
Predestination 171
Predigt 297 fn.
Presumption 6, 76
  Jewish 176
  of human powers 177
  of pride 226
  of righteousness 5
  of wisdom 5, 226
Pride 5, 51, 96, 97, 111, 131, 203, 225, 265, 322
  of flesh 63
  of Jews 81, 176
  presumption of 226
Priest(s) 60, 162, 292, 339
  high 3, 57, 113, 338
  of Baal 144
Priesthood 13, 115, 126, 127, 356
  Mosaic 77
Primogeniture 64
Prince(s) x, 114, 123, 126, 127, 131, 151, 153, 179, 182, 245, 270, 271, 340, 356
Princess 146
Prison 18, 179, 181
Procreation 135, 136, 152, 177, 205, 206, 208, 310
Prometheus Bound, by Aeschylus 49 fn.
Promiscuity 47
Promise(s) 4, 9, 13, 14, 15, 16, 17, 18, 19, 20, 21, 22, 23, 24, 25, 26, 27, 28, 29, 31, 32, 33, 35, 36,
37, 38, 39, 42, 43, 44, 45, 46, 54, 56, 58, 60, 62, 63, 64, 66, 67, 74, 75, 76, 77, 82, 83, 84, 85, 86, 87, 88, 89, 90, 92, 93, 94, 95, 97, 99, 102, 104, 105, 106, 110, 111, 112, 113, 116, 117 fn., 119, 120, 122, 123, 124, 125, 132, 135, 138, 139, 144, 145, 146, 147, 148, 149, 150, 151, 152, 153, 154, 155, 156, 157, 158, 161, 162, 163, 169, 176, 177, 180, 185, 186, 192, 200, 203, 208, 214, 216, 218, 220, 221, 222, 224, 225, 237, 242, 265, 285, 287, 289, 291, 302, 315, 316, 317, 318, 319, 324, 327, 328, 338, 343, 345, 346, 356, 357, 359
  definite 96
  indefinite 96
  of Satan 140
Promised Land 28, 32
Propagation 207
Prophecy 36, 141, 152, 212, 278
  three types of 10, 330
Prophet(s) 3, 10, 35, 36, 37, 38, 39, 60, 72, 76, 79, 82, 90, 94, 108, 109, 115, 116, 125, 147, 152, 153, 155, 156, 161, 163, 166, 167, 168, 191, 203, 212, 215, 218, 220, 221, 223, 239, 240, 255, 264, 274, 289, 300, 317, 338, 339, 345, 349, 350, 353, 356, 357, 359, 360, 364
  false 237, 355
  foolish and lying 224
  of Baal 320

Proportio
 finiti 158 fn.
 infiniti 158 fn.
Proselyte(s) 88, 89
Prostitutes 227, 249, 259
Prostitution 257
προσωπολήπτης 130
Proverbs 197, 201
Psalm(s) 5, 7, 27, 35, 50, 138, 140, 160, 164, 229, 244, 248, 283, 289, 290, 313, 334, 335, 336, 362, 364
Pseudo-Dionysius 166 fn., 274 fn.
Publishers x
Pugilist 146
Punishment(s) 10, 37, 40, 48, 59, 60, 68, 123, 132, 133, 135, 160, 166, 190, 218, 221, 222, 225, 226, 230, 234, 239, 243, 250, 252, 255, 256, 257, 264, 265, 267, 277, 279, 280, 281, 294, 295, 298, 300, 301, 302, 311, 328, 335, 341, 360
Puteoli x, 295
Pylades 189
Pythian Odes, by Pindar 189 fn.

Quarrel(s) 53, 54, 55, 354
 among philologians 83
 family 57
 of linguists 80
Queen of Sheba 112
Quintilian 73 fn.

Rabbi(s) 16, 21, 68, 70, 72, 73, 147, 209, 299, 312
 Kimalthi 71
 Solomon 71
Rachel 134
Rape 279
Raphael 80, 232
Rapine 62, 182, 203, 364
Razor 193

Reason 85, 86, 100, 107, 108, 131, 145, 170, 171, 172, 173, 174, 203, 221, 257, 265, 268, 282, 295, 320, 322, 323
Rebellion(s) 13, 16, 301
Reconciliation 12
Red Sea 221
Redeemer 69; *see also* Christ, Mediator, Messiah, Savior, Son of God
Redemption 38, 39, 43, 214, 338, 344
Reformation 6, 213 fn., 275 fn.
Regeneration 167
Regula ad servos Dei, by St. Augustine 130 fn.
Religion(s) 162, 316, 340
 self-elected 108
 true 118, 188, 219
 Turkish 37
Remission of sins 118, 124, 222, 237; *see also* Forgiveness of sins
Repentance 40, 170, 268, 340
Restraint 201, 202, 281
Resurrection 10, 38, 39, 141, 148
 Christ's 83
 into eternal life 142
Reuben 16
Reubenites 280
Revelation(s) 5, 6, 11, 12, 71 fn., 92, 120, 167, 170, 219, 275, 280, 285, 302, 330, 350
 three classes of 10
Reverence 14, 99, 185, 186, 189, 218, 228, 234, 247, 281
Reward(s) 132, 263, 257, 361
Rhetoric 9, 191, 196, 288, 341
 divine 343
 of Holy Spirit 347

Rhetorician(s) 73, 195, 213, 214
Riches 96, 100, 243, 248, 365
 eternal 125
Righteous 36, 227, 234, 235, 243, 295
Righteousness 9, 20, 22, 23, 24, 25, 26, 28, 29, 78, 80, 82, 84, 85, 88, 90, 93, 94, 96, 101, 102, 103, 104, 105, 106, 107, 112, 113, 122, 148, 156, 167, 179, 242, 252, 305, 331 fn.
 comes through faith in Christ 21
 eternal 87
 imperfect 79
 imputed 39
 of faith 177
 of Law 59
 of works 177
 perfect 79
 presumption of 5
Robbery 66
Rolls 197
Roman Catholicism 67 fn.
Roman pontiff 106
Romans 6, 18, 23, 67, 84, 94
Rome 108, 109, 168, 252, 254, 342, 344, 362
Rule, by St. Benedict 200 fn.
Ruth 133, 313

Sabbath 77, 141, 142
Sacrament(s) 37, 85, 87, 92, 110, 122, 155, 213, 272, 275, 288; *see also* Baptism, Communion, Eucharist, Holy Supper, Last Supper, Lord's Supper
 visible form of invisible grace 107
Sacramentarians 5, 13, 191, 272, 301
Sacred Scripture 37, 149;

see also Bible, Holy Scripture(s), Holy Writ, Scripture(s), Word of God
Sacrifice(s) 15, 22, 32, 33, 41, 80, 91, 106, 111, 112, 122, 143, 145, 164, 218, 237, 242, 250, 328, 359
  of Mass 128
  of praise and gratitude 227
  of thanksgiving 70
Sadducees 118
Sadness 7
Sadoleto, Jacob, cardinal 67 fn.
Sadoletus 67
Saint(s) 4, 5, 8, 9, 12, 14, 16, 17, 19, 25, 30, 31, 42, 51, 52, 76, 96, 134, 139 fn., 167, 168, 171, 174, 181, 188, 202, 215, 229, 233, 254, 259, 261, 264, 265, 267, 269, 271, 283, 292, 300, 305, 311, 317, 320, 321, 325, 328, 329, 333, 334, 335, 336, 337, 345, 351, 354, 355, 357
  canonization of 109
  church of 222
  Gentile 81 fn.
  true 13, 225
Salah 233
Sallust 283, 284 fn.
Salt 200, 300
  pillar of 298
Salt Sea 298
Salvation 76, 77, 79, 89, 90, 96, 97, 104, 106, 107, 110, 111, 112, 114, 120, 124, 128, 129, 133, 134, 143, 145, 154, 156, 161, 162, 163, 167, 220, 225, 262, 272, 273, 283, 286, 299, 359
Samaria 263
Samson 30
Samuel 30, 285

Sanctification 344
Sanctus 155
Sand 18
Santes 358
Saracens 63, 76, 161
  haughtiness of 65
Sarah 9, 13, 14, 42, 43, 44, 45, 46, 49, 51, 52, 53, 54, 55, 57, 58, 59, 61, 62, 63, 64, 65, 68, 70, 74, 75, 99, 135, 144, 145, 146, 147, 148, 150, 151, 152, 153, 154, 156, 157, 158, 161, 176, 188, 192, 200, 201, 202, 203, 204, 205, 206, 207, 208, 209, 210, 211, 212, 215, 216, 217, 228, 317, 319, 322, 323, 324, 327, 331, 332, 333, 336, 337, 349, 352, 354, 356, 357, 358, 359, 361
Sarai 146
Satan 8, 11, 19, 21, 34, 44, 45, 51, 57, 58, 63, 76, 108, 109, 120, 124, 138, 139, 146, 161, 166, 173, 179, 180, 184, 185, 214, 234, 265, 266, 270, 271, 277, 282, 296, 301, 319, 327, 330, 341, 345, 347, 350, 357, 363; see also Devil
  angel of 5
  craftiness of 167
  does not cease to drive on from sin to sin 255
  fury and malice of 158
  illusions of 168
  kingdom of 364
  leaves saints and church of God no peace 17
  messenger of 6
  plots of 291
  poisonous promise of 140

schemes and stratagems of 172
school of 227
slaves of 174, 256
snares of 276
thorn of 6
torture and tyranny of 342
works of 264
Satires, by Juvenal 48 fn.
Saul 30, 62, 172, 283, 285, 327, 339, 360
Savagery 256
Savior 82, 91, 117, 122, 162, 167, 359; see also Christ, Mediator, Messiah, Redeemer, Son of God
Saxony 66 fn., 340, 341 fn.
  electors of 356
Scabs 52
Scandals 234
Schenk, Jacob 243 fn.
Scholastics 274, 358
School(s) 42, 50, 118, 164, 248, 259, 274, 326, 331, 356
  of devil 362
  of Satan 227
Schoolmaster 117
Schrift 297 fn.
Schwenkfeld 273, 276
Schwiebert, E. G. 183 fn.
Scotuses 306
Scripture(s) ix, 10, 11, 16, 19, 24, 35, 38, 45, 59, 69, 70, 73, 98, 114, 166, 168, 177, 178, 191, 192, 195, 210, 217, 219, 220, 225, 229, 232, 237 fn., 239, 242, 249, 250, 261, 267, 270, 272, 289, 308, 310, 312, 316, 319, 322, 323, 325, 338, 357, 364; see also Bible, Holy Scripture(s), Holy Writ, Sacred Scripture, Word of God
  accommodates its way

INDEX 385

of speaking to human custom 230
analogy of 15
authority of 27, 57, 297
fount of all wisdom 306
fourfold sense of 27
Sea 18, 31, 33, 39, 89, 261
of blessings 343
Sebastian, St. 125
Second Table 5, 6, 98, 100, 159, 227, 240
Sect(s) 17, 55, 56, 76, 78, 147, 229
Seed 13, 14, 15, 28, 33, 35, 36, 37, 43, 45, 46, 57, 60, 66, 81, 82, 89, 90, 95, 100, 123, 134, 143, 144, 151, 163, 177, 200, 206, 208, 215, 220, 227, 281, 327, 338, 339, 346, 353, 359
Blessed 11, 94, 111, 112, 113, 152, 175, 225, 340
of the woman 19, 39, 92
physical 12, 19
promised to Adam 42
spiritual and heavenly 18, 20, 21
Semi-Pelagianism 67 fn.
Senate 233
Senators 253
Seneca 254, 287
Senility 268
Sense organs 10
Sententiae, by Peter Lombard 133 fn., 137 fn., 193 fn.
Seraphim 123
Sermones, by St. Augustine 288 fn.
Sermones condimenta ciborum 200 fn.
Sermones de diversis, by Bernard 291 fn.
Sermons on Genesis, by Luther 52 fn.
Serug 233, 319

Service(s) 118, 186, 187, 190, 197, 198, 203, 218, 245, 253, 270, 271, 273, 274, 279, 284
of love 196
of one's neighbor 125
Servus servorum Dei 188 fn.
Seth 96
Seventh Commandment 350
Sex(es) 44, 103, 104, 111, 129, 134, 135, 136, 144, 147, 200, 201, 310, 353, 360
Sexual intercourse 48, 208, 261, 308
Sheep 30, 78, 80, 197, 347, 356
lost 240
Shelah 319, 323, 338
Shell 149, 150, 151
Shem 3, 97, 233, 234, 319, 321, 323, 324, 338
Shem Hamphoras 296 fn.
Sheol 348
Shepherd(s) 78, 270, 285, 318
Shipwreck 290
Shoe 130
Shur 61, 318
Sickness 5, 156, 224
Sign(s) 17, 29, 30, 31, 32, 38, 70, 86, 87, 90, 93, 97, 99, 101, 105, 106, 107, 110, 111, 112, 113, 114, 116, 117, 123, 124, 125, 126, 129, 131, 134, 135, 136, 143, 145, 146, 150, 156, 166, 300, 337
false 108
true 108
Silence 200 fn.
Silver 190, 199, 359
Simeon 70, 120
Sin(s) 5, 9, 21, 22, 28, 30, 48, 54, 57, 60, 61, 63, 65, 75, 84, 87, 95, 99, 104, 105, 110, 112, 115, 131, 135, 141, 143, 154, 159, 167, 173, 181, 202, 211, 214, 216, 221, 222, 223, 224, 226, 233, 238, 239, 240, 242, 249, 251, 252, 254, 255, 256, 257, 258, 260, 261, 269, 278, 279, 280, 281, 282, 294, 295, 301, 302, 303, 304, 307, 309, 312, 313, 314, 323, 324, 326, 332, 334, 335, 336, 337, 339, 342, 343, 346, 347, 349, 352, 356, 360
forgiveness of 7, 12, 39, 109, 158, 214, 224, 228, 265, 333, 338
inborn 103
law of 6
mortal 73, 259, 339 fn.
mortification of 174
of commission 362
of omission 363
of weakness 296
original 56, 103, 133, 134, 136, 137, 138, 139, 144, 206 fn., 350
remission of 118, 124, 222, 237
that cry to heaven 230
unforgivable 296
venial 73, 208, 333
victory over 160
Sinai 223
Sinner(s) 26, 65, 107, 130, 134, 144, 159, 160, 214, 215, 224, 239, 243, 265, 269, 277, 295
Sirach 11, 138, 140, 171, 186
Sixth Commandment 331, 350
Slave(s) 52, 55, 64, 65, 127, 132, 142, 143, 147, 162, 175, 252, 281, 334, 360

of Satan 174, 256, 356
Slavery 32, 33, 63
Sluggishness 23
Smalcald 335
Smoke 304, 354
Smugness 14, 174, 222, 223, 226, 229, 238, 267, 311, 314, 336
Snakes 347
Sodom x, 61, 131, 176, 181, 187, 188, 190, 218, 222, 223, 224, 225, 226, 228, 231, 232, 233, 234, 237, 238, 239, 240, 242, 243, 244, 247, 248, 249, 250, 252, 253, 255, 256, 257, 262, 263, 264, 265, 266, 268, 285, 287, 292, 293, 294, 296, 303, 305, 306, 309, 311, 316, 319, 324, 330, 331, 333, 338, 341, 342, 344, 345, 346, 351, 352, 365
Sodomites 98, 140, 240, 241, 249, 264, 294, 296, 321, 324
Soldier 228, 251
Solomon 27, 112, 152, 165, 197, 227, 246, 249, 256, 285, 334
Son of God 7, 22, 25, 39, 87, 92, 95, 109, 115, 116, 118, 124, 154, 163, 168, 178, 189, 196, 199, 204, 214, 215, 219, 220, 222, 225, 265, 268, 276, 287, 293, 296, 297, 338, 343, 353, 355, 359, 363; see also Christ, Mediator, Messiah, Redeemer, Savior
incarnation of 136
Song of Solomon 8, 283
Sophist(s) 24, 29, 336, 339
have absolutely no understanding of sacred matters 118

Sorrow 7, 8, 12, 14, 68, 154, 238, 305, 309, 312, 314, 324, 356
Soul(s) 103, 132, 149, 168, 235, 236, 243, 271, 277, 285, 286, 300, 308, 327, 337, 346, 347
immortality of 11, 268
mortality of 268
of infant 137
Sow 243
Spain 16, 41 fn., 108, 168
Spears 191
Star(s) 10, 17, 18, 34, 164, 209, 261 fn.
Statues 109
Stephen, St. 119, 125
Stifft 163, 164
Strassburg 306 fn.
Straw 149, 295, 344
Strophis of Phocis 189 fn.
Students x
Suffering(s) 33, 102, 292
of Christ 72
of Son of God 124
Sulphur 295
Sun 50, 86, 91, 129, 184, 193, 273, 289, 292, 293, 316, 342, 347
Superstition 11
Suspensio gratiae 7 fn.
Swine 199, 308, 354
Sword(s) 59, 132, 190, 191, 192, 232, 271, 281, 328, 348, 357
Sybaris 281
Synagog(s) 70, 115, 164, 192
Synecdoche 360
Syria 16, 235, 332
Syrians 260, 263, 264

Tabernacle 163
Table Talk, by Luther 144 fn.
Tapestry 199
Tartar 183
Tautology 177, 205
Te Deum laudamus 7
Teacher(s) 8, 50, 68, 69, 87, 121, 128, 131, 132, 138, 143, 147, 160, 161, 164, 185, 192, 193, 194, 198, 217, 233, 234, 236, 260, 269, 272, 280, 281, 284, 301, 319, 324, 326, 338, 339, 340, 341, 344, 357, 363
fanatical 210
pernicious 222
scholastic 137
Teaching(s) 27, 28, 118, 137, 164, 178, 192, 221, 230, 292, 297, 299, 300, 349, 363
Teman 96
Temple(s) 81, 89, 101, 108, 121, 122, 126, 150, 188, 263, 364
Temptation 6, 42, 172, 278, 288, 307
Terah 319, 352
Terebinth 199
Terence 47 fn., 303
Terror(s) 3, 63, 135, 237, 330, 331, 345
of conscience 8 fn.
Tetragrammaton 296
Thanks 50, 120, 122, 145, 146, 227, 243, 276, 288, 336, 342, 344, 364
Thanksgiving 70, 99, 118, 128
The Mountain of Contemplation, by John Gerson 276 fn.
The Words of the Days 361
Theft 5
Theocracy 31 fn.
Theodosius 329
Theologian(s) 27, 42, 267, 306, 358 fn.
Theology 26, 94, 132, 136, 160, 262
Theses of the Disputations Against the Antinomians 223 fn.
Theseus 189
Thieving 233
Thirst 179, 180, 184
This Is My Body: These

INDEX

Words Still Stand,
  by Luther 110 fn.
Thomases 306
Thorn(s) 319
  of Satan 6
Timon 51
Tischreden, by Luther
  114 fn., 144 fn.
Tithe 35
Tobias 44
Tongue(s) 130, 136, 362
  venomous 194
Tortoise 201
Torture(s) 8, 125, 264
  of Satan 342
Tradition(s) 203, 206 fn.,
  250, 321
  human 121, 145, 155,
    204, 326
  Jewish exegetical
    232 fn.
  medieval 275 fn.
  of pope 121, 122
Trial(s) 3, 5, 6, 7, 8, 9,
  10, 12, 13, 14, 15,
  17, 42, 43, 46, 55,
  56, 58, 71, 76, 128,
  129, 135, 159, 174,
  185, 190, 229, 239,
  265, 282, 301, 302,
  303, 312, 325, 348
Tribulation(s) 36, 333,
  334, 356
Trinity 61, 190, 191, 192,
  193, 194, 219, 232,
  245, 353
  knowledge of 195
  unique evidence con-
    cerning 195
Truth(s) 16, 22, 36, 62,
  174, 213, 214, 265,
  268, 286, 295, 296,
  297, 313, 316, 332,
  333, 345
  begets hatred 281
Turk(s) 14, 35, 37, 40,
  59, 63, 64, 69, 98,
  121, 122, 158, 161,
  162, 173, 174, 183,
  229, 271, 290
Tyranny 172, 240, 326,
  329, 339, 349, 356
  of Satan 342

Tyrant(s) 34, 190, 235,
  242, 256, 319, 327,
  329, 356, 357

Ubi uber, ibi tuber
  248 fn.
Ulrich, St. 361, 362
Unbelief 30, 37, 136,
  148, 158, 170, 187,
  190, 199, 214, 229
Unbelievers 269, 286
Ungodliness 136, 324,
  335, 352
Ungodly 13, 14, 15, 22,
  40, 60, 70, 140, 173,
  235, 241, 244, 264,
  265, 268, 269, 270,
  284, 292, 293, 294,
  295, 296, 302, 304,
  311, 318, 320, 333,
  336, 340, 341, 347
Unity 147
University of Erfurt
  50 fn.
Unjust 234, 235
Unworthiness 25, 158,
  160, 161, 291
Ur of the Chaldeans 28,
  34, 35, 43, 112, 180,
  244
Uriel 80
Usurers 222, 279
Usury 231, 249, 324
Uterus 360

Vagrants 179, 180, 182
Vainglory 4, 5, 6, 9
Valerian 125 fn.
Vanity 63
Vegetius 132 fn.
Veil 98
Venice 41 fn.
Venus 201
Vergil 308 fn., 359 fn.
Vermin 52
Vestigia Trinitatis 192 fn.
Vices 132, 254
Victory 9, 31, 76, 225,
  226
  Abraham's 3, 4, 6, 7,
    13
  over death and sin 160
Vigils 316

Vincent of Lerins 125 fn.
Vineyard 129
Vipers 193
Virgin(s) 147, 202, 211,
  257, 259
  Mary 29, 136, 145,
    152, 206
Virginity 204, 208
Virtue(s) 22, 24, 25, 26,
  44, 49, 58, 132, 185,
  198, 200, 201, 203,
  208, 209, 210, 306,
  351, 354, 357
Vision(s) 10, 11, 12,
  17, 18, 164, 167,
  177 fn., 275, 330,
  350, 351
*Vita S. Hilarionis eremi-
  tae,* by Jerome
  355 fn.
Vitae patrum 217 fn.
Vocatio 62 fn.
Vocation(s) 62, 128, 142
Vow(s) 128, 158
  of poverty 203

Wantonness 179, 231
War(s) 30, 66, 114, 191,
  225, 290, 293
Warfare 171
*Warning to His Dear
  Germans,* by Luther
  252 fn.
Water 34, 59, 86, 87, 95,
  105, 108, 149, 181,
  184, 185, 186, 190,
  202, 204, 225, 245,
  249, 274, 355
Wax 28, 191
Waxen nose 191
Wealth 33, 153, 227,
  229, 248, 326, 328,
  362, 264
  of divine mercy 168
Weather 180
  April 123
Wedding(s) 251, 331
Weimar x
  edition 69 fn., 195 fn.,
    305 fn.
  editors 41 fn., 150 fn.,
    181 fn., 183 fn.,
    202 fn., 252 fn.,

256 fn., 263 fn., 320 fn., 324 fn.
Whoredom 243
Widow(s) 47, 183 fn., 202
   of Zarephath 81, 89
   wanton 182
Widowhood 204
Wife 13, 14, 42, 45, 46, 47, 49, 51, 53, 55, 57, 58, 133, 147, 179, 201, 204, 209, 210, 213, 227, 231, 253, 258, 261, 283, 288, 315, 317, 318, 320, 321, 323, 325, 326, 327, 329, 330, 333, 335, 340, 342, 349, 350, 351, 352, 353, 354, 360, 361
   Lot's 240, 264, 267, 286, 294, 298, 299, 300, 301, 302, 303, 304, 305, 307, 308, 312, 324
Wilderness 31, 60, 64, 66, 69, 71, 74, 107
Wine 190, 197, 204, 220, 248, 267, 309, 311, 312, 364
Wisdom 9, 96, 108, 109, 114, 126, 127, 128, 137, 162, 173, 241, 242, 243, 261, 262, 274, 300, 306, 342, 353
   above all wisdom 125
   carnal 172
   heavenly 338
   presumption of 5, 226
   supposed 209
Wittenberg x, 303 fn.
Witzel, Georg 193 fn., 275
Wolf 17, 67, 78, 271, 347
Womb(s) 45, 55, 64, 134, 148, 152, 205, 206, 208, 360
Wonder men 261, 262
Wonders 117, 166
Wood 86, 153, 191, 206, 214, 303

Word of God 14, 16, 19, 30, 37, 55, 64, 70, 77, 78, 86, 98, 108, 111, 116, 117, 118, 120, 121, 138, 140, 145, 146, 148, 155, 160, 163, 164, 167, 174, 180, 182, 214, 216, 219, 220, 227, 228, 232, 237, 239, 241, 273, 284, 286, 291, 297, 299, 302, 307, 326, 338, 343, 344, 348, 353, 357; *see also* Bible, Holy Scripture(s), Holy Writ, Sacred Scripture, Scripture(s)
   is never without fruit 69
   et passim
Work(s) 21, 23, 25, 26, 30, 34, 50, 80, 84, 87, 102, 106, 118, 128, 136, 146, 156, 162, 172, 176, 210, 212, 271, 290, 292, 315, 318, 320, 321, 322, 336, 348, 359, 362
   ceremonial 101
   childish 170
   divine 218
   domestic and civil 202, 216
   done for profit 122
   good 24, 85, 86, 169, 171, 173, 185, 190, 193, 196, 197, 200, 203, 204, 211, 217, 239, 326, 329, 335, 347, 349, 364, 365
   holy 174
   menial 211
   miraculous 167
   monkish 325
   moral 100, 101
   of Law 20, 22, 29
   of love 189
   of mercy 180, 225
   of nuns 201

   of repentance and love 170
   of Satan 264
   of the Lord 120
   of unbelief 170
   of wrath 225
   righteousness of 177
   self-chosen 218
   strange 209
Works and Days, by Hesiod 332 fn.
World 10, 13, 14, 19, 33, 43, 48, 49, 51, 52, 57, 59, 63, 66, 81, 82, 84, 91, 96, 105, 106, 108, 112, 114, 118, 120, 123, 124, 126, 129, 134, 141, 142, 145, 146, 150, 151, 152, 153, 154, 159, 161, 179, 180, 189, 200, 208, 212, 218, 221, 229, 231, 234, 237, 238, 240, 246, 247, 248, 262, 267, 268, 270, 279, 292, 294, 295, 300, 301, 315, 316, 317, 327, 329, 331, 338, 339, 340, 343, 344, 345, 346, 362, 363, 365
   dregs of 170, 233, 245
   foolish pomp of 199
   future 38
   last evil of 293
   original 293, 319
   thankless 342
Worldling 276
Worms 310
Worship 36, 74, 84, 94, 98, 108, 109, 116, 117, 118, 120, 121, 122, 144, 146, 150, 164, 172, 174, 200, 201, 202, 203, 204, 210, 242, 250, 284, 319, 325, 329, 339, 344, 345, 357, 362, 364
   hypocritical 181
   of angels 275

Wrath 6, 22, 59, 135, 138, 180, 220, 221, 222, 223, 227, 235, 256, 296, 305, 320
  against Christ 21
  children of 136
  doctrine of 242
  of God 8, 44, 60, 72, 134, 214, 224, 233, 234, 236, 237, 238, 239, 242, 243, 264, 269, 278, 281, 292, 294, 295, 302, 304, 308, 310, 313, 348, 351
  works of 225
Wrathfulness 9
Wrestler 146
Wundermänner 261 fn.

ξένος 198

Yahweh 296 fn.
Yeast 5

Youth(s) 6, 186, 279, 323, 327

Zacharias 208, 284
Zadok 13
Zarephath 81, 89
Zeal 13, 15, 137, 146, 197, 198, 218, 232, 246, 276, 290
Zechariah 58
Zoar 290, 292, 293, 298, 302, 306, 307
Zwingli 5

INDEX TO SCRIPTURE PASSAGES

Genesis
- 1:14 — 163
- 1:26 — 353
- 1:27 — 202
- 1:28 — 205
- 3:2 — 282
- 3:7 — 56
- 3:24 — 61 fn.
- 4:6 — 272
- 6:15 — 229
- 11:7 — 230
- 12:1 ff. — 316 fn.
- 12:3 — 28
- 12:20 — 356
- 13:18 — 316 fn.
- 14:18 — 267
- 15:1 — 116
- 15:4 — 16 fn.
- 15:6 — 23 fn.
- 15:7 — 27 fn.
- 15:13 — 34 fn.
- 15:13-16 — 36
- 16:4 — 47 fn.
- 16:11 — 64 fn.
- 16:12 — 71 fn.
- 16:16 — 72 fn.
- 17:4 — 102
- 17:7-9 — 91
- 18:2 — 188 fn.
- 18:10 — 205 fn.
- 18:21 — 230 fn.
- 18:22 — 232 fn.
- 19:1 ff. — 61 fn., 188
- 19:2 — 246 fn.
- 19:3 — 250 fn.
- 19:9 — 257 fn.
- 19:11 — 263 fn.
- 19:12 — 266 fn.
- 19:14 — 269 fn.
- 19:26 — 298 fn., 299 fn.
- 19:33 — 308 fn., 313 fn.
- 20:1 — 303
- 20:6 — 337 fn.
- 20:11 — 128, 303
- 20:13 — 353 fn.
- 21:12 — 94
- 23:16 — 317
- 29:16 — 266 fn.
- 30:1 — 134
- 31 — 146
- 37:2 — 280
- 41:1-7, 17-21 — 177 fn.
- 45:27 — 154
- 50:20 — 334

Exodus
- Book of — 35
- 1:8 — 182
- 1:8 ff. — 34
- 2:3 — 34
- 6:16 ff. — 34
- 12:36 — 259
- 12:40 — 34
- 20:2 — 117
- 20:2, 6 — 237
- 20:5 — 80
- 20:24 — 146
- 32:28 — 280

Leviticus
- 10:1 ff. — 300
- 10:2 — 285
- 19:18 — 25
- 26:36 — 8 fn., 264

Numbers
- 12:3 — 58
- 12:6-8 — 10
- 16 — 15
- 16:24 — 280
- 21:35 — 197

Deuteronomy
- Book of — 361 fn.
- 4:7 — 169
- 10:16 — 76, 82
- 13 — 166
- 18:15 — 90, 91
- 22:29 — 46
- 24:6 — 237
- 25:5 — 47
- 28:31 — 80
- 29:6 — 197
- 32:15 — 249
- 32:21 — 152

Joshua
- 22:10 ff. — 280

Judges
- 6:17 — 30 fn.
- 19, 20 — 279

Ruth
- 1:16 — 133

1 Samuel
- 1:10 — 134
- 2:6 — 348
- 11 — 30
- 11:2 — 228
- 15 — 283
- 15:22 — 172
- 19:11-17 — 327

2 Samuel
- 6:16 — 44 fn.
- 7:14 — 27
- 15:25, 26 — 13

1 Kings
- 13:24 — 284, 300
- 18:28 — 144
- 18:40 — 320
- 19:1-4 — 320
- 19:18 — 345

2 Kings
- 6:18 — 263
- 16:3 — 216
- 19:35 — 270
- 20:8 — 156

2 Chronicles
- 20:7 — 31

Job
- 2:9 — 44 fn.
- 23:15 — 348

Psalms
- 1 — 138
- 4:3 — 4, 8, 334, 336
- 6:1 — 358
- 8:5 — 4
- 12:1 — 345
- 12:5 — 345
- 14:1 — 229

INDEX

14:3 — 108
18:25 — 334, 336
18:26 — 334, 335
19:12 — 348, 350
21:1 — 4
23:4 — 190
26:9 — 235
27:14 — 223
28:1 — 230
30:5 — 140
30:6-9 — 4
31:16 — 72
31:22 — 72
32:9 — 149
35:16 — 197
41:9 — 50, 51
42:8 — 18 fn.
50:15 — 328
51 — 45, 117 fn.
51:17 — 236
51:19 — 242
52:2 — 193
62:10 — 248
69:22 — 37
74:4 — 164
74:8 — 164
86:17 — 30 fn.
89:26, 27 — 27
89:47 — 302
91:7 — 223
100:3 — 35
103:5 — 323
103:8 — 283
103:15 — 159
105:14 — 330
107:6, 7 — 328
107:27 — 8
108:1 — 283
116:15 — 292
118 — 120 fn.
118:10-12 — 132
118:17 — 120
119 — 138
127:3 — 134
139:1 — 36
139:16 — 36
145:19 — 289

Proverbs

2:14 — 249
3:27 — 80
7:10 ff. — 108
7:11 — 201
10:13 — 59
15:1 — 256
16:18 — 227
23:6, 7 — 246
23:35 — 285
24:16 — 261, 334
25:27 — 138, 140

Song of Solomon

2:9 — 8
5:2-5 — 283

Isaiah

1:18 — 358
3:9 — 249, 255
5:7 — 230
6:3 — 123
6:10 — 155, 193
7:10-14 — 30 fn.
8:14 — 70
11:10 — 107
18:2 — 69 fn.
26:10 — 318
28:29 — 54
29:11, 12 — 37
29:12 — 69
30:10 — 269 fn.
31:9 — 169
40:31 — 323
41:8 — 164
41:14 — 310
42:3 — 242
45:15 — 121
49:4 — 59
49:8 — 283
53:8 — 116
54:8 — 71
57:15 — 350 fn.
61:1 — 222, 281
61:1 ff. — 241
65:1, 2 — 107
66:2 — 236
66:3 — 108

Jeremiah

7:25 — 60
9:24 — 96
9:26 — 76, 82
23:29 — 348
26:9, 18 — 237 fn.
31:22 — 253
33:17 — 36
34:8 ff. — 41 **fn.**
35:15 — 60

Ezekiel

3:18 — 280
3:19 — 240
9:4-6 — 60
13:5 — 292
13:19 — 242
13:22 — 243
16:49 — 181
16:49, 50 — **247**
18:23 — 140
22:30 — 292
33:11 — 277
34:3, 4 — 223

Daniel

3:25 — 274
9:24 — 90

Hosea

2:17 — 330
2:23 — 152
4:6 — 153
6:6 — 153

Matthew

3:7, 9 — 96
3:12 — 150
4:10 — 118
5:42 — 178
5:45 — 50
6:6 — 18 fn.
6:12 — 349
7:11 — 138
8:21 — 299
9:2 — 155
10:10 — 361
10:15 — 294
10:42 — 203
11:28 — 223
11:29, 30 — **346**
12:32 — 295
12:35 — 252
12:49 — 165
13:3 ff. — 225
15:9 — 273
16:24 — 317

17:5 — 82
18:18 — 124
19:4, 5 — 272
19:6 — 204
19:17 — 132
20:12 — 129, 131
20:20-28 — 56
20:22 — 159
21:43 — 152
22:32 — 110, 118
23:8 — 147
23:15 — 89
23:24 — 321
24:23 — 108
25:31-46 — 187
25:35 — 178, 187, 244
25:40 — 178, 184, 187, 271
26:26, 27 — 124
26:41 — 8
26:53 — 270
28:19 — 91, 104

Mark

16:5 — 61 fn., 106
16:16 — 273

Luke

1:18-22 — 208
1:20 — 284
1:25 — 134
1:36 — 29
1:37 — 212
1:50 — 115
1:51 — 17
1:52 — 241
2:13 — 270
2:29 — 120
2:34 — 70, 241
8:5-15 — 281
8:6 — 317
9:62 — 299
10:16 — 271
11:10 — 359
11:13 — 138
11:21 — 179
12:32 — 160, 241
15:4 ff. — 240
16:19-21 — 65
17:11-19 — 183
17:18 — 50

17:32 — 294, 299, 300
18:9-14 — 9
19:22 — 290
22:19 — 163
24:16 — 263
24:28 — 327

John

1:13 — 93
1:16 — 90
3:3 — 95
3:5 — 105
3:6 — 95
4:22 — 97
5:19 — 297
6:63 — 272
7:7 — 221
7:16 — 297
7:48, 49 — 341
8:44 — 179
8:56 — 153, 194, 219
10:39 — 263
11:9 — 345
12:36 — 283
13:1 ff. — 245
13:4-17 — 245 fn.
13:6 — 172
13:18 — 50
13:20 — 186
14:9 — 297
14:10 — 297
14:12 — 364
16:5-7 — 205
16:20 — 238
16:23 — 359
16:24 — 339
18:23 — 57
20:15 — 263
21:18 — 127
21:20 — 299
21:21, 22 — 129

Acts

1:10 — 61 fn.
2:38 — 101 fn.
3:6 — 270
7:5 — 119
8:16 — 101 fn.
9:4 — 348
9:6 — 63
10:26 — 355

10:34 — 129, 130
10:48 — 101 fn.
12:7 ff. — 18
14:15 — 320, 322, 355
14:17 — 225
15 — 83
15:5 — 83
19:34 — 83 fn.
20:29, 30 — 17
27:43 — 290
28:15 — 264

Romans

Book of — 23
1:21 — 117
2:1 — 240
2:4 — 40
2:11 — 64
2:25 — 90
3:4 — 214
3:8 — 258
3:20 — 22
4:1 ff. — 176
4:4, 5 — 22
4:5 — 156
4:11 — 85, 101, 102, 105
4:11, 12 — 105
4:15 — 59
4:17 — 35
4:19 ff. — 147
4:23 — 19
4:23, 24 — 39, 148
5:12 ff. — 133
5:14 — 103
6:3 — 101 fn.
7:23 — 6, 333
7:24 — 334
8:8 — 224, 254
8:18 — 344
8:26 — 363
8:28 — 334, 336
9:6-8 — 94 fn.
9:8 — 19
9:11 — 103
10:10 — 273
11 — 94 fn.
11:17 — 152, 339
11:33 — 276, 348
12:6 — 130
12:10 — 197, 199
12:11 — 290

INDEX

12:19 — 286
13:1, 2 — 328
14:4 — 261
14:23 — 30
15:4 — 19, 222
16:18 — 197, 269

1 Corinthians

1:10 — 147
1:26 — 341
2:2 — 139, 276, 277
3:9 — 270
4:13 — 180
5:5 — 300
6:9 — 254
6:9, 10 — 224
7:2 — 47
9:9 — 149
10 — 222
10:6 — 239
11:31 — 225
11:32 — 300
13:7 — 31
15 — 239 fn.

2 Corinthians

1:9 — 4
1:20 — 88
1:24 — 326
4:17 — 343, 346
4:17, 18 — 343
6:1 — 288
6:2 — 283
6:17 — 286
11:14 — 108, 167
12:7 — 5, 6
12:9 — 130

Galatians

Book of — 23, 35
1:6 — 301
2:16 — 21
3:4 — 213 fn.
3:7 — 29
3:9 — 29
3:10 — 29
3:17 — 34
3:27 — 101 fn.
4:14 — 187
4:23 — 64
4:29, 30 — 55

4:30 — 70
5:2-4 — 77
6:10 — 185

Ephesians

2:2 — 271
2:3 — 136
2:19, 20 — 152
3:20 — 158
6:9 — 64

Philippians

2:3 — 199
2:14 — 291
3:13 — 300
3:18, 19 — 14

Colossians

2:3 — 276
2:9 — 90
2:11, 12 — 103 fn.
2:18 — 275
2:18, 23 — 108
3:25 — 64
4:6 — 200

2 Thessalonians

2:3 — 326
2:4 — 121

1 Timothy

2:1 — 291 fn.
2:4 — 138
3:2 — 98
5:16 — 182
5:17 — 361
6:4 — 213
6:5, 20 — 301
6:16 — 122, 138
6:17 — 83

2 Timothy

2:12 — 334
2:15 — 222, 239 fn., 241
2:26 — 271
3:16 — 70
3:16, 17 — 239

Titus

2:5 — 201

3:4 — 155
3:4 ff. — 167
3:10, 11 — 286

Philemon

7 — 181 fn.

Hebrews

4:12 — 348
7:9, 10 — 35
11:3 — 33
11:5, 6 — 79
11:6 — 20, 105
11:8-10 — 318
11:10 — 157
11:11 — 206
12:29 — 122
13:2 — 178, 220, 244 fn.
13:4 — 224, 254

James

3:1 — 147
3:2 — 348, 349
5:16 — 292
5:17 — 354

1 Peter

3:6 — 44, 209
3:7 — 58, 353
4:10 — 130
5:6 — 14
5:9 — 180

2 Peter

1:10 — 169
2:6 — 293, 294, 296
2:8 — 252, 346
2:9 — 295
2:14 — 231
2:21 — 112
3:3 — 305
3:7 — 40

1 John

1:1 — 229
1:8 — 333
1:24 — 300 fn.
3:8 — 179
5:19 — 189

Jude

3 — 301
22, 23 — 278

Revelation

2:9 — 227

18:4 — 280, 285
22:11 — 170

APOCRYPHA

Tobit

3:8 — 58 fn.
5:17 — 44 fn.

Wisdom of Solomon

3:7 — 8

Ecclesiasticus

3:22 — 138, 171
31:14 — 186
34:6, 7 — 11